Cryptocurrencies and Blockchain Technology Applications

Scrivener Publishing
100 Cummings Center, Suite 541J
Beverly, MA 01915-6106

Publishers at Scrivener
Martin Scrivener (martin@scrivenerpublishing.com)
Phillip Carmical (pcarmical@scrivenerpublishing.com)

Cryptocurrencies and Blockchain Technology Applications

Edited by
Gulshan Shrivastava
National Institute of Technology Patna, India
Dac-Nhuong Le
Haiphong University, Haiphong, Vietnam
Kavita Sharma
National Institute of Technology, Kurukshetra, India

Scrivener
Publishing

This edition first published 2020 by John Wiley & Sons, Inc., 111 River Street, Hoboken, NJ 07030, USA and Scrivener Publishing LLC, 100 Cummings Center, Suite 541J, Beverly, MA 01915, USA
© 2020 Scrivener Publishing LLC
For more information about Scrivener publications please visit www.scrivenerpublishing.com.

Wiley Global Headquarters
111 River Street, Hoboken, NJ 07030, USA

For details of our global editorial offices, customer services, and more information about Wiley products visit us at www.wiley.com.

Limit of Liability/Disclaimer of Warranty
While the publisher and authors have used their best efforts in preparing this work, they make no representations or warranties with respect to the accuracy or completeness of the contents of this work and specifically disclaim all warranties, including without limitation any implied warranties of merchantability or fitness for a particular purpose. No warranty may be created or extended by sales representatives, written sales materials, or promotional statements for this work. The fact that an organization, website, or product is referred to in this work as a citation and/or potential source of further information does not mean that the publisher and authors endorse the information or services the organization, website, or product may provide or recommendations it may make. This work is sold with the understanding that the publisher is not engaged in rendering professional services. The advice and strategies contained herein may not be suitable for your situation. You should consult with a specialist where appropriate. Neither the publisher nor authors shall be liable for any loss of profit or any other commercial damages, including but not limited to special, incidental, consequential, or other damages. Further, readers should be aware that websites listed in this work may have changed or disappeared between when this work was written and when it is read.

Library of Congress Cataloging-in-Publication Data

ISBN 978-1-119-62116-4

Cover image: Pixabay.Com
Cover design by Russell Richardson

Set in size of 11pt and Minion Pro by Manila Typesetting Company, Makati, Philippines

10 9 8 7 6 5 4 3 2 1

*Dedicated to our friends
and family for their
constant support during the
course of this book*

Contents

Part I   Cryptocurrencies and Blockchain Technology

List of Figures

List of Tables

Foreword

The concept of blockchain recently came into the limelight when the hype around Bitcoin and other cryptocurrencies gained momentum. Blockchain is the underlying principle behind cryptocurrencies. At the center of blockchain is a distributed ledger that records all the transactions that take place in the network. A blockchain network is usually described as decentralized because it is replicated across many network participants, each of which collaborates in its maintenance. In addition to being decentralized and collaborative, the information recorded on the blockchain is also immutable, which guarantees that once a transaction has been added to the ledger, it cannot be modified. This property of immutability assures the participants that their information is safe and secure.

The technology itself holds much more promise in various areas such as time stamping, logging of critical events in a system, recording of transactions, trustworthy e-governance, etc. With blockchain technology in the financial sector, participants can interact directly and can make transactions across the Internet without the interference of a third party. Such transactions through blockchain will not share any personal information regarding participants and it creates a transaction record by encrypting the identifying information. The most exciting feature of blockchain is that it greatly reduces the possibilities of a data breach. In contrast with the traditional processes, in blockchain there are multiple shared copies of the same database which makes it challenging to wage a data breach attack or cyber-attack. With all the fraud resistant features, the blockchain technology holds the potential to revolutionize various business sectors and make processes smarter, more secure, more transparent, and more efficient compared to traditional business processes.

Many researchers are working on multiple uses such as decentralized public key infrastructure, self-sovereign identity management, registry maintenance, health record management, decentralized authentication, decentralized DNS, etc. Also, corporations, such as IBM and Microsoft, are developing their own applications in diverse fields such as the Internet of Things (IoT), etc., even enabling blockchain platforms on the cloud.

With all the best available expertise and knowledge, the editors provide a complete and comprehensive collection of chapters that address the various aspects of blockchain technology such as decentralization computing, automation of content extraction and an assortment of business applications in blockchain using machine learning, evolutionary algorithms and other techniques.

By the end of the book, the reader will know everything one needs to know about blockchain technology and be ready use that information for future applications and investments.

Professor Nguyen Thanh Thuy
VNU University of Engineering and Technology, Vietnam
April 2020

Preface

Blockchain is in its early phase of development where experiments are performed on existing systems by developers working on reducing the cost and making user activities faster. Their support is limited in terms of computing power and the number of nodes within the network being small. The current situation is that solutions are usually designed to address where the decentralized system makes decisions. Coin offerings made by blockchain technology implemented using smart contract can deliver high proposition value to the solution over a decentralized network where each node will have equal importance and control over the decisions made by the system. In the future, real power is empowered by smart contract where advanced technologies will enable transactions at a faster rate. Satoshi Nakamoto published his paper titled "Bitcoin: A Peer-to-Peer Electronic Cash System" in October 2008 and released it in January 2009, which was a clear sign of the disruption of the financial and banking sectors to come. Since it is a practical solution with limiting technology, it seemed very unlikely to have drawbacks to its success and full-fledged implementation. With the exception of financial sectors, healthcare, supply chains, and governments look forward to implementing game-changing results. Companies acting as a middleman to conduct business can be eliminated using this technology. Thus, they are looking forward to utilizing blockchain technology to remove central authority over the network. It enables us to achieve transformative change but will take time to solve existing challenges with user scalability and complexity of transaction. Thus, the blockchain technology can be imagined as the ozone layer in the atmosphere where with its presence we can stop many malicious activities in the field of computer technology, where it acts as a protective shield to the users' data against attackers.

Objective of the Book

This book covers the latest cryptocurrencies and blockchain technologies and their applications. It discusses blockchain and cryptocurrencies related issues and also explains how to provide the security differently through algorithms, frameworks, approaches, techniques and mechanisms. This book explores blockchain in relation to other technologies like IoT, big data, artificial intelligence, etc.

Organization of the Book

This book consists of 15 chapters which are organized into two sections. The first section of the book contains eight chapters focusing mainly on blockchain technology and its impact on IoT and social networks. The second section consists of seven chapters that concentrate mostly on the cryptocurrencies and blockchain applications. A brief description of each of the chapters follows:

- **Section 1: Cryptocurrencies and Blockchain Technologies** (Chapters 1-8)

  - **Chapter 1**: In this chapter, the author discusses how the advent of Blockchain Technology has changed the lives of people, giving them a new dimension. It has changed the perspective of viewing things on the web and has been more user-centric and user-friendly. Blockchain, with its wide range of technology, has provided more data security. The hashing algorithms used security parameters that have a wide diversity in controlling the cybercrimes occurring in the world and also solve the problem of data breach and money, and property-related issues. With this, sectors like digital advertising, cybersecurity, forecasting, supply chain management, IoT, and networking have a fantastic future. It has a comprehensive perspective of the new occupation industry. In a client-server architecture, users experience a single point of failure and even it is prone to attackers to provide a better solution. The use of distributed network improves the efficiency of the system and provides more security to the system. The transactional activities can be performed much faster and can be efficiently used. The blockchain technology provides a sustainable and efficient method to the existing service structures where some are underperforming and have unreliable security. The authors discuss that the blockchain technology is going to be used in many more sectors in the future, such as in government systems, as these systems are slow, dense, and likely to be affected by corruption. Implementing blockchain technology in government systems can make their operations much more secure and efficient.

  - **Chapter 2:** In this chapter, the author discusses the blockchain technology architecture with the consensus algorithms involved in it. Also, the type of blockchain systems and applications, such as those in reputation systems and the internet of things (IoT), are discussed. Future directions in the field of blockchain are also discussed.

  - **Chapter 3:** In this chapter, the author discusses the ability of blockchain to reduce business costs, simplifying various processes and interactions with others. Blockchain can provide its users with a faster and safer way to verify essential information and establish trust. With the advent of 5G technology, which provides faster speed and faster communication, its impact can be seen everywhere. This chapter also discusses how blockchain makes supply chains trustful and trackable. Because of the enormous potential of blockchain, it can be thought of as the operating system of the future. It also helps in streamlining processes and removing intermediaries.

  - **Chapter 4:** This chapter discusses various blockchain-based social media platforms. Today's primary concern is social media platform security and privacy. Blockchain-based social media provides more benefits than just security and privacy. It assists in gaining control over the user's content and enables e-commerce, crowd-funding transactions as well as smart apps and contracts. This chapter also highlights the research challenges and issues facing the blockchain social network.

  - **Chapter 5:** In this chapter, the rapid advancement in connected and automated vehicle technologies are discussed. Cooperative adaptive cruise control (CACC)-based platooning is used as a case study. The CACC-based platooning can enhance safety and driving comfort, increase traffic throughput, and reduce fuel consumption and pollutant emissions. Various platooning maneuvers, such as merge, split, lane change, leave, etc., have been integrated with CACC-based platooning to meet the objectives mentioned above. In such a platooning, a platoon leader plays a crucial role in the execution of various functions such as synchronization, collision avoidance, coordination, and better route planning. However, if a malevolent vehicle becomes the leader, it may put the entire platoon in danger. Thus, vehicles must elect a trusted and reputed leader to lead the platoon. The unencrypted broadcast inter-vehicle communication of CACC exposes vehicles to several security threats. Establishing trust among vehicles is a critical challenge. The author states that the core features of the blockchain of decentralization, immutability, security, and high availability turn out to be a strong contender for addressing the challenge. Introduction of blockchain platforms supporting smart contracts helps build trust among untrusted parties and enhances the decision-making processes.

- **Chapter 6:** In this chapter, the author discusses various applications of IoT, followed by security and privacy issues. The internet of things (IoT) plays a significant role in the industry and is encouraging research to come up with various applications by bringing economic and social benefits to society. The impact of IoT can be seen in various environments like mission-critical applications, health, transport systems, video surveillance, banking, etc. The chapter discusses challenges for secure IoT followed by an introduction to blockchain technology along with various advantages of blockchain for IoT. The author discusses the application domains of blockchain technology in IoT, classification of threat models that are considered by blockchain protocols for IoT networks, and comparison of state-of-art secure models concerning blockchain. The IoT objects are interconnected to each other, but the functions of these vary from each other, which yield better results of security with the conventional approaches. To address the security and privacy concerns, the central server concept is eliminated and blockchain technology is introduced as a part of IoT, blockchain, which is used to provide security in a peer-to-peer network which is similar to IoT technology.

- **Chapter 7:** In this chapter, the author discusses the dynamics of worm propagation in cryptovirology. A nonlinear epidemic model is applied to study the viral propagation of worm in the cyber network system and the effect of rate of worm infection on the dynamics of the model is analyzed. In this chapter, the author discusses how the internet is used as a powerful tool for communication, cyber transactions and cyber networks; most computers are interconnected through the same operating software. Also, in the present era, the internet becomes the primary medium for cybercrime. Cybercrimes are committed by developing malicious codes or programs which invade private and public computers, gathering information and posing security threats. The highest risks faced by computer networks is from viral malware or worm propagation which target the software vulnerability. Like in cryptovirology, cryptography is used to design powerful malicious software. The security of critical networks is targeted and chaotic or erratic behavior is introduced in their performance, leading to disruption in the complete system.

Also, in recent times, blockchain security vulnerabilities have become an issue of distributed ledger technology.

– **Chapter 8:** In this chapter, the author shows the strength of Bitcoin value, even though it has many security threats. With the help of a case study, the major contributing security breach which caused a drop in the value of Bitcoin is identified. Also, there is a focus on the prediction of the future value of the Bitcoin. Bitcoin is the world's first virtual currency.

• **Section 2: Cryptocurrencies and Blockchain Applications** (Chapter 9-15)

– **Chapter 9:** In this chapter, the blockchain technologies are discussed that could be used to develop a lot of applications, which is similar to the internet. The information recorded on a blockchain can take on any form, whether it is denoting a transfer of money, ownership, a transaction, someone's identity, an agreement between two parties, or even how much electricity a light bulb has used. It can be done by getting confirmation from several devices such as the computer on the network. The data cannot be removed or altered by anyone without the knowledge and permission of those who made that record, as well as the wider community. In blockchain technology, rather than keeping information in one central point, as is done by traditional recording methods, multiple copies of the same data are stored in different locations and on different network devices, such as computers or printers, which is called peer-to-peer network. If one point of storage is damaged or lost, multiple copies remain safe and secure elsewhere and if one piece of information is changed without the agreement of the rightful owners, there are countless other examples in existence where the information is right, making the false record obsolete. Blockchain owes its name to the manner in which it works and where data is stored, that means the information is packed into blocks, which link to form a chain with similar blocks. Usually, each block contains the data it is recording. It also includes a digital signature linked to the account that made the recording and a unique identifying link, in the form of a hash (think of it as a digital fingerprint), to the previous block in the chain. It is this link that makes it impossible for any of the information to be altered or for a block to be inserted between two existing blocks. In order to do so, all the following blocks would need to be edited too. As a result, each block strengthens the previous block and the security of the entire blockchain because it means more blocks would need to be changed to tamper with any information. When combined, all of these create unquestionable storage of information which cannot be disputed or declared to be untrue. This chapter discusses the working of blockchain technology.

– **Chapter 10:** This chapter provides an outlook on big data and blockchain individually with viewpoints of various situations in which both Big Data and Blockchain coexist to ensure data quality in various sectors, including web, health, education and government through diagrams, working and inner implementations. The importance of Blockchain-Big Data in the national development with its various aspects in Industry 4.0 and some other future aspects that need to be addressed are also discussed. This chapter is designed to give insights into various facets of cryptocurrency, blockchain and big data, which are combined to perform certain operations pertaining to the task of any organization or institution that may be private or public.

– **Chapter 11:** In this chapter, the author proposes a smart farming environment based on artificial intelligence (AI) and blockchain technology. Artificial intelligence can be harnessed to automate and manage agricultural and related tasks while blockchain technology can help in intensifying agriculture food and supply chains. A sensational AI-based approach helps in developing the smart farming environment that can efficiently gather and monitor data for real-time monitoring to address the uncertain issues faced by the agricultural community. Because of the rapid increase in global population, there will be an increase of nearly 70% in the agricultural production by 2050 to meet the ever-increasing demands of people. To develop cost-effective agricultural solutions, 90% intensification is required on technological farming for achieving agricultural inputs and market demands. Today, the agricultural sector is affected by various factors like increased labor costs, increased population, crop failures, unpredictable yields, extreme weather, climate change, market fluctuations, etc. All these factors have directly or indirectly affected the socioeconomic status of farmers. With such a large number of challenges and increasing demands, there is a need to implement an artificial intelligence-based approach for developing the smart farming environment for real-time monitoring and management of agricultural issues. Blockchain can handle issues related to the increased demands for agricultural products with transparency and trust. It accompanies a variety of certification schemes on branded agricultural products that face issues related to claims, labels and adulterations. Blockchain can prove to be an efficient solution for agricultural products safety, quality and sustainability. Blockchain ensures the permanency of records during data sharing. ICT in the agricultural sector provides more efficient solutions for effective water and land usage, resulting in maximum agricultural yields. The author proposes a neoteric smart and sustainable farming environment incorporating the blockchain-based artificial intelligence approach.

– **Chapter 12:** In this chapter, the author states that many countries have quantified their purpose to create an ecosystem in which businesses can grow, which can only mean the continued growth of the sector in the predictable future. Simultaneously, it reduces the friction of making payments and transfers in fiat currency, facilitated by e-money. This has raised the bar of virtual currency and the cryptocurrency market. Bill Gates opined that *"Banking is essential, banks are not."* The early 21st century has seen a proliferation of financial technology and analytics firms, providing a wide and varied array of services, from payments and local and international money transmission to financing through P2P lending and crowdfunding. Venture capital funding in the U.K. for financial technology-related business increased to more than US$500 million in 2014, while the sector is estimated to contribute more than GBP 20 billion to the economy. Cryptocurrencies have come a long way from their relatively ambiguous origins. Even though the financial institutions have concerns about digital currencies as tools for criminals, terrorists or rebellious individuals frustrated with traditional money, the industry has significantly progressed in establishing their potential legitimacy.

– **Chapter 13:** In this chapter, the author discusses how blockchain technology can create ramifications across the investment banking ecosystem due to their cryptographic distributed ledger. The author evaluates the adaptation feasibility and predicts performance for a regulatory framework when investment banks apply blockchain technology. Random sampling is used with a sample size of 50 respondents from investment banks operating in urban Bangalore based on the primary data collected. Statutory impact (SI), compliance policy (CP), fiscal policy (FP), competitive edge (CE) and service-level agreement (SLA) are the variables. The statistical software used to test structural equation model (SEM) with confirmatory factor analysis (CFA), multiple linear regression analysis and one-way ANOVA (analysis of variance) are SPSS and SPSS AMOS. SI is the most influential variable and has a more significant impact on acceptability with beta value 0.899 at 0.001 percent significant level with Chi-square value of 3.14 and the estimated reliability post-adoption of 81 per cent. SI, CP, SLA, and CE are the significant predictors of performance with a higher association between the performance of the banks and regulatory framework indicators with significance at 0.01 percent level. The author discusses how technology can reduce the middle- and back-end operating cost and improves transparency.

– **Chapter 14:** In this chapter, the author discusses how blockchain technology could facilitate and help to implement a market, allowing the transformation of energy in a digital asset which could be tracked and traded. The author discusses the smart energy grid decentralization problem by proposing a blockchain-based energy market allowing the energy to be traded among prosumers in a peer-to-peer fashion. The main advantages brought by the blockchain technology, such as energy provenance, transaction privacy and immutability, are discussed and details on their implementation in our envisioned energy market are provided. To implement the energy market management operations, such as prosumers registration and permission control, bids and offers matching and financial settlement self-enforcing smart contracts are used. At the same time, the prosumers level smart contract is used to automatize the bids and offers registration and monitor their energy generation and demand.

– **Chapter 15:** In this chapter, the author discusses blockchain from an application point of view, throwing some light on mining mechanism, participants of the blockchain system, and organized and versatile use cases, while demystifying the related myths. Blockchain is an eccentric technology, in addition to being the most vaunted, least understood and most disrupting technology of the current era.

Gulshan Shrivastava
National Institute of Technology Patna, India
Dac-Nhuong Le
Hai Phong University, Hai Phong, Vietnam
Kavita Sharma
National Institute of Technology, Kurukshetra, India

Acknowledgments

First of all, we would like to thank the authors for contributing their excellent chapters to this book. Without their contributions, this book would not have been possible. Thanks to all our friends for sharing our happiness at the start of this project and following up with their encouragement when it seemed too difficult to complete.

We would like to acknowledge and thank the most important people in our life, our parents, and finally, give thanks to god. This book has been a long-cherished dream of ours which would not have been turned into reality without the support and love of our families, who encouraged us despite not giving them the proper time and attention.

Gulshan Shrivastava
National Institute of Technology Patna, India
Dac-Nhuong Le
Hai Phong University, Hai Phong, Vietnam
Kavita Sharma
National Institute of Technology, Kurukshetra, India

Acronyms

5G	The next (5th) Generation
AI	Artificial Intelligence
ACC	Adaptive Cruise Control
AMOS	Analysis of Moment Structure
ANOVA	Analysis of Variance
AGFI	Adjusted Goodness of Fit Index
API	Application Programming Interface
AWS	Amazon Web Services
ADEPT	Autonomous Decentralized Peer-to-Peer Telemetry
BCT	Blockchain Technology
BG	Byzantine Generals
CA	Certificate Authority
CACC	Cooperative Adaptive Cruise Control
CE	Competitive Edge
CFA	Confirmatory Factor Analysis
CFI	Comparative Fit Index
CP	Compliance Policy
C-DAC	Center for Development of Advanced Computing
CSS	Cross-Site Scripting
CP	Compliance Policy
CPU	Central Processing Unit
CoAP	Constrained Application Protocol
DApp	Decentralized Application
DHT	Distributed Hash Table
DPoS	Delegated Proof of Stake
dBFT	Delegated Byzantine Fault Tolerance
DLT	Distributed Ledger Technology
DNS	Domain Name System
DOSN	Distributed Online Social Network
DoS	Denial of Service
DDoS	Distributed Denial of Service
DTSL	Datagram Transport Layer Security
DSRC	Dedicated Short-Range Communications
EVM	Ethereum Virtual Machine
ECDSA	Elliptic Curve Digital Signature Algorithm
EHR	Electronic Health Record

ERP	Enterprise Resource Planning
EMR	Electronic Medical Record
FIR	First Information Report
FP	Fiscal Policy
GFI	Goodness of Fit Index
GUID	Global Unique Identification
HDAC	Hyundai Digital Access Currency
HTTP	Hypertext Transfer Protocol
HTML	Hypertext Markup Language
HD	High Definition
IANA	Internet Assigned Numbers Authority
IB	Investment Banks
ICT	Information and Communications Technology
IoT	Internet of Things
IPFS	InterPlanetary File System
I2V	Infrastructure-to-Vehicle
IP	Internet Protocol
IPv6	Internet Protocol version 6
IT	Information Technology
ICO	Initial Coin Offering
IoV	Internet of Value
IPO	Initial Public Offering
JSP	Java Server Pages
KYC	Know Your Customer
LPoS	Leased Proof-of-Stake
LoWPAN	Low-Power Wireless Personal Area Networks
LWM2M	Lightweight M2M
M2M	Machine to Machine
MBD	Misbehavior Detection
MQTT	Message Queuing Telemetry Transport
NAV	Net Asset Value
NIFTY	National Stock Exchange Index
NFI	Normed Fit Index
NHTSA	National Highway Transportation Safety Agency
NSA	National Security Agency
OBC	Open Blockchain
OS	Operating System
OBM	Original Brand Manufacturing
PKI	Public Key Infrastructure
PHP	Hypertext Preprocessor
PC	Personal Computer
P2P	Peer to Peer
PoW	Proof of Work
PoS	Proof of Stake
PBFT	Practical Byzantine Fault Tolerance
PoET	Proof of Elapsed Time

PoA	Proof of Activity
PoB	Proof of Burn
PL	Platoon Leader
RMSEA	Root Mean Square Error of Approximation
RMR	Root Mean Square Residential
RF1	Statutory Impact
RF2	Compliance policy
RF3	Competitive edge
RF4	Fiscal Policy
RF5	Service Level agreement
RFW	Regulatory Framework
REST	Representational State Transfer
RPC	Remote Procedure Call
RSU	Road-Side Units
RAT	Radio Access Technology
RPL	Routing Protocol for Low-Power and Lossy Networks
RFID	Radio Frequency Identification
RBAC	Role-Based Access Management
SIS	Susceptible, Infected, Susceptible Model
SEIR	Susceptible, Exposed, Infected and Recovered
SEI	Susceptible Exposed Infected
SC	Smart Contract
SCMS	Security Credential Management System
SIR	Susceptible, Infected, Recovered
SI	Statutory Impact
SLA	Service Level Agreement
S&P	Standard & Poor's (Index)
SEM	Structural Equation Model
SQL	Structured Query Language
SSL	Secure Sockets Layer
SCP	Stellar Consensus Protocol
SO	Social Overlay
SHA	Secure Hash Algorithm
TA	Trusted Authority
TCS	Tata Consultancy Service
TSL	Transport Layer Security
TCP	Transmission Control Protocol
UGV	Unmanned Ground Vehicle
UI	User Interaction
URL	Uniform Resource Locator
UTXO	Unspent Transaction Output
UNL	Unique Node List
VANET	Vehicular Ad-Hoc Networks
VVP	Virus-Vulnerable and Protected
V2X	Vehicle-to-Everything
V2V	Vehicle-to-Vehicle

V2I	Vehicle-to-Infrastructure
XHTML	Extensible Hypertext Markup Language
XMPP	Extensible Messaging and Presence Protocol
XAMP	X-Cross Platform
XSS	Cross-Site Scripting
W3C	World Wide Web Consortium
WAVE	Wireless Access in Vehicular Environment
WSN	Wireless Sensor Network

CRYPTOCURRENCIES AND BLOCKCHAIN TECHNOLOGY

PART I

CRYPTOCURRENCIES AND
BLOCKCHAIN TECHNOLOGY

CHAPTER 1

BLOCKCHAIN: A NEW ERA OF TECHNOLOGY

Gururaj H L,* Manoj Athreya A, Ashwin A Kumar, Abhishek M Holla, Nagarajath S M, Ravi Kumar V

Vidyavardhaka College of Engineering, Mysuru, India

* Corresponding author: gururaj1711@vvce.ac.in

Abstract

As the whole world is moving towards digital payments, ethers and transaction methods with quick payment, information is stored in a blockchain in a distributed network. The distributed network is a network system through which data, software and computer programming are spread across more than one node (computers) and these nodes are dependent on each other. It is nothing but a peer-to-peer network which eliminates a single point of failure. The blockchain is a growing list of records called blocks that are linked using cryptography. It is a decentralized, distributed and immutable ledger to store digital transactions. Its databases are managed using a peer-to-peer network where all the nodes in a network are equal and are the major concern in the types of network architecture. The consensus protocol is used for transacting and communicating between the nodes. In this chapter, an approach for storing data in a blockchain is investigated and reported whereby the record is kept safe and secure, preventing it from being manipulated by others. With the help of the above blockchain technology we are able to achieve data that is secure from manipulators.

Keywords: Blockchain, inter-planetary file system, Ethereum, Web 3.0, consensus protocol, mining, distributed P2P network, Ethereum transaction, SHA-256 algorithm, decentralized application

Blockchain is one of the booming words in the field of computer technology, which has the power to change the lives of people as the Internet did in the past twenty years. Blockchain is ready to make a big impact on the lives of people if we adhere to this technology. It is a fundamental and parallel part to the Internet and not just a use case like emails, e-commerce, etc. When people hear the term blockchain many come to a conclusion that it deals mainly with cryptocurrency and Bitcoin but it is not all about that. The cryptocurrency and Bitcoin can be compared to email where the backbone technology behind it is the internet. As such, blockchain is a technology. Blockchain can be broadly described as a digital form of the ledger where you can store whatever data you want and then later access it through the hash value you received. It's just like the acknowledgment number you get when you produce some documents. Consider a scenario where some person x needs to send money to person y who lives in a different country; it takes at least 5-6 working days to transfer the money because we have middle parties like banks which require time to process it. When it comes to blockchain we have an immutable universal ledger where it stores transaction details of all the individuals in a block. When a transaction is made it adds a new block into the existing set of blocks in the system which is authenticated by everyone. When it comes to security it uses the best cryptographic algorithms and is difficult to hack. It uses the SHA-256 algorithm to keep the hash value secured. When a hacker tries to hack a blockchain system, first of all, he needs computation power of more than 50% of the supercomputer in the word and he also needs to change all the blocks because they are cryptographically linked to each other; moreover, the blocks reside in a distributed node and every time it checks with other nodes to see whether they possess the same details which are based on the consensus protocol. As it is a collection of chained blocks you can trace back to the transactions that have occurred by going back block by block. They also have originated smart contracts which are the logic built into most blockchains, where when an event happens it triggers another event. Finally, all the blocks are not owned by anyone like a bank or any trusted authority. The blockchain is owned by all of us and to maintain it we need resources, electricity, computing power, time, money, etc. So for the people who maintained all these resources, in 2008 Satoshi Nakamoto introduced the concept of Bitcoins to give them as incentives, and the persons who looked after the blockchain mined it and hence they were called miners. In this blockchain the word TRUST plays an important role. Consider an example of a party where ten people put in a thousand rupees each and draw one name from the box; this lucky person will get the entire amount. Here, it is the trust between all ten people which works like a blockchain and brings the trust from a centralized to decentralized platform. The blockchain works on the following four major features:

1. Consensus

2. Security

3. Provenance

4. Trust

The countries which use this technology are Japan, Canada, Dubai, Estonia and many more. Dubai is transforming itself as the world's first blockchain-powered government. Estonia is being called Ethereum Island. When it comes to India we have certain blockchain information such as:

1. State Bank of India partnered with BankChain and Intel to develop blockchain solutions.

2. West Bengal and Andhra Pradesh is transitioning to using blockchain software for solving land property issues.

3. The Centre for Development of Advanced Computing (C-DAC) Hyderabad is working on blockchain projects.

4. Blockchain patents are claimed by the Indians and many more.

Some of the recent blockchain technology being hyped in the current industry are as follows:

1. Google is bringing blockchain technology to its cloud services.

2. Facebook has plans for blockchain-based authentication.

3. Microsoft Azure allows the development, testing, and deployment of secure blockchain apps.

4. IBM is now delivering blockchain service around the world.

5. Walmart has partnered with IBM to create a blockchain for tracking food globally through its supply chain.

6. Mastercard has started to build their own blockchain-based payment gateways.

7. Huawei's blockchain technology offers mobile carriers superb opportunities to subscribers.

Figure 1.1 shows the different sectors in which blockchain technology is being used.

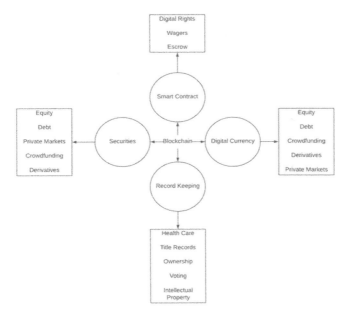

Figure 1.1   Sectors of blockchain.

Blockchain is making its way into many sectors like agriculture, power production, education, banking, voting and many more. Consider the example of power production where if you have solar panels installed in your home and if you produce electricity, the excess can be sent to others and in turn you get money through Blockchain; and where we can have the IoT also being used with it. Basically, blockchain comes into the picture when you can prevent data hoaxes and establish trust in the distributed network. The internet has solved many more problems like information searches (Google, Yahoo), distribution (YouTube, Amazon Prime, Netflix) and communication (email, chat applications) but it has not solved two major problems, which are trust and intermediation. On the internet, we find fake news and fake profiles which are not to be trusted; and in intermediaries, the big companies like Google, Amazon, Facebook, etc., have acquired the market and are not open to all, which means there is a middleman between producer and consumer. But with the advent of Blockchain, we can solve all these problems and bring back a trusted environment.

1.1   Introduction to Web 3.0

With the web entering a new phase of evolution, Web 3.0 is lined up to be the next big thing marking a fundamental change in how developers create websites and how people interact with those websites. Internet experts claim that these changes will make the internet smarter, thereby making our lives easier [2].

1.1.1   Web 1.0

This is referred to as the first generation of the web, invented by Tim Berners-Lee. It is often referred to as the read-only web as few people created content for the rest of the customers. Commonly used technologies are HTTP, XHTML, HTML, CSS, etc. It supports both server-side scripting (like JSP, PHP, etc.) and client-side scripting (JavaScript, VBScript, etc.) [3].

Web 1.0 has a lot of vulnerabilities, some of them are:

1. It is extremely slow.

2. Each time new content is pushed onto the webpage, it needs to be refreshed.

3. It doesn't support two-way communication as it can be initiated only by the client (HTTP).

1.1.2   Web 2.0

This is also referred to as the read-write web as the users can interact with websites that have predetermined behaviors according to the inputs. With the emergence of blogs in the 20th century, widgets and other instant and universal authorizing tools and sites are always ready to accept the content. These have played a substantial role in the democratization of the web. Commonly used technologies are Ajax, DOM, REST, etc. [6].

Web 2.0 has a lot of vulnerabilities, some of them are:

1. SQL Injection

2. Information Leakage

3. Cross-Site Request Forgery

4. Authentication and Authorization Flaws

5. Cross-Site Scripting

1.1.3   Web 3.0

This term was coined by the reporter John Markoff of *The New York Times* in 2006. It allows online applications to receive information from the web and provide new information (results) to the users [4].

Web 3.0 is made up of these 4 basic properties:

- *Semantic Web*: This deals with the meaning or the emotion conveyed by the data.

- *3D graphics*: This is being used to provide a realistic feel to the websites.

- *Universal*: This will allow accessing the content/service on the web from anywhere.

- *Artificial intelligence*: This will allow websites to filter and present users the best data possible.

1.2   Blockchain

The concept of blockchain was first introduced by Stuart Haber and W. Scott Stornetta while they were trying to build a system in which document timestamps could not be modified.

This was later implemented in the year 2008 by Satoshi Nakamoto, whose real identity is still unknown.

Blockchain can be defined as a growing list of records called blocks, which are linked and stored using cryptography. The first block of the chain is referred to as the genesis block [11].

Each and every block will have the following details in it:

1. *Data*: String of characters stored.

2. *Nonce*: A unique number related to mining.

3. *Previous hash*: Hash value of a block that came before the current block. This field establishes the cryptographic link with the subsequent block.

4. *Hash*: Fingerprint of some amount of data stored in the block.

As shown in Figure 1.2, the hash value of a block is calculated using all of the other three fields, i.e., data, nonce and the previous hash field.

The concept of blockchain can be understood with the help of the following:

1. Hash Cryptography

2. Immutable Ledger

3. Distributed P2P Network

4. Mining

5. Consensus Protocol

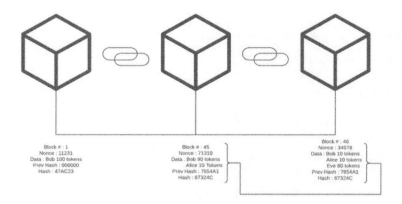

Figure 1.2   Cryptographically linked blocks.

1.2.1 Hash Cryptography

Each and every human being in this world will have a unique fingerprint and there exists a very minimal chance, i.e., one in 60 million, for this to be the same. Similarly, the digital document like an operating system, video, etc., can be identified uniquely with the hash value calculated using the SHA-256 algorithm [5]. This was first developed by the National Security Agency (NSA) and the expansion is as follows:

- SHA stands for secure hash algorithm.

- 256 is the total number of bits consumed in the memory.

The requirements for any hash algorithm are as stated below:

1. *One-way*: Every digital document will have a hash value associated with it. This can be retrieved through the digital document but the reverse cannot be achieved.

2. *Deterministic*: Every digital document will have a unique hash value generated by a hashing algorithm which will remain the same until the file content is not changed.

3. *Fast computation*: The hash value generation should be instantaneous and must not be sluggish.

4. *Avalanche effect*: Any change in the input file causes a radical change in the hash value generated previously.

5. *Must withstand collisions*: If a hash function generates the same value for two digital documents, this is referred to as collisions. Data integrity makes it obligatory that such collisions are prevented.

Figure 1.3 shows the conversion of message to hash value using SHA-256 algorithm where for each character change it generates a different hash value. The important feature is that we cannot obtain the message from hash value.

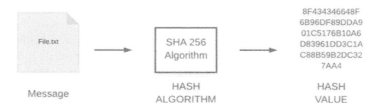

Figure 1.3   Hash function.

1.2.2 Immutability

Immutability refers to anything and everything that cannot be changed once recorded. For example, a mail sent to a bunch of people cannot be reversed. An additional field called timestamp is stored inside the block when a transaction is approved and appended onto the blockchain. If anyone tries to alter the data in a block the cryptographic link is broken [7]. This helps us to recognize the precise section of the chain where the data is manipulated. Thus, one has to compute the previous hash value of the entire chain again to restore the link. It requires a lot of computational power in order to do so. Therefore, making sure that the data stored is resistant to any kind of alterations. This feature is not available in the earlier databases which only provide an option to delete or modify records. Moreover, blockchains sustain the entire history and data path of any application. This acts as a backbone for any auditing process. Preserving a full historical record is not only a blessing for auditing, but also provides new chances in the query, analytics, and overall business processes [9].

Figure 1.4 shows the immutability feature of blockchain.

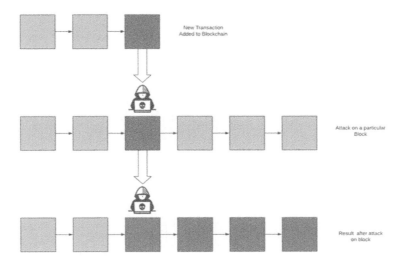

Figure 1.4   Immutability of blockchain.

1.2.3 Distributed P2P Network

The backbone of blockchain methodology is formed by P2P network architecture. This policy authorizes us to remove the dependency on a central decision-making source called a server [12]. The user has to completely trust networks and hope they don't have a backdoor to quietly read or manipulate the reports. Also, one should hope that they don't go out of business and shut down their servers. The nodes comprising tablets, routers, etc., interact and share data directly with one another; thus, distributing all the data across all nodes in the grid rather than using a server. All the nodes in the network will have a copy of the blockchain, thereby making it completely impossible for anyone to modify any value in the chain [10]. Hypothetically, all these nodes are joined via a path. None of the nodes have precise knowledge about the network topology and merely reroute messages to the designated node. Members of the P2P network share the resources between other members, including bandwidth, disk storage, etc. This is accomplished with the help of minimum resource contribution threshold defined for all peers in the network. The peer-to-peer network enables us to solve all the obstacles faced in client-server architecture, i.e., single source of failure and scalability, efficiently [13]. Table 1.1 below shows the contrasting characteristics of both the architectures.

Table 1.1 Difference between Client-Server and P2P.

Client-Server Architecture	P2P Architecture
The Server acts as the master and client as a slave	Peers are treated as nodes with equal capability
Adopted in small and large companies	Normally adopted small companies
Easy to set up and manage	Hard to set up and manage
Software installation is done on the server and it is accessed by the clients	Software installation is done on all the nodes and accessed by the nodes itself
Ex: Instagram	Ex: BitTorrent

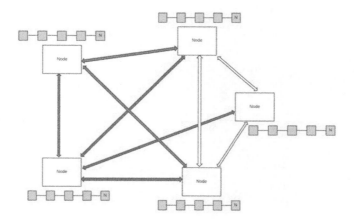

Figure 1.5 P2P network of blockchain.

1.2.4 Mining

This term picked up steam due to the recent surge of Bitcoin. It can be defined as the process of adding new transactions to the distributed system by predicting the value of the nonce such that the hash value generated is less than the target range. Miners compete against each other to figure out a hash value by solving a mathematical problem and receive a reward in terms of tokens or transaction fees. One of the solutions or mining algorithm used is proof-of-work [15]. This acts like a testament that the miner spent a substantial bulk of time and resources to figure out the solution to the problem. The miner needs to wait a while before his transaction is confirmed and added to the block. Afterward, the reward is credited to the miner. Going by the trend, the amount associated with a block mined decreases by half every 210,000 blocks. The decrease in the amount credited is evened up by the increase in the transaction fees. Subsequently, no new coins are generated or issued.

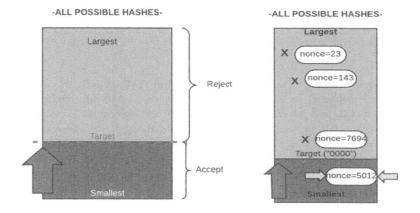

Figure 1.6 Process of mining.

1.2.5 Consensus Protocol

Blockchain consensus protocol creates an indisputable system of understanding between various nodes across a distributed network. This permits us to keep all the nodes on the grid synchronized with one another [16]. As a result of a distributed system, it becomes mandatory to maintain the same state of blockchain across the network. This is being challenged by two main factors:

a) *Attackers*: This nature of attack is prevalent when an attacker wants to disrupt the distributed chain by brute-force method. There are two probable ways in which the attacker can do it:

1. *Adding a new block between the chain*: Suppose the attacker adds a new block in between the blocks of the chain, then the entire cryptographic link will be broken. The chain on distribution will perceive that the chain that it contains is different from all the other copies in the network. Instantly, the node will recognize the same and replace the entire copy of the chain, thereby integrating the data across the grid.

2. *Adding a new vicious block at the end of the chain*: Each and every node performs a series of checks on the newly mined blocks before confirming it to the miner.

During this process, if some node feels that the block is malicious, it will soon bring it to the notice of the network and necessary actions will be taken against it.

b) *Competing chains*: This problem arises when two nodes mine a block into the chain at approximately the same time. With a large number of nodes present in the distributed network, a conflict crops up with the development of two competing chains and it thereby becomes imperative to make a call [17]. The solution to this dilemma is achieved with the help of a simple notion, i.e., to accept the chain which will add the next block. Now, a lot depends on the hashing power of the nodes and whichever set of nodes has the higher power will have a greater possibility of mining the next block. The entire copy of the accepted chain among the competing chains is now relayed across the network to retrieve what is known as the orphan blocks. These are mostly blocks (enclosing the miner's reward) now no longer a part of the chain [18].

This forms the core of the blockchain technology to exist and function methodically.

1.3   Bitcoin

Bitcoin, launched under the name Satoshi Nakamoto in 2008, is a digital currency which overcomes the inefficiency and greed of banks. Bitcoin's nature is resilient to the encroachment of banks and governments. It uses P2P technology that operates under no central adversaries where transactions are approved mutually by the network participants [22]. Here, a private key protects the access to the money of an individual account, which is contradictory in the case of fiat currency. Additionally, the number of bitcoins minted is limited to 21 million, unlike traditional currency minted by authorized central banking agencies. Blockchain is the underlying technology that stores each transaction on Bitcoin network globally in a shared ledger which is verifiable, accessible and constantly updated by a global fleet of computers. Once a transaction is done, its details are globally recorded, which provides no means to reverse the transaction. At the same time, Bitcoin requires no identity of one's personal information for participating in a network, thus it cannot be traced back to an individual until and unless he/she wishes to reveal it.

1.4   Ethereum

Ethereum is a decentralized, open-source, dynamic service that works on the properties of the blockchain. It was first introduced in 2013 through a white paper by Vitalik Buterin. This was obtained from the Bitcoin project which is primarily a tool intended towards monitoring transactions among people. He himself was an enthusiast of the Bitcoin project but firmly felt that this technology can be applied to diverse varieties of transactions [20]. The core of Ethereum largely revolves around smart contracts. They are small blocks of code that reside in the blockchain meant for accomplishing a specific task. This system went online in July 2015 and continues to thrive even today. Its main aim is to develop a platform which runs on DApps in order to create a more global, free and more mature internet, Web 3.0. Their intention is to give users and creators more control in developing their apps rather than the conglomerate. It runs on the same protocol as that of Bitcoin, proof of work (PoW), but the disadvantages are a 51% danger of attack and the enormous energy consumption required for the security. Thus, proof of stake [19] came into existence which works akin to PoW. Instead of nodes approval in the network, it makes use of token holders. *N%* of a block reward is received for *N%* of tokens (computing power in the case of PoW) for accounting on the network [21].

The concept of Ethereum can be understood with the help of the following:

1. Ethereum Network

2. Interfacing with Ethereum

3. Ethereum Account

4. Transaction

1.4.1 Ethereum Network

The infrastructure of a decentralized network is made up of an assortment of nodes interacting with each other. The Ethereum network is largely related to the transfer of money and storage of data, thus permitting us to build diverse exciting applications. This is achieved with the help of a cryptocurrency called ether. This is similar to bitcoin and is responsible for fueling the Ethereum ecosystem. There exist many Ethereum networks, some of which are:

1. *Main Network*: Production applications are deployed here so that they can be used by the user. It is in this network that ether coins have real value and can be turned into U.S. dollars.

2. *Rinkeby, Kovan, Ropsten Test Network*: These provide us with free ether coins to test code and contracts before deploying them to the main network.

3. *JSON RPC API*: This allows us to connect to the local Ethereum test network which runs at "localhost" on port 8445.

Figure 1.7 depicts the organization of the Ethereum network.

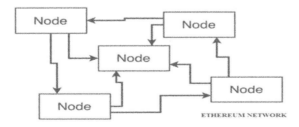

Figure 1.7   Ethereum network.

1.4.2 Interfacing with Ethereum

Interfacing refers to the process of interacting with the network. This can be accomplished in two ways:

1. *Web3 library*: This is an API predominantly used by the developers to interact with the network. It enables the performance of numerous operations like creating smart contracts, sending ethers, etc. It communicates with the blockchain through JSON

RPC and ensures that it is communicating with only one node in the distributed P2P network.

2. *MetaMask*: This is a browser extension used by users to interface with the network. Normally, it is preferred by users who do not have previous knowledge of Ethereum.

Figure 1.8 depicts the interfacing with Ethereum.

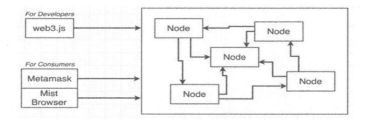

Figure 1.8   Interfacing with Ethereum.

1.4.3   Ethereum Account

MetaMask creates two distinct sorts of accounts:

1. *Externally owned accounts*: These are generated and managed by private keys and will have the following:

    a) No associated code

    b) Ether balance

    c) Help in triggering contract code

    d) Ether transfer

2. *Contract accounts*: These are generated and regulated by code and will have the following:

    a) Associated code

    b) Ether balance

    c) Code implementation is triggered by transactions

Ignoring the kind of account created, the following four essential elements are:

1. *Balance*: The amount of Wei possessed by this address.

2. *Nonce*: In case of externally owned accounts, it depicts the number of transactions carried out from a specific account address; whereas, in a contract account, it illustrates the number of contracts generated by the account.

3. *CodeHash*: The hash of the EVM code of this account. These codes are stored in the database supporting the respective hash value for future retrieval.

4. *StorageRoot*: A 256-bit value representing the encoded version of the data stored in the chain.

1.4.4 Ethereum Network Transactions

Any sort of transaction in the Ethereum network should possess a MetaMask account and some ethers in it. If the user makes an order, they will automatically be redirected to a payment gateway to confirm and pay with ethers. Upon confirmation, their balance is checked in the back-end server to confirm whether it meets the appropriate requirements or not. If the requirements are met then the transaction of ethers will take place. When the user pushes the submit button, it sends the ethereum address to the back-end server for validation. Then the back-end server uses the web3 library to create a transaction object. For demo purposes, the researchers use the test networks while in the real world it is done in the main network. After a successful transaction, the back-end server pushes the success message onto the user screen. The user needs to wait for a few seconds as the transaction object generated needs to be added to the network. This will be approved by the miners by randomly generating a nonce value and is added as a new block in the network. The block will have a unique hash value assigned to it and thus data integrity is ensured.

Figure 1.9 below shows all the steps followed throughout this process in detail.

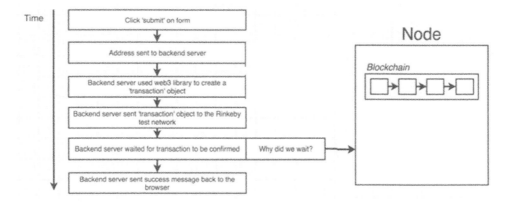

Figure 1.9   Transaction in Ethereum network.

1.5 InterPlanetary File System (IPFS)

The HTTP fails to merge with the modern file distribution techniques recently invented. Without affecting the current network the upgrades are nearly impossible because of the large involvement of the present HTTP model and the web. To overcome these challenges, IPFS network works on distributed peer-to-peer network which has a similar file data structure called Merkle DAG. IPFS works in a manner similar to BitTorrent where bitswap protocol is used. Clients can set their own Bitswap strategies using Bitswap protocol. A Bitswap strategy tells a node how it should request and send blocks to/from its peers. Through the collective use of distributed technologies, IPFS enables a unique file and data sharing in a decentralized fashion. IPFS has its file-system or directories mounted globally and provides high performance and cluster persistence, which is enough to store and organize the world's information [23].

IPFS as the distributed web also offers features like:

1. *Content Addressing*: The addressing data in IPFS is performed by addressing the content of the file or document in the network rather than addressing location where the addressing is different, which is performed using IP addresses. The IPFS address resolves the IPFS objects, the entities present which contain a list of links and content data which is being addressed. When the large files are added to IPFS, the file is decomposed into much smaller representation of data and stored into an array of links that points to the broken pieces of the original data. This type of addressing ensures that a particular address will always result in querying the same file. Content addressing also has an advantage over the content hosted by a node where the content can be retrieved from the IPFS network as long as the file is hosted in the network. Thus, a single copy of a file is enough to retrieve a file from the network.

2. *Distributed Hash Table (DHT)*: The DHT is the database distributed over a network which can be used to store data in terms of key/value pairs in a peer-to-peer network consisting of nodes. The distributed hash table has the mechanism of fault tolerance triggered when key/value pairs are duplicated or not accessible in the network. To evenly share the information across the network, DHT uses the concept of hashing where a hash function that serves as a randomized function accepts keys. Since DHT nodes don't store all the data, routing layer has to perform the necessary function which enables a client to contact other peers in the network that stores the certain key which then can be used to retrieve the value and access the content. The two routing protocols that are significantly used in the routing layer in DHT are iterative lookup and recursive lookup, which are classified on the manner in which they process a complete request.

3. *Versioned File System*: IPFS allows a versioned file system that is made use of in Git versioning which enables maintaining different versions of the same file and can be easily traced to the original file using commit objects. The commit object in the versioned file system has links to name ID which points to last committed object, and also the link which contains the object which points to the globally mounted file directory which is started by that commit.

1.6   Decentralized Applications (DApps)

Decentralized applications are completely open-source applications that work entirely on the smart contract code run on the blockchain. They are a type of software program designed to exist in such a way that is not controlled by any single entity but instead controlled by blocks of code known as smart contracts. DApps uses decentralized storage to store data and code. Decentralized application is a blockchain-based app, where the smart contract is what allows it to connect to the blockchain [1].

The main difference between Satoshi Nakamoto's bitcoin and Vitalik Buterin's ethereum is given in Table 1.2.

Table 1.2   Difference between bitcoin, ethereum, and hyperledger.

Characteristics	Bitcoin	Ethereum	Hyperledger
Permission Restriction	Permission less	Permission less	Permissioned
Access restriction for data	Public	Public or Private	Private
Consensus	Proof-Of-Work	Proof-Of-Work	Practical Byzantine Fault Tolerance
Scalability	High Block scalability	High Block scalability	Low Block scalability
Governance	Low, decentralized decision making by miners	Medium, core developer group, but EIP process	Low, Open governance model based on Linux model
Anonymity	Pseudo-anonymity, no encryption of data	Pseudo-anonymity, no encryption of data	Pseudo-anonymity, encryption of data
Native Currency	Yes, bitcoin	Yes, ether	No
Scripting	Stack-based scripting	Turing complete virtual machine with support to high-level language	Turing complete scripting of chain code in go language

1.7 Case Study: FIR

The first information report (FIR) is the written document maintained by the police department that has the information collected about any criminal offense. It is generally a complaint lodged with the police by the victim of a cognizable offense or by someone on his or her behalf, but anyone can make such a report either orally or in writing to the police, after which an investigation is started by the police. The person giving information has the right to see what is being mentioned and has to affix his signature to it, stating it's correct. The existing system is handwritten, time-consuming and less secure; and there is no way to track if events are being recorded properly. The FIR acts as sensitive data and provides clues for the investigation. Thus, the data stored must be secured and should not be tampered with or influenced by external pressure once the report is written. The FIR details are stored in a ledger where they can be manipulated. So, to mitigate this we can use blockchain technology once the data is stored in a block since it has its hash value and it is linked. Whenever anybody tries to change even a small character or even a space the hash value immediately changes due to the avalanche effect and hence indicates that data has been tampered with. This provides high security of data and eliminates the manipulation of information. The person who provided the information can keep track of it by using the hash value that is generated when the data block is added. The advantages of the FIR is that it reduces cost and time, eliminates manual errors, and online information can be seen by anybody. The FIR consists of information like place, time, date, and detailed descriptions, all of which are stored in a block of the blockchain and the hash value is given to the user to check whether the details are provided correctly and to make sure no information is misinterpreted. Thus, by using blockchain technology a major problem is solved and data integrity is ensured.

1.7.1 Project Description

The FIR dApp is a provable public crystal-clear platform based on decentralized and open source technologies that use blockchain to assure the authenticity of a report filed by the user. It aims to be the standard on decentralized projects communications. With this application, users can lodge a complaint and also protect their identity and publish what really matters to them. This application permits searching for the FIR based on the ID provided to them. This application is eternal and can't be stopped by anyone or anything. All data is securely encrypted before leaving your browser. Also, the code which runs the dApp is viewable by everyone and is free of politics and human error, thus making it secure, trustworthy, and accessible to anyone.

Secure: Ethereum blockchain is fully decentralized. Due to the immutability property of the blockchain, any record added via this application cannot be omitted. This system cannot be controlled by any single adversary or authority.

Trustworthy: All the documents are accumulated on Ethereum along with a timestamp. Neither the content nor the time of the document can be changed or mishandled in any way.

Accessible to anyone: Complaints lodged by the user can be viewed by anyone without incurring any transaction fees. All the vital data required to access the information regarding any application is publicly available.

This distributed application is able to :

- Save arbitrary documents on the InterPlanetary File System (IPFS).
- Receive a receipt for the submission.
- Prove time of submission (via block timestamp).

1.7.2 Tools Used

The tools cited below are needed for the development of the project.

1.7.2.1 Node.js

JavaScript runtime environment is built on Chrome's V8 JavaScript engine. The main strategy of Node.js is that it uses non-blocking and event-driven I/O which enables maintaining a lightweight state in the case of data-concentrated applications which are mainly run as real-time applications. Node.js comes with default package management and a tool called an NPM tool which is installed with every Node.js installation. Node.js can be installed through an installer available via an online repository, with version and dependency management.

1.7.2.2 Truffle

Truffle[1] is a smart contract development environment and framework used to deploy Ethereum DApps, which makes the smart contract development easy for ethereum developers. Since Truffle is a fully fledged framework with development and testing capabilities, it is also embedded with the Web3.0 library by default, which makes it more attractive to users with a Web 3.0 development background. Truffle is operated in the Terminal, using various commands at the different stages of developing a dApp. Contracts can be tested using popular testing frameworks like Mocha and Chai. Truffle supports the development of both web apps and console apps. It also has a feature of migration which helps in in-

---

[1] https://www.trufflesuite.com

stant rebuilding of assets during development. Contract compilation and deployment can be done using the RPC client.

1.7.2.3 Ganache

Ganache[2] is a simulation of blockchain nodes that works to set up a local ethereum node where smart contracts are compiled and can be migrated with a development tool such as Truffle. By using Ganache there is no additional set up of a geth client and other dependencies. It provides a total of 10 virtual accounts, each account loaded with 100 ethers which can be used for the purpose of development where the virtual accounts are used to pay for gas when running transactions on the blockchain. Along with the virtual accounts their private keys are also given and through these keys the transaction is signed and written in the blockchain. Ganache has both the visual user interface and command line interface, which allows users to see the current status of all accounts, including their addresses, private keys, transactions, and balances. Apart from these features, Ganache also provides blockchain log output, which displays the log output of Ganache internal blockchain, including responses and other vital debugging information and advanced mining controls.

1.7.2.4 Infura

Infura[3] provides a set of tools to connect the application to the Ethereum platform. These tools enable secure and reliable access to Ethereum APIs and the InterPlanetary File System. Through Infura one can host their application in the decentralized network of ethereum using the API key available through their platform. Infura also hosts IPFS nodes which connect to IPFS network and users can also connect to them using the URL provided. Infura has a scalable infrastructure with the ability to transfer 2.5 PB of data per month and handle over 10 billion user requests daily.

1.7.2.5 MetaMask

MetaMask[4] is a browser extension that offers crypto wallet and an interface for signing transactions for DApps.Through MetaMask, the transaction can be signed onto the ethereum network without actually running a full ethereum node. MetaMask also enables users to store the wallet-related data like public addresses and private keys similar to any other Ethereum wallet, and users can also interact with websites running DApps and smart contracts. MetaMask includes a feature called secure identity vault, which provides a user interface to handle their identities on different sites and sign transactions onto the blockchain.

1.7.2.6 Solidity

Solidity[5] is a contact-oriented, high-level language for writing smart contracts. Solidity code runs on Ethereum virtual machine (EVM), where once deployed cannot be changed or manipulated. It offers features like inheritance and libraries, and complex user-defined types are also supported. The programming style of Solidity is influenced through C++, JavaScript, and Python and is statically typed. Solidity also has development tools such as Solidity REPL, which is a Solidity interpreter with a command-line Solidity console and solgraph which is a visualization tool that visualizes control flow and highlights potential security vulnerabilities.

---

[2]https://github.com/trufflesuite/ganache
[3]https://infura.io
[4]https://metamask.io
[5]https://github.com/ethereum/solidity

1.7.3   Project Workings

1. *Lodge Complaint*: This facilitates the user to register a new accusation by specifying the required trivia. The information cannot be altered once submitted, thereby giving the end user the freedom of trusting the system and filing a case without bothering about the external influence.

2. *Fetch Complaint:* This element enables us to retrieve the details of a specific accusation using the unique ID number provided when it was first loaded onto the chain.

3. *Recent Complaints*: This element helps to retrieve all the recently added complaints, thereby making sure that the system is available publically.

Figure 1.10   Index page of the application.

Figure 1.10 depicts how a user can file a complaint on this distributed application by specifying the following mandatory details:

1. Police station name

2. Title

3. Detailed description of the complaint

All the aforementioned are considered as inputs for the transaction and are approved by the transfer of a nominal fee of 0.001 ETH.

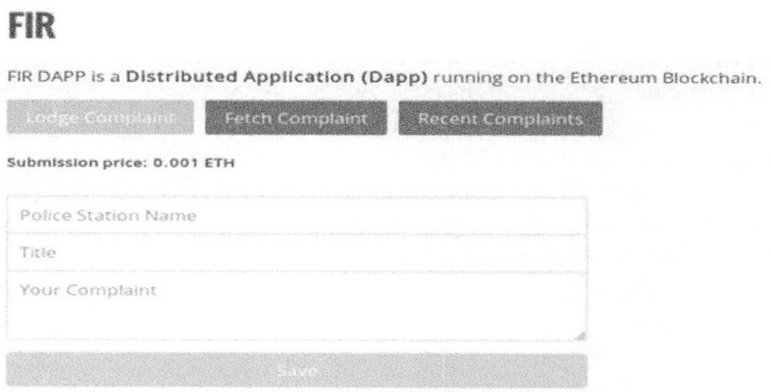

FIR

FIR DAPP is a **Distributed Application (Dapp)** running on the Ethereum Blockchain.

Lodge Complaint   Fetch Complaint   Recent Complaints

Submission price: 0.001 ETH

Police Station Name

Title

Your Complaint

Save

Figure 1.11   Fields for a complaint.

Figure 1.12 demonstrates how MetaMask browser extension pops up when the save button is pushed. A total cost of 0.001 ETH will be debited from the account as a sign of validation and the transaction will be attached to the block upon mining. The user has the choice of either confirming or declining the transaction.

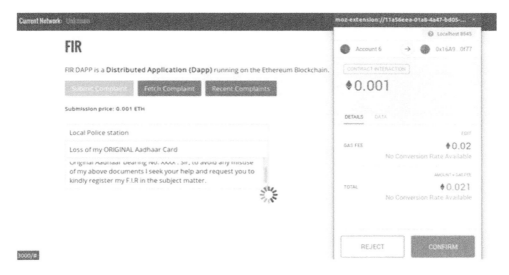

Figure 1.12   Submitting the complaint.

Figure 1.13 illustrates how a user can fetch details concerning any complaint on the network by using the ID number. On fulfilling the requirements, the entire report filed along with the Ethereum hash and timestamp is retrieved. IPFS hash is also revealed which confirms the storage of the report in the network.

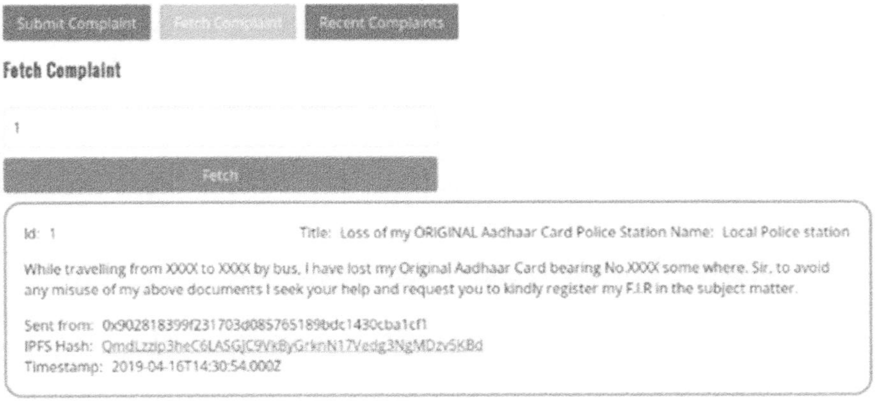

Figure 1.13   Fetching complaint by ID.

This component of the system serves in establishing transparency with pseudo-anonymity. Any user can check for recent submissions of complaints under this option. This would give users a possibility to view the pending cases in the network.

Figure 1.14   Fetching recent complaint.

1.8   Conclusion

The advent of blockchain technology has changed the lives of people, giving it a new dimension. It has changed the perspective of viewing things on the web and has been more user-centric and user-friendly. With its wide range of technology, blockchain has provided more data security, as mentioned in the above topics about how it works, its hashing algorithms, its security parameters and so on. In addition, it has a wide diversity in controlling the cybercrimes occurring in the world and also solves the problem of data breach and money- and property-related issues. With this, sectors like digital advertising, cybersecurity, forecasting, supply chain management, IoT, and networking have a fantastic future. Blockchain also has a wide perspective of the new occupations emerging in industry. With this, we can transform the whole world into a much smaller place. In a client-server architecture, users experience a single point of failure, and even it is prone to attacks; therefore, to provide a better solution to prevent these attacks the use of distributed network improves the efficiency of the system and provides more security to the system. The transactional activities can be performed much faster and efficiently using blockchain. Blockchain technology is going to be used in many more sectors in the future, such as in government systems, as these systems are slow, dense, and likely to be affected by corruption. Implementing blockchain technology in government systems can make their operations much more secure and efficient. Even though storing data on a blockchain is a slow and expensive process, in certain cases its benefits outweigh the cost, and in the future the Ethereum network will be faster and cheaper. The blockchain technology provides a sustainable and efficient method to the existing service structures whereas some other methods underperform and have unreliable security. Blockchain is in its early phase where experiments are performed on existing systems by developers working on reducing the cost and making user activities faster. Their support is limited in terms of computing power and the number of nodes within the network is small. Currently solutions are usually designed to address where solutions are made by the decentralized system. Coin offerings made by blockchain technology implemented using smart contract can deliver high proposition value to the solution over a decentralized network where each and every node will have equal importance and control over the decisions made by the system. In the future, real power is empowered by smart contract where advanced technologies will enable transactions at a faster rate. Satoshi Nakamoto's paper titled "Bitcoin: A Peer-to-Peer Electronic Cash System," was published in October 2008 and released in January 2009, which was a clear sign of the disruption of the financial and banking sectors to come. With an effective solution but limiting technology, it seemed too unlikely to have drawbacks to succeed and fully implement. With the exception of financial sectors, healthcare, supply chains and governments look forward to implementing game-changing results. Companies acting as a middleman to conduct business can be eliminated using this technology. Thus, they are looking forward to utilizing blockchain technology to remove central authority over the network. Blockchain technology enables transformative change but it will take time to solve existing challenges with user scalability and complexity in transaction processing systems. Thus, blockchain technology can be imagined as the ozone layer in the atmosphere whose presence can stop many malicious activities in the field of computer technology by acting as a protective shield to the users' data against the attackers.

REFERENCES

1. Buterin, V. (2017), A next-generation smart contract and decentralized application platform, *Ethereum White Paper*.

2. Aung, Y. N., & Tantidham, T. (2017, November). Review of Ethereum: Smart home case study. In *2017 2nd International Conference on Information Technology (INCIT)* (pp. 1-4). IEEE. https://doi.org/10.1109/incit.2017.8257877

3. Yavuz, E., Koc, A. K., Cabuk, U. C., & Dalkilic, G. (2018, March). Towards secure e-voting using ethereum blockchain. In *2018 6th International Symposium on Digital Forensic and Security (ISDFS)* (pp. 1-7). IEEE. https://doi.org/10.1109/isdfs.2018.8355340

4. Dinh, T. N., & Thai, M. T. (2018). AI and blockchain: A disruptive integration. *Computer*, 51(9), 48-53. https://doi.org/10.1109/mc.2018.3620971

5. Ming, Z., Yang, S., Li, Q., Wang, D., Xu, M., Xu, K., & Cui, L. Blockcloud: A Blockchain-based Service-centric Network Stack.

6. Ehmke, C., Wessling, F., & Friedrich, C. M. (2018, May). Proof-of-property: a lightweight and scalable blockchain protocol. In *Proceedings of the 1st International Workshop on Emerging Trends in Software Engineering for Blockchain* (pp. 48-51). ACM.

7. Sambra, A., Guy, A., Capadisli, S., & Greco, N. (2016, April). Building decentralized applications for the social Web. In *Proceedings of the 25th International Conference Companion on World Wide Web* (pp. 1033-1034). International World Wide Web Conferences Steering Committee. http://dx.doi.org/10.1145/2872518.2891060

8. Dinh, T. T. A., Liu, R., Zhang, M., Chen, G., Ooi, B. C., & Wang, J. (2018). Untangling blockchain: A data processing view of blockchain systems. *IEEE Transactions on Knowledge and Data Engineering*, 30(7), 1366-1385. https://doi.org/10.1109/tkde.2017.2781227

9. Bartoletti, M., Lande, S., Pompianu, L., & Bracciali, A. (2017, December). A general framework for blockchain analytics. In *Proceedings of the 1st Workshop on Scalable and Resilient Infrastructures for Distributed Ledgers* (p. 7). ACM. https://doi.org/10.1145/3152824.3152831

10. Wichtlhuber, M., Heise, P., Scheurich, B., & Hausheer, D. (2013, October). Reciprocity with virtual nodes: Supporting mobile peers in Peer-to-Peer content distribution. In *Proceedings of the 9th International Conference on Network and Service Management (CNSM 2013)* (pp. 406-409). IEEE. https://doi.org/10.1109/cnsm.2013.6727866

11. Nakamoto, S. (2008). Bitcoin: A peer-to-peer electronic cash system, http://bitcoin. org/bitcoin. pdf.

12. Dai, P., Mahi, N., Earls, J., & Norta, A. (2017). Smart-contract value-transfer protocols on a distributed mobile application platform. URL: https://qtum.org/uploads/files/cf6d69348ca50dd985b60425ccf282f3.pdf, 10.

13. Wright, C., & Serguieva, A. (2017, December). Sustainable blockchain-enabled services: Smart contracts. In *2017 IEEE International Conference on Big Data (Big Data)* (pp. 4255-4264). IEEE. https://doi.org/10.1109/bigdata.2017.8258452

14. Eyal, I., Gencer, A. E., Sirer, E. G., & Van Renesse, R. (2016). Bitcoin-ng: A scalable blockchain protocol. In *13th USENIX Symposium on Networked Systems Design and Implementation (NSDI 16)* (pp. 45-59).

15. Kokoris-Kogias, E., Jovanovic, P., Gasser, L., Gailly, N., Syta, E., & Ford, B. (2018). OmniLedger. A secure, scale-out,decentralized ledger via sharding. In *IEEE Symposium on Security and Privacy (SP)*, IEEE. https://doi.org/10.1109/sp.2018.000-5

16. Dang, H., Dinh, T. T. A., Loghin, D., Chang, E. C., Lin, Q., & Ooi, B. C. (2019, June). Towards scaling blockchain systems via sharding. In *Proceedings of the 2019 International Conference on Management of Data* (pp. 123-140). ACM. https://doi.org/10.1145/3299869.3319889

17. Poon, J., & Buterin, V. (2017). Plasma: Scalable autonomous smart contracts. White paper, 1-47. http://plasma.io/plasma.pdf.

18. Wu, K. (2019). An Empirical Study of Blockchain-based Decentralized Applications. arXiv preprint *arXiv:1902.04969*. https://doi.org/10.3390/computers8030057

19. Chang, J., Gao, B., Xiao, H., Sun, J., Cai, Y., & Yang, Z. (2019). sCompile: Critical Path Identification and Analysis for Smart Contracts. *Lecture Notes in Computer Science*, 286-304. https://doi.org/10.1007/978-3-030-32409-4_18

20. Chen, W., Zheng, Z., Cui, J., Ngai, E., Zheng, P., & Zhou, Y. (2018, April). Detecting Ponzi schemes on ethereum: Towards healthier blockchain technology. In *Proceedings of the 2018 World Wide Web Conference* (pp. 1409-1418). International World Wide Web Conferences Steering Committee. https://doi.org/10.1145/3178876.3186046

21. Liu, B., Yu, X. L., Chen, S., Xu, X., & Zhu, L. (2017, June). Blockchain based data integrity service framework for IoT data. In *2017 IEEE International Conference on Web Services (ICWS)* (pp. 468-475). IEEE. https://doi.org/10.1109/icws.2017.54

22. Benet, J. (2014). Ipfs-content addressed, versioned, p2p file system. arXiv preprint *arXiv:1407.3561*.

23. Storj: A Decentralized Cloud Storage Network Framework (2018) v3.0 https://github.com/storj/whitepaper

CHAPTER 2

BLOCKCHAIN: A PATH TO THE FUTURE

Avinash Kaur,[1] Anand Nayyar,[2] Parminder Singh[1]

[1] Lovely Professional University, Punjab, India
[2] Duy Tan University, Da Nang, Vietnam

*Corresponding author: anandnayyar@duytan.edu.vn

Abstract

Blockchain, which was invented by Satoshi Nakamoto to serve as the public transaction ledger of Bitcoin, has received a great amount of attention. Blockchain allows transactions to be performed in a decentralized manner. It is currently being applied in various fields such as reputation systems, internet of things (IoT) and financial services. There are still many challenges in blockchain yet to be solved such as security and scalability. This chapter presents the blockchain technology architecture along with the consensus algorithms involved in it. Also, types of blockchain systems and applications are also discussed. Finally, future directions in the field of blockchain are discussed.

Keywords: Blockchain, consensus algorithm, Bitcoin, Ethereum, consortium, mining, Bitcoin smart contracts

2.1 Introduction

Nowadays, the buzzword in industry and academia is cryptocurrency. The highly successful cryptocurrency bitcoin is a huge success, with the market reaching as high as 10 billion dollars [1]. Bitcoin with a specific data storage structure and transactions occurs without the involvement of a third party. The core technology for Bitcoin is blockchain. Blockchain was first proposed in 2008 and implemented in 2009 [2]. All transactions in blockchain are stored in blocks. It is regarded as the public ledger. The chain grows with the addition of new blocks. In order to maintain consistency in the ledger and for user security, a distributed consensus algorithm and asymmetric cryptography algorithms are implemented. The key attributes in blockchain technology are persistency, decentralization, audit-ability and anonymity. With all these characteristics, blockchain saves costs and improves efficiency.

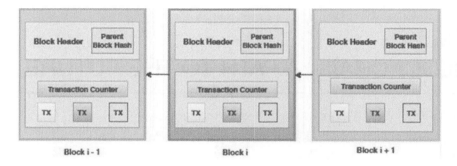

Figure 2.1   Continuous sequence of blocks in blockchain.

The payment in blockchain can be made without involvement of any intermediary, so it can be used in various financial services such as remittance, digital assets and online payment [3, 4]. It can be used in various other fields such as public services, smart contracts [5], security services [6], reputation systems [7], internet of things [8], etc. The blockchain is favored in multiple ways by these fields. The transaction information cannot be tampered with in a blockchain. Businesses with high privacy and security requirements use blockchain for attracting users. It uses a distributed form of computing and avoids the situation of single point of failure. The contract is executed automatically in smart contract, once deployed on blockchain. The future use of blockchain technology for the internet faces numerous technical issues. First there is the challenge of scalability. The size of block in Bitcoin is limited to 1MB while the size of block increases every 10 minutes. The network restriction of bitcoin is 7 transactions per second, which does not have the capability to deal with high-frequency trading. Hence, the larger the block the larger is the storage space required with slower diffusion into the network. Therefore, the need arises for decentralization in blockchain. The most difficult challenge is the trade-off between security and size. Secondly, the miners can achieve higher revenues through a selfish mining strategy [9]. In order to generate higher revenues the miners hide their blocks. This hinders the development of blockchain as branches could take place frequently. Solutions need to be proposed to find a solution to this problem. Also, privacy leakage can happen in blockchain if the users use a private key [10] and public key. Furthermore, the present proof-of-stake or proof-of-work consensus algorithm is facing some serious issues. For example, a lot of electrical energy is wasted in proof-of-work while the process to become richer could happen in proof-of-stake consensus. A large amount of literature exists on blockchain from various modes like wikis, journal articles, blogs, forum posts and codes. A technical survey has been conducted for the Bitcoin decentralized digital currencies [11]. This research article focuses on blockchain technology.

2.2 Blockchain Architecture

A blockchain is a mesh of computers interconnected to each other and not to the central system. The protocol for the computers in a network is to agree upon and define a state of shared data and also obey the constraints imposed on the data. Each and every block in the blockchain makes a change to that shared state.

A block sequence containing a complete list of transactions as a public ledger is called a blockchain. Figure 2.1 illustrates a blockchain. A block has only one parent block with a previous block hash in block header. The Ethereum blockchain consists of uncle blocks (children of block's ancestors). The first block of blockchain with no parent is called the genesis block [12]. The blockchain is further explained below.

2.2.1 Block

A block consists of a block body and block header, as in Figure 2.2.

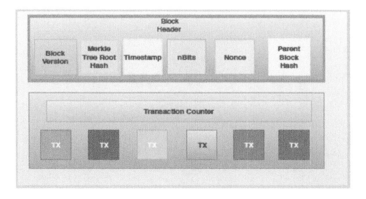

Figure 2.2   Block structure.

The block header consists of:

- *Block Version*: It indicates protocols to be followed for block validation.

- *Merkle Tree Root Hash*: It consists of the value of hash for all transactions in a block.

- *Timestamp*: It represents the current time in units of seconds.

- *nBits*: It represents the threshold value of valid hash block.

- *Nonce*: It is a 4-byte field. It starts with zero and the value increases with every calculation.

• *Parent Block Hash*: This field is directed towards the previous block with 256 bit hash value.

The body of block contains transactions and transaction counter. The number of transactions in a block is dependent on the size of transaction and size of block. The asymmetric cryptography technique is used for validating the authenticity of transactions [13]. In an untrustworthy environment, digital signature based on asymmetric cryptography is applied.

2.2.2   Digital Signature

Each user has a pair of private and public keys. Confidentiality is maintained in the private key and it is used for signing the transactions. In the network, digitally signed transactions are broadcasted. Digital signature consists of two phases: Signing and Verification. For example, user Tom wants to send a message to another user Jerry. So, in the signing phase, Tom's data is encrypted using his private key and encrypted data with the result is sent to Jerry. In the verification phase, using the public key Jerry validates the value. So, tampering with data can be easily checked by Jerry. Elliptic curve digital signature algorithm (ECDSA) is an algorithm used in blockchain [14].

As in Figure 2.3, a hash value is generated when Tom wants to sign a transaction. Using the private key hash value is encrypted. The original data with encrypted hash is sent to another user Jerry. The verification of received transaction is performed by Jerry by comparing the decrypted hash and value of hash derived from received data using the same hash function.

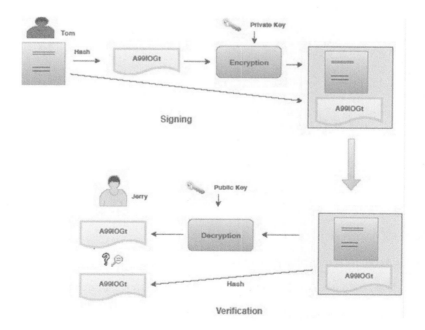

Figure 2.3   Digital signature.

2.2.3   Main Attributes of Blockchain

Blockchain has the following attributes:

a) *Decentralization*: In central transaction systems, the validation of each transaction is performed by a central agency, thus leading to bottlenecks of performance and cost. Contrarily, no central system is required in Blockchain. In a distributed network, consistency of data is maintained through consensus algorithms in blockchain.

b) *Persistency*: The validation of transactions can be performed in an instant and invalid transactions are not entertained by honest miners. Once a transaction is included in Blockchain, it cannot be deleted or rolled back. Blocks consisting of invalid transactions are immediately discovered.

c) *Anonymity*: The identity of the user is hidden in blockchain. Interactions between the users are performed by generated address in Blockchain. Privacy is not guaranteed in blockchain due to intrinsic constraint.

d) *Auditability*: On the basis of unspent transaction output (UTXO) model, bitcoin blockchain stores the data about the balance of the user. Previous unspent transaction is to be referred by the transaction. The state of referred unspent transaction is changed from unspent to spent when the transaction is rolled out in blockchain. So, verifying and tracking the transactions is easy.

2.3   Types of Blockchain Systems

The categories of blockchain systems are [15]:

Table 2.1   Classification of blockchain systems.

PROPERTIES	PUBLIC	PRIVATE/FEDERATED
SPEED	Slow	Fast
ACCESS RIGHTS	Open: Read / Write	Permissioned: Read/Write
IDENTITY	Anonymous	Identifiable
SECURITY	Work Proof, Stake Proof, Consensus Mechanism	Pre-Approved User
ASSEST	Native	Any

1. *Public Blockchain*: Visibility of records is public and everyone can participate in the consensus process. In consortium blockchain, in the consensus process only a group of pre-selected nodes can participate. Likewise, in a private blockchain, nodes from a particular organization can join the consensus process. The examples of public blockchain are Ethereum,[1] Bitcoin, Dash, Litecoin,[2] etc.

2. *Private Blockchain*: It is a centralized network blockchain that is completely controlled by one organization. The examples are Monox and MultiChain.

---

[1] https://ethereum.org
[2] https://litecoin.org

3. *Consortium Blockchain*: It is partially decentralized blockchain as only some of the nodes are selected for determination of consensus. The examples are EWF (energy),[3] R3 (banks),[4] Corda and B3i (insurance).[5]

4. *Hybrid Blockchain*: It is a combination of private and public blockchain. The determination for information to be private or public is made in it. The example is Dragonchain.[6]

2.4 Consensus Algorithms

The transformation of the Byzantine Generals Problem is raised in blockchain [16]. In the case of the Byzantine Generals Problem, some of the Byzantine army circled the city with a group of command generals. The command generals had two viewpoints. Some wanted to retreat and some wanted to attack. However, if only some of the generals attacked then it would fail. So, agreement either to choose attack or retreat has to be reached. Similarly, in distributed environment reaching a consensus is a challenge. So, the same challenge exists for blockchain, as it also consists of distributed environment. No central node exists in blockchain that determines similarity of ledgers on distributed nodes. To ensure the consistency of ledgers in different nodes some protocols need to be followed [16]. The different methods to reach consensus in blockchain is further explained in this section.

In this section, proof-based consensus algorithms are discussed. The first algorithm is proof of work. Different alternatives of Proof of Work are introduced and the algorithms are explained.

2.4.1 Proof of Work (PoW)

Proof of Work is a strategy of consensus applied in a Bitcoin network [2]. To record the transactions in a decentralized network, someone has to be selected. The easiest way is random selection method but it is the most vulnerable to attacks. So, to validate a node for publishing transactions, a large process is involved to validate the node so that it will not attack the network. The amount of computations in a computer is called work. The block header hash value is calculated by each node. The block header is composed of miners and nonce. The miners obtain the different hash values by changing the nonce frequently. The requirement of consensus is that the generated value needs to be either equal or smaller than the certain given value. When target value is reached by one node, then other nodes are broadcasted with a block; hence, the correctness of hash value is confirmed by all nodes. The miners append the new block to their own blockchain if the block is validated. Miners are the nodes that calculate the hash values and the PoW procedure is known as mining in Bitcoin.

At nearly the same time, when multiple nodes and the appropriate nonce are chosen then valid block is generated in a decentralized network. The generation of branches can be as represented in Figure 2.4.

---

[3] https://www.energyweb.org
[4] https://www.r3.com
[5] https://b3i.tech
[6] https://dragonchain.com

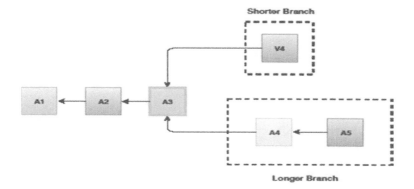

Figure 2.4   Blockchain branches scenario.

However, it is not possible that branches will be generated simultaneously by two forks. In PoW protocol, the chain is authentic if it becomes long thereafter. Consider two forks created by simultaneously validated blocks V4 and A4. The mining is performed by miners until a longer chain is found. The longer chain is formed by A4, A5. So, the miners on V4 switch to the longer chain. Miners perform a lot of computations in PoW, but a lot of resources get wasted. To overcome the loss, some PoW protocols with side applications in the work are designed. For example, Primecoin [17] is used for mathematical research searches for a special chain of prime numbers.

Analysis shows that the limitations of PoW are that there can be some security or usage issues. So, different alternatives are suggested for these limitations. The speed of appending the blocks is increasing day by day, which further enhances the hardness of the puzzles. Hence, miners are bound to invest in hardware in order to be the first solvers of the puzzle. The miners with lower investments are unable to cope with the market needs. Tromp [18] introduced a method for replacing puzzle work by using Cuckoo Hash Function [19], which involves fewer efforts of miners with easy appending of blocks. The hash table is used with two different hash functions to get all the possible results from the hash table. The input that is provided in this hash table results in two positions in the hash table.

The blank position is traced and the value of hash generated is placed into one of the positions. If none of the blank positions are found then one of the old hash values is replaced. Then, the input to two hash functions is given an old replaced result. The process is repeated until no blank value remains in the hash table. A graph is created by Cuckoo hash function with edges as the removed value and nodes as the replaced value position or hashed position. In PoW, to replace the puzzle work, many nonces have to be guessed by the miner. These are given as an input to a defined hash function. When there are enough cycles in a graph with the guessed nonces, then the block is broadcasted by the miner.

An idea has been put forward that the miners have to find a longest chain of prime numbers satisfying some requirements instead of finding a meaningless nonce. The length needs to be larger than the given value is the first requirement. Then, the next requirement is that it needs to be in the form of a Cunningham chain. Lastly, the origin value needs to be defined, which is the center of the first and second prime number in a chain. An algorithm for Fermat primality testing [20] is used to verify the block. This method not only verifies transactions but is also dedicated to mathematics for ending distributed values of Cunningham chain.

The limitation of PoW is known as a double-spending attack [21], as shown in Figure 2.5.

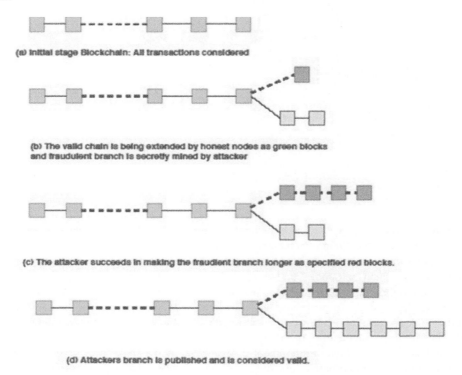

(a) Initial stage Blockchain: All transactions considered

(b) The valid chain is being extended by honest nodes as green blocks and fraudulent branch is secretly mined by attacker

(c) The attacker succeeds in making the fraudient branch longer as specified red blocks.

(d) Attackers branch is published and is considered valid.

Figure 2.5   Double-spending attack script.

(a) *Initial stage Blockchain*: All transactions are considered.

(b) The valid chain is being extended by honest nodes as green blocks and fraudulent branch is secretly mined by attacker.

(c) The attacker succeeds in making the fraudulent branch longer, as specified with red blocks.

(d) The attacker's branch is published and is considered valid. The attacker tries to make the transaction invalid and makes his fork longer than the other forks by attacking a valid node and reversing the transaction. At least 51% of computing power of verified network needs to be used to perform such an attack [22]. Hence, a double-spending attack can also be known as a 51% attack. It possesses such a large amount of computing power that it is difficult for an individual node.

The introduction of mining pools [23] makes this kind of attack possible. In this method voting is done by a group for a pool operator and the work is also made easier by finding the nonce value in a group. The rewards appear in a coinbase and are distributed equally between each miner. This kind of 51% attack by a mining group is presented [24]. A method is introduced to overcome this limitation. Each individual node needs to own a private coinbase signature before finding the nonce. This is dangerous work, as miners can transfer the rewards freely inside the pool [25].

The miners have to solve an extra PoW puzzle if a private signature is not provided. To overcome the limitation of pool mining, Miller *et al.* [26] proposed a method for modifying the original puzzles to non-outsourceable puzzles for increasing the chance of miners winning with any effort. The signing key is used to evolve this puzzle. Along with the issues of security, PoW is not suited for real-time payment [27]. For example, a person goes to drink a cup of coffee but has to wait 15 minutes for creating block speed, as payment has to be verified by the seller. So, it becomes necessary to reduce latency in transactions. The solution introduced previously was increasing the size of block for executing more transactions; thus, reducing the complexity of puzzle solving. A new consensus model called Bitcoin-NG was introduced in which traditional block is divided into two types: micro block and key block [27]. If the best suitable nonce is found by the miner for his puzzle, then the miner becomes the leader for all other miners. When a miner is leader, micro blocks will be published by nodes containing transaction information. The Ghost technique is suggested for reducing the time it takes to append new block in chain. This technique prevents the double-spending attack problem and handles the fork [28, 29]. It chooses the most contributing fork instead of the longest one. Figure 2.6 depicts the protocol for Ghost technique.

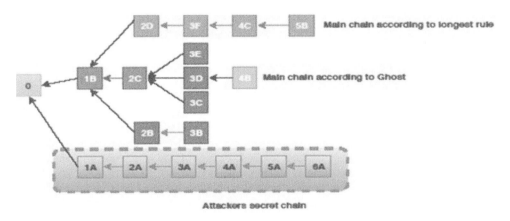

Figure 2.6   Technique for choosing main chain when fork appears.

Another strategy is proposed by Liu *et al.* [30]. It is a generalized form of proof of work in which the committee chooses to append a block on the basis of luck factor. It finds the number of nonces with the computing power of each. The nonce is sent with the block to the committee for approval. The validated block is put into a temporary array. The random number is chosen at the end of the round. The miners index in the block matches the random number that is allowed to append the block. After the completion of each round, rewards are distributed equally to all committee members.

2.4.1.1 *Proof of Stake (PoS)*

Proof of Stake is one energy-saving alternative to PoW. The ownership of the currency amount has to be proved by miners in PoS. Those less likely to attack the network are the people possessing a very large number of currencies. The selection of a candidate on the basis of an account balance is unfair, as the richest person becomes dominant in the network. So, various solutions are proposed combining stake size to decide the next block to be forged. Particularly, randomization is used by BlackCoin [31] for predicting the next generator. The formula used combines the lowest hash value with the size of stake. Coin-based selection process is favored by Peercoin [32]. In Peercoin, the greater probability of mining the next block is by older and larger set of coins. In comparison to PoW, the energy is saved by PoS and is more effective. The attack can be a consequence, as mining cost is zero. In many of the blockchains, PoW is adopted at the beginning and then a transformation is made to PoS. For example, Ethereum plans to transform from Ethash (PoW kind) [33] to Casper (PoS kind) [34].

2.4.2 Pure Stake-Based Consensus

NextCoin [35] is the pure form of PoS. The bigger the stake available to the miner, the more chances the miner has to mine a block. For example, if the total number of coins is "n" and those available with the miner are "a," then the chance for miner M to mine is a/n. Another method is proposed for finding the miner on the basis of pure stake. Also, a "follow-the-satoshi" rule is applied. A Satoshi value, the smallest unit of bitcoin, is considered. The Satoshi index is provided as an input to Satoshi procedure. The value of the Satoshi index is between 0 and total number of Satoshi. The block that created the Satoshi is found. These are the rewards of the miners who created the block. The one who appends the block to the chain is the last owner of Satoshi. The Satoshi is chosen on the basis of hash function. The inputs are taken on the basis of present status of chain. The first input is obtained from comb function as bits. The current blocks in a chain provide second input and finally third input is a random integer.

Another method [36] is proposed to handle the problem. In it the block is not created by the Satoshi owner during his chance. Three chances are provided to choose the Satoshi. If these chances are missed then the owner is blacklisted and not allowed to append the block. The idea of Bentov is used by follow-the-satoshi procedure for execution of PoS consensus [37]. According to it, the leader should be chosen randomly by using entropy value. This calculated value needs to be secured, as it would be difficult to simulate protocol and predict the value for manipulating leader election. The entropy value is calculated on the basis of Bentov election [36]. Epoch, a snapshot of each stakeholder, is taken. The numbers of stake holders are chosen in each epoch for execution of coin-flipping protocol.

2.4.3 Leased Proof of Stake (LPoS)

Leased proof of stake is a variant of PoS introduced by Waves Platform.[7] It offers better catch with limited energy consumption. The disadvantage in PoS is that the users with limited amount of coins are not able to participate in staking. This algorithm overcomes this disadvantage and allows smallholders a chance to stake.

2.4.4 Delegated Proof of Stake (DPOS)

The DPOS is a representative democracy while PoS is a direct democracy. The delegates are elected by stakeholders for generation and validation of blocks. As there are fewer numbers of nodes for block validation, transactions are confirmed quickly due to quick

---

[7]https://wavesplatform.com/

conformation of blocks. Also, the network parameters block intervals and block size are tuned by delegates. The dishonest delegates can be voted out easily. The backbone of bitshare is DPOS [38].

2.4.5 Hybrid Form of PoS and PoW

Peercoin, also known as PPCoin, is the first variant of PoS using PoW. It uses "coin age" of the miner calculated as his/her stake multiplied by the amount of time owned. For getting priority to append new block to the chain, stake coins are created by the miner for appending new block to the chain. Stake coins hold many transactions but one special one from the miner him/herself. The greater the amount spent, the greater the chances.

2.4.6 Practical Byzantine Fault Tolerance (PBFT)

Practical Byzantine fault tolerance is one of the replication techniques for Byzantine faults [39]. It is utilized by Hyperledger Fabric [40] as a consensus algorithm. A third of the malicious Byzantine replicas can be handled by PBFT.

Furthermore, a determination of new block is made. In every round, a primary is selected as per the protocols and it orders the transaction. There are three phases in the whole process: pre-prepare, prepare and commit. In each of these phases the node enters the next state if the voting is received from over 80 percent of nodes. So the requirement of PBFT is that every node is to be known to the network. Stellar consensus protocol (SCP) [41] is also a Byzantine agreement protocol. In PBFT, each and every node is queried, but in SCP, it is the right of participants to choose another set of participants to believe. Delegated Byzantine fault tolerance (dBFT) is implemented by Antshares [42] on the basis of PBFT. Some professional nodes are voted to record the transactions in dBFT.

2.4.7 Ripple

Ripple [23] is one of the consensus algorithms.[8] In the larger network, it uses collectively-trusted subnetworks. There are two types of nodes in the network: server node for participating consensus processes and client node for fund transfer. There is a unique node list (UNL) in each server that is important to the server. The decision to put the transaction into the ledger is dependent upon the response of node query in UNL. If 80% of the nodes reach agreements then transactions are put into a ledger. The ledger will remain appropriate in a node till the faulty nodes are less than 20%.

2.4.8 Tendermint

Tendermint [24] is one of the consensus algorithms. An unconfirmed block is broadcasted in the network by the selected proposer. It occurs in three steps;

a) Prevote step: Validators decide to broadcast their prevote for the proposed block.

b) Precommit step: If more than 80% of the prevotes are received for the block proposed, then precommit is broadcasted for the block. If 80% of precommits are received then the node enters the step of commit.

---

[8]https://ripple.com/

c) Commit step: The block is validated by the node and commit is broadcasted for the block. If 80% of commits are received then the block is broadcasted. In contrast to PBFT, nodes have to lock their coins to become validators. The validator who is found to be dishonest is punished.

2.4.9   Proof of Elapsed Time

Proof of elapsed time (PoET) [43] is one of the best consensus algorithms used on permissioned blockchain network. The permissioned network decides on the principles of voting or mining rights. There is transparency in the entire network. The system login is secured as miners are identified before joining. So, winners are selected by fair means only. In this, the limit for the waiting time of an individual is random. The participant that completes the fair share of waiting time can be allocated a ledger to create a new block. An example of this is the Intel SGX system[9] [44].

2.4.10   Proof of Activity (PoA)

Proof of Activity [45] is a combination of PoW and PoS. The advantages it exhibits are a) it is more secure against attacks, and b) it isn't a power-hungry system. It begins like the PoW algorithm, with miners solving a critical puzzle for the reward. Only the block templates are mined by miners. The header inside a block specifies random stakeholders. The greater the stakes of the stakeholder, the better the chances of approving blocks.

2.4.11   Proof of Burn (PoB)

In the PoB algorithm, to protect cryptocurrency, a portion of the coins are burnt. Some coins are sent to the eater address.[10] The coins sent to the eater address cannot be used again. The ledger keeps track of burnt coins, making them genuinely unspendable. Although burning is a loss, the damage is only temporary as the coins are safeguarded in the long run from cyber attacks by hackers. Also, it increases the stakes of other coins. This increases the chances of mining the next blocks and also increases rewards. So, burning is a privilege in mining [46].

A comparison of different consensus algorithms is shown in Table 2.2.

---

[9]https://software.intel.comen-ussgx
[10]http://slimco.in/

Table 2.2 Consensus algorithms comparison.

Consensus Algorithm	Year	Platform of Blockchain	Programming Language	Smart Contracts	Advantages	Disadvantages
PoW [47]	2009	Bitcoin [2]	C++	No	DDoS protection	More energy consumption, Miners centralization
PoS [48]	2013	NXT [49]	Java	Yes	Energy efficient, Decentralization	Fully Decentralization
PBFT [50]	2015	Hyperledger Fabric	JavaScript, Python, Java REST and Go	No confirmation needed, Energy reduction	Communication Attack, Sybil Attack	-
DPoS [51]	2016	Lisk [52]	JavaScript	No	Energy Efficient, Scalable, More Security	-
LPoS [53]	2016	Waves	Scala	Yes	Lease Coin fair usage	-
PoET [55]	2018	Hyperledger Sawtooth [56]	Python, JavaScript, Go, C++, Java, and Rust	Yes	Cheap Participation, Different levels of protection	
PoB [57]	2014	Slimcoin [46]	Python, C++, Shell, JavaScript	No	Preservation of the network	

2.5 Blockchain Applications That Are Transforming Society

Business: The traditional systems are slower and more prone to errors. Intermediates are required for resolving conflicts that cause stress and cost money and time. One of the examples of business is Asset Management: Trade Processing and Settlement [58]. The traditional process is risky and expensive for cross-border transactions. Inefficient records are maintained with errors. These errors are reduced in blockchain ledgers by encryption of records. Another example are insurance claims. These are more prone to error as the processors have to go through the fraudulent claims and also process forms manually. Risk-free management and transparency is provided by blockchain. The global sector of payment is open to money laundering and is error prone. Solutions to this problem are being provided by blockchain with companies such as Align Commerce, Bitspark and Abra. Blockchain is merged with payment application [59].

Smart Property: All the intangible or tangible property, such as property titles, company shares or patents, also houses or cars, can have embedded smart technology. The storing of registration details can be performed on a ledger along with the details of the contract of ownership of property. Smart property decreases risk of fraud and increases the efficiency and trust [4].

Blockchain Internet of Things (IoT): A network of internet connected objects is known as the internet of things. When an object is connected to a network of computers it becomes a thing. The IoT affects the user in many ways. For example, when cartridges in a printer become low, they can automatically be ordered from any shopping website via printer. Blockchain and IoT can be applied in smart appliances, supply chain sensors, etc. [60, 61].

Smart Contracts: These are digital with embedded if-this-then-that (IFTTT) code for self-execution. In real environment, the intermediary ensures the following of protocols. Blockchain removes the need for an intermediary with all the contract details available to the users. It can be used in insurance premiums, financial derivatives, etc. It can also be implemented in blockchain healthcare. All personal health records can be stored and encoded on blockchain with a private key. The access rights would be available to specific individuals. The ledger can be used for drug supervision, managing healthcare supplies and testing results [5].

Blockchain Identity: The blockchain protects the identity of the user by encrypting data and securing it from spammers. One of the examples is a passport. The digital passport was introduced in 2014 to help users identify themselves. The blockchain ensures reliability in keeping records of birth, death, anniversary, etc. It encrypts the information of birth and death [62].

Financial Services: Blockchain technology called distributed ledger technology (DLT) allows optimization of business processes by the financial industry by sharing data in a secure and efficient manner. Blockchain technologies are reshaping the landscape of financial services as a key mechanism for digital cash transactions. The present inefficient profit pools and business models are going to face risks of inefficient blockchain financial platforms. The distributed ledger improves the security and transparency in back-office operations using blockchain technologies. This is favored from a regulatory and auditing perspective. The existing infrastructure of capital markets is expensive and slow. It requires intermediates. The new blockchain inventions for capital markets are improving workflow and decreasing overhead.

Government: Blockchain is one of the potential processes for the improvement of government services. It fosters the transparent relation between citizen and government. It optimizes the business processes through secure sharing of data. It has numerous applications for public sector. With blockchain technology government can improve methods of delivering services, reducing waste, eliminating bureaucracy and preventing tax fraud. The intervention of blockchain in government processes has a huge impact on health services, social security benefits, etc. The government procedures become streamlined.

2.6 Future Scope

Blockchain has potential in academia and industry. The future directions are as follows:

(a) *Blockchain Testing*: Different types of blockchain exist and there are more than 700 cryptocurrencies [63]. The investors can be fooled by developers by the huge performance of blockchain. Also, there needs to be known knowledge of the blockchain to involve it in a business. So, a blockchain testing procedure needs to test the blockchains. There are two phases in it. First is the standardization phase and second is the testing phase. In the standardization phase, all protocols have to be met and agreed upon. The introduced blockchain needs to be tested as to whether it obeys the required protocols as desired by the developer.

(b) *Limit Tendency to Centralization*: The design of blockchain is a decentralized system. In the mining pool, miners are centralized. In a Bitcoin network, the total hash power of 51% is owned by 5 mining pools [42]. In selfish mining technique, pools with 25% of computing power get more shares. So, a blockchain method needs to be introduced for other individuals.

(c) *Big Data Analytics*: Blockchain and big data can be combined. The categories of data analytics and data mangement can be combined. In data management, the important data can be stored by blockchain, as it is secure and distributed. It also ensures the originality of data. For example, tampering with and stealing the stored information of patients becomes difficult. In the case of analytics, transactions can be used for big data analytics. For example, depiction of most suitable patterns can be made by users [64].

(d) *Blockchain Applications*: Numerous financial applications exist but more are being introduced. The blockchain can be implemented in different fields for enhancing the systems. For example, storing the reputation of users on blockchain. The new industry can use the blockchain for performance improvement. Smart contracts are computerized transaction protocols that can execute terms of a contract [65]. This can be implemented by blockchain.

REFERENCES

1. Hileman, G. (2016), *State of blockchain Q1 2016: Blockchain funding overtakes bitcoin*. Coin-Desk, New York, NY, May 2016; 11.

2. Nakamoto, S. (2008). *Bitcoin: A peer-to-peer electronic cash system*.

3. Peters, G., Panayi, E., & Chapelle, A. (2015). Trends in cryptocurrencies and blockchain technologies: a monetary theory and regulation perspective. *Journal of Financial Perspectives*, 3(3).

4. Foroglou, G., & Tsilidou, A. L. (2015, May). Further applications of the blockchain. In *12th Student Conference on Managerial Science and Technology*.

5. Kosba, A., Miller, A., Shi, E., Wen, Z., & Papamanthou, C. (2016, May). Hawk: The blockchain model of cryptography and privacy-preserving smart contracts. In *2016 IEEE Symposium on Security and Privacy (SP)* (pp. 839-858). IEEE.

6. Akins, B. W., Chapman, J. L., & Gordon, J. M. (2014). A whole new world: Income tax considerations of the Bitcoin economy. *Pitt. Tax Rev.*, 12, 25.

7. Sharples, M., & Domingue, J. (2016, September). The blockchain and kudos: A distributed system for educational record, reputation and reward. In *European Conference on Technology Enhanced Learning* (pp. 490-496). Springer, Cham.

8. Zhang, Y., & Wen, J. (2015, February). An IoT electric business model based on the protocol of bitcoin. In *2015 18th International Conference on Intelligence in Next Generation Networks* (pp. 184-191). IEEE.

9. Eyal, I., & Sirer, E. G. (2018). Majority is not enough: Bitcoin mining is vulnerable. *Communications of the ACM*, 61(7), 95-102.

10. Biryukov, A., Khovratovich, D., & Pustogarov, I. (2014, November). Deanonymisation of clients in Bitcoin P2P network. In *Proceedings of the 2014 ACM SIGSAC Conference on Computer and Communications Security* (pp. 15-29). ACM.

11. Tschorsch, F., & Scheuermann, B. (2016). Bitcoin and beyond: A technical survey on decentralized digital currencies. *IEEE Communications Surveys & Tutorials*, 18(3), 2084-2123.

12. Buterin, V. (2014). A next-generation smart contract and decentralized application platform. *White paper*, 3, 37.

13. Zheng, Z., Xie, S., Dai, H. N., Chen, X., & Wang, H. (2018). Blockchain challenges and opportunities: A survey. *International Journal of Web and Grid Services*, 14(4), 352-375.

14. Johnson, D., Menezes, A., & Vanstone, S. (2001). The elliptic curve digital signature algorithm (ECDSA). *International Journal of Information Security*, 1(1), 36-63.

15. Pilkington, M. (2016). 11 Blockchain technology: principles and applications. In *Research Handbook on Digital Transformations*, (p. 225), Edward Elgar Publishing Limited.

16. Lamport, L., Shostak, R., & Pease, M. (1982). The Byzantine generals problem. In *ACM Transactions on Programming Languages and Systems (TOPLAS)*, 4(3), 382-401.

17. Burks, C. (2017). Bitcoin: Breaking bad or breaking barriers?. *North Carolina Journal of Law & Technology* 18(5), 244.

18. Tromp, J. (2014). Cuckoo Cycle: a memory-hard proof-of-work system. *IACR Cryptology ePrint Archive*, 2014, 59.

19. Nguyen, G. T., & Kim, K. (2018). A survey about consensus algorithms used in blockchain. *Journal of Information Processing Systems*, 14(1).

20. Liskov, M. Fermat primality test. In *Encyclopedia of Cryptography and Security* 2011: 455-456.

21. Hurlburt, G. F., & Bojanova, I. (2014). Bitcoin: Benefit or curse?. *IT Professional*, 16(3), 10-15.

22. Bhme, R., Christin, N., Edelman, B., & Moore, T. (2015). Bitcoin: Economics, technology, and governance. *Journal of Economic Perspectives*, 29(2), 213-38.

23. Zohar, A. (2015). Bitcoin: under the hood. *Communications of the ACM*, 58(9), 104-113.

24. Sirer, E. G., & Eyal, I. (2014). How to Disincentivize Large Bitcoin Mining Pools. Blog post: http://hackingdistributed.com/2014/06/18/how-to-disincentivize-large-bitcoin-mining - pools 2014.

25. Bastiaan, M. (2015, January). Preventing the 51%-attack: a stochastic analysis of two phase proof of work in bitcoin. Available at http://referaat. cs. utwente. nl/conference/22/paper/7473/preventingthe-51-attack-a-stochasticanalysis-oftwo-phase-proof-of-work-in-bitcoin.pdf.

26. Miller, A., Kosba, A., Katz, J., & Shi, E. (2015, October). Non-outsourceable scratch-off puzzles to discourage bitcoin mining coalitions. In *Proceedings of the 22nd ACM SIGSAC Conference on Computer and Communications Security* (pp. 680-691). ACM.

27. Eyal, I., Gencer, A. E., Sirer, E. G., & Van Renesse, R. (2016). Bitcoin-ng: A scalable blockchain protocol. In *13th USENIX Symposium on Networked Systems Design and Implementation (NSDI 16)* (pp. 45-59).

28. Sompolinsky, Y., & Zohar, A. (2013). Accelerating bitcoin's transaction processing. Fast money grows on trees, not chains.

29. Sompolinsky, Y., & Zohar, A. (2015, January). Secure high-rate transaction processing in bitcoin. In *International Conference on Financial Cryptography and Data Security* (pp. 507-527). Springer, Berlin, Heidelberg.

30. Tang, S., Liu, Z., Chow, S. S., Liu, Z., Long, Y., & Liu, S. (2017). Forking-free hybrid consensus with generalized proof-of-activity. *IACR Cryptology ePrint Archive*, 2017, 367.

31. Vasin, P. (2014). Blackcoins proof-of-stake protocol v2. URL: https://blackcoin.co/blackcoin-pos-protocol-v2-whitepaper.pdf 2014; 71.

32. King, S. (2013). *Primecoin: Cryptocurrency with prime number proof-of-work.* July 7th, 1, 6.

33. Wood, G. (2014). Ethereum: A secure decentralised generalised transaction ledger. *Ethereum Project Yellow Paper*, 151(2014), 1-32.

34. Zamr, V. (2015). Introducing Casper the friendly ghost. Ethereum Blog URL: https://blog. ethereum. org/2015/08/01/introducing-casper-friendly-ghost.

35. dos Santos, R. P. (2019). Consensus algorithms: A matter of complexity?. In *Blockchain Economics: Implications of Distributed Ledgers- Markets, Communications Networks, and Algorithmic Reality*, (1, 147). World Scientific.

36. Bentov, I., Gabizon, A., & Mizrahi, A. (2016, February). Cryptocurrencies without proof of work. In *International Conference on Financial Cryptography and Data Security* (pp. 142-157). Springer, Berlin, Heidelberg.

37. Kiayias, A., Russell, A., David, B., & Oliynykov, R. (2017, August). Ouroboros: A provably secure proof-of-stake blockchain protocol. In *Annual International Cryptology Conference* (pp. 357-388). Springer, Cham.

38. Chauhan, A., Malviya, O. P., Verma, M., & Mor, T. S. (2018, July). Blockchain and scalability. In *2018 IEEE International Conference on Software Quality, Reliability and Security Companion (QRS-C)* (pp. 122-128). IEEE.

39. Castro, M., & Liskov, B. (1999, February). Practical Byzantine fault tolerance. In *Proceedings of the Third Symposium on Operating Systems Design and Implementation (OSDI '99)* (Vol. 99, No. 1999, pp. 173-186).

40. Androulaki, E., Barger, A., Bortnikov, V., Cachin, C., Christidis, K., De Caro, A., ... & Muralidharan, S. (2018, April). Hyperledger fabric: a distributed operating system for permissioned blockchains. In *Proceedings of the Thirteenth EuroSys Conference* (p. 30). ACM.

41. Mazieres, D. (2015). The stellar consensus protocol: A federated model for internet-level consensus. Stellar Development Foundation, 32.

42. Zheng, Z., Xie, S., Dai, H., Chen, X., & Wang, H. (2017, June). An overview of blockchain technology: Architecture, consensus, and future trends. In *2017 IEEE International Congress on Big Data (BigData Congress)* (pp. 557-564). IEEE.

43. Chen, L., Xu, L., Shah, N., Gao, Z., Lu, Y., & Shi, W. (2017, November). On security analysis of proof-of-elapsed-time (poet). In *International Symposium on Stabilization, Safety, and Security of Distributed Systems* (pp. 282-297). Springer, Cham.

44. *Consensus Algorithms: The Root of The Blockchain Technology.* URL: https://101blockchains.com/consensus-algorithms-blockchain/6 2019.

45. Bentov, I., Lee, C., Mizrahi, A., & Rosenfeld, M. (2014). Proof of activity: Extending bitcoin's proof of work via proof of stake. *IACR Cryptology ePrint Archive*, 2014, 452.

46. Milutinovic, M., He, W., Wu, H., & Kanwal, M. (2016, December). Proof of luck: An efficient blockchain consensus protocol. In *Proceedings of the 1st Workshop on System Software for Trusted Execution* (p. 2). ACM.

47. Vukoli, M. (2015, October). The quest for scalable blockchain fabric: Proof-of-work vs. BFT replication. In *International Workshop on Open Problems in Network Security* (pp. 112-125). Springer, Cham.

48. Saleh, F. (2019). Blockchain without waste: Proof-of-stake. Available at SSRN 3183935.

49. Alharby, M., & van Moorsel, A. (2017). Blockchain-based smart contracts: A systematic mapping study. *arXiv preprint arXiv:1710.06372.*

50. Sukhwani, H., Martnez, J. M., Chang, X., Trivedi, K. S., & Rindos, A. (2017, September). Performance modeling of pbft consensus process for permissioned blockchain network (hyperledger fabric). In *2017 IEEE 36th Symposium on Reliable Distributed Systems (SRDS)* (pp. 253-255). IEEE.

51. Mingxiao, D., Xiaofeng, M., Zhe, Z., Xiangwei, W., & Qijun, C. (2017, October). A review on consensus algorithm of blockchain. In *2017 IEEE International Conference on Systems, Man, and Cybernetics (SMC)* (pp. 2567-2572). IEEE.

52. Bashir, I. (2017). *Mastering Blockchain: Deeper Insights into Decentralization, Cryptography, Bitcoin, and Popular Blockchain Frameworks.* Packt Publishing Ltd.

53. Atton M (2018). *Blockchain – Implications for Legal Practice.*

54. Laurence, T. (2019). *Blockchain for Dummies.* John Wiley & Sons.

55. Baliga, A. (2017). *Understanding Blockchain Consensus Models.* Persistent Systems Ltd.

56. Dhillon, V., Metcalf, D., & Hooper, M. (2017). The hyperledger project. In *Blockchain Enabled Applications* (pp. 139-149). Apress, Berkeley, CA.

57. Dubovitskaya, A., Xu, Z., Ryu, S., Schumacher, M., & Wang, F. (2017). Secure and trustable electronic medical records sharing using blockchain. In *AMIA Annual Symposium Proceedings* (Vol. 2017, p. 650). American Medical Informatics Association.

58. Rosic, A. (2019). 17 blockchain applications that are transforming society URL: https://blockgeeks.com/guides/blockchain-applications.

59. Mougayar, W. (2016). *The Business Blockchain: Promise, Practice, and Application of the Next Internet Technology*. John Wiley & Sons.

60. Huckle, S., Bhattacharya, R., White, M., & Beloff, N. (2016). Internet of things, blockchain and shared economy applications. *Procedia Computer Science*, 98, 461-466.

61. Kaur, A., Gupta, P., & Singh, M. (2019). Hybrid balanced task clustering algorithm for scientific workflows in cloud computing. *Scalable Computing: Practice and Experience*, 20(2), 237-258.

62. Rivera, R., Robledo, J. G., Larios, V. M., & Avalos, J. M. (2017, September). How digital identity on blockchain can contribute in a smart city environment. In *2017 International Smart Cities Conference (ISC2)* (pp. 1-4). IEEE.

63. Bariviera, A. F., Basgall, M. J., Hasperue, W., & Naiouf, M. (2017). Some stylized facts of the Bitcoin market. *Physica A: Statistical Mechanics and Its Applications*, 484, 82-90.

64. Liu, P. T. S. (2016, November). Medical record system using blockchain, big data and tokenization. In *International Conference on Information and Communications Security* (pp. 254-261). Springer, Cham.

65. Szabo, N. (1997). The idea of smart contracts. *Nick Szabo's Papers and Concise Tutorials*, 6. URL http://www.fon.hum.uva.nl/rob/Courses/InformationInSpeech/CDROM/Literature/LOTwinterschool2006/szabo.best.vwh.net/idea.html

CHAPTER 3

BLOCKCHAIN IN 5G

C. Mageshkumar,[1] J. Rajeshkumar,[2] L. Godlin Atlas,[1] P. Hamsagayathri[3]

[1] Department of Computer Science & Engineering, Sri Shakthi Institute of Engineering and Technology, Coimbatore, India

[2] Department of Information Technology, SNS College of Technology, Coimbatore, India

[3] Department of Electronics and Communication Engineering, Bannari Amman Institute of Technology, Sathyamangalam, India

*Corresponding authors: mageshchinna@gmail.com; rajeshkumarjmtech@gmail.com; godlin88@gmail.com; raji1anju@gmail.com; palanisamy.hamsagayathri@gmail.com

Abstract

5G is the enabler for all technologies to maximize their impact. The incredible speed of 5G will assist devices in communicating in almost real-time, embedded with Connected Intelligence. Data explosion in the digital space has thrown open an opportunity where rich insights can solve big problems. It can help massively transform businesses and deliver rich, meaningful and immersive experiences to their customers. With the data economy in full play, work and life will be fundamentally changed. New applications like autonomous vehicles, telemedicine, and precision manufacturing robots will finally have the bandwidth to meet their true potential and, as a result, businesses will run more efficiently. Workers will spend less time on operations and more time focusing on ways to innovate and grow the business. Those who prepare well to understand 5G technologies will greatly benefit by delivering unique experiences to their end customers, which will disrupt the marketplace and create strategic differentiation for their businesses. Blockchain has the power to solve many of the world's most pressing problems. In its most basic form, the blockchain is a decentralized ledger that is immutable and provides its users with a faster and safer way to verify key information and establish trust.

Blockchain has the ability to change the way we buy and sell, interact with others and verify everything from voting, to property records, to even where our vegetables come from. It allows us to simplify processes, reduce costs, and hold businesses and each other accountable. Because of its enormous potential, we expect that Blockchain will be the operating system of the future. Much of the excitement about blockchain is about removing intermediaries and streamlining data management processes. Blockchain can enable a transformation of business to predict the modern day supply chain. Supply chains are fragmented and extremely fragile on account of the multiple parties that are involved. Blockchain makes supply chains trustful and trackable.

Keywords: Bitcoin, 5G, cryptography, data explosion, quasi protocol

3.1 Introduction

A blockchain is a growing list of records, called blocks, which are linked using cryptography. Each block contains a cryptographic hash of the previous block, a timestamp, and transaction data (generally represented as a *Merkle tree*). By design, a blockchain is resistant to modification of the data. It is "an open, distributed ledger that can record transactions between two parties efficiently and in a verifiable and permanent way." By allowing digital information to be distributed but not copied, blockchain technology created the backbone of a new type of internet. Originally devised for the digital currency, Bitcoin, the tech community has now found other potential uses for the technology.

Figure 3.1   Blockchain − the invisible technology.

The development of technology in the current era is no longer single-stranded. It involves the combination of multiple technologies − and particularly so in the case of blockchain and 5G, alongside the IoT. Blockchain happens to belong and participate in more and more of our daily transactions and documentations, transforming the immutable distribution of data to make online registration of encrypted transactions even more secure. Whether they are contracts, documents, or certificates, stored and distributed in public, or private, they are unalterable by man [1].

The blockchain is an undeniably ingenious invention − the brainchild of a person or group of people known by the pseudonym, Satoshi Nakamoto. But since then, it has evolved into something greater, and the main question every single person is asking is: *What is Blockchain?*

Along with IoT, blockchain has been another one of those buzzwords over the last couple years with a lot of promise but little in terms of concrete results, outside of cryptocurrencies. Blockchain is an immutable, distributed ledger.

Blockchain technology's application as a cryptocurrency (including most famously Bitcoin) is well accepted, if not always well understood. We are still looking for that "killer app" for non-cryptocurrency applications of the technology. Numerous startups as well as large corporations have been making huge strides on this front [2].

3.1.1 What Is Blockchain Technology?

In their book, *Blockchain Revolution*, Don and Alex Tapscott define the blockchain as "an incorruptible digital ledger of economic transactions that can be programmed to record not just financial transactions but virtually everything of value" [62].

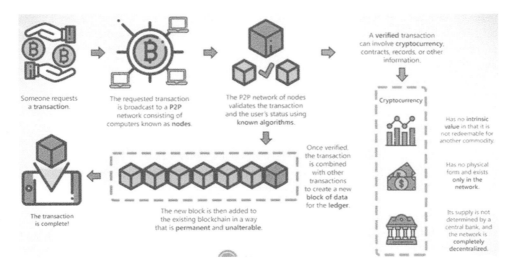

Figure 3.2   Transaction cycle of blockchain.

A blockchain is, in the simplest terms, a time-stamped series of absolute record of data that is managed by a cluster of computers not owned by any single entity. Each of these blocks of data (i.e., block) are protected and bound to each other using cryptographic principles (i.e., chain).

So, what is so special about blockchain and why are we saying that it has the capability of disrupting some areas of industry? The blockchain network has no central authority – it is the very definition of a democratized system. Since it is a shared and absolute ledger, the information in it is open for anyone and everyone to see. Hence, anything that is built on the blockchain is by its very nature translucent and everyone involved is accountable for their actions [3-5].

3.1.2 Blockchain in Real-Time World

A blockchain carries no transaction costs. The blockchain is a simple yet ingenious way of passing information from *A* to *B* in a fully automated and safe manner. One party to a transaction initiates the process by creating a block. This block is verified by thousands, perhaps millions, of computers distributed around the net. The verified block is added to a chain, which is stored across the net, creating not just a unique record, but a unique record with a unique history. Falsifying a single record would mean falsifying the entire chain in millions of instances. That is virtually impossible. Bitcoin uses this model for monetary transactions, but it can be deployed in many other ways.

Think of a railway company. We buy tickets on an app or the web. The credit card company takes a cut for processing the transaction. With blockchain, not only can the railway operator save on credit card processing fees, it can move the entire ticketing process to the blockchain. The two parties in the transaction are the railway company and the passenger. The ticket is a block, which will be added to a ticket blockchain. Just as a monetary transaction on blockchain is a unique, independently verifiable and unfalsifiable record (like Bitcoin), so too can your ticket be. Incidentally, the final ticket blockchain is also a record of all transactions for, say, a certain train route, or even the entire train network, comprising every ticket ever sold, every journey ever taken. But the key here is this: it's free. Not only can the blockchain transfer and store money, but it can also replace all processes and business models which rely on charging a small fee for a transaction or any other transaction between two parties.

The gig economy hub Fivver charges 0.5 dollars on a 5 transaction between individuals buying and selling services. Using blockchain technology, the transaction is free. Ergo, Fivver will cease to exist. So will auction houses and any other business entity based on the market-maker principle. Even recent entrants like Uber[1] and Airbnb[2] are threatened by blockchain technology. All you need to do is encode the transactional information for a car ride or an overnight stay, and you have a perfectly safe way that disrupts the business model of the companies which have just begun to challenge the traditional economy. We are not just cutting out the fee-processing middleman; we are also eliminating the need for the matchmaking platform.

Because blockchain transactions are free, you can charge minuscule amounts, say 1/100 of a cent for a video view or article read. Why should I pay *The Economist* or *National Geographic* an annual subscription fee if I can pay per article on Facebook or my favorite chat application? Again, remember that blockchain transactions carry no transaction cost. You can charge for anything in any amount without worrying about third parties cutting into your profits.

Blockchain may make selling recorded music profitable again for artists by cutting out music companies and distributors like Apple or Spotify. The music you buy could even be encoded in the blockchain itself, making it a cloud archive for any song purchased. Because the amounts charged can be so small, subscription and streaming services will become irrelevant.

In the financial world the applications are more obvious and the revolutionary changes more imminent. Blockchains will change the way stock exchanges work, loans are bundled, and insurances contracted. They will eliminate bank accounts and practically all services offered by banks. Almost every financial institution will go bankrupt or be forced to change fundamentally, once the advantages of a safe ledger without transaction fees is widely understood and implemented. After all, the financial system is built on taking a small cut of your money for the privilege of facilitating a transaction. Bankers will become mere advisers, not gatekeepers of money. Stockbrokers will no longer be able to earn commissions and the buy/sell spread will disappear.

---

[1] https://www.uber.com/
[2] https://www.airbnb.com/

3.1.3 Working Process of Blockchain

Picture a spreadsheet that is duplicated thousands of times across a network of computers. Then imagine that this network is designed to regularly update this spreadsheet and you have a basic understanding of the blockchain. Information held on a blockchain exists as a shared – and continually reconciled – database. This is a way of using the network that has obvious benefits. The blockchain database isn't stored in any single location, meaning the records it keeps are truly public and easily verifiable. No centralized version of this information exists for a hacker to corrupt. Hosted by millions of computers simultaneously, its data is accessible to anyone on the internet [6].

Based on his research study, the venture advisor, 4x entrepreneur, marketer, strategist and blockchain specialist William Mougayar described the benefits of blockchain compared to the traditional collaborative way of sharing documents. The traditional way of sharing documents with collaboration is to send a Microsoft Word document to another recipient and ask them to make revisions to it. The problem with that scenario is that you need to wait until receiving a return copy before you can see or make other changes because you are locked out of editing it until the other person is done with it. That's how databases work today. Two owners can't be messing with the same record at once. That's how banks maintain money balances and transfers; they briefly lock access (or decrease the balance) while they make a transfer, then update the other side, then re-open access. With Google Docs[3] (or Google Sheets), both parties have access to the same document at the same time, and the single version of that document is always visible to both of them. It is like a shared ledger, but it is a shared document. The distributed part comes into play when sharing involves a number of people.

Imagine the number of legal documents that should be used that way. Instead of passing them to each other, losing track of versions, and not being in sync with the other version, why can't "all" business documents become shared instead of transferred back and forth? So many types of legal contracts would be ideal for that kind of workflow. You don't need a blockchain to share documents, but the shared documents analogy is a powerful one.

The reason why the blockchain has gained so much admiration is that:

- It is not owned by a single entity, hence it is decentralized,

- The data is cryptographically stored inside,

- The blockchain is immutable, so no one can tamper with the data that is inside the blockchain,

- The blockchain is transparent so one can track the data if they want to.

3.2 Data Economy of Blockchain and 5G

5G is the next next (fifth) generation of wireless networks. As with previous next-generation networks, we should see the customary speed increase on our cell phones and tablets. However, what is different this time around is that in addition to the speed increase, 5G promises reduced latency (for quicker response time) and higher capacity (so more devices can be connected). This is in addition to the requisite security enhancements. Of all the new features of 5G, the ability to connect a vastly larger number of devices, including smaller, less

---

[3]https://docs.google.com/

expensive, lower powered devices, has the potential to truly transform the way we live. The ever forthcoming Internet of Things "revolution" can finally happen!

Not only will 5G be the evolution of the broadband network, but a unique network with completely new features, as well. These features will provide the user with a number of performance enhancements in terms of network capacity increase, shorter latency, more mobility and increased network reliability and security [7-9].

What makes 5G even more exciting is that this evolution from 4G will allow mobile carriers to lower their costs at approximately 10 times less per gigabyte as compared to the current 4G networks we have today. This means they can expand to underserved suburban areas and recoup their expansion investment in less than two years. This makes for easy expansion decisions.

This new connectivity for households and businesses will allow more people to be connected and therefore be a part of this growing innovation. Not only will videos play seamlessly on mobile devices, and your Skype or FaceTime calls will sound much clearer and without interruption, but now more people will have access to the upcoming innovations which blockchain will serve.

Blockchain has the potential to be the framework on which business is conducted and 5G will be the network it runs on. Networks are at the heart of accelerating digital transformation and a fully functional 5G network will deliver unprecedented productivity gains, redefine competitive advantages and reshape every industry vertical [10]. Simply put, 5G is the enabler for all technologies to maximize their impact. The incredible speed of 5G will assist devices in communicating in almost real-time, embedded with Connected Intelligence. Data explosion in the digital space has thrown open an opportunity where rich insights can solve big problems. It can help massively transform businesses and deliver rich, meaningful and immersive experiences to their customers. With the data economy in full play, work and life will be fundamentally changed [11].

New applications like autonomous vehicles, telemedicine, and precision Manufacturing Robots will finally have the bandwidth to meet their true potential and, as a result, businesses will run more efficiently. Workers will spend less time on operations and more time focusing on ways to innovate and grow the business. Those who prepare well to understand 5G technologies will greatly benefit by delivering unique experiences to their end customers, which will disrupt the marketplace and create strategic differentiation for their businesses.

Demystifying Blockchain – The Operating System of the Future

Blockchain has the power to solve many of the world's most pressing problems. In its most basic form, the blockchain is a decentralized ledger that is immutable and provides its users with a faster and safer way to verify key information and establish trust.

Blockchain has the ability to change the way we buy and sell, interact with others and verify everything from voting, to property records, to even where our vegetables come from. It allows us to simplify processes, reduce costs, and hold businesses and each other accountable. Because of its enormous potential, we expect that Blockchain will be the operating system of the future. Much of the excitement about blockchain is about removing intermediaries and streamlining data management processes.

There is no better example of where the blockchain can transform business than in the modern day supply chain. Supply chains are fragmented and extremely fragile on account of the multiple parties that are involved. Blockchain makes supply chains trustful and trackable. The pace of innovation over the last few decades has been remarkable and we are on the cusp of a monumental shift in the way the world lives, works and plays. While still in their early stages, 5G and Blockchain will shape our lives remarkably. The 5G and Blockchain economy is here, it is time for us to make it count [12].

The argument is that 5G will drive IoT deployment and that IoT devices will utilize Blockchain as a layer of security [13]. The W3C however is already securing DNS and HTTP in order to deliver greater security using the public/private key pairs also utilized by blockchain – so Blockchain may not be needed for security but may prove beneficial for data distribution – if it can be made to operate faster, much faster.

Figure 3.3   Collaboration of Blockchain with 5G.

Today we have a number of Blockchain solutions, some that operate over fast trusted networks and some others that claim to work faster, some much faster, over those unreliable networks. If the new Blockchain does operate quickly and efficiently over unreliable and insecure networks then 5G won't make any real difference to Blockchain operations. However, there has yet to be an independent mathematical proof that states those fast solutions will work and we have witnessed major challenges associated with rolling out a faster Ethereum, so perhaps we will be best served by relying on trusted nodes, connected by trusted and fast networks – so 5G can help [14].

Analysts, such as Ben Whittle, have been anticipating the implications of the internet of things (IoT) for several years. However, there have been two main impediments to its success: capacity and security. But now, the introduction of a new technology could change that. This year, major carriers like AT&T and Verizon will be introducing 5G, the latest generation of cellular mobile communications. The 5G platform brings a high data rate, reduced latency, energy savings, cost reduction, higher system capacity and massive device connectivity, according to the analysts.

The combination of 5G and blockchain technology has the potential to unleash a surge of economic value. In order to understand this connection between 5G and blockchain, one must think of the relationship as multifold. The power of 5G coverage through its reduced latency, high speeds and capacity allows for IoT devices to become widely used. Simultaneously, these devices can leverage the security, decentralization, immutability and consensus arbitration of blockchains as foundational layers. That means smart cities, driverless vehicles, smart homes and other sensor-driven enhancements will finally have a technology that can handle their needs [15].

3.3 Combination of Blockchain Technology and 5G Mobile Connection

Blockchain technology now has several sectors under its wings, from agriculture to health-care, virtual gaming to media, and banking to foreign exchange. Mass adoption of blockchain continues to revolutionize business processes across industries. However, a need for in-novation in the space has been felt for the past few years. Especially with the growing popularity of modern techs like Artificial Intelligence, Machine Learning and Internet of Things, the need for newer developments in blockchain technology is deeply felt.

Experts have predicted that the introduction of 5G mobile cellular data connection can help the further development of blockchain. The latest generation of mobile data is all set to launch sometime soon. 5G connection boasts data connection with unheard-of speeds. And as more and more people start entering the mobile space, the use of 5G will grow sig-nificantly. Integration of blockchain with 5G is still quite far from happening, but experts are already suggesting that it will possibly create great economic value. Especially with mobile phone-based payment solutions becoming the norm, that's one area which can be completely revolutionized by the two innovative techs collaborating.

Also, 5G is expected to bring down latency considerably, which will further help blockchain achieve shorter block times, resulting in improved scalability. These features will help in projects related to the internet of things (IoT), a futuristic concept which has been gaining significant traction recently. Blockchain is already being used by companies in Europe for developing sensors for driverless cars through machine learning. 5G can speed up the underlying blockchain in sensors for making them more secure and safe. Apart from these, there are several blockchain-based projects aimed at creating smart cities, smart homes, and other similar concepts, which heavily depend on IoT [16].

Transparency, security and immutability are the main characteristics of the blockchain technology, while 5G will be more focused on data speed, sizeable data transfer and low latency, which are what the blockchain space somewhat lacks. The big corporations which have taken a keen interest in distributed ledger technology have the capital and infras-tructure to conduct research on the tech: especially the tech giants like IBM, TCS and Microsoft are likely to test the integration of blockchain with 5G. Demand for blockchain has been growing exponentially in the past few years. In 2018, investment companies poured in over $5.2 billion in blockchain based startups, an amount significantly more than the preceding year's $1.5 billion.

Banking giants like HSBC and JPMorgan have also established their respective blockchain divisions. HSBC alone executed forex transactions worth over $250 billion in 2019 using blockchain. As the use of blockchain expands, the amount of data transfer will also go up.

Currently, the amount of data being transferred is much less than what the future holds. This is a potential problem for blockchain, as carrying that much data will hinder block speeds, creating latency. Integration with 5G connectivity will help solve this issue, as the latest generation mobile connection tech is capable of transferring huge amounts of data at lightning speed.

3.4 How to Use 5G and Blockchain Together

Blockchain technology could operate at this level, which, with its characteristic of un-changeability and intrinsic security, allows the transmission of data and payment activities to be carried out in a safe and non-infringing manner. The problem at this point, however, is the scalability of the blockchain: if applied extensively to the IoT, the DLT must be able to tolerate an extremely high number of transactions per second, and we know that this is the weak point of this type of technology.

5G will allow implementations on blockchain to run smoothly and efficiently while remaining in the secure environment it requires. The new mobile data standard will become the data transmission infrastructure upon which blockchain – as a quasi protocol – will run.

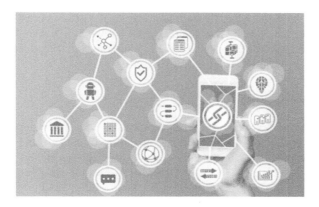

Figure 3.4   The fusion of Blockchain and 5G.

The point at which 5G and blockchain technologies intersect is at the micro-data level enabled through the internet of things (IoT). A number of prominent blockchain projects, such as IOTA,[4] VeChain[5] and Walton Chain,[6] are pursuing a use case in supply chain management and the emerging machine-to-machine (M2M) economy. These projects are geared towards the collection of data from what will become an inordinate number of sensors along the supply chain.

For example, Bitcoin can support 7 TPS, Litecoin 56, Ethereum 25, BCH 61 and Tron 2000. The choice, however, may not fall directly on a blockchain but on a second-layer blockchain, overlapping the main one, as is the case with Lightning Network on BTC or LTC, able to provide the scalability that the main one cannot provide. The public blockchain could act as a contact element between the widespread IoT in cities, homes and means of transport and the 5G network, thus becoming the protector of our privacy and payments.

This type of technology is still in its infancy, but the 5G will not have a profound impact if not accompanied by the DLT. Of course, there must be a safety assessment of 5G networks at the level of possible health damage, as highlighted by the recent blockade of the experiment in Brussels, which occurred due to doubts about the possible danger of long-term electromagnetic waves, much more dangerous in a network that needs to be spread with great depth. But once these problems are solved, we could see a real revolution in the everyday life of people.

[4] https://www.iota.org/
[5] https://www.vechain.org/
[6] https://www.waltonchain.org/

3.5   Applications of Blockchain and 5G

3.5.1   Smart Contracts

Distributed ledgers enable the coding of simple contracts that will execute when specified conditions are met. Ethereum is an open source blockchain project that was built specifically to realize this possibility. Still in its early stages, Ethereum has the potential to leverage the usefulness of blockchains on a truly world-changing scale. At the technology's current level of development, smart contracts can be programmed to perform simple functions. For instance, a derivative could be paid out when a financial instrument meets certain benchmarks, with the use of blockchain technology and Bitcoin enabling the payout to be automated.

3.5.2   Data Management

Today, in exchange for their personal data people can use social media platforms like Facebook for free. In the future, users will have the ability to manage and sell the data their online activity generates. Because it can be easily distributed in small fractional amounts, Bitcoin – or something like it – will most likely be the currency that gets used for this type of transaction.

The MIT project Enigma understands that user privacy is the key precondition for creating a personal data marketplace. Enigma uses cryptographic techniques to allow individual data sets to be split between nodes, and at the same time run bulk computations over the data group as a whole. Fragmenting the data also makes Enigma scalable (unlike those blockchain solutions where data gets replicated on every node). A Beta launch is promised within the next six months.

3.5.3   Supply Chain Auditing

Consumers increasingly want to know that the ethical claims companies make about their products are real. Distributed ledgers provide an easy way to certify that the backstories of the things we buy are genuine. Transparency comes with blockchain-based timestamping of a date and location on ethical diamonds, which, for instance, corresponds to a product number.

The UK-based provenance offers supply chain auditing for a range of consumer goods. Making use of the Ethereum blockchain, a Provenance pilot project ensures that fish sold in Sushi restaurants in Japan has been sustainably harvested by its suppliers in Indonesia.

3.5.4   Entertainment and Multimedia

5G will offer a high definition virtual world on your mobile phone. High speed streaming of 4K videos only takes a few seconds and it can support crystal clear audio clarity. Live events can be streamed via wireless network with high definition. HD TV channels can be accessed on mobile devices without any interruptions. The entertainment industry will hugely benefit from 5G wireless networks.

5G can provide 120 frames per second, high resolution and higher dynamic range video streaming without interruption. Audiovisual experience will be rewritten after the implementation of the latest technologies powered by 5G wireless. Augmented reality and virtual reality require HD video with low latency. 5G network is powerful enough to power

AR and VR with amazing virtual experience. HD virtual reality games are becoming popular and many companies are investing in VR-based gaming. High speed 5G network can offer better gaming experience with high speed Internet.

3.5.5 Smart Home

Smart home appliances and products are catching up with today's market. The smart home concept will utilize 5G networks for device connectivity and monitoring of applications. 5G wireless network will be utilized by smart appliances which can be configured and accessed from remote locations, and closed-circuit cameras will provide high quality real-time video for security purposes.

3.5.6 Logistics and Shipping

The logistics and shipping industries can make use of smart 5G technology for tracking of goods, fleet management, centralized database management, staff scheduling and real-time delivery tracking and reporting.

3.5.7 Drone Operation

Drones are becoming popular for multiple operations ranging from entertainment, video capturing, medical and emergency access, smart delivery solutions, security and surveillance, etc. 5G network will provide strong support with high speed wireless internet connectivity for drone operations in a wide range of applications. During emergency situations like natural calamities, humans have limited access to many areas where drones can reach out and collect useful information.

3.6 Conclusion

The transition to a data-driven world is being accelerated by the pace of the technological advances of an internet-enabled global world, the rise of societal challenges, and an increasing competition for scarce resources. In this ecosystem, blockchain can offer a 5G platform for distributing trusted information that defies non-collaborative organizational structures.

And for anyone who has heard of 5G, in other words, the 5th generation of mobile internet, but has not yet used it or tried it, it might already jump right into 6G, which is already accessing the Blockchain mobile network. In the future we will depend on many transactions using blockchain. The future of technology heavily relies on data management; therefore, blockchain and 5G integration can create wonders in tech-driven industries.

REFERENCES

1. Downes, L., and Nunes, P (2014), *Big-Bang Disruption*, vol. 91. New York, NY, USA: Penguin Group

2. Mougayar, W. (2016). *The Business Blockchain: Promise, Practice, and Application of the Next Internet Technology*. John Wiley & Sons.

3. Whittle, B. (2019). Reinsurance blockchain: Simplifying the complex insurance industry. CoinCentral.

4. Shrivastava, G., Peng, S. L., Bansal, H., Sharma, K., & Sharma, M. (Eds.). (2020). *New Age Analytics: Transforming the Internet through Machine Learning, IoT, and Trust Modeling.* Apple Academic Press.

5. Ahokangas, P., Matinmikko, M., Yrjola, S., Okkonen, H., & Casey, T. (2013). Simple rules for mobile network operators' strategic choices in future cognitive spectrum sharing networks. *IEEE Wireless Communications, 20*(2), 20-26.

6. Jaffrey, H. (2015). *Crypto 2.0 Lenses.* LinkedIn Pulse blog, April, 17. Available: https://www.linkedin.com/pulse/crypto-20-lenseshyder-jaffrey

7. Amit, R., & Han, X. (2017). Value creation through novel resource configurations in a digitally enabled world. *Strategic Entrepreneurship Journal, 11*(3), 228-242.

8. Kumar, P., Shrivastava, G., & Tanwar, P. (2020). Demistifying Ethereum technology: Application and benefits of decentralization. In *Forensic Investigations and Risk Management in Mobile and Wireless Communications* (pp. 242-256). IGI Global.

9. Backman, J., Yrjola, S., Valtanen, K., & Mammela, O. (2017, November). Blockchain network slice broker in 5G: Slice leasing in factory of the future use case. In *2017 Internet of Things Business Models, Users, and Networks* (pp. 1-8). IEEE.

10. C. P. Gurnani, Managing Director and CEO of Tech Mahindra.

11. Mattila, J. (2016). ETLA-Res. Inst. Finnish Economy, Helsinki, Finland, ETLA Working Papers. *Industrial blockchain platforms: An exercise in use case development in the energy industry.* [Online]. Available: http://pub.etla.fi/ETLA-Working-Papers-43.pdf

12. Gupta, R., Shrivastava, G., Anand, R., & Tomazic, T. (2018). IoT-based privacy control system through android. In *Handbook of e-Business Security* (pp. 341-363). Auerbach Publications.

13. Tim Sloane (2019). Will The Melding of 5G And Blockchain Add Enormous Economic Value? [Online]. Available: https://www.paymentsjournal.com/5g-and-blockchain-add-economic-value/

14. Kumar, P., Quadri, M., Sharma, K., Gia, N. N., & Ranjan, P. (2018). Persistent cellular telephony: Enhanced secure GSM architecture. *Recent Patents on Engineering*, 12(1), 23-29.

15. BOND. (2019). The Blockchains Boosting Finnish Industry Project Web Pages. Accessed. [Online]. Available: https://www.vtt.fi/sites/BOND

16. Shrivastava, G., Kumar, P., Gupta, B. B., Bala, S., & Dey, N. (Eds.). (2018). *Handbook of Research on Network Forensics and Analysis Techniques.* IGI Global.

CHAPTER 4

BLOCKCHAIN IN SOCIAL NETWORKING

T. Poongodi,[1] R. Sujatha,[2] D. Sumathi,[3] P. Suresh,[4] B. Balamurugan[1]

[1] School of Computing Science & Engineering, Galgotias University, Greater Noida, Uttar Pradesh, India
[2] School of Information Technology & Engineering, Vellore Institute of Technology, Vellore, India
[3] School of Computer Science and Engineering, VIT-AP University, Amaravati, Andhrapradesh, India
[4] School of Mechanical Engineering, Galgotias University, Greater Noida, Uttar Pradesh, India

*Corresponding authors: tpoongodi2730@gmail.com; r.sujatha@vit.ac.in; sumathi.research28@gmail.com; psuresh2730@gmail.com; kadavulai@gmail.com

Abstract

Since the last decade, the social media platform has served as an entry point for establishing connections, content sharing and social interactions for many users. Exploiting customer's information is very prevalent nowadays by gaining insight into user's habits, preferences, connections, behaviors, content and location. Logging into a social media website paves the way to becoming a target of marketing campaigns for advertising. Primarily, most social media sites available today are centralized and provide opportunities for exploiting the user's content well. Privacy and data security are of great concern in social media platforms. Blockchain, with distributed ledger and decentralized concept, secures users' content by encrypting it. The social media platforms such as Whatsapp, iMessage, Signal, Wire, Threema, etc., follow end-to-end encryption for security. A problem occurs when metadata is exchanged along with messages, thereby providing an opportunity for third parties to steal the user's personal details. Blockchain-based social media provide more benefits than just security and privacy: Cryptocurrencies are used for secure communication by paying and buying content in peer-to-peer marketing. Blockchain assists in gaining control over the user's own content. A decentralized approach to blockchain technology in social networking ensures privacy and enables e-commerce, crowdfunding transactions as well as smart apps and contracts. Nowadays, the digital social network media platforms, such as Facebook, LinkedIn, Instagram, Twitter, Reddit, etc., provide free access. Obviously, development and server infrastructures are vital to social networking platforms and their profit focuses on advertising and analytics in the social network business era. The fundamental problems facing social networking includes fake news (Facebook), excessive trolling (Twitter), censorship and demonetization (YouTube).

Keywords: Blockchain, social network, social data

4.1 Overview of Blockchain and Social Networking Platform

Obsidian Messenger follows Stratis-based blockchain in storing data in a decentralized manner and it uses end-to-end encryption with a 256-bit encryption algorithm for encrypting pictures, videos, files, payment and messages. It works with Windows, Linux, macOS, iOS app, Android app and uses nodes to obtain cryptocurrency by maintaining resilient, reliable network. Steemit is a decentralized network which supports social interaction with cryptocurrency rewards and users get paid for their contributions. Nexus is a decentralized blockchain approach which handles many operations in social media. Blockchain eliminates the external payment mechanisms because of internal currency in crowdfunding websites such as Kickstarter,[1] Indiegogo,[2] etc. Synereo employs blockchain that uses WildSpark where the users get paid for their creations. Indorse is equivalent to LinkedIn, which is on the top of Ethereum blockchain, where users can own their rights to create their own content, build profile, connections and get paid for their contributions. It also encourages a skills economy by providing Indorse Rewards and Indorse Score reputation system to build the platform for improving privacy and security of user's data.

Blockchain social network offers:

   i) Transparency and governance; it implements transparent democratic process that allows transactions to be verified by different servers and developers.

  ii) Content monetization; no intervention of third party to use the cryptocurrency.

 iii) Data control; ensures "secure identity ecosystem."

 iv) Single point failure is avoided because of decentralized concept.

Blockchain social networks have to be focused on overcoming plagiarism, bots, token economics and first-mover advantage. The blockchain changes social media from the aspect of

   i) Verifying online identities.

  ii) Verification of marketplaces.

 iii) Combining cryptocurrencies and blockchain technology.

 iv) Cryptocurrency collectibles.

  v) Blockchain smart contract blocks fake content.

---

[1]https://www.kickstarter.com
[2]https://www.indiegogo.com

According to Gartner's recent "Hype Cycle for Emerging Technologies" report, blockchain is entering the "trough of disillusionment." Blockchain platform is anticipated to reach maturity in the next 10 years, according to Mike Walker at Gartner. A survey conducted by Deloitte says that 44% of "blockchain savvy" U.S. executives and 39% of executives from U.K, Germany, France, China and Canada believe that "blockchain is overhyped." This chapter overviews various blockchain-based social media platforms. It also highlights the research challenges and issues facing in blockchain social network.

4.1.1   Basic Structure of Blockchain

The potential increase in the online transaction of money has paved the way to the requirement of trust-based structure. Due to constraints, financial institutions have been met with unavoidable disputes. This has led to stopping the small transactions and some percentage of fraudulent ones. The need for a third party is considered unnecessary by introducing a cryptographic approach that enables a secured transaction between the concerned parties without intermediaries. By considering all these pros and cons, Nakamoto defined an "electronic coin" which is a chain of digital signatures. This unique concept appends the previous transaction hash along with the next owner public key as a digital signature to make secure payments. Block or node is the name coined to indicate each part involved in the flow. In the primary work carried in 2008, SHA-256 is utilized to show the effectiveness of an innovative approach. The network begins with fresh transaction information being passed towards all nodes followed by making the transaction into a block by nodes. When all is perfect, the block is transferred to all nodes and passes only when valid and not used before. The process flows with the hash concept [1]. Cryptocurrency is a modest way of enabling end-to-end cash transaction in the digital format. The need for substitute currencies is due to localism, financial institutions' inefficiencies, speculation, technology, and other political economy uncertainties. There are a variety of blockchain stakeholders, including researchers, investors, regulators, and merchants. Cryptocurrency's success is because of open-source software which is global, fast, secure, reliable, automated, peer-to-peer, flexible, scalable and has highly convincing integration. Bitcoin is the first type of cryptocurrency followed by various national levels like SpainCoin (SPA), IrishCoin (IRL), and the list goes on [2].

Bitcoin rocked capital marketing. Thus, without any third party, the transaction happens. Figure 4.1 exemplifies the blockchain idea that holds a sequence of blocks.

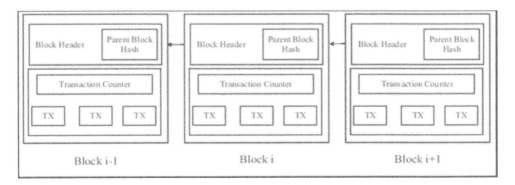

Figure 4.1   An example of blockchain.

Block structure consists of the block header and block body. Block header consists of block version, Merkle tree root hash, timestamp, nonce and parent block. Similarly, the block body consists of a transaction counter and transactions. The initial block of the blockchain is popularly called the Genesis block. Figure 4.2 illustrates the structure of the block.

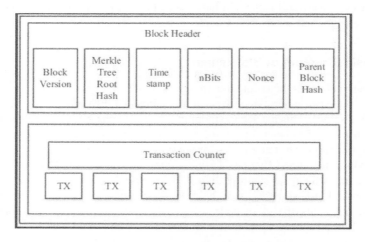

Figure 4.2 Block structure.

Based on the property of consensus determination, read permission, immutability, efficiency, and consensus process the blockchain is classified into public, consortium and private. Various algorithms rule the different types of blockchain [3].

A blockchain works in a decentralized approach encompassing six layers to carry out different services. Data-related manipulation like collecting and collating is carried out by data and network layer. Consensus layer and contract layer work in techniques pertaining to making decisions in a synchronized manner among blockchain users with the proof-of-work, proof-of-stake, and proof-of-importance concepts along with contract-related matter. Finally, implementation and deployment of blockchain are carried out by the service layer and application layer. Data and information in the blockchain are arranged in a chronological fashion. Since blocks are synced in sequence the data structure resembles a chain. In the private chain category, a complete distributed system is less permissioned in nature where any node can participate in any file actions. In the consortium chain, it is centralized and controlled by the authority, so it is specifically meant for small target groups or organizations. The consortium chain is a mix of the public and private chain [4]. Blockchain is a trending research and is applied to various sectors, such as public service, entertainment, particularly in the music industry, education, healthcare, cybersecurity, voting, and the list goes on. It was initially deployed in business and industry and slowly found its way to all thematic areas. It's embedded with IoT, big data concepts, and deep learning ideas to make the system highly informative and interesting [5, 6].

4.1.2 Review of Social Networking Platform

The features of the social networking platform enable relationships among people who share similar interests and activities. It is broadly classified into four types: social network where friends get together, distributed social network where users get connected through the internet, non-social interpersonal linking, and social navigation to search based on specific resources [7]. Social networking finds its path in the versatile domain and uses different sets of people like government agencies, business, dating, education, finance, crowdsourcing, medical and health, social and political. The popularity of social networking can be inferred from more user engagement and an increase in the number of people spending more time on sites. The data collated by statistics is given as a graph in Figure 4.3;[3] Facebook and YouTube are used in the comparison.

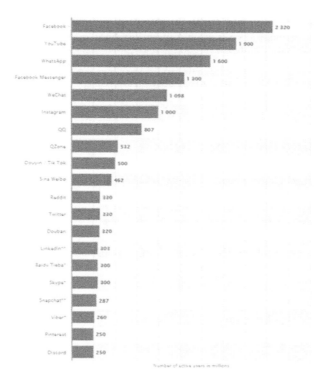

Figure 4.3 Popular social networks as of April 2019.

A social network connects people or organizations and helps in collaborating with people of the same or different fields. It also helps in solving complex problems such as giving reviews, citations and conference invitations on a large scale. Statistical analysis helps researchers of social network get an insight into the subnetworking and patterns of individuals. The adjacency matrix method is used for publication and for authors to combine work on the same topic. Symmetric and asymmetric methods are applied to the adjacency matrix for analysis. With analogy, the users get a better idea of the ultimate aim of social networking platforms [8].

Muller and Peres write about how people become passionate about an innovative product and the way in which distributors market their product to achieve their target. The pro-

[3]https://www.statista.com/statistics/272014/global-social-networks-ranked-by-number-of-users/

cess is carried out primarily by creating awareness about the product and learning about the product. The motivation for the social network theory is to construct a high performing network. Creation of dyadic connections enables connecting a large number of ties to a large number of nodes. Seeding strategy is the most important way to achieve the target. Referral programs help in bringing new customers [9].

4.1.3   Relationship between Social Media and Blockchain

Content is the rocking item in social media and by imparting it with blockchain the control over the content is optimized and the level of security is improved. By continues monitoring of the flow of events, popular posts will be highlighted. Fake entities are controlled, thus highly authenticated legitimate content will be available. Verification of online entities is done with proper checking. The future of social media will be highly influenced by cryptocurrency. The user control mechanism is highly appraisable in blockchain-based development. Crowdfunding and P2P sales are maximized.

4.2   Decentralized Online Social Network

4.2.1   Distributed Online Social Network Architecture

An online social network is the buzzword of this generation. Due to the growth of the social network, the level of interaction across the globe has invariably increased, leading to both pros and cons of its use. The big data generated by way of this social networking is exponential. Data Never Sleeps shows the voluminous amount of data generated via online social networking sites. The data generated every minute is shown in Figure 4.4.

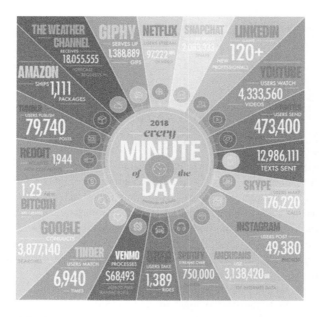

Figure 4.4   Data generated every single minute (Courtesy of Domo, Inc.).

A distributed online social network (DOSN) is the up-gradation of traditional central-ized architecture to the deployment of different distributed models based on the require-ment of social networking [10]. Social networking is governed by various stakeholders beginning with users, providers, advertising companies and other media consumers [11]. By the process of decentralization, benefits regarding ownership, such as privacy, dynamic choice of resources, and openness, are gained in comparison with online social networking. Distributed online social network is the 3-layered model.

Figure 4.5 illustrates the components in the core and extension consisting of two sublay-ers. Core component consists of access control, profile storage, and overlay. The extended layer holds API, recommender system, search scheme and social network connector [12]. The recommender system is social-aware, tag-based, and location-aware [13].

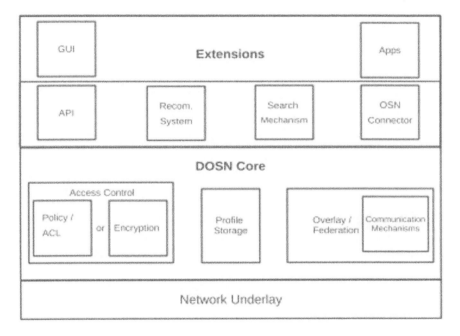

Figure 4.5   DOSN architecture.

The structure begins with a social network layer on the top that provides common func-tionalities like chat, posts, mail, etc. The intermediate layer helps in peer transaction of data. The bottom is the communication and transport layer that holds the internet and other related infrastructure. A distributed online social network is classified based on peers into three categories: distributed hash table based (DHT-based), social overlay based (SO-based) and external resource based. Management of data in the DHT is encrypted whereas others make use of trusted nodes for storing. A data management service revolves around the idea of data availability, information diffusion, privacy and security [14-16].

4.2.2   Social Data Representation

Similar to the online social network structure, DOSNs also works around users with a unique profile identity to show their individuality. Representation of social data is an interesting phenomenon in the distributed social networking environment. The special thing about it is that it consists of multiple social sites that work in an interoperable manner.

A social profile is maintained in a hierarchical manner, with each node holding social contents. The root is the entry point. Each node holds a binary branch with one holding the unique identifier and the other the privacy policy. Figure 4.6 shows the flow of various activities.

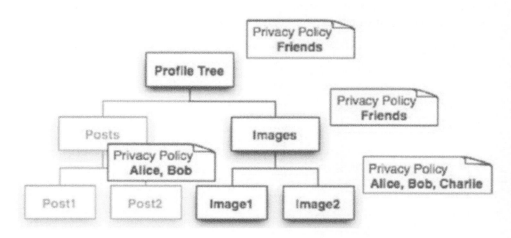

Figure 4.6   Hierarchical organization of social content.

Architecture for an online social network is highly revolutionizing due to the rapid speed in which it gives the best output to users across the world. User privacy is a great concern and can be said to be the main problem in an online social network. Breaches happening make it a necessity to have the best design that tackles all the hurdles in the social network. A distributed hash table (DHT) is deployed in DECENT architecture for security and confidentiality. Modularity in the design phase helps to segregate cryptographic execution from an elementary object model and utilize DHT of any type. Each object possesses three access policies, namely attribute-based, identity-based or a hybrid of both. Participants are arranged in DHT. The version number is used to ensure new or fresh node enters. The digital signature algorithm is considered for the write policy. DECENT DHT guarantees requests like read, write and append. To illustrate a sequence it begins with join, which establishes contact, followed by post and comment for handling each object.

Figure 4.7 shows an instance of an object structure [17]. In LifeSocial.KOM, distributed linked lists are deployed for storing the objects to the unique atomic object. Several plugins are introduced and its first fully executable social network with various functions in the P2P network [18]. In the diaspora network, hover card (hCard) is used to store user profiles. Various P2P network booms in the market substantiate growth and the need for versatile users in the competitive and interactive world.

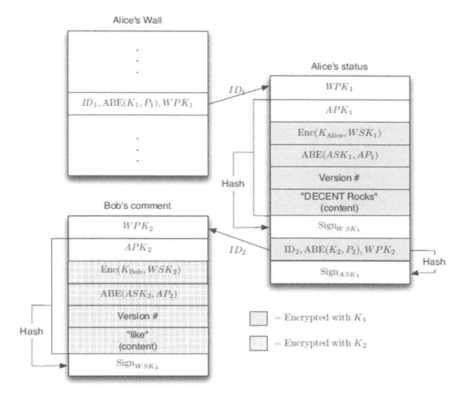

Figure 4.7   An instance of an object structure.

4.2.3 Security Issues

Typical threats in the internet era are spam attacks (unwanted messages); malware (malicious software); phishing attacks (intruder invades and acquires personal details); and cross-site scripting. Modern threats are click jacking (UI redress attack); de-anonymization attacks (tactics based on data mining approach, fake profiles, identity clone, and inference attacks, information and location leakage); cyberstalking (harass individual or set via internet); and user profiling (analyze regular users with machine learning concepts and surveillance that monitors the human activities in which privacy of the user is trapped). Deploying blockchain consensus delay sends the wrong information to peers, such as denial of service (DoS) and double transaction [19, 20].

4.3 Trusted Social Network with Blockchain Technology

Rumor spreading in large-scale systems will have a huge impact in e-economic and e-social platforms. However, there is a need for the effective mechanisms of rumor spreading in both theoretical and practical aspects. With the help of blockchain, rumor spreading can be limited. Particularly, a novel paradigm for social media equipped with the blockchain technology is driven. It incorporates decentralized contract to secure information exchange and motivate trusted networks. A blockchain-based sequential algorithm is designed which uses virtual information credit for all peer-to-peer information exchange. The effectiveness on minimizing the rumor spreading in blockchain-based social network is validated.

Rumor has been persistent in human history for thousands of years across the world. A rumor is defined as a unit of unverified information (e.g., information exchange, media coverage, etc.) circulated among persons which pertains to a particular event, object or issue of public concern [21]. Rapid transmission rate and denser connections pave the way for triggering rapid rumor propagation, causing more negative effects and increasing social panic [22]. The techniques for preventing and avoiding rumor spreading were emphasized in recent studies.

The diversity of social network, complexities of dynamic rumor transmission, drastic growth of information transmission media, and the root cause of a rumor taking off are not identified and an effective approach is not available to eliminate the dissemination of a rumor [23]. Hence, the blockchain technology is well suited and has reached success in the financial sector for secure and trusted contracts. The information exchange process has to be redesigned as a contract-based process in the current social networks. The blockchain-based pair-wise rumor spreading style is more suitable for information exchange and propagation in the future.

The blockchain-based smart contract design was introduced for information exchange; a virtual accumulated credit is allocated for each member participating in the social network. The gathered credits are the credibility of both members and the corresponding information in the social network. In order to avoid the propagation of fake news on a large scale through the network, a graphical model with nonlinear systems was designed for the social networks.

Individuals are more cautious regarding the authenticity of their information in blockchain-based peer-to-peer information exchange. The proposed approach effectively reduces the economic and social damage that occurs due to the exchange and propagation of fake information. The features of blockchain are incorporated in order to address the rumor spreading problems with appropriate solutions in the social network. The architecture of blockchain-based information exchange is depicted in Figure 4.8.

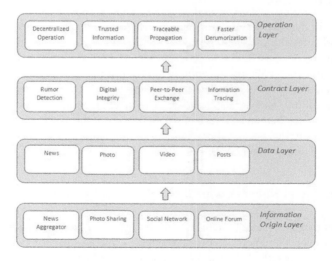

Figure 4.8   Architecture of blockchain-based information exchange.

4.3.1 Rumor Spreading Model

Rumor is a portion of unverified information which is circulated in the social network. Past research on rumors engaged multidisciplinary efforts from sociology, physics and psychology. Various approaches for modeling rumor spreading and managing its severity were discussed [24, 25]. Rumors were propagated in classic rumor models with heterogeneous social network. In their review, Moreno *et al.* provided a better understanding of the stochastic process used to simulate rumor spreading [26].

Numerous influential rumor spreaders exist in social networks [27] and there are higher probabilities for spreading the untrusted information. SIR (Susceptible, Infected, Recovered) is proposed as a rumor spreading model to control the severity of rumors in social media and networks. In the SIR process susceptible nodes are infected by infected neighbors, and recover to removed. In this work, it is assumed that the ignorant are highly influenced by the spreader, whereas the spreader is really converted into a stifler.

The blockchain technology is leveraged for the social network and the impact on the spread of rumors is examined. Blockchain technology has an interlinked chain of increasing list of blocks [28]. Every block holds the record and timestamp. It is purely a peer-to-peer network, where the records in each node are propagated to other nodes. The unvalidated modification of data is prevented in this model and it serves as a core component of Bitcoin. The significant advantages of blockchain are its high security, decentralization, and trustworthiness, which pave the way for Bitcoin as an innovative currency. Blockchain-based protocols are implemented to construct a decentralized network [29].

Blockchain is adopted in supply chain management for achieving better quality and trustability; traceability problems are solved in such a scenario [30]. Blockchain is also preferred in the power grid industry [31] and consumers are benefited by validating the information reliably and affordably in a distributed network. Meanwhile, the convergence of internet of things (IoT) and blockchain typically increases the usage of cloud storage [32]. It also plays a role in many applications in identity management, notarization, and online transaction [29].

An SIR epidemiological model is presented to analyze the rumor spreading dynamics with a set of fixed participants in the social network. The temporal characteristics such as peak value, convergence rate and final state are analyzed in this stochastic model. The practical issues in the real-world scenario and how the influence of blockchain technology decreases the spread of rumors are discussed [33].

An undirected graph $G = (V, E)$ is considered, where V and E refer to the set of vertices and edges that represent the individuals and social interactions in the social network. The fixed number of homogeneous population is assumed and the degree distribution for all the nodes in the graph G conforms to the Poisson distribution:

$$P(k) = e^{-\overline{k}}\frac{\overline{k}^k}{k!} \tag{4.1}$$

where $\overline{k}$ denotes the average degree for the graph G and $P(k)$ refers to the probability of observing k degrees for the set of vertices $v \in V$.

The rule-based classification method categorizes the vertices into 3 convertible sets such as spreader set S, ignorant set I and stifler set R. The three classes are as follows:

4.3.1.1 Ignorant with Density $I(t)$

The susceptible individuals are referred to as ignorants in classic SIR models. An ignorant has a probability λ to form as a spreader at time $t > 0$, when it is in touch with a spreader who is quite related to the truth of rumor. Meanwhile, there is a probability η for the ignorant to become a stifler, who does not show interest in the rumor anymore.

4.3.1.2 Spreader with Density $S(t)$

The contribution of spreader lies in the rumor propagation within G. If a spreader involved in a pair-wise meeting tries to infect the other individuals with the rumor, and the spreader is communicating with a stifler at time $t > 0$, the probability of the spreader is γ to be converted into a stifler. At a certain time, a spreader may forget the rumor then converts into a stifler at a rate δ.

4.3.1.3 Stifler with Density $R(t)$

The significant contribution of the stifler lies in the final purging of rumor. It is considered as the absorbing state in this stochastic model and the density of stifler is accumulated by converting both ignorants as well as spreaders into stiflers.

The differential equations for $I(t)$, $S(t)$ and $R(t)$ are derived respectively,

$$\frac{dI(t)}{dt} = -(\lambda + \eta)\overline{k}I(t)S(t) \tag{4.2}$$

$$\frac{dS(t)}{dt} = \lambda\overline{k}I(t)S(t) - \gamma\overline{k}S(t)(S(t) + R(t)) - \delta S(t) \tag{4.3}$$

$$\frac{dR(t)}{dt} = \eta\overline{k}I(t)S(t) + \gamma\overline{k}S(t)(S(t) + R(t)) + \delta S(t) \tag{4.4}$$

4.3.2 Blockchain Protocols for Rumor Spreading

Blockchain protocol integrated into the social network for information exchange has been proposed. A blockchain technology is adopted in social network for enabling privacy and security in order to prevent large-scale spreading of rumors, as well as for efficient information exchange. A protocol is designed by including private and public contract. The main objective of this protocol is to prevent or avoid the propagating of untrusted information. Accumulated virtual information credit is introduced and allocated for each participant in order to motivate the spreading of trusted information only.

4.3.2.1 Private Contract

For exchanging information between two parties, the private contract is negotiated and agreed upon between the spreader and the receiver. A private contract is negotiated at timestamp t. For instance, If the receiver's desires are accomplished, virtual credit $cred_{rs}(t)$ is paid to the spreader s, meanwhile the spreader in turn sends the information $info_{sr}(t)$ to the receiver r. The investment of the credit can be paid once the unit of information is validated as trustworthy. Hence, the accumulated credit would be increased for receiver r. Suppose that the information is validated as untrusted information (rumor), then the accumulated credit would be decreased automatically for receiver r.

The algorithm for private contract in peer-to-peer information exchange is given below:

Algorithm Private contract in peer-to-peer information exchange

---

Begin

    Step 1: Initialize the Spreader set S, $info \leftarrow \theta$, $cred \leftarrow \theta$

    Step 2: Receive the input as receiver r, accumulated credit of $r - c(t)$

    Step 3: **For** s_i in connection of r **do**

    Step 4:   **if** $s_i \in S$ **then**

    Step 5: s_i and r construct a secure channel to negotiate contract;

    Step 6:   **if** contract done **then**

    Step 7: $c(t + 1) = c(t) - credrs(t)$;

    Step 8: $info \leftarrow infos_i r(t)$;

    Step 9: $cred \leftarrow cred_{rsi}(t)$;

    Step 10:   break;

    Step 11:   **end if**

    Step 12:   **end if**

    Step 13: **end for**

end

4.3.2.2 Public Contract

The public contract is updated continuously at every time slot which records credit flows and links of information propagation in the social network. It acts as a public ledger for recording all information transactions. The public contract announces the highest transaction credit (C_{max}) publicly to all the participating users in the information exchange that is available in every private contract for decision-making.

The algorithm for public contract in peer-to-peer information exchange is given below:

Algorithm Publish contract in peer-to-peer information exchange

---

Begin

    Step 1: Initialize the highest credit C_{max} as 0;

    Step 2: Again initialize $infolist \leftarrow \theta$,

    Step 3: $credlist \leftarrow \theta$;

    Step 4: **for** $t \in T$ **do**

    Step 5:   Update $C_{max}, infolist, credlist$;

    Step 6: **end for**

end

The 2-layer contract design is employed for information exchange; hence, a distributed contract network is constructed that is more resilient and secure. Moreover, if the network is evolved, C_{max} automatically increases and it specifies a higher risk to trust the given information for the ignorant. The public transaction information helps the participants make the private decision in the blockchain contract. The proposed contract-based blockchain architecture is not only useful for contractors but also for normal participants in the social network who want to process the original information exchange.

4.3.3 Comparison of SIR and Blockchain-Based SIR

A trusted model is introduced which defines how the blockchain technology inhibits the propagation of untrusted information on social networks. In this model, a set of participants in the social network who have signed blockchain-based trusted contract is identified. The comparison between SIR and blockchain-based SIR is shown in Figure 4.9.

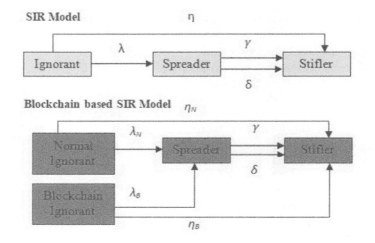

Figure 4.9   Comparison of SIR and Blockchain-based SIR model.

Initially, the density of initial participants of such trusted contract is denoted as I_B and the participants who have not signed the contract is given as I_N. I_N conforms to the ignorants' dynamics and the probability of converting an ignorant into a spreader and stifler is referred to as λ_N and η_N. If there is an information exchange among tow members with minimum one belonging to I_B, the reliable and secure consensus protocol is used to consent upon the predefined credits for participants in the trusted contract. Hence, the individual participant from I_B has the privilege of accessing the public information defined in the blockchain contract; the members have a different estimate in their virtual credits during information exchange. Therefore, there would be a difference in the dynamics of I_B and I_N and the probability is denoted as λ_N and η_N, respectively.

The dynamics of $S(t)$, $R(t)$, $I_N(t)$ and $I_B(t)$ are derived based on blockchain-based social network:

$$\frac{dI_B(t)}{dt} = -(\lambda_B + \eta_B)\overline{k}I_B(t)S(t) \tag{4.5}$$

$$\frac{dI_N(t)}{dt} = -(\lambda_N + \eta_N)\overline{k}I_N(t)S(t) \tag{4.6}$$

$$\frac{dS(t)}{dt} = \lambda_B\overline{k}I_B(t)S(t) + \lambda_N\overline{k}I_N(t)S(t) - \gamma\overline{k}S(t)(S(t) + R(t)) - \delta S(t) \tag{4.7}$$

$$\frac{dR(t)}{dt} = \eta_B\overline{k}I_B(t)S(t) + \eta_N\overline{k}I_N(t)S(t) - \gamma\overline{k}S(t)(S(t) + R(t)) - \delta S(t) \tag{4.8}$$

4.3.3.1   *Rumor Spreading Rate*

If an individual member has signed a trusted contract, it has an additional record for the blockchain transactions in the entire network. An extra estimate for the information exchange is calculated by accumulating the virtual credits and it provides a better authentication for the missing credits in certain transactions. In common, if the private contract between two individual members reaches a higher value, the participants from I_B should be very careful about the current information exchange. Then the participants from I_B are not vulnerable to a spread rumor. Meanwhile, the members who are losing interest in terms of terms will be converted into stiflers directly.

The ignorants from I_B category make good contributions to the stifler R but limited contributions to the spreader S.

$$\eta_B > \eta_N, \ \lambda_B < \lambda_N \qquad (4.9)$$

4.3.3.2 Forgetting Mechanism

The forgetting mechanism under blockchain-based SIR model takes into account both the spreaders and the "forget" process of spreaders. Thus, it reduces the likelihood of keeping fake information in the public records. The δ achieves a higher value for the given group G, which is enabled with blockchain technology. Hence, the blockchain-based social network could attain a higher absorbing rate from spreaders S to stiflers R.

4.4 Privacy-Preserving Services for Social Network

The modern world is driven by the huge generation of data due to the prevalence of smart energy grid and cities, internet of things (IoT), ubiquitous mobile computing and more in social media. Interaction among the users has been done and sharing of data among themselves also happens. The concept of Blockchain has attracted many users and researchers to focus on the adoption of various cryptographic techniques to provide control over the system. In 2013, the Ethereum, a transaction-based state machine, was devised to program the blockchain technologies. The distinctive and remarkable features of blockchain, such as security, the immutability of data, integrity, authorization, system transparency, auditability and fault tolerance, has been implemented in several domains like Industry 4.0 [34-35], agriculture [36], intelligent transportation [37-39], identity management [40], mobile crowdsensing [41], and security in mission critical systems [42]. Blockchain cryptocurrencies have attracted users and received a great deal of attention. The security depends on the computing power rather than the central authority, which in turn eliminates the risks of one taking control of the system [43].

Usually information spreading is a common phenomenon in the natural world. Conventional methods like offline communications were followed in the good old days. But, with the progress in web technologies, information spreading done through online social media is rapid in nature. Recently, social networks have become a common platform for people to communicate with each other. Many researchers have analyzed the propagation of information due to the social network structure [44]. The incorrect information that spreads in public is identified as rumor [45]. Mechanisms to avoid the spreading of rumors [46] is the modeling technique grabbing the attention of researchers nowadays. Rumor generation and transmission is done over extended periods of time. Due to this, the authenticity of the information is essential. Normally the development of Blockchain technology is implemented in financial transactions between the two parties at the peer level. Hence, this could be extended to implement trusted contract-based propagation on the social network. A technique has to be developed to evaluate the authenticity of the information with the help of Blockchain technology in social media so that there is no possibility of spreading rumors.

The incorrect information within the network has to be blocked by applying new techniques. When Information Dynamics is considered for verification and authenticity at the initial phase of the communication process, then an instantaneous action must be taken in order to eliminate the unverified information if it is found. This is an essential strategy so that the issues at the starting stage itself can be resolved to a certain extent. Moreover, the source of the information also must be determined so that proper action can be taken against the misinformation initiators. Various methodologies have to be implemented for performing certain actions like identifying trusted friends, authenticity check of information being shared, connections and information that has been collected. Information can be about anything and can be shared among the friends. The mutual friend relationship is the conventional strategy that has been followed to determine the trusted mutual link in most social networking sites. But following this method is not suitable or proper for finding the trustworthy friends.

The focus of researchers should be on certain privacy issues in social media that are yet to be solved, as outlined in Table 4.1 below.

Table 4.1   Issues and techniques related to different areas of social media.

S.No	Area	Issues and techniques
1	Data Privacy Preserving	• Generation of data rapidly increases. From a recent report [55], it has been predicted that 20%of the world's data has been gathered in the past couple of years. From the largest online social network Facebook, about 300 petabytes of personal data has been collected right from its origin. • Hence, a better encryption algorithm is required to enforce the "Decentralizing privacy" • Due to the emergence of more social network sites, preserving the data is too critical. When an adversary possesses the knowledge about the friends of a target victim and their relationships, it becomes an easy task for the adversary to attack the victim easily.
2	Trust Based user Credibility	• Nowadays users use the social media for posting and collecting the information. It is a tough task for the users to trust on the credibility of the information. When the source of the information is not known, then it becomes a tough task for the users still.
3	Economic challenge	• Money could not be generated by the social media company without selling your data.
4	Autonomy	• The control over the rests in few hands
5	Trust	• A centralized power makes all the decisions.
6	Single point of failure	• It is known that traditional social networks are exposed to attacks. Hackers have a chance of attacking at one point which results in accessing all the users' information. For instance, in 2012, a hacker bust into the LinkedIn network and flooded with 6.5 million encrypted passwords. He posted them on a Russian hacker forum

4.4.1 Blockchain-Based Social Media

There are many issues related to social media like its centralized nature, exploitation of user information, less privacy and data security. Due to these issues, the ultimate solution to privacy and security is to make a transition to the blockchain-based social media networks. Due to their decentralized property, social media networks possess a strong end-to-end encryption. Therefore, the third party would not be able to track the user. In addition, digital currencies could be used for processing in-platform transactions. This section describes a few blockchain-based social networking sites.

4.4.1.1 Steemit

Steemit[4] is one of the important blockchain-based social media platforms that provides the users an opportunity to make use of the features of both Facebook and Reddit. This makes the publishers pay for content, such as posts, music, videos and pictures, that has been posted. Steemit currency units are created and distributed to the active users on the platform.

4.4.1.2 SocialX

SocialX[5] is a decentralized blockchain platform where everyone can earn cryptocurrency SOCX token rewards. It allows users to have their videos, photos and groups on a secured platform. Moreover, it also possesses a built-in license management. This feature provides the facility of users being able to keep their photos or selling them to other users. Exchanging photo rights for SOCX tokens is possible if the user is willing to sell the photos to others.

4.4.1.3 Indorse

Indorse[6] is a blockchain-based social network. It is mainly built for professionals and is similar to LinkedIn. User verification is done with the help of blockchain technology and supports the skills of a particular user anonymously. In addition, reputations could be increased through the efforts taken by the participants. Advertisements and company pages could be purchased with the IND tokens that could be earned on the platform. Chat bots have been deployed for automated real-time validation.

4.4.1.4 onG.Social

Through onG.social blockchain-based social media, both centralized and decentralized social media networks could be easy to control and in addition it also endorses social interaction with cryptocurrency rewards and community building. It works on two blockchains, namely Ethereum and Waves Platform. The significant feature is that the content of an individual could be shared in all networks through this media at the same time. The efforts of the participants have been monetized inside the network. Posts are authenticated by determining the global impact of a submission. In addition, the public could be very motivated to produce quality content so that fake news could be eliminated.[7]

4.4.1.5 Minds

Minds is a decentralized and open source social network in which users are able to earn crypto tokens for the contributions made by them to the network. This media is constructed with the principle of privacy, free expression and transparency. Through the Blockchain technology, security and transparency is provided. In addition, it constructs a mobile-first commerce infrastructure with a smooth user experience and perspective interface between the users.

4.4.2 Impact of Blockchain in Social Media

4.4.2.1 Verification of Information and News

Blockchain can perform activities such as identity and information verification and

[4]https://steem.com
[5]https://socialx.network
[6]https://indorse.io
[7]https://www.ongcoin.com

checking for the posted data. A framework developed through the 0xcert protocol constructs decentralized apps which enable the user to authenticate and manage their digital assets, such as educational certificates or in-game item, on the blockchain. This framework could be used to verify the data and news that has been shared online.

4.4.2.2 Better User Control Mechanisms

Manipulation of information, information given to the third parties, and building of revenue streams for social media owners which should not be shared with the users whose information has been sold might sometimes lead to hacking of both personal and financial information. Implementing blockchain could disturb all these activities. It is the choice of users to select the persons to access the information. Moreover, users can directly contact the advertisers and third parties to share the information by paying a fee.

4.4.2.3 Blockchain Leverages and Crowdfunding

Through crowdfunding, social media that runs on the blockchain could raise money. Making the payments, tracking the contracts, and user verification could be done with the infrastructure provided by the blockchain. The decentralized ledgers which are used for storing the information provide safety and transparency for each transaction, which in turn makes the users crowdfund or sell their products and services.

The market value of blockchain technology will attain a massive growth in the upcoming years; globally it may reach 23.3 billion U.S. dollars by 2023. Focusing on the potential of blockchain technology and its tamper-evident distributed ledger nature, it offers enormous uses in different sectors. The size of the blockchain technology market from 2018 to 2023 is depicted in the graph below.

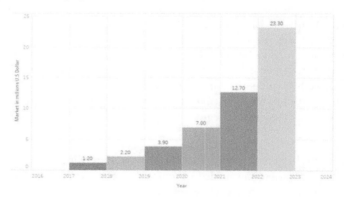

Figure 4.10   Blockchain technology market size.

4.5   Issues and Challenges of Blockchain in Social Network

Issues like data harvesting, privacy and content censorship are highly challenging in social networks such as Facebook, Instagram, Twitter, LinkedIn, etc. The blockchain technology fixes the primary bottlenecks that arise in conventional social networks.

i) Control over data: There is no control currently available for the content which is floated in social network. If there is a personal account for the users in the social network, they would have control over their personal information and content. The social network owners have complete control of what is to be viewed or not viewed by the users. Blockchain's decentralized nature eliminates the role of intermediaries and the content posted on the social network could be easily tracked. It never permits duplication and the content is deleted by the particular user; unauthorized third parties are not able to access and benefit from the erased content.

ii) Recently, users involved in social network are susceptible to different types of attacks which could expose the user's personal information.

iii) Conventional social networks are highly vulnerable to various attacks due to their centralized nature.

iv) Blockchain eliminates the single entity influence by its distributed nature. Each transaction is clearly tracked and audited with the blockchain which avoids tampering with data.

v) Once the user has gained control of their content in the social network platform, irrelevant content, such as unwanted advertisements, will not be visible in the specified platform.

There are two main significant trends that shift social media to being more interesting with blockchain technologies:

- Online identities are validated and verified.

- Fake content is restricted with its smart contracts.

4.6 Conclusion

The dynamics of rumor spreading with and without blockchain technology for social networks were discussed. How the blockchain technology with virtual credits can be incorporated for peer-to-peer information exchange has been clearly illustrated. Thus, blockchain technology avoids large-scale rumor spreading and encourages the exchange of trustworthy information in the social network. A rapid increase in the usage of social networks results in the construction of the potential infrastructure which assures better privacy and a prospective approach to performing more actions with smart contracts and apps. Moreover, an increase in the e-commerce transactions and crowdfunding transactions is also possible.

REFERENCES

1. Nakamoto, S. (2008). *Bitcoin: A peer-to-peer electronic cash system.*

2. Chuen, D. L. K. (Ed.). (2015). *Handbook of Digital Currency: Bitcoin, Innovation, Financial Instruments, and Big Data.* Academic Press.

3. Zheng, Z., Xie, S., Dai, H., Chen, X., & Wang, H. (2017, June). An overview of blockchain technology: Architecture, consensus, and future trends. In *2017 IEEE International Congress on Big Data (BigData Congress)* (pp. 557-564). IEEE.

4. Lu, Y. (2019). The blockchain: state-of-the-art and research challenges. *Journal of Industrial Information Integration.*

5. Atlam, H. F., & Wills, G. B. (2018). Technical aspects of blockchain and IoT. In *Advances in Computers* (pp. 1-39). Elsevier.

6. Casino, F., Dasaklis, T. K., & Patsakis, C. (2018). A systematic literature review of blockchain-based applications: current status, classification and open issues. *Telematics and Informatics*.

7. Thelwall, M. (2009). Social network sites: Users and uses. *Advances in Computers*, 76, 19-73.

8. Dunn, T. J., Baguley, T., & Brunsden, V. (2014). From alpha to omega: A practical solution to the pervasive problem of internal consistency estimation. *British Journal of Psychology*, 105(3), 399-412.

9. Muller, E., & Peres, R. (2019). The effect of social networks structure on innovation performance: A review and directions for research. *International Journal of Research in Marketing*, 36(1), 3-19.

10. Tanenbaum, A. S., & Van Steen, M. (2007). *Distributed Systems: Principles and Paradigms*. Prentice-Hall.

11. Falch, M., Henten, A., Tadayoni, R., & Windekilde, I. (2009, November). Business models in social networking. In *CMI Int. Conf. on Social Networking and Communities*.

12. Paul, T., Famulari, A., & Strufe, T. (2014). A survey on decentralized online social networks. *Computer Networks*, 75, 437-452.

13. Campana, M. G., & Delmastro, F. (2017). Recommender systems for online and mobile social networks: A survey. *Online Social Networks and Media*, 3, 75-97.

14. Strufe, T. (2009). Safebook: A privacy-preserving online social network leveraging on real-life trust. *IEEE Communications Magazine*, 95

15. Mega, G., Montresor, A., & Picco, G. P. (2011, August). Efficient dissemination in decentralized social networks. In *2011 IEEE International Conference on Peer-to-Peer Computing* (pp. 338-347). IEEE.

16. Guidi, B., Conti, M., Passarella, A., & Ricci, L. (2018). Managing social contents in Decentralized Online Social Networks: A survey. *Online Social Networks and Media*, 7, 12-29.

17. Jahid, S., Nilizadeh, S., Mittal, P., Borisov, N., & Kapadia, A. (2012, March). DECENT: A decentralized architecture for enforcing privacy in online social networks. In *2012 IEEE International Conference on Pervasive Computing and Communications Workshops* (pp. 326-332). IEEE.

18. Graffi, K., Gro, C., Mukherjee, P., Kovacevic, A., & Steinmetz, R. (2010, August). LifeSocial. KOM: A P2P-based platform for secure online social networks. In *2010 IEEE Tenth International Conference on Peer-to-Peer Computing* (P2P) (pp. 1-2). IEEE.

19. Taylor, P. J., Dargahi, T., Dehghantanha, A., Parizi, R. M., & Choo, K. K. R. (2019). A systematic literature review of blockchain cyber security. *Digital Communications and Networks*.

20. Ali, S., Islam, N., Rauf, A., Din, I., Guizani, M., & Rodrigues, J. (2018). Privacy and security issues in online social networks. *Future Internet*, 10(12), 114.

21. Peterson, W. A., & Gist, N. P. (1951). Rumor and public opinion. *American Journal of Sociology*, 57(2), 159-167.

22. Bordia, P. (1996). Studying verbal interaction on the Internet: The case of rumor transmission research. *Behavior Research Methods, Instruments, & Computers*, 28(2), 149-151.

23. Doerr, B., Fouz, M., & Friedrich, T. (2012). Why rumors spread fast in social networks. *Communications of the ACM*, 55(6), 70-75.

24. Allport, G. W., & Postman, L. (1947). *The Psychology of Rumor*. New York: Henry Holt.

25. Rosnow, R. L., & Fine, G. A. (1976). *Rumor and Gossip: The Social Psychology of Hearsay*. Elsevier.

26. Moreno, Y., Nekovee, M., & Pacheco, A. F. (2004). Dynamics of rumor spreading in complex networks. *Physical Review E*, 69(6), 066130.

27. Vega-Oliveros, D. A., da F Costa, L., & Rodrigues, F. A. (2017). Rumor propagation with heterogeneous transmission in social networks. *Journal of Statistical Mechanics: Theory and Experiment*, 2017(2), 023401.

28. Brito, J., & Castillo, A. (2013). *Bitcoin: A Primer for Policymakers*. Mercatus Center at George Mason University.

29. Zyskind, G., & Nathan, O. (2015, May). Decentralizing privacy: Using blockchain to protect personal data. In *2015 IEEE Security and Privacy Workshops* (pp. 180-184). IEEE.

30. Chen, S., Shi, R., Ren, Z., Yan, J., Shi, Y., & Zhang, J. (2017, November). A blockchain-based supply chain quality management framework. In *2017 IEEE 14th International Conference on e-Business Engineering (ICEBE)* (pp. 172-176). IEEE.

31. Basden, J., & Cottrell, M. (2017). How utilities are using blockchain to modernize the grid. *Harvard Business Review*, 23.

32. Shafagh, H., Burkhalter, L., Hithnawi, A., & Duquennoy, S. (2017, November). Towards blockchain-based auditable storage and sharing of IoT data. In *Proceedings of the 2017 on Cloud Computing Security Workshop* (pp. 45-50). ACM.

33. Chen, Y., Li, Q., & Wang, H. (2018). Towards trusted social networks with blockchain technology. *arXiv preprint arXiv:1801.02796*.

34. Li, Z., Kang, J., Yu, R., Ye, D., Deng, Q., & Zhang, Y. (2017). Consortium blockchain for secure energy trading in industrial internet of things. *IEEE Transactions on Industrial Informatics*, 14(8), 3690-3700.

35. Ahram, T., Sargolzaei, A., Sargolzaei, S., Daniels, J., & Amaba, B. (2017, June). Blockchain technology innovations. In *2017 IEEE Technology & Engineering Management Conference (TEMSCON)* (pp. 137-141). IEEE.

36. Tian, F. (2016, June). An agri-food supply chain traceability system for China based on RFID & blockchain technology. In *2016 13th International Conference on Service Systems and Service Management (ICSSSM)* (pp. 1-6). IEEE.

37. Huang, X., Xu, C., Wang, P., & Liu, H. (2018). LNSC: A security model for electric vehicle and charging pile management based on blockchain ecosystem. *IEEE Access*, 6, 13565-13574.

38. Dorri, A., Steger, M., Kanhere, S. S., & Jurdak, R. (2017). Blockchain: A distributed solution to automotive security and privacy. *IEEE Communications Magazine*, 55(12), 119-125.

39. Lei, A., Cruickshank, H., Cao, Y., Asuquo, P., Ogah, C. P. A., & Sun, Z. (2017). Blockchain-based dynamic key management for heterogeneous intelligent transportation systems. *IEEE Internet of Things Journal*, 4(6), 1832-1843.

40. Wilson, D., & Ateniese, G. (2015, November). From pretty good to great: Enhancing PGP using bitcoin and the blockchain. In *International Conference on Network and System Security* (pp. 368-375). Springer, Cham.

41. Wang, J., Li, M., He, Y., Li, H., Xiao, K., & Wang, C. (2018). A blockchain based privacy-preserving incentive mechanism in crowdsensing applications. *IEEE Access*, 6, 17545-17556.

42. Kshetri, N. (2017). Blockchain's roles in strengthening cybersecurity and protecting privacy. *Telecommunications Policy*, 41(10), 1027-1038.

43. He, Y., Li, H., Cheng, X., Liu, Y., & Sun, L. (2017, June). A bitcoin based incentive mechanism for distributed P2P applications. In *International Conference on Wireless Algorithms, Systems, and Applications* (pp. 457-468). Springer, Cham.

44. Doerr, B., Fouz, M., & Friedrich, T. (2012). Why rumors spread fast in social networks. *Communications of the ACM*, 55(6), 70-75.

45. Peterson, W. A., & Gist, N. P. (1951). Rumor and public opinion. *American Journal of Sociology*, 57(2), 159-167.

46. Jin, F., Dougherty, E., Saraf, P., Cao, Y., & Ramakrishnan, N. (2013, August). Epidemiological modeling of news and rumors on twitter. In *Proceedings of the 7th Workshop on Social Network Mining and Analysis* (p. 8). ACM.

47. Srivastava, S. R., Dube, S., Shrivastaya, G., & Sharma, K. (2019). Smartphone triggered security challenges issues, case studies and prevention. *Cyber Security in Parallel and Distributed Computing: Concepts, Techniques, Applications and Case Studies*, 187-206.

48. Ahmad, F. A., Kumar, P., Shrivastava, G., & Bouhlel, M. S. (2018). Bitcoin: Digital decentralized cryptocurrency. In *Handbook of Research on Network Forensics and Analysis Techniques* (pp. 395-415). IGI Global.

49. Shrivastava, G., Kumar, P., Gupta, B. B., Bala, S., & Dey, N. (Eds.). (2018). *Handbook of Research on Network Forensics and Analysis Techniques*. IGI Global.

50. Sharma, K., & Shrivastava, G. (2014). Public key infrastructure and trust of Web based knowledge discovery. *Int. J. Eng., Sci. Manage.*, 4(1), 56-60.

51. Sharma, K., Rafiqui, F., Attri, P., & Yadav, S. K. (2019). A two-tier security solution for storing data across public cloud. *Recent Patents on Computer Science*, 12(3), 191-201.

CHAPTER 5

INTEGRATING BLOCKCHAIN WITH CACC FOR TRUST AND PLATOON MANAGEMENT

Pranav Kumar Singh,[1,2] Roshan Singh,[2] Sunit Kumar Nandi,[1,3] Sukumar Nandi[1]

[1] Department of Computer Science and Engineering, Indian Institute of Technology, Guwahati, Assam, India

[2] Department of Computer Science and Engineering, Central Institute of Technology, Kokrajhar, Assam, India

[3] Department of Computer Science and Engineering, National Institute of Technology, Arunachal Pradesh, India

Corresponding authors: snghpranav@gmail.com; roshansingh3000@gmail.com; sunitnandi834@gmail.com; sukumar@iitg.ac.in

Abstract

With the rapid advancement in connected and automated vehicle technologies, a widespread use case cooperative adaptive cruise control (CACC)-based platooning is gaining momentum. The CACC-based platooning can enhance safety and driving comfort, increase traffic throughput, and reduce fuel consumption and pollutant emissions. Various platooning maneuvers, such as merge, split, lane change, leave, etc., have been integrated with CACC-based platooning to meet the objectives mentioned above. In such a platooning, a platoon leader plays a crucial role in the execution of various functions such as synchronization, collision avoidance, coordination, and better route planning. However, if a malevolent vehicle becomes the leader, it may put the entire platoon in danger. Thus, it is very crucial for vehicles to elect a trusted and reputable leader to lead the platoon. The unencrypted broadcast inter-vehicle communication of CACC exposes vehicles to several security threats. Establishing trust among vehicles is a critical challenge. Blockchain, with its core features of decentralization, immutability, security, and high availability, turns out to be a strong contender for addressing the challenge. Introduction of blockchain platforms supporting smart contracts helps build trust among untrusted parties and enhance the decision-making processes. In this chapter, we address the challenges in CACC-based platooning, such as leader election and platoon management, which have been mostly centralized in nature until now and contribute a blockchain-based framework for trust and platoon management. To achieve these objectives, we propose maintaining two blockchains: A PoW-based blockchain at the RSU plane and a permissioned blockchain among the vehicles in the platoon. The PoW-based blockchain will be used for vehicle trust and reputation management and for implementing ITS-related services, whereas the permissioned blockchain at the vehicular plane will be used for collaborative decision-making and leader election in the platoon. Besides, we provide experimental results along with a detailed analysis of the proposed approach.

Keywords: Cooperative adaptive cruise control, vehicle-to-vehicle communication

5.1   Introduction

Cooperative adaptive cruise control (CACC) is an extension of adaptive cruise control (ACC) [1], which enables automated controls via vehicle-to-everything (V2X) communication. A platoon consists of a group of vehicles traveling together in the same direction. Platooning is common for heavy-duty vehicles such as trucks and lorries. Usually, a platoon is initiated by a group of vehicles belonging to the same organization or a transportation company. In CACC-based platooning, the cooperation among vehicles is implemented mainly via vehicle-to-vehicle (V2V) communication [2]. Once the members of the platoon are chosen, the platoon begins its journey to its destination. However, a platoon should allow any CACC-enabled vehicle which is not initially a member of the platoon to join, be the member of the platoon and allowed to leave the platoon once its destination has been reached. These requirements lead to making different maneuvers by the members of the platoon such as lane change, merge, and split. Each maneuver requires changes to be made to the platoon and disturbs the platoon string stability. Performing frequent maneuvers, such as merge and split, may degrade the performance of the platoon. Often a platoon is headed by a Platoon Leader which is the first vehicle in the platoon. The remaining vehicles are also known as the follower vehicles that act upon the information received from the Platoon Leader. It is often required that an experienced driver should drive the first vehicle or the platoon leader, and the vehicle should be well-conditioned. Although CACC requires the presence of drivers in the vehicle, the contribution of the driver in the following vehicles is conditional, such as in the case of lane change when the vehicle needs to be steered manually in another lane. Since in CACC-based platooning, only longitudinal control of vehicle motions is provided, it represents automation Level-1 on both the NHTSA and SAE scales of automated driving. The primary communication in the platoon takes place on a hop-to-hop basis where the information is shared from a preceding node to its immediate successor node. Also, sometimes, multicast communication takes place where a node sends information directly to another node in the platoon. This multicast communication is mainly utilized by the Platoon Leader to communicate with a specific vehicle in the platoon and vice versa.

The CACC-based platooning offers various benefits, which are as follows: It improves fuel efficiency, safety, and roadway throughput. It also provides comfort, convenience, and satisfaction to drivers. In various pilot projects, it has been observed that air resistance has a significant impact on fuel economy. In CACC-based platooning, follower vehicles face less air resistance (reduction in air drag) due to shorter following gaps, which reduces fuel consumption; thus, it reduces the carbon emission [3].

Over the years, various CACC-related projects have been initiated in the USA, Europe, and Japan. Some of them are as follows: "Chauffeur" [4] in 1996 and "Chauffeur2" in 2004 [5] have dealt with the coupling of trucks together on European roads. In these projects, the platoon leader was driven manually, and the following vehicles (trucks) were either partially or fully automated. The main goal of the project was to demonstrate truck platooning, estimate the reduction in fuel consumption, and also estimate the associated costs and its benefits. The "California PATH" program [6] was started at the beginning of 2000 to conduct experiments on truck platooning. The main goal was to assess its impact on highway capacity and energy saving. In 2011, they tested it with three trucks at a gap of 6 m. The improvement of 10% (on average) fuel consumption was noted in this experiment [7]. "KONVOI" was initiated in Germany in the year 2005 [8]. In this project, the German scientists developed a platoon of four trucks. The main goal was to enhance roadway capacity and reduce fuel consumption. "Energy ITS" is a Japanese truck platooning project initiated in 2008 [9]. The main aim of the project was to save energy and consequently reduce CO_2 emission. The "SARTRE" project [10] was initiated in 2009 and funded by the European Commission. Unlike other projects, the SARTRE project considered platooning with mixed vehicles, i.e., heavy and light vehicles. However, the platoon leader would be a heavy vehicle, such as a truck or bus, and must be driven by a well-trained professional driver. The follower vehicles need to be fully automated, but the drivers would need to remain available for unforeseen circumstances. There are several other popular projects such as "GCDC 2011" (Grand Cooperative Driving Challenge), "COMPANION 2013," "INFLO 2012" (Intelligent Network Flow Optimization), etc. More details of these projects can be found in [1].

The V2V communication plays a vital role in a CACC-based platoon because it enables the information sharing among the vehicles, which improves the ability of the following vehicles for their autonomous driving and helps the controller to make a better decision. Thus, it enhances safety, efficiency, stability, and overall performance. The three popular protocol stacks which enabled V2V and V2I communications in regions of the USA, Europe, and Japan are wireless access in vehicular environment (WAVE), cooperative-ITS (C-ITS) and ARIB-based, respectively [3]. These stacks operate over dedicated short-range communications (DSRC). Although these communication protocol stacks have matured over time, they still face security issues. The security credential management system (SCMS) architecture is one of the leading candidates for V2V security design in the USA. The security frameworks in these regions are immune to most of the outside attackers but not mature enough in dealing with the adversarial and misbehaving peers.

False information dissemination, attacks on communication and control protocol, and compromised sensors can lead to wrong decisions made by following vehicles. Since the platoon leader's actions have a direct implication on other follower vehicles, the election of the malevolent vehicle as platoon leader can also disturb the stability of the platoon and can have devastating effects [11]. Thus, it is crucial to design a system which can ensure availability, integrity, authenticity, non-repudiation and must be able to detect misbehaviors. We need to have a mechanism, which can elect the trusted and best node as a platoon leader.

As an emerging decentralized technology, Blockchain has those capabilities which can provide required security in the form of authentication, integrity, and non-repudiation, etc. It can also be utilized in reputation management, which in turn will help in leader election of the platoon. However, towards this end, very little attention has been given. In this chapter, we introduce two blockchains, one at the vehicular level for platoon management and intra-platoon communication and another at the RSU level for trust and reputation management. With this, more transparency in the proceedings of a CACC platoon can be achieved. The rest of this chapter is organized as follows. Section 5.2 discusses the related works. In Section 5.3, we provide the background details and discuss the consensus mechanism in Section 5.4. Our proposed mechanism is presented in Section 5.5. The experimental setup details are given in Section 5.6. We discuss obtained results in Section 5.7, and, finally we conclude with a summary of the chapter in Section 5.8.

5.2 Literature Review

There are few studies [12-16] which considered malicious insiders and demonstrated the impact of attacks on the safety and stability of the platoon. In these studies, the authors have shown how the vulnerabilities of the communication protocol stacks can be exploited by an attacker to perform attacks, such as eavesdropping, falsification, replay, jamming, etc., on CACC-based platooning. They have shown that such attacks can cause significant instability in the CACC platoon. However, there are very few studies which proposed some mechanism to deal with trust, reputation, and misbehavior. In [17], the authors proposed a reliable trust-based platoon service recommendation scheme called REPLACE. The aim is to help the user vehicles to avoid electing a badly behaved platoon leader. The authors have designed a reputation system for the platoon leader vehicle, which collects and models their user vehicle's feedback. In [11], we demonstrated how badly behaving platoon leader could affect the string stability, which can also put the entire platoon in danger. We also proposed an architecture mechanism for leader election to elect the best leader of the platoon efficiently.

In [18], the authors evaluated the impact of abrupt degradation from CACC to ACC on safety. The degradation may happen due to failures in communication, manipulations made by the driver, cyberattacks, etc. The authors found that sudden degradation has severe negative influences on longitudinal safety. In [19], the authors proposed a model for the unmanned ground vehicle (UGV) platoon to deal with inaccurate information, i.e., platoon, which is under attack. The authors proposed RoboTrust algorithm to analyze the trustworthiness of the vehicle and eliminate low credit information.

In [20], the authors proposed a collaborative control strategy to enhance the protection level of autonomous platoons. The authors tested the strength of the proposed mechanism against the application and network layer attacks because attacks at these layers can severely affect platoon safety. In [21], the authors proposed a Vouch location proof scheme to detect position falsification attacks and also several reaction strategies to mitigate such attacks.

In [22, 23], the authors proposed a hybrid intrusion detection system which incorporates artificial intelligence techniques to detect flooding attack in VANETs. The attacks were detected with high accuracy and precision, and the false alarm rate was found to be negligible.

Misbehavior detection (MBD), trust management, and reputation models have been studied extensively in VANET [24-26]. Several data-centric and node-centric mechanisms have been proposed for MBD, and numerous centralized and decentralized models have also been proposed for reputation and trust management [17, 27, 28]. However, there are no such studies which model reputation management in a decentralized way and also provide a mechanism for secure communication. In this work, the authors utilize the power of blockchain to achieve their goals. There are blockchain-based studies [29, 30], which provide a solution to trust and privacy in VANETs. However, to the best of our knowledge, this is the first work in which blockchain has been used for CACC platooning.

5.3 Background

In the following section, we discuss the elementary details of the technologies used and the use case where the technology has been applied.

5.3.1 CACC Platooning

The core concept of CACC is the integration of cooperation to Level-1 automated vehicles using V2X communication. At its heart, it is automated longitudinal control with two cooperative elements, V2V or Infrastructure-to-Vehicle (I2V) communication. The V2V mode of communication provides mobility such as speed, direction, location, and other related information about the other vehicle(s). The I2V mode provides information about the traffic ahead or speed restrictions due to congestion, etc. Thus, the key information sources for CACC are onboard sensors (lidar, radar, and cameras), roadway infrastructure (I2V information), and other vehicles (V2V information).

The key radio access technology (RAT) which enables V2V communication is DSRC. DSRC is specially designed for VANETs and standardized in IEEE 802.11p [31], and it is one of the key enablers of CACC-based platooning. Another upcoming RAT is cellular-V2X (C-V2X), which is in its evolution phase and can be one of the potential facilitators in the future. The active communication between CACC-enabled vehicles is enabled via beaconing, using necessary parameters for their longitudinal control which are exchanged over DSRC. It is a periodic single-hop message broadcast by platoon vehicles.

There are three key variants of CACC-based platooning: One-vehicle look-ahead communication, CACC platoon with communication from platoon leader, and bidirectionally assisted platoon. However, the third one is not that popular. The first two variants are shown in Figure 5.1. In this work, we consider the CACC-based platoon with communication from platoon leader.

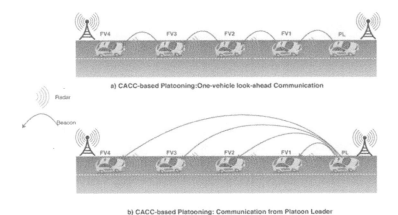

a) CACC-based Platooning:One-vehicle look-ahead Communication

b) CACC-based Platooning: Communication from Platoon Leader

Figure 5.1   CACC platooning variants.

5.3.2 Blockchain

Blockchain is one of the cutting edge technologies of the 21st century. Bitcoin [32, 33] blockchain, a peer-to-peer, decentralized, and cryptographically secure payment system, was the first successful implementation of the technology. Blockchain is a new technology which is based upon some core principles of computer science, mathematics and cryptography that have been in existence for a long time.

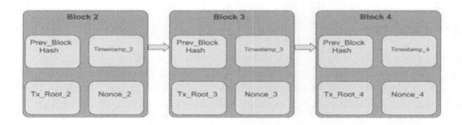

Figure 5.2   Blockchain.

As shown in Figure 5.2, a blockchain is formed of blocks which are connected with the help of cryptographic hashes. Transactions are the fundamental components of the blockchain. A blockchain transaction denotes a change in the state of the blockchain. Transactions are bundled and are placed in the blocks. Blockchain utilizes PKI for providing security. It ensures authenticity with the help of cryptographic signatures and uses the concepts of hashes for providing data integrity.

5.3.3 Smart Contracts

Smart contracts [34] are a well-defined, programmatically implemented set of conditions and actions that can be deployed onto the blockchain. The smart contract allows the integration of logic governing blockchain transactions. With its self-executing and immutable characteristics, it ensures bias-free implementation of the use case logic and thus eliminates the need for a third party. It can be used as a tool for automated decision-making process without an intermediary in an untrusted environment.

5.3.4 Ethereum

Ethereum [35] is a global, public, and permissionless blockchain platform. That means anyone can voluntarily come, join, and leave the network. It provides its users with both read and write permissions. A user can download the entire copy of the blockchain and can execute transactions independently. The support of smart contracts makes the platform open for a wide variety of use cases. The platform is ideal for developers who want to implement their smart contract for a certain problem-specific use case. The Ethereum blockchain is based upon a state-transition-based model, where each node executes a set of transactions in the same order to reach a common consensus. Ether is a cryptocurrency, which is used as a medium of exchange on the Ethereum blockchain. The platform uses the notion of GAS (a unit of measuring the computational complexity) and GAS LIMIT while processing the transactions. The idea of GAS is used to curb the menace of an attacker who can embed an infinite loop in his smart contract and execute a transaction. The absence of GAS and GAS LIMIT will lead to a halting problem in the blockchain and may result in a crash of the chain. The Ethereum blockchain platform currently provides its support for the two types of accounts named below.

5.3.4.1 Externally Owned Accounts

These are the accounts owned by the users on the blockchain. An externally owned account is associated with a set of public/private key pairs. These are used by the user to sign and verify the transactions.

5.3.4.2 Contract Accounts

These are the accounts where the code of the smart contract resides. It acts as an address for the contract. The smart contract can be accessed with its contract address. An externally owned account can send and receive ether to and from other externally owned accounts or contract accounts. The contract accounts cannot do anything on its own. It depends upon the transactions executed from the externally owned accounts, which trigger the execution of the code present in the contract account.

5.4 Consensus in Blockchain

The nodes in a blockchain need to come to a common agreement on a particular state of the blockchain. This agreement on a particular state is called a consensus, and the mechanism/algorithm for reaching the agreement is called the consensus mechanism. Although there are several consensus mechanisms for blockchain available, in this work, we consider two predominant consensus mechanisms; those are Proof-of-Work (PoW) and Proof-of-Authority (PoA).

5.4.1 Proof-of-Work (PoW)

Proof-of-Work is a challenge-response-based consensus mechanism ideally used for reaching a consensus in public and permissionless blockchain. PoW uses the concept of practical resource utilization to protect the blockchain from malicious and cheating nodes in the network. For reaching a consensus in PoW, the nodes maintaining the blockchain, often known as the miner nodes, compete among themselves to solve a cryptographically hard problem. The node which solves the problem first is allowed to propose a block. The proposer node is also required to broadcast the block in the network to make sure that the block has been examined by other nodes. Once the nodes have found the block to be a valid one the block is added onto the chain, otherwise the block is dropped, and the competition starts again. The cryptographic problem is assigned a difficulty level, which keeps on changing depending upon the analysis of previously added blocks over a period of time. The miner nodes perform the problem-solving tasks independently. In case two or more miner nodes mine a block at the same time, then forks may happen in the blockchain. Some nodes in the network might verify and add the block received from miner A whereas some may add the block received from miner B. The block being received by a node from a miner depends upon several parameters such as geographic locations and network performance. Forks are undesirable in blockchain and hence need to be resolved as soon as possible. The PoW algorithm resolves the fork by using the longest chain rule. That means the one blockchain out of B1 and B2 which adds a valid block on top of the received block is considered to be the valid blockchain, and the other one is treated as a fork of the original chain and is thus ignored. And the process goes on.

5.4.2   Proof-of-Authority (PoA)

Proof-of-Authority is a blockchain consensus algorithm used for establishing consensus in permissioned and private blockchains. The algorithm uses the concept of authorities (nodes having special powers) where authority is provided with the right to create and add a block in the blockchain. These authorities are sometimes also called validators; they collect the transactions generated by the users in the network, then bundle these transactions and seal them in a block. The block is then propagated in the network for its addition. The addition of a block onto the chain takes place turn by turn, wherein each round is an authority which is allowed to propose a block once. Once an authority has proposed a block, the charge of proposing the next block goes to the next authority. This cycle continues, and each authority gets an equal opportunity to propose a block. Before the addition of a block onto the chain, the block has to undergo a validity check by the rest of the validator nodes in the network. The addition takes place once the block is verified by the validator nodes. If the block is found to be invalid during the validity check, it is dropped, and the validator nodes vote out the proposer, thus restricting the proposer by not allowing them to propose any more blocks. The lightweight and low power consumption characteristics of PoA makes it an ideal contender as a blockchain consensus mechanism for IoT use cases.

5.5   Proposed Framework

This section describes our blockchain-based approach in CACC. We propose introducing two blockchains; one at the vehicular plane within the platoon for intra-platoon communication and platoon management, and the other at the RSU plane for trust and reputation management. We incorporate our logic for platoon management and trust management in the smart contracts (SC) and deploy them on both the blockchains, respectively.

5.5.1   Blockchain at the Vehicular Plane for Intra-platoon Communications

Maintaining an authoritative blockchain among the members of the platoon can help reduce and prevent such attacks and, moreover, will make the platoon management more efficient. We propose maintaining a private blockchain among the members of the platoon. In particular, we make the initial members of the platoon maintain a private and authoritative blockchain. We are calling the blockchain a private one as we do not allow any unauthenticated nodes to be a part of the blockchain and authoritative, as we allow only a set of authorized entities to verify and propose a block. Permanent members of the platoon will maintain the private authoritative blockchain in the platoon, which means that the blockchain will be maintained from the very beginning, as when the platoon leaves from its source towards its destination. Another good reason for allowing the initial members of the platoon to maintain the blockchain is that the initial members of the platoon will belong to the same organization and thus will have better trust among themselves and can be considered as more genuine than any random vehicle entering the platoon. Each message exchanged in the platoon is considered to be a transaction at the blockchain level. Figure 5.3 shows the framework in the vehicular plane.

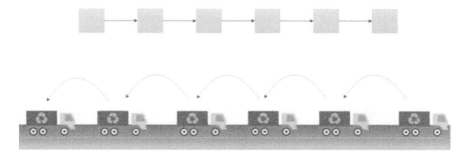

Figure 5.3   Blockchain in the platoon for intra-platoon communication and platoon management.

The vehicle sending a message will sign the message and will then broadcast the message to the blockchain. Say a vehicle *V1* wants to share a message *M* with its immediate successor vehicle *V2*, then *V1* will sign the message with its private key as typically happens in a blockchain transaction. As the message *M* will be broadcasted, all the vehicles in the platoon will be able to receive the message. Every vehicle including *V2* will check for the validity of the signature and the integrity of the message *M*. If *M* is found to be authentic and a valid transaction, each vehicle acting as a blockchain node will put the transaction in their pool of pending transactions where the transaction *M* will wait its turn to be committed. Intuitively, one of the sealers will put the transaction *M* into its block, and thus the block will be committed. However, the information in the message may be time-critical and may require the receiver to act upon it as soon as possible or as soon as it receives the message. Waiting for the transaction to be committed on the blockchain and then acting upon the committed transaction will be a bottleneck for our approach of introducing blockchain among the platoon members.

Our aim in introducing a blockchain is to make the platoon management more efficient, but not at the cost of human life. For countering this problem, we urge that the actual recipient of the message should take action on the information in the received transaction as soon as the transaction is found to be authentic. As much less time is required to verify a signature, the time for signature verification can also be considered as negligible here if a signature is found to be valid that implicitly guarantees that the transaction will be eventually committed to the blockchain sooner or later. Thus, with the introduction of a private blockchain among the platoon vehicles, each initial vehicle in the platoon will be able to record everything happening in the platoon. As the blockchain will be authoritative, each of the initial members in the platoon can be designated as the signer. Each initial vehicle will be provided an opportunity to seal a block. The block sealing will proceed in rounds where in each round a vehicle will be chosen as the sealer and is allowed to seal a block. The sealer vehicle will collect the transactions coming from the platoon members and will try to form a block. After sealing a block, the sealer needs to ensure that their sealed block is committed to the chain. For this, the sealer vehicle will send his sealed block to the rest of the platoon members maintaining the blockchain. After receiving the block, each vehicle will verify the validity and authenticity of the block. If the vehicles found the block to be a valid one, then each of them will commit the received block to their local copy of the blockchain. And as all the nodes commit the block, a global consensus on the block is reached, and the next sealer vehicle is allowed to seal the next block. However, if the block proposed by a sealer vehicle is found to be invalid or violates any of the desired properties of a block, then the detecting node calls for voting among the sealer nodes in the platoon. If a majority of the sealer vehicles votes against the proposed vehicle, then the proposed vehicle is assumed to be compromised and is kicked out of the list of sealers and thus is not further allowed to seal any blocks.

Each vehicle in the platoon periodically executes a status-update transaction, as shown in Figure 5.4. This contains information about its current system status that includes real-time information such as remaining fuel, tire pressure, engine status, etc. The executed transaction updates the information of the vehicle in the smart contract deployed on the local blockchain being maintained in the platoon.

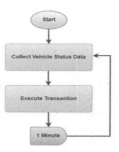

Figure 5.4   Periodic self-status update in a smart contract by vehicle.

As we previously mentioned, the blockchain in a platoon would be maintained only among the initial members of the platoon. However, this does not restrict any member coming from outside to join the platoon.

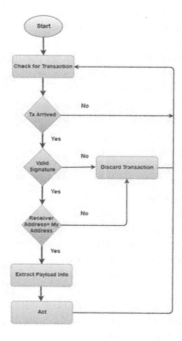

Figure 5.5   Operations performed by the initial vehicles (validator nodes) in the CACC platoon.

Figure 5.5 shows the operations performed by the initial members of the platoon, whereas Figure 5.6 shows the operation performed by the non-initial or the newly joined CACC vehicle in the platoon.

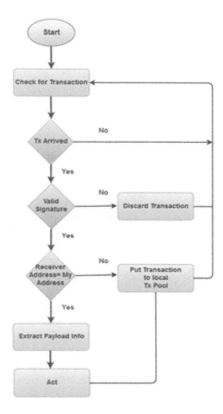

Figure 5.6   Operations performed by non-initial platoon members.

Any CACC-enabled vehicle having a valid blockchain account and satisfying the requirements of the platoon for its addition, such as availability of the position, destination, etc., can opt to merge into the platoon. The merge request should be sent to the platoon leader (PL).

5.5.1.1 New Vehicle Merge

After receiving a merge request from a CACC-enabled vehicle, the platoon leader polls the smart contract maintained among the platoon members for getting the platoon-related details such as availability of vacant space, the position where the vehicle will be added, etc. Based on the information received from the smart contract, the platoon leader decides whether the merge request should be accepted or not. If the requirements of the addition of a new vehicle are met, the platoon leader begins verifying the trust and reputation score of the requesting vehicle; for this, the platoon leader polls the blockchain maintained at the RSU level with the address of the requesting vehicle. If it has a satisfactory trust and reputation score, the requesting vehicle is allowed to join the platoon. The trust score represents the behavior of the vehicle when participating in a platoon. Where the reputation of the vehicle specifies the behavior of the vehicle when operating as an individual, such as obeying the traffic rules, cases of any traffic violation, and hit and run cases, all of these determine the reputation score of a vehicle. The joining instruction is sent by the platoon leader to the requesting vehicle explicitly. Accordingly, the platoon leader makes changes to the platoon configuration details in the smart contract to reflect the addition of a new member.

5.5.1.2   *Vehicle Leaving the Platoon*

As a CACC-enabled vehicle joins a platoon, similarly, it may also want to leave the platoon as it might have reached its destination or it may want to leave voluntarily. Before leaving the platoon, a vehicle needs to inform the platoon leader. Once the PL has accepted a leave request, it executes a transaction modifying the smart contract state. The PL also provides the ratings to the leaving vehicle in terms of trust score. The ratings depend upon the contribution and the behavior of the leaving vehicle in the platoon like a contribution to message forwarding, maintaining platoon string stability, etc.

5.5.1.3   *Platoon Leader Election*

As mentioned earlier, the platoon leader is the first vehicle in the platoon. The platoon leader has to bear most of the burden of platoon management such as initiating and managing maneuvers. Also, the driver of the platoon leader vehicle constantly needs to pay more attention while driving as compared to the driver of the follower vehicles. With such burdens, it is obvious that the driver may get tired and require a break from the responsibilities. Making a tired driver continue its operations may result in accidents. During such circumstances, a platoon leader change is required. The current platoon leader initiates a request for platoon leader change. When such a request is made the vehicles in the platoon need to vote for a new platoon leader. For this, the vehicles' information is available at both the blockchains at the RSU level as well as the platoon level.

The RSU level blockchain is utilized to find the trust and reputation score of each vehicle in the platoon, whereas the platoon level blockchain is used to check for the behaviors, contributions and the status of the vehicle until now in the platoon along with some other required information such as fuel level, tire pressure, etc. We consider an initial maximum score a default minimum score that no vehicle can ever have. Based on this information, each vehicle proposes its favored platoon leader. The vehicle receiving the highest proposals is provisionally selected as the new platoon leader. The provisionally selected platoon leader is confirmed as soon as all the platoon members agree on the newly selected platoon leader. Once the election of a new PL is made, the current platoon leader hands over the authority to the new platoon leader to take charge of and control the platoon. This handover is made via the smart contract. We developed a leader election Algorithm 5.1 based upon the data present on both the blockchains.

Algorithm for New Leader Election

Algorithm 1 Platoon Leader Election

1: $maximum \leftarrow -1000$ // default lowest value
2: **for** each v_i in V **do**
3:     **for** each $j \leftarrow 0$ to $j \leftarrow MEMBER.length$ **do**
4:         $vehicle \leftarrow MEMBER[j]$
5:         $localScore \leftarrow getLocal(vehicle, localSC)$
6:         $trustScore \leftarrow getTrust(vehicle, globalSC)$
7:         $reputationScore \leftarrow getReputation(vehicle, globalSC)$
8:         $total \leftarrow localScore + trustScore + reputationScore$
9:         **if** total > maximum **then**
10:             $maximum \leftarrow total$
11:             $contenderPL \leftarrow vehicle$
12:         **end if**
13:     **end for**
14:     $Propose(contenderPL)$
15: **end for**

- V: Set of all vehicles in the platoon.

- `localSC`: Smart contract deployed on the blockchain maintained within the platoon for platoon management.

- `globalSC`: Smart contract deployed on the blockchain maintained by the RSUs for trust and reputation management.

- `MEMBER`: A list maintained in `localSC` containing the addresses of the platoon member.

How can the authoritative blockchain in the platoon help?

As we have already seen, the implementation of a blockchain at the platoon level can help in better platoon management as it allows each vehicle to have knowledge about the behaviors of the other platoon members. Also, we saw how the blockchain helps in an efficient PL election and making platooning decisions such as a new vehicle merge. Also, the notion of signature-based transactions for communication among the platoon members makes the entire communication secure, whether or not there is any significant delay. Invalid transactions will never be accepted. The performance can be much improved by allowing the vehicles in the platoon to access the list of valid addresses (MEMBER) in the platoon via the smart contract. A vehicle receiving transactions from one of the addresses in the list can start checking the signature. Otherwise, it can simply drop the transaction without verifying the signature.

5.5.2   Blockchain at the RSU Plane for Trust and Reputation Management

As stated earlier, our approach aims to bring transparency and security in a CACC platoon. The efficiency of a CACC platoon highly depends on the behavioral intention of the vehicles in the platoon. Establishing trust in a vehicular environment where the nodes are open to communicating with each other and are not under constant monitoring is a challenging task. There exist approaches for trust management in vehicular networks. However, most of these approaches are data-centric or node-centric. These approaches are highly centralized and have disadvantages such as a single point of failure. What if the centralized authority becomes unavailable or tampers with the data present in it? It's impractical to believe that a third party will never tamper with your data and will not utilize it for their personal gain. Also, tracking the changes made to the data once it has been tampered with is quite difficult. One may need to involve another legal and trusted third party as an intermediary to resolve the issues. It not only results in a waste of time and effort but also at the same time leads to severe financial losses. We address the problem by introducing a permissionless blockchain at the RSU plane.

Figure 5.7 shows the framework in the RSU plane.

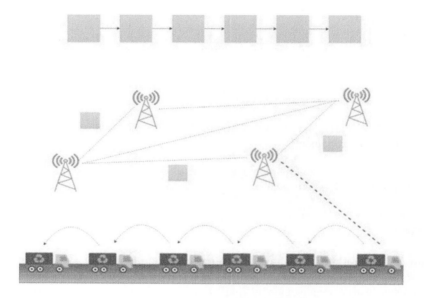

Figure 5.7   Blockchain for trust and reputation management at RSU plane.

A blockchain at the RSU plane is maintained by the RSU and the infrastructure deployed by the trusted authority (TA). The blockchain is a public blockchain based on computationally extensive proof-of-work consensus mechanism, where anyone, such as the insurance company and service providers, can voluntarily come up and participate in the mining procedure by using their own resources. Primarily, the task of maintaining the blockchain is with the RSUs deployed by the TA. The participation of the insurance company and the service providers is not always necessary; however, their participation will help to make the system truly decentralized.

The blockchain maintained at the RSU plane consists of transactions about the trust and reputation scores of the vehicles. However, it may also contain transactions related to the use of various ITS-related services that the vehicle may have utilized. The blockchain uses the proof-of-work (PoW) as the consensus mechanism.

5.6 Experiments

We performed experiments on a private Ethereum blockchain network. The testbed details are listed in Table 5.1.

Table 5.1 Testbed details.

Device Name	Specification	Role
Dell-Vostro PC	8GB RAM, i7-7700 CPU, 1 TB HDD	RSU
Raspberry Pi 3 B+	**SoC:** Broadcom BCM2837B0 quad-core A53 (ARMv8) 64-bit @ 1.4GHz. **RAM:** 1GB LPDDR2 SDRAM. **GPU:** Broadcom Videocore-IV. **Networking:** Gigabit Ethernet (via USB channel), 2.4GHz and 5GHz 802.11b/g/n/ac Wi-Fi. **Bluetooth:** Bluetooth 4.2, Bluetooth Low Energy (BLE) **Storage:** Micro-SD, 32GB **GPIO:** 40-pin GPIO header, populated.	Vehicle OBU

5.6.1 Experiment 1: Blockchain for Intra-platoon Communication and Platoon Management

We implemented our blockchain-based approach for intra-platoon management with a prototype implementation. We used Raspberry Pi[1] 3 as the processing unit of a vehicle. We demonstrated a platoon with three vehicles with the help of 3 Raspberry Pis. All the Raspberry Pis run Geth (Go Ethereum), a client for Ethereum blockchain. We used Clique Ethereum proof-of-authority consensus mechanism for reaching the consensus in the blockchain. The Geth[2] version chosen was: geth 1.8.18 ARMv7. We used the puppeth utility for setting up the blockchain. All the vehicles were designated as the initial vehicles, and each of them was allowed to seal blocks. The block generation time was set to 2 seconds. That means every 2 seconds a new block is added to the blockchain. One of the three vehicles was chosen as the platoon leader and the blockchain configuration was done by the platoon leader.

5.6.2 Experiment 2: Blockchain for Trust and Reputation Management

For implementing trust and reputation management, we performed experiments on a prototype setup. We used PCs denoting RSUs. The experiments are performed with 3 PCs representing 3 RSUs. All the PCs run Geth (a Go Ethereum client for Ethereum blockchain). We used Ethash, an Ethereum proof-of-work-based consensus mechanism, for reaching the consensus in the blockchain. The Geth version chosen was: 1.8.17-stable release. We used autodiscovery mode for connecting and peering the RSUs (blockchain nodes). The testbed setups for these two experiments are shown in Figure 5.8 and Figure 5.9, respectively.

---

[1] www.raspberrypi.org
[2] https://geth.ethereum.org/

Figure 5.8 Testbed setup for the CACC platoon of vehicular plane.

Figure 5.9 Testbed setup for maintaining blockchain at the RSU plane.

5.7 Results and Discussion

We analyzed the performance of the blockchain node (vehicle) for demonstrating the feasibility of our proposed blockchain-based approach for intra-platoon communication and platoon management in CACC.

Figure 5.10 shows the CPU utilization of Raspberry Pi 3 B+ (blockchain validator node at the vehicular plane). The figure shows an average CPU utilization when the validator node is active and is taking part in the sealing procedure.

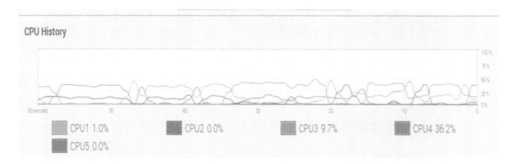

Figure 5.10   CPU utilization of blockchain node (vehicle) when running the PoA blockchain consensus mechanism.

This demonstrates the feasibility of PoA algorithm as a choice of consensus mechanism to be used for maintaining the blockchain in the platoon.

We evaluated the performance of our blockchain-based approach for trust and reputation management by analyzing the system performance of one of the blockchain nodes (RSU). We compared the system performance in terms of CPU utilization, temperature, power consumption, and clock frequency when the system is in idle mode and when it is taking part in the mining procedure. Figure 5.11 shows the performance plots when the RSU is in idle mode, whereas Figure 5.12 shows the performance plots when the RSU is participating in mining procedure.

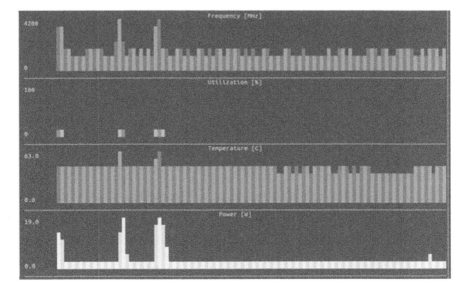

Figure 5.11   System performance of blockchain node (RSU) when idle.

From Figure 5.12, one can observe that the system resources are utilized at their maximum. This is because of the computation extensive and power exhaustive PoW consensus algorithm chosen for maintaining the blockchain.

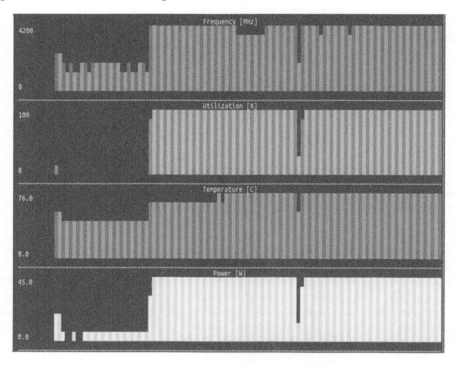

Figure 5.12   System performance of blockchain node (RSU) when mining.

5.8 Conclusion

In this work, firstly, we have proposed a novel blockchain-based approach for intra-platoon communication and platoon management and secondly proposed a decentralized blockchain-based approach for trust and reputation management of the vehicles. We enhanced the communication security and provided a better platform for platoon management by introducing an authoritative blockchain at the vehicular plane. Introduction of a completely decentralized public blockchain ensured the integrity of the trust and reputation scores of the vehicles and guaranteed the availability of the score data all the time. We also performed and analyzed the performance of both the approaches at different planes with proper testbed implementation. Lower CPU consumption of the blockchain nodes at the vehicular plane for intra-platoon communication demonstrates the feasibility of the approach. But, the blockchain implementation at the RSU plane seems to be quite expensive both in terms of system performance and power consumption. As already explained, this is because of the chosen state-of-the-art and a well-established consensus mechanism for an open public blockchain. However, with the choice of the used consensus mechanism at the RSU plane, one can guarantee complete decentralization, which is most desired to maintain the data integrity.

REFERENCES

1. Shladover, S. E., Nowakowski, C., Lu, X. Y., & Hoogendoorn, R. (2014). *Using Cooperative Adaptive Cruise Control (CACC) to Form High-Performance Vehicle Streams*. California Partners for Advanced Transportation Technology.

2. Amoozadeh, M., Deng, H., Chuah, C. N., Zhang, H. M., & Ghosal, D. (2015). Platoon management with cooperative adaptive cruise control enabled by VANET. *Vehicular Communications*, 2(2), 110-123.

3. Singh, P. K., Nandi, S. K., & Nandi, S. (2019). A tutorial survey on vehicular communication state of the art, and future research directions. *Vehicular Communications*, 100164.

4. Fritz, H. (1999, August). Longitudinal and lateral control of heavy duty trucks for automated vehicle following in mixed traffic: experimental results from the CHAUFFEUR project. In *Proceedings of the 1999 IEEE International Conference on Control Applications* (Cat. No. 99CH36328) (Vol. 2, pp. 1348-1352). IEEE.

5. Fritz, H., Gern, A., Schiemenz, H., & Bonnet, C. (2004, June). CHAUFFEUR Assistant: a driver assistance system for commercial vehicles based on fusion of advanced ACC and lane keeping. In *IEEE Intelligent Vehicles Symposium, 2004* (pp. 495-500). IEEE.

6. Shladover, S. E. (2010, June). Truck automation operational concept alternatives. In *2010 IEEE Intelligent Vehicles Symposium* (pp. 1072-1077). IEEE.

7. Lu, X. Y., & Shladover, S. E. (2014). Automated truck platoon control and field test. In *Road Vehicle Automation* (pp. 247-261). Springer, Cham.

8. Kunze, R., Ramakers, R., Henning, K., & Jeschke, S. (2011). Organization and operation of electronically coupled truck platoons on german motorways. In *Automation, Communication and Cybernetics in Science and Engineering 2009/2010* (pp. 427-439). Springer, Berlin, Heidelberg.

9. Tsugawa, S. (2014, June). Results and issues of an automated truck platoon within the energy ITS project. In *2014 IEEE Intelligent Vehicles Symposium Proceedings* (pp. 642-647). IEEE.

10. Davila, A., & Nombela, M. (2011). Sartre-safe road trains for the environment reducing fuel consumption through lower aerodynamic drag coefficient (No. 2011-36-0060). *SAE Technical Paper*.

11. Singh, P. K., Sharma, S., Nandi, S. K., Singh, R., & Nandi, S. (2018, October). Leader election in cooperative adaptive cruise control based platooning. In *Proceedings of the 1st International Workshop on Communication and Computing in Connected Vehicles and Platooning* (pp. 8-14). ACM.

12. Dadras, S., Gerdes, R. M., & Sharma, R. (2015, April). Vehicular platooning in an adversarial environment. In *Proceedings of the 10th ACM Symposium on Information, Computer and Communications Security* (pp. 167-178). ACM.

13. Van der Heijden, R., Lukaseder, T., & Kargl, F. (2017, November). Analyzing attacks on cooperative adaptive cruise control (CACC). In 2017 *IEEE Vehicular Networking Conference (VNC)* (pp. 45-52). IEEE.

14. DeBruhl, B., Weerakkody, S., Sinopoli, B., & Tague, P. (2015, June). Is your commute driving you crazy?: a study of misbehavior in vehicular platoons. In *Proceedings of the 8th ACM Conference on Security & Privacy in Wireless and Mobile Networks* (p. 22). ACM.

15. Amoozadeh, M., Raghuramu, A., Chuah, C. N., Ghosal, D., Zhang, H. M., Rowe, J., & Levitt, K. (2015). Security vulnerabilities of connected vehicle streams and their impact on cooperative driving. *IEEE Communications Magazine*, 53(6), 126-132.

16. Singh, P. K., Tabjul, G. S., Imran, M., Nandi, S. K., & Nandi, S. (2018, October). Impact of security attacks on cooperative driving use case: CACC platooning. In *TENCON 2018-2018 IEEE Region 10 Conference* (pp. 0138-0143). IEEE.

17. Hu, H., Lu, R., Zhang, Z., & Shao, J. (2016). REPLACE: A reliable trust-based platoon service recommendation scheme in VANET. *IEEE Transactions on Vehicular Technology*, 66(2), 1786-1797.

18. Tu, Y., Wang, W., Li, Y., Xu, C., Xu, T., & Li, X. (2019). Longitudinal safety impacts of cooperative adaptive cruise control vehicle's degradation. *Journal of Safety Research*, 69, 177-192.

19. Li, F., Mikulski, D., Wagner, J. R., & Wang, Y. (2019). Trust-based control and scheduling for UGV platoon under cyber attacks. *SAE Technical Paper*, 01-1077.

20. Petrillo, A., Pescape, A., & Santini, S. (2018). A collaborative approach for improving the security of vehicular scenarios: The case of platooning. *Computer Communications*, 122, 59-75.

21. Boeira, F., Asplund, M., & Barcellos, M. P. (2018, December). Mitigating position falsification attacks in vehicular platooning. In *2018 IEEE Vehicular Networking Conference (VNC)* (pp. 1-4). IEEE.

22. Aneja, M. J. S., Bhatia, T., Sharma, G., & Shrivastava, G. (2018).Artificial intelligence based intrusion detection system to detect flooding attack in VANETs. In *Handbook of Research on Network Forensics and Analysis Techniques* (pp. 87-100). IGI Global.

23. Shrivastava, G., Kumar, P., Gupta, B. B., Bala, S., & Dey, N. (Eds.). (2018). *Handbook of Research on Network Forensics and Analysis Techniques*. IGI Global.

24. Singh, P. K., Dash, M. K., Mittal, P., Nandi, S. K., & Nandi, S. (2018, December). Misbehavior detection in C-ITS using deep learning approach. In *International Conference on Intelligent Systems Design and Applications* (pp. 641-652). Springer, Cham.

25. Singh, P. K., Gupta, R. R., Nandi, S. K., & Nandi, S. (2019, March). Machine learning based approach to detect wormhole attack in VANETs. In *Workshops of the International Conference on Advanced Information Networking and Applications* (pp. 651-661). Springer, Cham. DOI: 10.1007/978-3-030-15035-8_63

26. Singh, P. K., Gupta, S., Vashistha, R., Nandi, S. K., & Nandi, S. (2019, January). Machine learning based approach to detect position falsification attack in VANETs. In *International Conference on Security & Privacy* (pp. 166-178). Springer, Singapore. DOI: 0.1007/978-981-13-7561-3_13

27. Marmol, F. G., & Perez, G. M. (2012). TRIP, a trust and reputation infrastructure-based proposal for vehicular ad hoc networks. *Journal of Network and Computer Applications*, 35(3), 934-941.

28. Wang, J., Zhang, Y., Wang, Y., & Gu, X. (2016). RPRep: A robust and privacy-preserving reputation management scheme for pseudonym-enabled VANETs. *International Journal of Distributed Sensor Networks*, 12(3), 6138251.

29. Yang, Z., Yang, K., Lei, L., Zheng, K., & Leung, V. C. (2018). Blockchain-based decentralized trust management in vehicular networks. *IEEE Internet of Things Journal*, 6(2), 1495-1505. DOI: 10.1109/jiot.2018.2836144

30. Lu, Z., Liu, W., Wang, Q., Qu, G., & Liu, Z. (2018). A privacy-preserving trust model based on blockchain for vanets. *IEEE Access*, 6, 45655-45664.

31. IEEE 802.11 p Working Group. (2010). IEEE Standard for Information Technology-Local and Metropolitan Area Networks-Specific Requirements-part 11: Wireless LAN Medium Access Control (MAC) and Physical Layer (PHY) Specifications Amendment 6: Wireless Access in Vehicular Environments. IEEE Std; *IEEE: Piscataway*, NJ, USA.

32. Nakamoto, S. (2008). *Bitcoin: A Peer-to-Peer Electronic Cash System*. Available at https://bitcoin.org/bitcoin.pdf

33. Ahmad, F. A., Kumar, P., Shrivastava, G., & Bouhlel, M. S. (2018). Bitcoin: Digital decentralized cryptocurrency. In *Handbook of Research on Network Forensics and Analysis Techniques* (pp. 395-415). IGI Global.

34. Szabo, N. (1997). Formalizing and securing relationships on public networks. *First Monday*, 2(9).

35. Wood, G. (2014). Ethereum: A secure decentralised generalised transaction ledger. *Ethereum Project Yellow Paper*, 151(2014), 1-32.

CHAPTER 6

IMPACT OF BLOCKCHAIN FOR INTERNET OF THINGS SECURITY

BHAWANA RUDRA

Department of Information Technology, National Institute of Technology Karnataka, India

Corresponding author: bhawanarudra@nitk.edu.in

Abstract

The Internet of Things (IoT) is playing a major role in the industry and is encouraging researchers to come up with various applications by bringing economical and social benefits to society. This is having an incredible impact on various environments using common operating picture ranging from mission-critical applications to business-oriented applications like healthcare, transportation, video surveillance, banking, etc. Common operating picture is achieved with the help of advancements seen in WSN devices, which are able to communicate with each other for the exchange of information and allow the data analysis for various purposes. The information is exchanged among the devices using the central server of cloud or fog, raising various security vulnerabilities. Not only the servers, but the IoT devices themselves will have security vulnerabilites which can be exploited by attacks like device spoofing, false authentication, etc. Taking into consideration the predicted evolution of IoT in the coming years, it is required to provide confidence in the users that the data they store or exchange and the devices they use for the purpose of security and privacy is preserved. The IoT objects are interconnected to each other but the functions of these vary from each other, which will not yield better security results with the conventional approaches. To address security and privacy concerns, the central server concept is eliminated and blockchain technology is introduced as a part of IoT. Blockchain, which is used for Bitcoin, has been recently used to provide security in peer-to-peer network, which is similar to IoT technology. This chapter explains the various applications of IoT followed by the security and privacy issues. It discusses the challenges involved in securing IoT followed by an introduction to blockchain technology along with various advantages of blockchain for IoT. It also discusses the application domains of blockchain technology in IoT, classification of threat models that are considered by blockchain protocols for IoT networks, and a comparison of state-of-the-art secure models with respect to blockchain. At the end, the chapter highlights the open challenges and further research directions in blockchain technology for IoT.

Keywords: Blockchain, IoT, security and privacy

6.1   Introduction

The use of the Internet to connect physical things that operate on a single network under IoT was estimated to be around 28 billion by 2020 [1]. Gartner even predicted that 20% of the businesses will have deployed security solutions for the protection of their IoT devices by 2017 [2, 12, 13]. The connectivity of the devices all over the world makes it easy to collect information with higher granularity. This helps to deliver sophisticated services in a wide range of applications that includes healthcare, smart cities, etc. Data collected by these devices are stored and can be used to provide a wide range of advanced services to users. As there is an increase in IoT usage day by day, like all communication networks, IoT suffers from various kinds of vulnerabilities and security issues. The IoT is being combined with other technologies like wireless sensor networks and mobile networks, among others, and the flexibility of the devices to interact with the environment without any external factors leads to security and privacy issues and makes it difficult to manage [3]. The security challenges are due to lack of central control, device resource heterogeneity, and multiple attacks. For these reasons, many researchers have studied the various security and privacy challenges of IoT [4, 5]. Some have discussed possible threats and their countermeasures, some have provided solutions to the protocols used by IoT [2, 3], and others some specific mechanisms. Many have suggested access control to sensitive information [6]. IPsec and TLS are used to provide authentication and privacy. A privacy management method was proposed to measure the risk [7]. Researchers have suggested security principles like confidentiality, integrity, availability, and authenticity as the security requirements of IoT. Researchers have proposed countermeasures for the IPv6 over LoWPAN, routing protocol for low power and lossy networks (RPL), and constrained application protocol (CoAP). They have investigated various technologies, like Bluetooth, ZigBee, Z-Wave, etc., to provide security in an efficient way. Celebucki *et al.* suggested the methods to enhance the privacy and robustness of the systems in the IoT [8]. The experts have studied and provided a detailed survey of the security protocols for eight various IoT frameworks [9, 10]. Although they have suggested many countermeasures based on the principles, it is still an ongoing problem. The network devices will obtain a large amount of data from the applications they are meant for. These devices will communicate within the network using various communication protocols and analytics platforms, which is done using the internet and one central storage server. This gives a scope to the generation of a huge amount of data using rich interactions among them. This allows the reliability and trustworthiness of the interactions among the things and central server. Security and privacy issues will be raised due to the data sensitivity provided by the things which are interconnected for the exchange of information. There is a possibility of release of sensitive data using false authentication and device spoofing. To handle the security and privacy issues in IoT, the centralized maintenance concept is eliminated by introducing distributed ledger technology known as blockchain. Before proceeding with Blockchain technology, we will briefly discuss the challenges and issues in the IoT.

6.2 Challenges and Issues in IoT

Although the Internet of Things has lots of benefits to solve a wide range of problems in various sectors, there still exist many issues and challenges. The challenges that are associated with IoT are security and privacy concerns. The other concerns are interoperability, lack of standards, legal issues, emerging IoT economic issues and so on. The report prepared by Rose *et al.* based on the Internet Society is discussed in detail [9-11].

- *Security issues*: The challenges involved in design practices are due to the lack of resources to train for the future. Cost and security trade-offs have to be considered for informed decisions and cost-benefit analysis. Due to lack of optimal control in IoT device communication models there are confidentiality, authentication, security issues and related cyberattacks. There is no sufficient information and maintenance due to lack of field upgradeability. The shared responsibility in IoT has a security vulnerability.

- *Privacy concerns*: Strict rules not being implemented in the data collection lead to privacy concerns. Multi-party models are not available which enable transparency, expression, and enforcement of rules leading to privacy.

- *Interoperability issues*: These issues arise due to the proprietary ecosystem and open ecosystem provided in data collection and use of data as per user choice. If security protocols can be implemented then technical and cost constraints are a challenge and create an issue of interoperability.

- *IoT standard and legal issues*: These issues are due to lack of effort in developing standard protocols; no standard trust policies, no laws, no control on data collection or sharing.

- *Emerging economic issues and developmental issues*: Infrastructure challenges due to the burden of the IoT devices and their communications on the internet are increasing day by day. Only limited study is available for the evaluation of the technical and economic benefits along with less awareness of the policies of IoT.

6.2.1 Attacks on IoT

Attacks on the Internet of Things are broadly divided into four types, namely physical and datalink attacks, network attacks, software attacks, and encryption attacks. A brief explanation of all these categories is given below [14, 15].

6.2.1.1 Physical and Datalink Attacks of IoT

In these attacks the attackers focus on the hardware system as the attacker is close to the device. This will affect the device for a lifetime or change the functionality of the system. The main types of attacks are non-invasive and invasive attacks. A non-invasive attack is where the attacker is very close to the device to sense the electrical characteristics and is able to change the behavior of the device. Some of the attacks are side-channel analysis, optical, EMFI, BBI, tamper attacks, power glitching, clock or reset glitching, frequency tampering, voltage attacks, temperature attacks and so on. In an invasive attack the chip of the device is replaced or manipulated. Some of the physical and data link attacks are explained below.

- *Node Tampering*: A node is damaged physically or by replacing the node partially or fully to gain access to sensitive information. It can even affect the operations of the communication layer [15].

- *RF Interference on RFIDs*: A noise signal can be sent to the RFID tag over a radio frequency that is used for RFID communication. Denial of service attack can be implemented using the radio frequency interference [15, 16].

- *Node Jamming Adversaries*: The attacker will interfere with the radio frequencies by not allowing the communication among the nodes. This leads to deterioration of the network by not allowing the device to follow any protocols. This will affect the data sent or received by the legitimate users, resulting in a change of behavior in the system. The physical layer will be affected with this kind of attack [17-19].

- *Malicious Node Injection*: A new node can enter into the network which is malicious and can control the data flow from and to the network and its operations [15].

- *Physical Damage*: This attack completely damages the system. This attack generally happens when there is no security in that particular area or in a building which has an IoT system. It is different from a node tampering attack as the attacker will damage the system to impact the availability of service [14, 15].

- *Insecure Initialization*: The secure initialization of the devices will ensure the proper funtioning of the system without violating the rules of privacy. The physical layer needs to be secured by making it unaccessible without permission. This attack damages the physical layer [20, 21].

- *Sleep Deprivation Attack*: The IoT devices are made to stay awake, which drains their energy. The devices will be asleep when they are not in use but the attacker will wake them so that the power will be consumed and depletion of the battery takes place. The devices will not perform well when a large task is assigned to be executed. This will affect the link layer of the IoT system [22, 15].

- *Social Engineering*: The users who are present in the IoT system are manipulated and the sensitive information is extracted. The attacker will interact physically with IoT users to achieve its goals [15].

- *Sybil and Spoofing Attacks*: These kinds of attacks are caused by fake nodes present in the network to degrade the IoT functionality. A Sybil attacker uses the forged MAC values to present itself as a different device aimed at depletion of the resources. This affects the physical layer of the IoT [23, 24].

- *Malicious Code Injection*: A node will be compromised by injecting the malicious code that allows the attacker to access the system [15].

6.2.1.2 *Network Attacks*

The attackers concentrate on the routing and session management along with communication of the devices of IoT. The attacks are performed on the network and transport layer of the IoT. Some of the possible attacks are discussed below.

- *Duplication Attacks*: These occur due to the fragmentation of IPv6 packets that are necessary for devices conforming to IEEE 802.15.4 that use small frame sizes. The construction of packet fragment fields at 6LoWPAN layer sometimes may result in resource depletion, overflow of buffers and device reboot. The duplicate packets sent by the malicious agents will affect the packet reassembly, thus not allowing the legitimate packets. This attack will affect the 6LowPAN adaptation layer and network layer [25, 26].

- *Insecure Neighbor Discovery*: Each device will be uniquely identified in the network and the communications which take place must be secure. The end-to-end communication should be secure and reaches the destination safely and securely. Before performing a transmission, the neighbor will be discovered based on the router discovery and using address resolution. The neighbor discovery packet will perform verification but may result in severe implications along with DoS attack. This attack will affect the network layer of IoT [27].

- *Buffer Reservation Attack*: The receiver node must reserve the buffer space for the reassembly of the packets which are coming from the other side. In this attack, the attacker can exploit the buffer space by sending incomplete packets. As denial-of-service attack occurs, the fragment packets are discarded. This will affect both adaptation layer of 6LoWPAN and network layer of IoT [26].

- *RPL Routing Attack*: Routing protocol for low-power and lossy networks (RPL) is exposed to various attacks. The hacker can deplete the resources or compromise the devices present in the network and perform eavesdropping attack. This affects the IPv6 network layer [29, 30].

- *Sinkhole and Wormhole Attacks*: The attacker establishes connection between the two parties. The information from sender has to pass to the receiver via attacker node. The attacks gain the information and perform malicious activity in the network. The operations of 6LoWPAN can be exploited due to the wormhole attack. In this attack, a tunnel is created between the nodes to receive the packets once they arrive at the other node immediately. Some attacks are eavesdropping, privacy violations and DoS attack. These attacks will affect the network layer [31-33].

- *Sybil Attacks on Network and Transport Layer*: Sybil nodes are deployed in the network to degrade the performance as well as violate the data privacy. The Sybil nodes use fake identity and result in spamming attack, phishing attacks, etc., and affect the network layer [34, 35, 49]

- *Authentication and Secure Communication*: The devices get authenticated using key management systems present in the network. Any loophole will lead to security issues. As there are constrained resources, the overhead of DTLS has to be minimized. The devices must ensure the secure communication of the data in IoT by considering efficiency and scarcity of the things and its related resources in the network. This attack affects the 6LoWPAN adaptation layer along with transport and network layer [36-38].

- *Transport Level End-to-End Security*: This provides reliable security from sender node to the desired destination node. For this, it has to provide comprehensive authentication mechanisms for message communication without violating privacy. The transport and network layers will be affected by this kind of attack [39, 40].

- *Session Establishment and Resumption*: Session hijacking can result in DoS attack. A node impersonation attack can continue the session among the two nodes. The nodes may alter the sequence numbers in the messages that are transmitted in the network. Network layer will be affected by this kind of attack in IoT [41, 42].

- *Privacy Violation on Cloud-Based IoT*: It is easy to compromise the cloud privacy with violation attacks that reveal the identity and location of users. The malicious cloud node will access confidential information being transmitted and received at destination [43, 44].

- *Traffic Analysis Attacks*: The attacker sniffs the data flowing from RFID due to its wireless characteristics. Before deploying the attack, the attacker tries to gain some network information. This kind of attack happens by sniffing the applications like port scanner, packet sniffer, etc. [16, 45].

- *RFID Spoofing*: RFID signals are spoofed to record the data which is transmitted from a RFID tag. The data is sent by the attacker that contains RFID, making it appear to be valid so that the attacker will have full access to the system pretending to be the main source [15, 46].

- *RFID Cloning*: Cloning can be done with RFID tag by photocopying data from the victims tag. Although everything, such as date, etc., matches, it does not duplicate the original ID, making it impossible to identify original and compromised data [15, 46].

- *Sinkhole Attack*: The attacker lures the traffic and creates a sinkhole. There will be a breach in confidentiality by denying the services and dropping all the packets instead of forwarding them to the destination due to this attack [47].

- *Man-in-the-Middle Attack*: The hacker will interfere with the communication occurring between the two nodes to access the restricted data by monitoring, eavesdropping and controlling the communication. The attacker will rely on the network protocols for the attack [48].

- *Denial of Service*: More traffic can be sent to an IoT device making it unable to fulfill other requests, leading to a successful DoS attack.

- *Routing Information Attacks*: Hello and Black-Hole attacks are examples of these types of attacks. These are direct attacks that are implemented by altering the information, replaying the routing information, creating routing loops, dropping of traffic, sending flag error messages, etc. [15].

6.2.1.3 Software Attacks

These kinds of attacks mainly occur on the applications being executed on the IoT devices. Software attacks can enter into the system by using code-based programs like Trojan horse, worms, etc., which are discussed below.

- *Constrained Application Protocol (CoAP) Security with Internet*: CoAP is a web-based interface for the constrained devices that uses DTLS. DTLS combines with various security modes to provide end-to-end security. It follows a specific format to pass information which will be encrypted for the purpose of secure communication. The multicast support requires authentication mechanisms to perform secure communication. The application and network layers will be affected by this kind of attack [50-52].

- *Insecure Interfaces*: The interfaces used to communicate among IoT devices, like Web, Mobile, and Cloud, are vulnerable to attacks which affect the privacy of the data. This affects the application layer of IoT [53].

- *Insecure Software/Firmware*: Vulnerabilities can be caused by insecure software used in IoT. The software code developed for the proper functioning of IoT is to be tested carefully in a secure manner. The updates are to be performed and carried out in a secure environment. Attacks due to insecure software/firmware affect the application, transport, and network layers of IoT [53].

- *Middleware Security*: The middleware is designed to deliver the communications among various devices in a secure manner for providing various services. Different environments use different middleware technologies and they must able to provide secure communication. The application, transport, and network layers will be affected by this attack of the IoT system [54, 55]

- *Phishing Attacks*: The hacker will gain access to data by user credential spoofing in the network using phishing websites [15].

- *Malicious Scripts*: The user who controls the gateway can be deceived into running an executable ActiveX script which can result in complete damage of the system [15].

- *Denial of Service*: DoS or DDoS is implemented on the affected systems through the application layer. It can block the legitimate users by not allowing full application layer access and allowing the hacker to access the databases and sensitive data [15].

6.2.1.4 Encryption Attacks

These attacks will work to break the encryption method used by the IoT device in the network [15].

- *Side-Channel Attacks*: Concentrating on a particular method of the set of devices and observing the pattern of data, the hacker can regain the encryption key for the encryption and decryption of the information.

- *Cryptanalysis Attacks*: In these attacks, the hacker will perform known plaintext attack, chosen plaintext attack, chosen ciphertext attack and ciphertext only attack.

With the emergence of IoT as a mainstream industry, challenges are also emerging. The IoT is not just data, but depends on how, why and when you collect it. The network is able to interact with other devices and request a service without human intervention, which raises many issues related to security. One of the key areas is security of the infrastructure and its services. The first and foremost challenge associated with IoT is the identification of the devices, authentications and security of the devices. It is expensive to consider a centralized security model as it is easy for the attackers to target a single point of failure, which results in great destruction of devices and information. It is difficult to implement the centralized network as the end nodes are distributed geographically. To overcome these attacks, the experts have suggested that Blockchain be incorporated with Internet of Things.

6.3 Blockchain

Blockchain is a distributed ledger which offers secure, transparent transactions and is open to everyone in the network. This technology is a technique which consists of cryptography, algorithms and is economical along with use of mathematics. Blockchain uses a consensus algorithm to solve the synchronization problem in distributed databases in peer-to-peer networks [56-58]. It enables new business models as it is efficient, highly resistant to attacks and public. It is public as the transactions are seen in the form of blocks which are stored in the database. The actual content will be protected using a private key. It has a database that maintains data records continuously. It doesn't contain a master, the participant nodes will have a copy of the chain in order to communicate. The data records will be added to the chain continuously. The records can be extended, but records present in the database cannot be changed. Transactions are created by the participants present in that system. The system will maintain a timestamp to verify when the transaction was added. Blocks will verify the transaction by recording them to check whether the correct sequence is present or not. It is very difficult to change or alter any information once it is entered in the blockchain [59, 60]. The transactions in the blockchain are encrypted using the encryption techniques and digital signature which prove authenticity. The network participants will agree, which is commonly known as consensus. All the records available to all the participants will not allow any duplication of the records. For example, in order to perform a bank transaction, a third party will be used for the transfer of money from one to the other, which is not safe as the third party may be hacked as well, wasting money in the form of commission. With the implementation of blockchain, third party involvement is not present for the transfer of money, which makes the process easy and secure. As the records are not stored in one place, corruption of the information is not possible by any hacker. Bitcoin is one of the applications of blockchain.

The blockchain consists of blocks which have data or information. The implementation of digital cyrptocurrency called Bitcoin was popularized by Satoshi Nakamoto in 2008 [59]. The blocks in the Blockchain consist of a hash with some information of their previous block. Hash is a unique mathematical code which is different for different blocks. If the information is changed, hash has to be changed. All the blocks are connected with hash keys that make the blockchain secure. When transactions take place in the network, their respective nodes will validate these transactions. If we use Bitcoin, the nodes present in the network are called miners and work on proof-of-work concept in order to validate the transactions. To validate a transaction in the network, hash of the previous node will be refereed and if the hash is correct then the transaction will take place. If any change is performed by the hacker, the hash will also get changed and will not be validated and the breach will be detected. This technique will ensure the blockchain is unalterable, as any change in the block will reflect the entire network transaction. To produce hash value, Blockchain uses Merkle tree function and the Merkel root field that presents the hash value of the current block [61, 62]. The transaction procedure in the Blockchain is as follows:

- Blockchain uses public and private keys in order to form a digital signature for ensuring security.

- Authentication is achieved using these keys and authorization is given.

- It allows the participants to perform mathematical verifications of the network and reach a consensus on any particular value.

- The sender uses the private key and announces the transaction over the network. The block consists of a timestamp, digital signature and the public key of the receiver to perform a transaction.

- Once the information is broadcasted, the validation of the process starts.

- The nodes that are present in the network try to solve the puzzle related to the transaction in order to process it. Nodes spend computational power in order to solve the puzzle.

- Once the puzzle is solved, the nodes will receive the bitcoins in the form of rewards. This kind of work is known as proof-of-work problems.

- Once the nodes in the consensus agree to a solution, the timestamp is added to the existing block. The block can contain anything, from money to data.

- If a new block is added to the chain, the existing nodes are updated in the network. The new data will be broadcasted in the network and all the nodes are updated.

Mesh network can use Blockchain that will allow IoT to connect safely and securely with the avoidance of spoofing and impersonation attacks. Every device will be issued a unique ID to connect others in the network. Blockchain ID can be used as URL and its wallet can be used to raise the identity request [64, 65]. This wallet will create a digitally signed request which is forwarded to the target device. Thus, the devices validate the signatures using the public keys of the sender. If a device is constrained by the resources, they can be connected to the proxies where a wallet can be created [66-68]. There are two kinds of peers in blockchain, namely: endorsing peers and committing peers. Endorsing peers specify the rules and policies for the execution of the transaction related to the endorsement, and simulate and endorse transactions. Committing peers receive the transactions of the endorsement peers that are endorsed, verify the ledger and update the records. The peers are also ordered nodes which receive the endorsed transactions of the endorsed nodes, sequence them and forward the transactions to the committing peers. Once a miner or a node enters into the network, it has to synchronize with the network; it should validate the transaction and block, support the creation of new blocks, perform proof of work, and fetch the reward [69].

6.3.1 Features

In the context of IoT, smart contracts play a major role in managing, controlling and securing the IoT devices. Some essential features of Blockchain that are useful for the IoT are [59-72]:

- *Decentralization*: Blockchains are decentralized, which means that everyone in the network stores one copy of the ledger and no one can modify it. This feature of blockchain provides transparency and security. This will also improve fault tolerance and scalability.

- *Peer-to-Peer Network*: The participants interact using the P2P model without any third party. It uses P2P protocol, allowing the participants to have a copy of transactions.

- *Immutability*: Once data is written in blockchain it cannot be changed. The best example to explain this is group mail, where if there are any changes all the recipients need to be asked to delete the sent mail, which is tedious work. If we try to change the data in one block, the entire block has to be changed. One block hash change will result in a change in all the blocks' hash values. It is not easy to change all the values as it requires much of the computational power. The data stored cannot be altered or be attacked by the attackers due to immutability.

- *Tamper Proof*: Due to the property of immutability, it is easy to detect any kind of tampering in the data of the block. Any small change in the data will be detected and addressed smoothly. Each hash function is associated with block ID, which is unique. Any change in data leads to change in hash function.

- *Address Space*: Blockchain consists of 160-bit address space, as opposed to IPv6 address space that consists of 128-bit space. Blockchain address consists of a 20-byte hash of the public key generated by Elliptic curve signature algorithm. Due to this, it can allocate 1.46×1048 devices at once. The probability of colliding with an address is 1048, which is considered secure enough to provide a global unique identifier and doesn't require any registration on the network. No centralized authority is required as that of IPv4 and IPv6 by Internet Assigned Numbers Authority (IANA). Blockchain provides 4.3 billion addresses, providing a scalable solution for IoT. The devices are constrained in memory and computation capacity, and therefore will be unfit to run an IPv6 stack.

- *Identity of Things in IoT Environment*: Identification of things and access control management has to be handled in an efficient and secure way. The main challenge is associated with the ownership and identity of the IoT devices. The lifetime of the ownership changes from producer to merchant and purchaser. The consumer ownership is changeable if the device is for resale, decommissioned or compromised by any attacker. IoT relations include human-to-device, device-to-device or device-to-service. The relationships among these devices and humans can be deployed, used, sold, upgraded, repaired and so on. Blockchain has the capacity to solve these kinds of challenges easily and securely as it provides tracking by owners, authorized identity, and monitoring of the goods. The concept of trust chain provides trusted transactions along with integrity in a distributed environment. Blockchain provides tracking of the transactions at each and every point. Blockchain can allow the IoT to register where an identity (ID) is given with an attributes set and their relationships which are stored in the distributed ledger.

- *Authentication and Integrity*: Data is cryptographically signed by the sender. The sender holds the public key and global unique identification (GUID) which ensure the authentication and integrity of the information. All the transactions performed using blockchain will be recorded and tracked securely.

- *Authentication, Authorization and Privacy*: Blockchain provides single and multi-party authentication for the IoT device. Smart contracts will provide authorization with less complexity when compared with traditional methods. Some of the protocols used for authorization are role-based access management (RBAC), OAuth 2.0, OpenID, OMADM, and LWM2M. Privacy can be achieved by using some rules and conditions and time of individual or group of users entry into the network.

- *Secure Communications*: Application protocols like MQTT, HTTP, XMPP, and CoAP, etc., are not designed with security features. The protocols are wrapped with other protocols like DTLS or TLS for providing secure communication. Due to the presence of centralized management, key management ID is performed using PKI protocol. With the help of blockchain, key management is eliminated, and IoT devices use GUID and asymmetric key pairs once installed in the network. There is no requirement for handling the protocols like DTLS, TLS, and exchange of PKI certificates. A lightweight security protocol suite for IoT devices makes computations and memory management feasible. The usage of GUID simplifies the security protocols usually used for the exchange of PKI certificates. Filament was an adopted hardware and software solution for the payments based on Bitcoin and smart contracts of the IoT. Some of the protocols supported by Filament devices are Blockname, Telehash, Pennyback and Bittorrent. Blockname is used to identify the device, Telehash is an opensource of Kademlia DHT and smart contracts define the device usage.

- *Scalability*: Latency consensus is improved by using the new Byzantine fault tolerant protocol, as the consensus has a direct effect on scalability. Litecoin, which is identical to Bitcoin, allows fast transaction confirmation and improves storage efficiency. It uses scrypt, which is a memory-intensive, password-based key derivation function. GHOST is another protocol meant to improve scalability by changing its chain selection rule. Rather than increasing the scalability, BigchainDB adds blockchain characteristics of big data, distributed databases with immutability. The interplanetary file system (IPFS) is used to store decentralized and shared files enabling peer-to-peer file system. IPFS increases efficiency and removes duplication and helps to track the version history of each file.

- *Anonymity and Privacy*: All the transactions are transparent in blockchain and each and every transaction can be checked and tracked from the very first level. This helps to build trust between the wallets and individuals, as there is no direct relationship between each other. In order to solve this problem in Bitcoin, a Zerocash and Zerocoin is used that support anonymous transactions which hide sender and receiver details along with the information. To make transactions untraceable Monero uses ring signatures. Mixing of services that are provided by Bitcoin, like Bitcoin Fog and Bit Laundry, will lead to anonymity. The services are broken into small transactions and scheduled accordingly for a fee. There are plenty of protocols to increase security such as DarkWallet, Dash, MixCoin, CoinShuffle, and CoinSwap. To increase privacy, data is encrypted and Hawk stores encrypted transactions. To limit the visibility of the sensitive data a permissioned blockchain called Quorum is used. A data-centric approach is used by Rockchain based on Ethereum where public calculations are performed on private data. This approach allows distributed file system to manage data privacy [70, 73].

- *Persistency*: As the transactions will be spread across the network, it is not possible to tamper with the information. Each block that is broadcasted in the network is validated and recorded and checked, so there is no falsification in the transactions.

- *Auditability*: As each transaction is validated with a timestamp, users have the accessibility to trace previous records using any node in the network. The transaction can be traced whenever required. Traceability and transparency of stored data is improved.

6.3.2 Blockchain Types

There are two categories of blockchains that will be used for performing the transactions over the network based on the requirements of the user. No matter what kind of blockchain is being used, some similarities exist in both private and public networks that are used in the decentralized system. All the peers present in that network will maintain a ledger copy. The ledgers are updated with the help of consensus. The rules of immutability and safety are applied in the network for the avoidance of attacks [69, 70, 72].

1. *Public Blockchain*: This is a permissionless ledger which can be accessed by anyone. A person connected to internet can download the public blockchain and access it. One is able to check the history of transactions. Public blockchains will reward the participants whenever a transaction is performed. The best examples for this kind of blockchain are Bitcoin and Ethereum. The rules decided initially will have little scope for modification. Everyone can check and verify each and every transaction.

2. *Private Blockchain*: This type of blockchain is shared among trusted parties. The control will be in the hands of the owners of the network. The rules can be changed according to the levels of permissions, members involved, etc. These will run independently or can be integrated with other blockchains present in the network. This kind of Blockchain is helpful between companies belonging to the same mother entity.

Usage of both blockchains is helpful as some transactions require private blockchains and other public blockchains based on conviction and depending on the services offered to the users in the network.

6.4 IoT Blockchain Approaches

Many studies were conducted to check the suitability of blockchain for the IoT. Marco Conoscenti conducted a survey and suggested that the applicability of blockchain in IoT provides more security [77]. Blockchain-enabled IoT deployment adds great value for large-scale real-world deployment of Fog and Cloud that yields good results in terms of providing security. This will help to understand the network latency, and among fog and cloud, fog is found to be performing well. The use of an Ethereum account to manage the networked IoT yielded good results, as suggested by Huh *et al.* [79]. A smart home was considered as a case study by Dorri *et al.* [76] who explained how blockchain provides security and privacy for various applications that involve transactions. The IoT can utilize the blockchain and provide security to its services. The Blockchain approaches towards IoT and layer-wise mechanisms are as follows [69, 77-80]:

- *End-to-End Blockchains*: In this kind of approach the source creates the first transaction block containing data. Other network elements will be appended to the next block and continue the process till it reaches the destination. The data gathered on the cloud is utilized to analyze the process. These are application specific and consist of a vast variety of application domains; some of the applications include smart city, intelligent transport, smart building, among others.

- *Analytics/Storage-Level Blockchains*: The analytics engine analyzes the transactions from the data source. Storage of information does not require integrity, but for some applications it is required. Two layers, like data centralization and data analytics, will use these blockchains. The blockchain is used for storage- and analytics-based applications. These layers describe core networking functions. The functionality includes industry owned extranets. This functionality is achieved using carrier provided connectivity by both wired and wireless networks.

- *Gateway Level Blockchains*: Once the gateway receives the data, the blockchain is incorporated into it along with data for other users. Data summarization points exist in the network that support IoT devices to connect with others. This works at the data aggregation layer where protocol conversion takes place, along with edge computing network capabilities. The gateway device handles the data aggregation function. Edge network represents the network infrastructure employed with networking protocols.

- *Fog Network*: This supports fog computing that is localized network with first hop of IoT user connectivity. Fog network optimizes IoT operating environment and sometimes may use specialized protocol. This can be connected using wired or wireless link. The initial communication link used by the devices is supported by this network.

- *Site Level Blockchains*: The devices at a given site develop data that doesn't require immediate protection of integrity. Once the local node receives the data, it is incorporated with blockchain from other site users. This deals with aggregation of authorization and authentication. The data acquisition layer is made up of sensors, embedded devices, sensor hubs, etc.

- *Device Level Blockchains*: Blockchains for the data can be built by each device present in the network for the protection of the data. This includes device level authorization and authentication. It also includes encryption and key management, and deals with trust and identity management. All the devices that are connected to the internet require these security features. This level consists of all the things that are subjected to automation offered by IoT. This is a large domain which includes people, wearable devices, smartphones, appliances, surveillance cameras, smart homes and buildings, and so on.

6.4.1 Blockchain Platforms for IoT

Blockchain is a technology that may affect many industries by providing security services. This technology offers many advantages in diverse areas. Since there are many available platforms which are constantly changing it is not easy to analyze all of them at one time. Some of the famous and suitable platforms for the IoT domains are as follows [14, 70, 80]:

- *Bitcoin*: This is the first blockchain platform and supports the monetary transactions. It is fast, cheap and reliable and can be integrated into the various applications. IoT can use bitcoins for the micro payments and applications that are attached to the currency. But the depreciation of the coin can be a drawback that affects the application negatively. Smart contracts can be a solution when integrating the blockchain with IoT. They contain a scripting language which sets some particular conditions when performing transactions. This scripting language is limited compared to smart contract platforms. Deployment of private blockchain is allowed by the multichain platform. An API is used which extends the original Bitcoin through new functionalities by allowing assets, permissions, transactions, etc. This recommends a command line tool to interact within the network. It allows other clients to interact with JSON-RPC using networks such as .js, Java, C# and Ruby. Multichain BC can be deployed on three nodes in the cluster, one on Arduino, one on Proof-of-Concept, and one on IoT application. This acts as a fork of Bitcoin and source code uses 64-bit architecture to compile.

- *Ethereum*: Ethereum is one of the BC Bitcoin initiatives that includes smart contracts. This is a built-in programming language of BC and runs consensus-based virtual machine globally. Inclusion of smart contracts allows the blockchain to integrate itself in areas other than only currencies. Ethereum has become popular due to its active and broad community which allows a variety of applications to develop. Most of the IoT applications use Ethereum as they are compatible. This approach will help to publish the measures and policies which react to changes in the environment.

- *Hyperledger*: This is an open platform where various projects can be developed which are applied for commercial implementations like IBM's blockchain. IBM use to derive the permissions without cryptocurrency. It provides a consensus and membership. Distributed applications are developed using blockchain. Blockchain receives the data from IoT devices using IBM Watson, which is an IoT platform that manages the devices and allows for further analysis.

- *IBM Open Blockchain (OBC)*: IBM sourced open Blockchain in 2016 as a part of Linux's new blockchain project. OBC allows organizations to work with enterprise level technology for the creation of applications which will help in solving common business problems. The main goal of IBM is to improve business workflow using blockchain as a platform. The automation of the business processes can be performed by deploying business rules as in the form of smart contracts. OBC includes REST and JSON-RPC, and an SDK that allow custom applications to communicate with each other in the network. The OBC's documentation is available in GitHub[1] repository. IBM allows the deployment of applications using OBC on its Bluemix cloud platform. The target is to reach 100,000 transactions per second in a standard production environment of about 15 validating nodes running in close proximity.

- *IBM's Bluemix*:[2] It allows the integration of blockchain, allowing it to be offered as a service. This helps in speeding up application prototyping and its use cases to be developed. For food traceability uses, this platform is an ongoing project.

- *Litecoin*[3]: This is identical to Bitcoin but with improved storage efficiency and faster transaction, which improve the block generation time from almost 10 times to 2.5 times that based on scrypt. It uses a memory-intensive password-based key derivation. The computational requirements are much less suitable for IoT.

- *Lisk*:[4] It offers a blockchain platform where sub-blockchains can be created for decentralized blockchain applications and use of cryptocurrencies provides good results. This platform allows the users to create and deploy decentralized applications with the help of JavaScript. The use of Lisk currency creates the tokens. It uses the delegated proof-of-stake consensus. This helps in developing the security within IoT.

---

[1] https://github.com/
[2] https://cloud.ibm.com/
[3] https://litecoin.org/
[4] https://lisk.io/

- *Quorum:*[5] This platform provides financial services with permissioned implementation of Ethereum and provides privacy. It uses the consensus mechanisms to provide privacy using cryptography and segmentation. Recently, it was integrated with Zero-Cash technology to obtain required information about any transaction. This provides secure links between the blockchain and physical objects.

- *HDAC*: This system uses both public and private blockchains and for secure transactions it uses quantum random number generation. It can be used for IoT contract and M2M transactions based on blockchain. To enable public blockchain, HDAC can be used with multiple private blockchains. Smart contracts are being used in many transactions, enabling applications beyond the cryptocurrency transactions. The blockchain can be used with or without cryptocurrency based on the application requirement. Ethereum provides required infrastructure for an IoT application. This can be deployed on cloud infrastructure or can be used using Amazon Web Services (AWS) or Google Cloud Platform. Non-cryptocurrency-based Hyperledger Fabric joins the consortium and starts a blockchain. This allows consortium and global applications to be created.

- *Eris*: Eris uses the Ethereum Virtual Machine and also uses Solidity or the Serpent programming languages. It requires finding participants to find its own key signers daemons that also requires knowledge of the particular domain. It works well with the recommended components of the applications. It is a modular platform that uses a docker for supporting various components of the network. The default components that Eris support are Tendermint socket protocol and Ethereum Virtual Machine for the multiclient support and the protocol for consensus. The Eris documentation is expensive. The scalability of Eris depends on the components. Eris can be used as a process auditor rather than transaction auditor; it tracks processes, such as when they have been created and executed.

- *Tendermint*: It is a software used to develop replicates of the applications in many machines. There are two components, namely, blockchain consensus engine and the generic application interface. The consensus engine is the core of Tendermint and makes sure of the transaction being recorded on all the machines. The Application interface will allow the transactions to run using any programming language. It is designed to be easily used, is simple to understand, and can be used for many distributed applications.

Ethereum and OBM are used more than other platforms. Both can interact using multiple methods and more are planned for the near future. OBC contracts are programmed in Java and JavaScript and require knowledge of Solidity and Serpent, as these are specifically meant for Ethereum VM. Ethereum consists of extensive documentation and supports the options of all the platforms. These two were part of the Linux Hyperledger project, with Ethereum being the oldest platform. Eris is a highly flexible platform because of modularity. Ethereum platforms are not extensible or modular, but they are flexible, as proved by hundreds of applications. The dynamic limit allows adjusting to meet the requirements of the network and blocks. Ethereum gives rewards to its participants, not unlike Bitcoin, and even unsuccessful participants also get rewards due to the addition of blocks in the network. Tokens are issued that represent the other values of the network. The Eris currency depends on logic and how it is composed.

---

[5]https://www.goquorum.com/

6.4.2 Applications

Bitcoins and the cryptocurrencies were the first to be introduced by Blockchain but they are not the only ones. Blockchain, with its features and advantages, slowly entered into various applications that led to businesses, industries and entrepreneurs connecting all around the world. The idea of transparency along with privacy and trust has created lots of hype in the market. Blockchain has several advantages for the Internet of Things like tamper-proof data, trustless and P2P communication, robust and highly reliable support of distributed file sharing, maintains records of historic actions, eliminates single control authority, provides trust and so on.

Alternative cryptocurrencies for financial applications other than Bitcoin and Ethereum have emerged, like Ripple, Litecoin, etc., that encouraged the market to enable new forms of payments and their investments. This has encouraged new modes of trading infrastructure for these new currencies. For the traceability-based systems, trustless ledger is identified as a solution. The chain stores will allow the object traceability along with the changes that occur with complete reliability. Some projects are still underway to track vehicles, history maintenance and so on by companies like IBM, Unilever, Walmart and Nestle for food traceability. Identity verification is also a famous technology where blockchain provides open trusted ledger to store the identities. The use of blockchain in Dubai for passport verification, e-identity in Estonia, birth certificate digitization in Illinois, and land registration in India are famous examples of blockchain. The integration of smart contracts of blockchain creates a new path for many industries to incorporate with blockchain like energy, real estate, betting, and many more. Other blockchain applications like cloud storage, education, or e-health have been proposed.

Blockchain can be applied in various sectors of IoT along with financial applications and some of the other applications are agriculture, for gathering soil data, secure data processing, shipping of agro products, etc.; business, for maintaining import and export data, energy raw materials, supply on demand, and financial values; and distribution, food, finance, healthcare, manufacturing and so on [70, 75, 82-84, 86].

- *Digital Currency*: Bitcoin has become a digital currency and a mode of online payment which doesn't need any central authorities. Bitcoin users will use pseudonyms instead of real names. Bitcoin uses three components like transaction, consensus protocol and communication network. It uses an encrypted technique for the funds transfer and operates independently of a central bank. It uses public keys to send and receive the information, and also records the transaction and its ID. The transaction confirmation needs the others computing power to get the consensus, and record the transaction in the network.

- *Smart Contract*: Ethereum is used for the exchange of services or products and the business deals occurring between users in society or the network. The parties will sign the terms and conditions of the contract or the agreements. The paper-based contracts are error prone and trusts can be contested or subject to fraud by both parties, raising risks. Smart contracts can be used to overcome these kinds of problem. Smart contracts perform work similar to paper-based agreements. The only difference is that they are digital and self-executable in nature. When some conditions are met by the contracts, they are deployed into the system. This will control the digital assets of the user, formulating the users rights and limits, executed by the system itself. It can be seen as a response to the message that a system receives and stores. Smart contracts hold the assets temporarily and follow the order they have been assigned and can be trusted. Ethereum is an open source blockchain that combines smart contract and uses the currency called ETH. Using this platform, people can develop different services, applications or contracts.

- *Internet of Healthcare*: The IoT has entered into e-healthcare to handle the information related to patients and healthcare providers. The data is stored by the healthcare provider and this electronic data storage is called electronic medical records (EMRs). Portable data is available to patients by using electronic health records (EHRs). These EHRs are in a more structured format than the EMRs. A blockchain-based IoT healthcare model was designed by Sicuranza and Esposito [91] using the concept of distributed database. This model creates a new block when new healthcare data is instantiated. This provides privacy and trust in the patients' records. Liang *et al.* [92] used the blockchain network for mobile healthcare applications and for protecting the integrity of the records. Smart contract can be used for shipping drugs to a pharmacist. The smart contract will contain information about the drug, quantity created data and so on. The contract will be responsible for the maintenance of the entries among various pharmacists throughout the supply chain. Contracts work based on some conditions, therefore no one can modify or perform changes, thus ensuring authenticity and trust.

- *Hyperledger*: Hosted by the Linux Foundation, it has been made available to all its users since 2015 in an open source form that can support the distributed ledgers. It can be used for global business that includes major technological, financial and supply chain companies that want to improve performance and reliability. The modular framework of this will support different components of the users. This can be used for the identification, access control, and contracts of the devices.

- *Smart City Energy Consumption*: Blockchain is a strong concept that can be applied for a smart city as it is based on the IoT that works automatically. Blockchain creates an open ledger and makes it easy to interact and coordinate among the IoT devices which increase the autonomy of the devices. Trusted information can be queried with reliability, and it favors creating new IoT markets [85, 87-89]. Ethereum is famous for its IoT blockchain applications. It has more features compared to Bitcoin and the use of smart contracts expands the possible applications. Use of blockchain by LO3 Energy was demonstrated in Brooklyn, Southern Germany and Australia and yielded good results. Microgrids used in LO3 are grouped based on the localization of the electricity generation, energy storage and the loads. It establishes a energy community market that develops a decentralized P2P energy network with the help of border power grid. This is a foist blockchain that allows the devices at the grid edge to interact for energy sales safely and securely among the microgrid participants. A hybrid device can measure buildings energy production in use and sends this information to the network. Liang *et al.* [91] proposed an architecture based on the Blockchain concept that can resist data manipulation attacks. The energy blockchain proposed by Li *et al.* [85] is based on consensus and a Stackelberg game. Aitzhan and Svetinovic have come up with a token-based private decentralized trading system that can be applied on the Internet of Energy [93].

- *Government Elections*: The current system of voting relies on the manual process and trust. It may eliminate the security breaches and frauds but manual errors can occur which cannot be ignored. Using smart contracts, these common issues can be eliminated. The entries in the smart contracts not only automate the process but provide transparency and security along with privacy, thus performing fair elections.

- *Identity Management*: When financial transactions are conducted over the network, hackers can access the account and draw money if they obtain your username and password. Therefore, there is a need for a system that can manage individual identification on the web. The distributed ledger used in blockchain offers public and private encryption through which a user can prove their identity and digitize the accounts. The gap between the government and private bodies can be filled using online identification based on blockchain.

- *Intellectual Property Protection*: With the help of the internet, digitized content can be easily reproduced and distributed as required. Due to which the users all around the world hold the power to copy and use it without allocating credit to the actual owner. Although there are copyright laws to protect and deal with such issues, there are no appropriate global standards. Even if copyright control exists, people lose control over their ideas and suffer in financial terms. With the help of blockchain, all the copyrights can be stored in the form of smart contracts which will enable automation in businesses along with an increase in online sales, thereby eliminating the redistribution risk. The IP registry will help authors and owners get a clear idea about the copyright. Once they are registered, they own the evidence that is tamper-proof. Blockchain is immutable in nature; once any entry is performed, it cannot be changed. The owner has the authority over the ownership and distribution of the content.

- *Autonomous Decentralized Peer-to-Peer Telemetry (ADEPT)*: This project was started by IBM and Samsung [80] to promote device autonomy and use blockchain at the end for the code execution on the edge devices. The three protocols used by this are Telehash, Bittorrent and Ethereum for the purpose of messaging, file sharing and blockchain. Blockchain provides authentication, contracts and the checklists. The first experiment for the implementation of blockchain was used for the smart washing machines as a proof of concept which used the contracts to buy the detergents from the suppliers.

- *Internet of Things in the 5G Era*: The 5G network will become a fully enabled mobile network connected with the billions of objects in society. To solve the privacy issue in 5G, Fan *et al.* [94] developed a blockchain-based, privacy-preserving sharing scheme for the 5G era.

- *Internet of Vehicles*: This allows vehicle-to-vehicle, vehicle-to-road, vehicle-to-human, and, in general, vehicle-to-everything communication. For providing privacy and security, the researchers proposed the frameworks based on blockchain known as blockchain ecosystem models. Some of the uses are the electric charge of the electric vehicle pile management. In order not to track the location of the vehicles, Dorri *et al.* [76] proposed a privacy-preserving framework where overlay nodes manage the blockchain. Lei *et al.* [95] developed a dynamic key management protocol for the vehicular communication. Kang *et al.* [96] proposed a P2P electric trading system called PETCON. Li *et al.* [85] proposed a Creditcoin concept to send the announcement anonymously. This helps to build trust in IoV communications. Noor *et al.* [97] proposed a reputation system using the blockchain concept, and used it to judge the messages based on the reputation values of the sender received by the receiver.

- *Internet of Things Devices*: A malware detection called CB-MDEE was proposed by Gu *et al.* [98] which works on the consortium blockchain. This method uses a fuzzy comparison along with multiple marking functions for the reduction of the false positive in order to improve detection ability. For the protection of the IoT devices, Lee *et al.* has suggested performing response verification to a request node and response from a response node.

- *Access Management in IoT*: Noor *et al.* [98] has come up with a distributed access control method using blockchain for the management of the IoT devices. The basic framework consists of sensor nodes, managers, agent nodes, smart contracts, Blockchain network and the management of the hubs. This provides mobility, accessibility and lightweight along with scalability and transparency.

- *Collaborative Video Delivery*: Decentralizing brokering system for collaborative blockchain-based video delivery was proposed by Herbaut and Negru [99] which depends on the advanced network services. The proposed system consists of content brokering, delivery monitoring and provisioning blockchains. It is deployed with the Hyperledger Fabric platform, which is a open source where the results obtained are that if the number of nodes slightly increases then there will be an increase in convergence time.

- *Cloud Storage*: If smart building or smart city devices would like to store information in the cloud, an analysis can be performed based on stored data for providing smart services. The users data is stored in the form of identical blocks using a unique block ID. For the purpose of user authentication, block ID and the hash of the data are used. If the user retrieves the data using the block ID and hash, user is authenticated. The packets received from users are stored in the form of Queue, i.e., first in, first out order, along with the hash. Once the data is stored, the new block ID is encrypted using shared key derived from Diffie-Hellman algorithm. If the key is known, the same person will know the block ID and as the hash used in this is collision resistant, only the true user will be able to know the block ID. This provides a guarantee that only the true user is able to access the particular block and chain fresh data to an existing ledger. Each user in the network can create a new ledger or can update the existing one for each device or for all the devices.

- *Intrusion Detection*: Using machine learning, intrusion detection techniques were proposed for IoT. For the improvement of the systems, a blockchain-based collaborative intrusion detection system (IDS) that can secure the exchange of alerts was introduced [53]. The application of blockchain in IDS was discussed by Bhattasali *et al.* [22]. The future IDS should be based on collaboration among the distributed systems, due to the demand in data sharing and trust computation. Blockchain can be applied to overcome the issues of privacy and can suppress insider attacks.

- *Software-Defined Networking*: This is used to provide intelligent routing. The decision-making process is made simple by the SDN controller. DistBlockNet based on blockchain distributed IoT network architecture provides scalability and flexibility without the need of any central server. This uses the verification codes and maintains an updated flow table and request-response node that updates the flow rules in the blockchain network.

- *Fog Computing*: Also known as edge computing, it is a highly visualized platform. It enables storage between users and data center based on traditional cloud computing.

Blockchain can be used to provide a link between fog nodes and IoT devices. Ibrahim suggested a fair payment scheme for outsourcing of the fog devices [41].

- *Distributed P2P Applications*: The IoT devices will self-organize and will cooperate for a new breed of applications. Applications include forwarding files, electronic commerce, and uploading data using sensors. A truthful incentive mechanism based on blockchain was proposed by He *et al.* [100]. This works well in the distributed P2P environments. The work proposes a pricing strategy to ovecome attacks, like collusion attacks, and obtain rewards upon successful delivery of the transaction.

- *Crowdsensing Applications*: These are based on mobile IoT applications. Using blockchain cryptocurrencies, Wang *et al.* [34] proposed a mechanism for preserving privacy in the crowd. The use of miners' verifiable data eliminates security and privacy and deals with impersonation attacks in the open and transparent blockchain.

- *Data Storage*: Dealing with heterogenous data resources leads to security issues for sensitive data. Using blockchain technology, Li *et al.* [85] proposed Searchain for the decentralized storage of data. This is based on a private keyword search and includes two components such as transaction nodes in a peer-to-peer structure and blockchain of ordered blocks. This provides privacy, accountability, and indistinguishability.

Blockchain framework aims to provide coordination among the devices, identity of the devices, and privacy for the billions of devices present in the network. The main objective is to develop a sharing economy where the IoT can be rented securely. Researchers are even working on the charging of vehicles called BlockCharge. It uses a SmartPlug and Android app to activate the plug and control the charge and the concept of blockchain to pay the charges. They are also working on providing a smart lock to access rented apartments.

Aigang is an autonomous insurance network for IoT assets. Smart contracts were deployed over the Ethereum testbed to issue policies, check the risk assessment, and process claims automatically. This created a virtual custom currency (AIX), offering the opportunity to invest in various products using different risk levels and gains. Smart contracts are used to connect devices with the underlying insurance policy, where maintenance and payment is performed automatically. With the help of Oracle, reporting events and claim handling will be easy.

MyBit plans to develop a system that can track the IoT assets owned by the group so that the revenues are shared accordingly. This is a new financial model that can be used by everyone to invest. Ethereum can be used to automate the process so that when the IoT generates revenue, the investors receive their share. The contract is responsible for controlling and updating the platform along with the maintenance of the system. Once the platform is installed, the information is communicated using an API to send and request. The devices can be connected using Oracle's IoT cloud service.

AeroToken has developed a real-time navigation along with a property access system for the services that it provides for low-altitude drones. The services are provided voluntarily, sharing airspace by solving the problem of permissions. The property owners use a blockchain-based smart contract and the service providers pay for their access. This application is based on Ethereum and smart contracts.

Maru was developed in the IoT research lab of Chain of Things, an integrated blockchain and IoT hardware solution. It focuses on providing blockchain-based security to IoT, a Chain of Solar to connect the panels to the blockchain for storing the produced energy, and a Chain of Shipping that improves the security in the shipping and logistics industry. The proof of concepts are developed using Ethereum and the data logging devices are used to send the data over the network.

Chronicled has invented many IoT products with the incorporation of cryptographic capabilities in order to create the most trusted IoT supply chain ecosystems. This platform consists of a blockchain synchronization server that has a capability of synchronizing the multiple BC systems. Registration and the verification of the devices are performed using smart contracts.

Modum.io sensor devices provide integrity for physical products, improving the supply-chain processes. Modum.io sensors are used to record environmental conditions during the shipments. They are designed to work on various platforms. Ethereum was used for the distribution of medical products. This was helpful to verify the data when the goods change ownership. To operate this kind of application and collect measurements at the time of transit, a mobile application was used to activate sensors and connect to them along with ownership changes on a dashboard to analyze the collected data.

Blockchain of Things is being used for industrial IoT integration. Many industries are using Catenis, a webservice for rapid Bitcoin blockchain integration along with encryption. This can be adopted by Ethereum, Hyperledger and other blockchains. Each IoT device is a virtual device in the respective hubs and gateways. The virtual device will manage to host Catenis services for the IoT.

In addition to these applications, some other apps used in smart cities are:

- *Smart Payments*: Municipal payments blockchain-based solution for city programs, assistance, welfare, etc.

- *Identity*: Uses blockchain to store and validate the users by reducing identity theft and fraud.

- *Government Services*: Smart contracts are implemented for identification, tracking property ownership, taxes, etc., by removing the paperwork and digitizing it in a more secure manner.

- *Waste Management*: The use of IoT devices and prediction models can improve efficiency.

6.5 Research Challenges

This section discusses various challenges and issues which could improve the efficiency of Blockchain-based IoT devices [14, 70, 72, 74].

- *Blockchain Vulnerabilities*: Although blockchain provides robust approaches for providing security to the IoT devices, these systems are also vulnerable [136]. The miners hashing can be compromised using the consensus mechanism, allowing the attacker to host and create a blockchain. The private keys can be exploited as they are limited. To ensure privacy, effective mechanisms need to be addressed in order to avoid attacks, like race attacks, that result in double-spending while performing a transaction.

- *Identity-Based Attacks*: The attackers will forge identities to masquerade as authorized users for gaining access and performing a modification attack. The types of identity-based attacks include key attack, replay attack, impersonation attack, and Sybil attack.

- *Manipulation-Based Attacks*: These attacks deal with data tampering or unauthorized access and fall under four categories. The categories of attacks are: false data injection attack, tampering attack, overlay attack, and modification attack.

- *Cryptanalytic Attacks*: Quantum attacks are designed to derive private keys from the elliptic curve digital logarithm public key. Using this, the attacker will sign the unauthorized transactions by forging all the required transactions. A lattice-based signature scheme proposed by Yin *et al.* [101] allows deriving numerous sub-private keys from the seed of the deterministic wallet of blockchain.

- *Reputation-Based Attacks*: The mediator in the network can manipulate his/her reputation from negative to positive, which can be done using Whitewashing or Hiding Blocks attacks.

- *Service-Based Attacks*: In these types of attacks, the service is made unavailable or the device is made to behave differently from its features. Some of the attacks that fall under this category and need to be addressed are DDoS attack, refusal-to-sign attack, double-spending attack, and collision attack of the keys.

- *Resiliency against Combined Attacks*: The security solutions based on Blockchain for IoT handle different security issues, but the challenge still remains the same; How to design a resilience against combined attacks while considering the feasibility of the solution under low-power resource-constrained devices.

- *Dynamic and Adaptable Security Framework*: The IoT devices deployed range from low-power to high-end server. A multilayer security is required rather than a single security solution. The security solution must be able to adapt to the existing resources, and make decisions regarding the security solution selection before providing services to the users. Dynamic and adaptable security mechanism requires intelligence based on the standardization of resources.

- *Energy-Efficient Mining*: Powerful miners are required because the blockchain grows as transactions increase. This increase uses storage resources and power-constrained IoT devices which are not able to meet the substantial computational and power consumption for the processing of blockchain. Efficient energy consensus protocols are required and are a significant research challenge.

- *Social Networks and Trust Management*: The large-scale spreading of rumors may be economically damaging to an organization. Blockchain can be a means of limiting the rumors.

- *Blockchain-Specific Infrastructure*: The blockchain stores the data that is not even useful for their own transactions. The decentralized storage of a large-block-size blockchain is a challenging issue.

- *Vehicular Cloud Advertisement Dissemination*: Many anonymous schemes have been proposed for hiding the identities of vehicles using IoV. The main challenges consist of designing a single attribute-based access control protocol, a privacy-preserving secret sharing scheme, and a low-complexity-based authentication scheme for the IoT using blockchain.

- *Skyline Query Processing*: This is a crucial issue in terms of database research. Research is still going on to study the feasibility of using skyline query processing for blockchain-based IoT. If a skyline database is constructed for many processing queries on blockchain, the security and privacy issues need to be addressed.

- *Hardware/Firmware Vulnerabilities*: As the devices are ubiquitous and low cost, there exist vulnerabilities with respect to hardware. The routing algorithms, security algorithms, and the packet processing mechanisms, along with physical malfunctioning, are to be verified before deploying any device. The vulnerabilities found after the deployment of devices are difficult to avoid or detect. A standard verification protocol is required for harnessing the IoT security.

- *Trusted Updates and Management*: A major issue is the updating of software in billions of devices by providing trust and scalability. Issues like ownership of the device, supply chain and data privacy are to be addressed by the researchers for a wide-ranging adoption of IoT. The research issues in this regard are scalability, efficiency, regulations, and key collisions.

6.6 Conclusion

The IoT devices are highly vulnerable to many types of attacks. The rise in use of IoT for various applications, like smart cities, healthcare, industry, agriculture and so on, is indirectly encouraging attackers to gain sensitive data. These loopholes are due to the constrained resources, immature standards, and the lack of proper methods to secure hardware and software. We discussed various attacks and challenges involved in IoT with respect to security. These problems were identified based on observations made during the interaction among the various components of IoT. Blockchain is recognized as a solution for addressing the issues of IoT. Although blockchain was originally designed for currency, its features are encouraging for various applications. By providing integrity, privacy, and trust in the emerging technology, it is possible to integrate it with IoT, providing security to the IoT devices and its communications. The integration of Blockchain with IoT and the various applications based on blockchain were discussed along with the open challenges for encouraging the research community to provide reliable, efficient, and scalable IoT security solutions in this area.

REFERENCES

1. Atzori, L., Iera, A., & Morabito, G. (2017). Understanding the Internet of Things: definition, potentials, and societal role of a fast evolving paradigm. *Ad Hoc Networks*, 56, 122-140. DOI: 10.1016/j.adhoc.2016.12.004

2. Rivera, J., & van der Meulen, R. (2013). Gartner says the internet of things installed base will grow to 26 billion units by 2020. Stamford, conn., December, 12., (https://www.gartner.com/newsroom/id/2636073).

3. Cheng, C., Lu, R., Petzoldt, A., & Takagi, T. (2017). Securing the Internet of Things in a quantum world. *IEEE Communications Magazine*, 55(2), 116-120., DOI: 10.1109/M-COM.2017.1600522CM.

4. Granjal, J., Silva, R., Monteiro, E., Silva, J. S., & Boavida, F. (2008, September). Why is IPSec a viable option for wireless sensor networks. In *IEEE 5th International Conference on Mobile Adhoc and Sensor Systems (MASS) 2008* (pp. 802-807). DOI: 10.1109/MAHSS.2008.4660130

5. Granjal, J., Monteiro, E., & Silva, J. S. (2015). Security for the internet of things: a survey of existing protocols and open research issues. *IEEE Communications Surveys & Tutorials*, 17(3), 1294-1312. DOI: 10.1109/COMST.2015.2388550

6. Nguyen, K. T., Laurent, M., & Oualha, N. (2015). Survey on secure communication protocols for the Internet of Things. *Ad Hoc Networks*, 32, 17-31. DOI: 10.1016/j.adhoc.2015.01.006

7. Krejci, R., Hujnak, O., & Svepes, M. (2017, November). Security survey of the IoT wireless protocols. In *2017 25th Telecommunication Forum (TELFOR)* (pp. 1-4). IEEE. DOI: 10.1109/TELFOR.2017.8249286.

8. Celebucki, D., Lin, M. A., & Graham, S. (2018, January). A security evaluation of popular internet of things protocols for manufacturers. In *2018 IEEE International Conference on Consumer Electronics (ICCE)* (pp. 1-6). IEEE. DOI: 10.1109/ICCE.2018.8326099.

9. Chen, L., Thombre, S., Jarvinen, K., Lohan, E. S., Alen-Savikko, A., Leppakoski, H.,... & Lindqvist, J. (2017). Robustness, security and privacy in location-based services for future IoT: A survey. *IEEE Access*, 5, 8956-8977. DOI: 10.1109/ACCESS.2017.2695525.

10. Ammar, M., Russello, G., & Crispo, B. (2018). Internet of Things: A survey on the security of IoT frameworks. *Journal of Information Security and Applications*, 38, 8-27. DOI: 10.1016/j.jisa. 2017.11.002.

11. Rose, K., Eldridge, S., & Chapin, L. (2015). The internet of things: An overview understanding the issues and challenges of a more connected world. The *Internet Society (ISOC)*, 22. https://www.internetsociety.org/wp-content/uploads/2017/08/ISOC-IoT-Overview-20151221-en.pdf

12. Van Der Meulen, R. (2016). Gartner says 6.4 billion connected "things" will be in use in 2016, up 30 percent from 2015. Stamford, Conn (2015). http://www.gartner.com/newsroom/id/3165317.

13. ITU. (2015). Measuring the Information Society Report. International Telecommunication Union (ITU).

14. Salah, K., & Khan, M. (2017). IoT security: Review, blockchain solutions, and open challenges. *Future Generation Computer Systems*. DOI: 10.1016/j.future.2017.11.022.

15. Sopori, D., Pawar, T., Patil, M., & Ravindran, R. (2017, March). Internet of things: security threats. *International Journal of Advanced Research in Computer Engineering & Technology (IJARCET)* 6(3). March, ISSN: 2278-1323.

16. Khoo, B. (2011, October). RFID as an enabler of the internet of things: Issues of security and privacy. In *2011 International Conference on Internet of Things and 4th International Conference on Cyber, Physical and Social Computing* (pp. 709-712). IEEE.

17. Mpitziopoulos, A., Gavalas, D., Konstantopoulos, C., & Pantziou, G. (2009). A survey on jamming attacks and countermeasures in WSNs. *IEEE Communications Surveys & Tutorials*, 11(4), 42-56.

18. Xu, W., Trappe, W., Zhang, Y., & Wood, T. (2005, May). The feasibility of launching and detecting jamming attacks in wireless networks. In *Proceedings of the 6th ACM International Symposium on Mobile Ad Hoc Networking and Computing* (pp. 46-57). ACM. http://dx.doi.org/ 10.1145/1062689.1062697.

19. Noubir, G., & Lin, G. (2003). Low-power DoS attacks in data wireless LANs and countermeasures. *ACM SIGMOBILE Mobile Computing and Communications Review*, 7(3), 29-30.

20. Chae, S. H., Choi, W., Lee, J. H., & Quek, T. Q. (2014). Enhanced secrecy in stochastic wireless networks: Artificial noise with secrecy protected zone. *IEEE Transactions on Information Forensics and Security*, 9(10), 1617-1628. http://dx.doi.org/10.1109/TIFS.2014.2341453.

21. Hong, Y. W. P., Lan, P. C., & Kuo, C. C. J. (2013). Enhancing physical-layer secrecy in multiantenna wireless systems: An overview of signal processing approaches. *IEEE Signal Processing Magazine*, 30(5), 29-40.

22. Bhattasali, T., & Chaki, R. (2011, July). A survey of recent intrusion detection systems for wireless sensor network. In *International Conference on Network Security and Applications* (pp. 268-280). Springer, Berlin, Heidelberg.

23. Xiao, L., Greenstein, L. J., Mandayam, N. B., & Trappe, W. (2009). Channel-based detection of sybil attacks in wireless networks. *IEEE Transactions on Information Forensics and Security*, 4(3), 492-503.

24. Chen, Y., Trappe, W., & Martin, R. P. (2007, June). Detecting and localizing wireless spoofing attacks. In *2007 4th Annual IEEE Communications Society Conference on Sensor, Mesh and Ad Hoc Communications and Networks* (pp. 193-202). IEEE.

25. H. Kim, (2008) Protection against packet fragmentation attacks at 6LoWPAN adaptation layer. In *2008 International Conference on Convergence and Hybrid Information Technology*, pp. 796-801. http://dx.doi.org/10.1109/ICHIT. 2008.261.

26. R. Hummen, J. Hiller, H. Wirtz, M. Henze, H. Shafagh, K. Wehrle, (2013)6LoWPAN Fragmentation attacks and mitigation mechanisms. In *Proceedings of the Sixth ACM Conference on Security and Privacy in Wireless and Mobile Networks, WiSec '13*, ACM, New York, NY, USA, pp. 5566. http://dx.doi.org/10.1145/2462096.2462107.

27. Riaz, R., Kim, K.-H., & Ahmed, H.F. (2009). Security analysis survey and framework design for IP connected LoWPANs. In *2009 International Symposium on Autonomous Decentralized Systems*, pp. 1-6. http://dx.doi.org/10.1109/ ISADS.2009.5207373.

28. Dvir, A., Holezer, T., & Buttyan, L. (2011). VeRA - version number and rank authentication in RPL. In *2011 IEEE Eighth International Conference on Mobile Ad-Hoc and Sensor Systems*, pp. 709-714. http://dx.doi.org/10.1109/MASS.2011.76.

29. Le, A., Loo, J., Lasebae, A., Vinel, A., Chen, Y., & Chai, M. (2013). The impact of rank attack on network topology of routing protocol for low-power and lossy networks, *IEEE Sensor Journal*, 13 (10) 3685-3692. http://dx.doi.org/10.1109/JSEN.2013.2266399.

30. Weekly, K., & Pister, K., (2012). Evaluating sinkhole defense techniques in RPL networks. In *Proceedings of the 2012 20th IEEE International Conference on Network Protocols (ICNP), ICNP '12*, IEEE Computer Society, Washington, DC, USA, pp.1-6. http://dx.doi.org/10.1109/ICNP.2012.6459948.

31. Ahmed, F., & Ko, Y. B. (2016). Mitigation of black hole attacks in routing protocol for low power and lossy networks, *Security and Communication Networks*, 9(18), 5143-5154. SCN-16-0443.R1.

32. Pirzada, A.A., & McDonald, C. (2005). Circumventing sinkholes and wormholes in wireless sensor networks. In *International Workshop on Wireless Ad-Hoc Networks*.

33. Zhang, K., Liang, X., Lu, R., & Shen, X. (2014). Sybil attacks and their defenses in the internet of things. *IEEE Internet of Things Journal*, 1(5), 372-383. http://dx.doi.org/10.1109/JIOT.2014.2344013.

34. Wang, G., Mohanlal, M., Wilson, C., Wang, X., Metzger, M., Zheng, H., & Zhao, B.Y. (2013). Social turing tests: Crowdsourcing sybil detection. In *Symposium on Network and Distributed System Security*, NDSS.

35. Granjal, J., Monteiro, E., & Silva, J. S. (2014). Network-layer security for the Internet of Things using TinyOS and BLIP. *International Journal of Communication Systems*, 27(10), 1938-1963. http://dx.doi.org/10.1002/dac.2444.

36. Raza, S., Duquennoy, S., Chung, T., Yazar, D., Voigt, T., & Roedig, U. (2011, June). Securing communication in 6LoWPAN with compressed IPsec. In *2011 International Conference on Distributed Computing in Sensor Systems and Workshops (DCOSS)* (pp.1-8). IEEE. http://dx.doi.org/10.1109/DCOSS.2011.5982177.

37. Granjal, J., Monteiro, E., & Silva, J. S. (2010, December). Enabling network-layer security on IPv6 wireless sensor networks. In *2010 IEEE Global Telecommunications Conference GLOBECOM 2010* (pp. 1-6). IEEE. http://dx.doi.org/10.1109/GLOCOM.2010.5684293.

38. Brachmann, M., Garcia-Morchon, O., & Kirsche, M. (2011). Security for practical coap applications: Issues and solution approaches. In *10th GI/ITG KuVS Fachgesprch Sensornetze (FGSN 2011)*. University Stuttgart.

39. Raza, S., Voigt, T., & Jutvik, V. (2012, March). Lightweight IKEv2: a key management solution for both the compressed IPsec and the IEEE 802.15. 4 security. In *Proceedings of the IETF workshop on smart object security* (Vol. 23).

40. Park, N., & Kang, N. (2016). Mutual authentication scheme in secure internet of things technology for comfortable lifestyle. *Sensors*, 16(1), 20.

41. Ibrahim, M. H. (2016). Octopus: An edge-fog mutual authentication scheme. *International Journal Network Security*, 18(6), 1089-1101.

42. Zhou, J., Cao, Z., Dong, X., & Vasilakos, A. V. (2017). Security and privacy for cloud-based IoT: Challenges. *IEEE Communications Magazine*, 55(1), 26-33. http://dx.doi.org/10.1109/MCOM.2017.1600363CM.

43. Henze, M., Wolters, B., Matzutt, R., Zimmermann, T., & Wehrle, K. (2017, August). Distributed configuration, authorization and management in the cloud-based internet of things. In *2017 IEEE Trustcom/BigDataSE/ICESS* (pp. 185-192). IEEE. http://dx.doi.org/10.1109/Trustcom/BigDataSE/ICESS.2017.236.

44. Thakur, B. S., & Chaudhary, S. (2013). Content sniffing attack detection in client and server side: A survey. *International Journal of Advanced Computer Research*, 3(2), 7.

45. Mitrokotsa, A., Rieback, M. R., & Tanenbaum, A. S. (2010). Classification of RFID attacks. *Gen*, 15693(14443), 14.

46. Soni, V., Modi, P., & Chaudhri, V. (2013). Detecting Sinkhole attack in wireless sensor network. *International Journal of Application or Innovation in Engineering & Management*, 2(2), 29-32.

47. Padhy, R. P., Patra, M. R., & Satapathy, S. C. (2011). Cloud computing: security issues and research challenges. *International Journal of Computer Science and Information Technology & Security (IJCSITS)*, 1(2), 136-146.

48. Newsome, J., Shi, E., Song, D., & Perrig, A. (2004, April). The sybil attack in sensor networks: analysis & defenses. In *International Symposium on Information Processing in Sensor Networks, 2004. IPSN 2004* (pp. 259-268). IEEE.

49. Brachmann, M., Keoh, S. L., Morchon, O. G., & Kumar, S. S. (2012, July). End-to-end transport security in the IP-based internet of things. In *2012 21st International Conference on Computer Communications and Networks (ICCCN)* (pp. 1-5). IEEE. http://dx.doi.org/10.1109/ICCCN.2012.6289292.

50. Granjal, J., Monteiro, E., & Silva, J. S. (2013, June). Application-layer security for the WoT: Extending CoAP to support end-to-end message security for Internet-integrated sensing applications. In *International Conference on Wired/Wireless Internet Communication* (pp. 140-153). Springer, Berlin, Heidelberg.

51. Sethi, M., Arkko, J., & Keranen, A. (2012, October). End-to-end security for sleepy smart object networks. In *37th Annual IEEE Conference on Local Computer Networks-Workshops* (pp. 964-972). IEEE. http://dx.doi.org/10.1109/LCNW.2012.6424089

52. OWASP, Top IoT Vulnerabilities, (2016). URL https://www.owasp.org/index. php/-Top_IoT_Vulnerabilities.

53. Conzon, D., Bolognesi, T., Brizzi, P., Lotito, A., Tomasi, R., & Spirito, M. A. (2012, July). The virtus middleware: An xmpp based architecture for secure iot communications. In *2012

21st International Conference on Computer Communications and Networks (ICCCN) (pp. 1-6). IEEE. http://dx.doi.org/10.1109/ICCCN.2012.6289309.

54. Liu, C. H., Yang, B., & Liu, T. (2014). Efficient naming, addressing and profile services in Internet-of-Things sensory environments. *Ad Hoc Networks*, 18, 85-101. http://dx.doi.org/10.1016/j.adhoc.2013.02.008.

55. Puthal, D., Malik, N., Mohanty, S. P., Kougianos, E., & Das, G. (2018). Everything you wanted to know about the blockchain: Its promise, components, processes, and problems. *IEEE Consumer Electronics Magazine*, 7(4), 6-14.

56. Swan, M. (2015). *Blockchain: Blueprint for a New Economy*, 1st ed. O'Reilly Media.

57. Tschorsch, F., & Scheuermann, B. (2016). Bitcoin and beyond: A technical survey on decentralized digital currencies. *IEEE Communications Surveys & Tutorials*, 18(3), 2084-2123.

58. Nakamoto, S. (2018). Bitcoin: A peer-to-peer electronic cash system, 2008. Available online: https://bitcoin.org/bitcoin.pdf. (Accessed 1 February 2018).

59. Antonopoulos, A. M. (2014). *Mastering Bitcoin: Unlocking Digital Cryptocurrencies*, O'Reilly Media, Inc.

60. Zheng, Z., Xie, S., Dai, H. N., Chen, X., & Wang, H. (2018). Blockchain challenges and opportunities: A survey. *International Journal of Web and Grid Services*, 14(4), 352-375.

61. Pilkington, M. (2016). Blockchain technology: principles and applications. In *Research Handbook on Digital Transformations*. Edward Elgar Publishing.

62. Tapscott, D., & Tapscott, A. (2016). *Blockchain Revolution: How the Technology behind Bitcoin Is Changing Money, Business, and the World*. Penguin Random House LLC, New York, NY.

63. Kosba, A., Miller, A., Shi, E., Wen, Z., & Papamanthou, C. (2016, May). Hawk: The blockchain model of cryptography and privacy-preserving smart contracts. In *2016 IEEE Symposium on Security and Privacy (SP)* (pp. 839-858). IEEE. doi: 10.1109/SP.2016.55.

64. Wright, A., & De Filippi, P. (2015). Decentralized blockchain technology and the rise of lex cryptographia. Available at SSRN 2580664. https://ssrn.com/abstract=2580664.

65. Xu, X., Pautasso, C., Zhu, L., Gramoli, V., Ponomarev, A., Tran, A. B., & Chen, S. (2016, April). The blockchain as a software connector. In *2016 13th Working IEEE/IFIP Conference on Software Architecture (WICSA)* (pp. 182-191). IEEE. doi: 10.1109/WICSA.2016.21.

66. Merkle, R. C. (1987, August). A digital signature based on a conventional encryption function. In *Conference on the Theory and Application of Cryptographic Techniques* (pp. 369-378). Springer, Berlin, Heidelberg. Lecture Notes in Computer Science. vol.293. p.369. doi:10.1007/3-540-48184-2_32.

67. Atzei, N., Bartoletti, M., Lande, S., & Zunino, R. (2018, February). A formal model of Bitcoin transactions. In *International Conference on Financial Cryptography and Data Security* (pp. 541-560). Springer, Berlin, Heidelberg. Available at https://eprint.iacr.org/2017/1124.pdf

68. Minoli, D., & Occhiogrosso, B., (2018). Blockchain mechanisms for IoT security. *Internet of Things*. 1-2, 1-13. DOI: 10.1016/j.iot.2018.05.002.

69. Reyna, A., Martin, C., Chen, J., Soler, E., & Diaz, M. (2018). On blockchain and its integration with IoT. Challenges and opportunities. *Future Generation Computer Systems*, 88, 173-190. DOI: 10.1016/j.future.2018.05.046.

70. Lin, I. C., & Liao, T. C. (2017). A survey of blockchain security issues and challenges. *International Journal Network Security*, 19(5), 653-659.

71. Kumar, N. M., & Mallick, P. K. (2018). Blockchain technology for security issues and challenges in IoT. *Procedia Computer Science*, 132, 1815-1823. 132. 1815-1823. 10.1016/j.procs.2018.05.140.

72. Bonneau, J., Narayanan, A., Miller, A., Clark, J., Kroll, J. A., & Felten, E. W. (2014, March). Mixcoin: Anonymity for bitcoin with accountable mixes. In *International Conference on Financial Cryptography and Data Security* (pp. 486-504). Springer, Berlin, Heidelberg.

73. Kshetri, N. (2017). Can blockchain strengthen the internet of things?. *IT professional*, 19(4), 68-72. DOI: 10.1109/MITP.2017.3051335

74. Ferrag, M. A., Derdour, M., Mukherjee, M., Derhab, A., Maglaras, L., & Janicke, H. (2018). Blockchain technologies for the internet of things: Research issues and challenges. *IEEE Internet of Things Journal*, 6(2), 2188-2204.

75. De La Rosa, J. L., Torres-Padrosa, V., El-Fakdi, A., Gibovic, D., Hornyk, O., Maicher, L., & Miralles, F. (2017, December). A survey of blockchain technologies for open innovation. In *Proceedings of the 4th Annual World Open Innovation Conference* (pp. 14-15).

76. Dorri, A., Kanhere, S. S., Jurdak, R., & Gauravaram, P. (2017, March). Blockchain for IoT security and privacy: The case study of a smart home. In *2017 IEEE International Conference on Pervasive Computing and Communications Workshops (PerCom workshops)* (pp. 618-623). IEEE.

77. Conoscenti, M., Vetro, A., & De Martin, J. C. (2016, November). Blockchain for the Internet of Things: A systematic literature review. In *2016 IEEE/ACS 13th International Conference of Computer Systems and Applications (AICCSA)* (pp. 1-6). IEEE. DOI: 10.1109/AICCSA.2016.7945805

78. Samaniego, M., & Deters, R. (2016, December). Blockchain as a service for IoT. In *2016 IEEE International Conference on Internet of Things (iThings) and IEEE Green Computing and Communications (GreenCom) and IEEE Cyber, Physical and Social Computing (CPSCom) and IEEE Smart Data (SmartData)* (pp. 433-436). IEEE. DOI: 10.1109/iThings-GreenCom-CPSCom-SmartData.2016.102

79. Huh, S., Cho, S., & Kim, S. (2017, February). Managing IoT devices using blockchain platform. In *2017 19th international conference on advanced communication technology (ICACT)* (pp. 464-467). IEEE. DOI: 10.23919/ICACT.2017.7890132

80. Macdonald, M., Liu-Thorrold, L., & Julien, R. (2017). The blockchain: A comparison of platforms and their uses beyond bitcoin. *COMS4507-Adv. Computer Network Security*. DOI: 10.13140/RG.2.2.23274.52164.

81. McGoogan, C. (2017). The end of passport gates? Dubai to test "invisible" airport checks using facial recognition, in: *The Telegraph*, http://www.telegraph.co.uk/technology/2017/06/13/end-passport-gates-dubai-test-invisible-airport-check s-using/. (Accessed 20 October 2017).

82. How to get an Illinois Birth Certificate online, (2017). https://vital-records.us/order-an-illinois-birth-certificate/. (Accessed 20 October 2017).

83. Biswas, K., & Muthukkumarasamy, V. (2016, December). Securing smart cities using blockchain technology. In *2016 IEEE 18th International Conference on High Performance Computing and Communications; IEEE 14th International Conference on Smart City; IEEE 2nd International Conference on Data Science and Systems (HPCC/SmartCity/DSS)* (pp. 1392-1393). IEEE.

84. Zheng, Z., Xie, S., Dai, H. N., Chen, X., & Wang, H. (2018). Blockchain challenges and opportunities: A survey. *International Journal of Web and Grid Services*, 14(4), 352-375.

85. Li, X., Jiang, P., Chen, T., Luo, X., & Wen, Q. (2017). A survey on the security of blockchain systems. *Future Generation Computer Systems*. DOI: 10.1016/j.future.2017.08.020.

86. Srivastava, S. R., Dube, S., Shrivastava, G., & Sharma, K. (2019). Smartphone triggered security challenges - Issues, case studies and prevention. *Cyber Security in Parallel and Distributed Computing: Concepts, Techniques, Applications and Case Studies*, 187-206.

87. Ahmad, F. A., Kumar, P., Shrivastava, G., & Bouhlel, M. S. (2018). Bitcoin: Digital decentralized cryptocurrency. In *Handbook of Research on Network Forensics and Analysis Techniques* (pp. 395-415). IGI Global.

88. Shrivastava, G., Kumar, P., Gupta, B. B., Bala, S., & Dey, N. (Eds.). (2018). *Handbook of Research on Network Forensics and Analysis Techniques*. IGI Global.

89. Sharma, K., & Shrivastava, G. (2014). Public key infrastructure and trust of Web based knowledge discovery. *Int. J. Eng., Sci. Manage.*, 4(1), 56-60

90. Sharma, K., Rafiqui, F., Attri, P., & Yadav, S. K. (2019). A two-tier security solution for storing data across public cloud. *Recent Patents on Computer Science*, 12(3), 191-201.

91. Sicuranza, M., & Esposito, A. (2013, December). An access control model for easy management of patient privacy in EHR systems. In *8th International Conference for Internet Technology and Secured Transactions (ICITST-2013)* (pp. 463-470). IEEE.

92. Liang, X., Shetty, S., Tosh, D., Kamhoua, C., Kwiat, K., & Njilla, L. (2017, May). Provchain: A blockchain-based data provenance architecture in cloud environment with enhanced privacy and availability. In *Proceedings of the 17th IEEE/ACM International Symposium on Cluster, Cloud and Grid Computing* (pp. 468-477). IEEE Press.

93. Aitzhan, N. Z., & Svetinovic, D. (2016). Security and privacy in decentralized energy trading through multi-signatures, blockchain and anonymous messaging streams. *IEEE Transactions on Dependable and Secure Computing*, 15(5), 840-852.

94. Fan, K., Ren, Y., Wang, Y., Li, H., & Yang, Y. (2017). Blockchain-based efficient privacy preserving and data sharing scheme of content-centric network in 5G. *IET Communications*, 12(5), 527-532.

95. Lei, A., Cruickshank, H., Cao, Y., Asuquo, P., Ogah, C. P. A., & Sun, Z. (2017). Blockchain-based dynamic key management for heterogeneous intelligent transportation systems. *IEEE Internet of Things Journal*, 4(6), 1832-1843.

96. Kang, J., Yu, R., Huang, X., Maharjan, S., Zhang, Y., & Hossain, E. (2017). Enabling localized peer-to-peer electricity trading among plug-in hybrid electric vehicles using consortium blockchains. *IEEE Transactions on Industrial Informatics*, 13(6), 3154-3164.

97. Noor, S., Yang, W., Guo, M., van Dam, K. H., & Wang, X. (2018). Energy demand side management within micro-grid networks enhanced by blockchain. *Applied Energy*, 228, 1385-1398.

98. Gu, J., Sun, B., Du, X., Wang, J., Zhuang, Y., & Wang, Z. (2018). Consortium blockchain-based malware detection in mobile devices. *IEEE Access*, 6, 12118-12128.

99. Herbaut, N., & Negru, N. (2017). A model for collaborative blockchain-based video delivery relying on advanced network services chains. *IEEE Communications Magazine*, 55(9), 70-76.

100. He, Y., Li, H., Cheng, X., Liu, Y., Yang, C., & Sun, L. (2018). A blockchain based truthful incentive mechanism for distributed P2P applications. *IEEE Access*, 6, 27324-27335.

101. Yin, W., Wen, Q., Li, W., Zhang, H., & Jin, Z. (2018). An anti-quantum transaction authentication approach in blockchain. *IEEE Access*, 6, 5393-5401.

CHAPTER 7

CHAOS CONTROL DYNAMICS OF CRYPTOVIROLOGY IN BLOCKCHAIN

RASHMI BHARDWAJ[1] AND SAUREESH DAS[2]

[1]Non-Linear Dynamics Research Lab, University School of Basic & Applied Sciences, Guru Gobind Singh Indraprastha University, Dwarka, Delhi, India
[2]University School of Basic & Applied Sciences, Guru Gobind Singh Indraprastha University, Indraprastha University, Delhi, India

Corresponding authors: rashmib@ipu.ac.in; rashmib22@gmail.com

Abstract

The study in this chapter deals with the dynamics of worm propagation in cryptovirology. An epidemic SEI nonlinear model is applied to study the viral propagation of worm in cyber networks and systems and the effect of rate of susceptibility of vulnerable system on the dynamics of the model is analyzed. Using stability and bifurcation analysis, the parameter values for stable limit cycle and chaotic states are determined and observed through numerical simulation. The stable and chaotic dynamic for worm propagation in cyber network is simulated for different values of rate or coefficient of decay (d); susceptibility of system (b) and coefficient of encounter with infected system during worm attack (k). From time series and phase plots, it is observed that for $d_1 = 5$, $d_2 = 1$, $d_3 = 1$, $b_1 = 11$, $b_2 = 6$, $k_1 = 2$, and $k_2 = 1$, a stable limit cycle exists and for $T = 0.4$, $d = 0.08$ and $U = 0.8$ chaotic state exists. As b1=16 or susceptibility of vulnerable system is increased the system becomes chaotic.

For controlling of chaotic dynamics, two identical chaotic systems are synchronized using active control scheme. For stabilizing the synchronization errors and to control chaos controllers, Lyapunov function is used. The controllers are applied to the system and through simulation controlling of chaos is observed. Time instant by which controllers are synchronized and chaos is controlled after activation at $t = 1000$ is tabulated and given below: It is concluded that the Controller 1 is faster and has lesser level of interaction terms than Controller 2. The increase in susceptibility of vulnerable system leads the system to chaotic state from which the stability of the system can be restored by synchronizing it with another identical system in stable state using controllers derived from Lyapunov function. The proposed controllers are useful for controlling the chaotic state to stable state in cryptovirology in blockchain.

Keywords: Security, blockchain, cybersecurity

7.1   Introduction

Today's era is an internet era; the internet is used as a powerful tool for communication and cyber transactions, and in cyber networks most computers are interconnected through the same operating software. Also, in the present era, the internet has become the primary medium for cybercrime. Cybercrimes are committed by developing malicious codes or programs which invade private and public computers, gathering information and posing a security threat. The highest risks faced by computer networks are from viral malware or worm propagation which target the software vulnerability. This powerful malicious software is designed in Cryptovirology using cryptography. In a study by Kephart *et al.*, computer epidemiology is discussed elaborately [1]. They drew analogies from the biological disease propagation and showed that the spread of computer virus can be modeled with epidemiological models. The study also shed light on the fact that the computer virus propagation can be contained and many viruses fail to thrive in the presence of effective centralized response system in defense. The effect of infection dynamics on scale-free networks was studied by May and Lloyd [2] where the effect of finite population sizes was discussed, showing that infection cannot spread in the case of low transmission probabilities. In cybercrimes the security of critical networks is targeted and chaotic or erratic behavior is introduced in their performance, leading to disruption in the complete system. In most of the cases, the malware is sent to the targeted computer in the network through an email. The spread of computer viruses in email network was studied by Newman *et al.* [3]. Zhou *et al.* modeled and analyzed the worm propagation under quarantine defense [4]. The connection between the networks and epidemic models is discussed in the work of Keeling and Eammes [5]. In their study, Yuan and Chen analyzed the network virus epidemic model in the case of a point-to-point infection propagation. It is shown through simulation that a proposed model can be significant in understanding the viral epidemics in network systems [6]. The threshold case in viral networks was discussed by Drief *et al.* [7]. In the work of Picqueria, a modified epidemiological model for computer viruses is introduced [8]. The dynamical behavior of computer viruses on the internet was studied by Ham and Tan [9]. The worm transmission model and its nonlinear dynamics in cyber warfare was analyzed by Mishra and Prajapati [10]. In 2019, for understanding the working aspects of blockchain systems a queuing-theory-based model was proposed and discussed in [11].

Bitcoin currencies are not considered an ideal means of payment due to the fact that in the short term the bitcoin prices fluctuate a lot, while in the long term the prices tend to rise higher. In the work of Saito and Iwamura, measures for stabilization of the Bitcoin prices were proposed for which design checks were developed through simple simulations [12]. But besides the pricing issues, the security of a blockchain system such as Bitcoin's is under serious threat. In recent times, blockchain security vulnerabilities have become an issue to distributed ledger technology. The distributed ledger technology is not immune to vulnerabilities from malware or worm propagation, though the security features inherent in blockchain make it resistant to attacks. The malware is sent to the user through emails in the network [3]. The spread of the virus can be considered to be analogical with the biological viral spread and the whole system can be modeled based on an SEI (Susceptible-Exposed-Infected) model. The global stability of an SEI epidemic model with general contact rate was studied by Li and Zhen [13]. The study of malware propagation by modeling is significant, as the spread of virus can be contained within limits in time, optimizing the cost borne due to damaging of computers in the network. The SIS model of worm infection with cost optimization was analyzed by Kim *et al.* [14]. The identification of chaos in the system is crucial to contain the spread of computer virus in the network from reaching a state of randomness. The first mathematical observation of chaos was made by Lorenz [15]. Chaos is encountered in different kinds of nonlinear systems in different fields of science like chemistry [26], physics [17-20], and finance [21, 22].

Another important aspect is synchronization of epidemic networks for the control of chaos through synchronization. Bai and Lonngren demonstrated the synchronization of two Lorenz systems using active control [23]. Different kinds of synchronization are feasible to control chaos. The concept of mixed synchronization using scalar coupling is discussed in the work of Bhomick *et al.* [24]. In the work of Das *et al.* [15], hybrid phase synchronization between identical and non-identical systems using active control method is shown. The anti-synchronization via sliding control for a four-dimensional system for control of chaos is demonstrated in a study of Sundarapandian and Sivaperumal [25]. Active control is one of the most utilized schemes of synchronizing both identical and non-identical systems. In their study, Ablay and Aldemir studied synchronization of different chaotic systems using generalized active control [26]. An identical Sprott system just by using active control synchronization is discussed in the work of Daskiwicz [27]. Synchronization can be helpful in restoring stability of cyber networks in chaotic state under viral attack.

The present study deals with the dynamics of worm propagation in cryptovirology based on SEI nonlinear epidemic model. The epidemic nonlinear model [10] is applied to study the viral propagation of worm in cyber network systems and the effect of rate of worm infection and rate of crashing nodes on dynamics of the model is analyzed. Stability analysis is carried out to determine the equilibrium points and their stability conditions using the Routh-Hurwitz theorem. Phase portraits are obtained for the limit cycle and chaotic state through numerical simulation. Bifurcation analysis is carried out to observe the change in dynamics with change in values of rate of crashing node as the bifurcation parameter. The Lyapunov exponent and Hurst exponent are calculated to substantiate the observations in bifurcation analysis. For controlling chaotic dynamics, two identical chaotic systems are synchronized using active control scheme. For stabilizing the synchronization errors and to control chaos controllers, the Lyapunov function is used. The controllers are applied to the system and through simulation controlling of chaos is observed. The increase in rate of worm infection leads the system to chaotic state from which the stability of the system can be restored by synchronizing it with another identical system in stable state using controllers derived from Lyapunov function. The proposed controllers are useful for controlling the chaotic state to stable state in cryptovirology in blockchain [28-30].

7.2   Mathematical Modeling and Stability Analysis

In this section the basic system of the blockchain distributed ledger technology and modeling of the system of study is explained. For modeling malware propagation in blockchain system it is important to first understand the participants and their interactions in the system network. A blockchain system is public digital, distributed, and decentralized ledger which is used to handle records transactions between several computers. Without the alterations of all subsequent blocks no individual record can be altered in a block. Collectively adhering to protocol of inter-node communication and validating new blocks on a peer-to-peer network basis the blockchain is managed for its use as a distributed ledger. Malware propagation is one of the potential threats to the blockchain systems. In 2016, families of ransomware primarily used for acquiring cryptocurrency exploded in number. In the case of cryptocurrencies like Bitcoin, blockchain technology is employed to maintain a distributed decentralized public ledger of all the bitcoin transactions. After verification, the new batch of bitcoin transactions get uploaded to the blockchain. As blockchain is decentralized ledger, this data gets downloaded to every computer which runs the Bitcoin software. The problem is that besides the bitcoin transactions all kinds of files including malware can be uploaded to the blockchain. Once the file gets uploaded in blockchain and hence on every computer of the Bitcoin network, it is hard to get rid of it. The blockchain network possesses security features to make it resistant to malware viral attacks, but with the variety of malware evolving, the system remains vulnerable and thus is potentially threatened by the viral spread of malware. It is thus significant to model and analyze the dynamics of virus propagation in such cyber networks based on analogies of biological models.

Let us now consider a Bitcoin network to which computers are connected as nodes of the network with their transactions getting recorded in the blockchain decentralized ledger. As the malware file is uploaded in the blockchain it spreads to all the computers connected in the bitcoin network. Some of the computers might have an antivirus software which is capable of handling the malware attack and protects the system. This class of computers are defined as protected computers in the model. Contrary to this there can be computers in the network with antivirus software which is not upgraded enough to counter the malware and protect the system. Such systems fall into the category of the vulnerable class in the model. The malware files effectively ensure their sustenance on the vulnerability of the host computer and they evolve fast. Thus, malware and the vulnerable class of computers in the system promote each other's existence and growth. If the number of vulnerable class of computers is high in the system, malware spreads more and effects the network. As the number of malware viruses in the network system increase, more computers enter the vulnerable class with high susceptibility. The old malware leaves the network as the new variety of malware gets introduced. The decay rate of malware viruses is assumed to be higher, as they get replaced faster by new varieties. Each system in the network has a crashing or decay rate by which it leaves the network irrespective of presence of a malware or not. On one side, a direct interaction between the malware virus and vulnerable class of computers takes place; while on the other side, the malware virus encounter with protected class of computers takes place in the network. If the encounter between the malware virus and protected class of computers is high then the number of computers in the vulnerable class is reduced. While if the interaction between the virus and vulnerable class of computers is increased, it leads to an upgrade in the defense system of affected vulnerable systems which leads to the protected class of computers, increasing the number of protected systems in the network.

The whole model of virus propagation in blockchain network thus comprises population of virus class of malware, vulnerable class of computers with old antivirus software and protected class of computers with effective antivirus to counter the malware. The VVP model discussed in this study is based on basic Type I population interactions between the Virus-Vulnerable and Protected class. It is different from other epidemiological models like SEIR (Susceptible, Exposed, Infected and Recovered) or SIR (Susceptible, Infected and Recovered) or SIS (Susceptible, Infected and Susceptible), as it also takes into account the evolution of virus class over time, which is crucial while modeling the blockchain, as malware viral class is highly evolving, increasing the cybersecurity risk of cryptocurrency network like Bitcoin. In Figure 7.1 a schematic diagram of the model is shown.

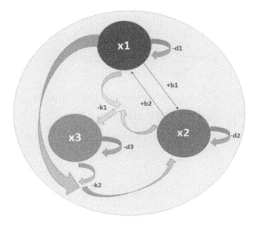

Figure 7.1 Schematic diagram of the VVP model.

Let x_1, x_2 and x_3 represent the three population levels of the malware virus, vulnerable systems and protected systems class. The model is described by the following equations:

$$\dot{x_1} = -d_1 x_1 + b_2 x_2 \tag{7.1}$$

$$\dot{x_2} = -d_2 x_2 + b_1 x_1 - k_2 x_1 x_3 \tag{7.2}$$

$$\dot{x_3} = -d_3 x_3 + k_1 x_1 x_2 \tag{7.3}$$

where the parameters are defined as

- d_1 is the coefficient of decay of virus;

- d_2 is the coefficient of decay of vulnerable systems;

- d_3 is the coefficient of decay of protected systems;

- b_1 is the coefficient of susceptibility of vulnerable system;

- b_2 is the coefficient of availability of vulnerable system;

- k_1 is the coefficient of encounter between virus and protected systems;

- k_2 is the coefficient of interaction between virus and vulnerable system.

As the model is based on interaction between the malware viral classes, the vulnerable class of computers with inefficient antivirus and protected class of computer with efficient antivirus are being developed. It will be interesting to see how the dynamics of the system evolve as the above-mentioned parameter values change. The basic nonlinear tools are applied to study the system evolution such as stability analysis, phase space analysis, time series analysis, bifurcation analysis and Lyapunov exponent analysis. The methodology is briefly described as follows:

- Stability analysis yields the parametric conditions which govern the stability of the steady-state solution of the system or fixed points of the system.

- After this, in phase space analysis and time series analysis the phase space plots and time series plots are plotted, through which the theories of system dynamics evolution obtained from stability analysis are verified.

- As the chaotic stage is detected, we next move to bifurcation analysis and determination of Hurst exponent and Lyapunov exponent.

- The bifurcation analysis give us the parametric condition for which either Hopf bifurcation or period-doubling bifurcation take place which serve as routes to chaos.

- The Hurst exponents help verify the increase in anti-persistence behavior of the time series due to increase in randomness of system as the dynamic state enters chaotic regime.

- The evaluation of Lyapunov exponent gives the final confirmation of existence of chaos as it measures the rate at which trajectories diverge.

- Finally, the chaos is controlled by synchronizing the chaotic systems by applying controllers designed from Lyapunov function.

7.2.1 Fixed-Point Analysis

The equations of the system mentioned above describe a nonlinear system and so it is required to carry out its fixed-point or stability analysis. It is important to recall the basic concepts of the stability theory before starting with the fixed-point analysis. Let us consider the first-order system of ordinary differential equation given as follows:

$$\frac{dv}{dt} = f(v), \quad v(t_0) = v_0 \tag{7.4}$$

where $v \in D$, $t \in R^+$. D is an open subset of R^n and $D = R^n$ in most cases. The system of differential equation is autonomous as there is no explicit dependency of the system on time (t). The point v^* is the fixed point of $\frac{dv}{dt} = f(v)$, i.e., $f(v^*) = 0$.

In analyzing fixed point it is important to linearize the differential equation in the neighborhood. Let f be analytic so it can be Taylor expanded about the neighborhood of v^*. In linearizing, the higher order terms are neglected. In the case of $\frac{dv}{dt} = f(v)$ it can be written in the neighborhood of the fixed point v^* as:

$$\frac{dv}{dt} = \frac{\partial f}{\partial v}(v - v^*) + \text{terms of higher order} \tag{7.5}$$

where the linear differential equation $\frac{dy}{dt} = \frac{\partial f}{\partial v}(v^*)(x - v^*)$ is studied. The Jacobian or functional matrix is defined as the $n \times n$ matrix $\frac{\partial f}{\partial v}$. The fixed point v^* is shifted by

$\overline{y} = u - a$ for simplifying of notation. This implies $\frac{d\overline{y}}{dt} = \frac{\partial f}{\partial v}(v^*)\overline{y}$, which leads to the linearized form of the system in the neighborhood of fixed point v^* can be written as:

$\Rightarrow \frac{dy}{dt} = Ay$, where A is a $n \times n$-dimensional matrix with constant coefficients.

In stability analysis the first step is to determine the fixed or equilibrium points of the system. The Jacobian matrix of the model and the characteristic equation are then evaluated. From the Jacobian the characteristic equation is formed. The parametric conditions for the stability of the fixed points from the Jacobian is derived by putting the fixed points in the Jacobian and characteristic equation using the Routh-Hurwitz criteria, which states that if for a fixed point v^* the characteristic equation is given by:

$$\lambda^3 + e_1\lambda^2 + e_2\lambda + e_3 = 0 \tag{7.6}$$

Then the fixed point v^* is stable if:

- Condition 1: $e_1 > 0$

- Condition 2: $e_3 > 0$

- Condition 3: $e_1 e_2 - e_3 > 0$

The fixed points for the system in equation (3.1) are evaluated by simultaneously equating all the individual differential equations in equation (3.1).

The evaluated three fixed points are as follow:

- Fixed Point 1: $(0, 0, 0)$,

- Fixed Point 2: $\left(\sqrt{\frac{(b_1 b_2 - d_1 d_2)d_3}{d_1 k_1 k_2}}, \frac{d_1}{b_2}\sqrt{\frac{(b_1 b_2 - d_1 d_2)d_3}{d_1 k_1 k_2}}, \frac{(b_1 b_2 - d_1 d_2)}{b_2 k_2} \right)$

- Fixed Point 3: $\left(-\sqrt{\frac{(b_1 b_2 - d_1 d_2)d_3}{d_1 k_1 k_2}}, -\frac{d_1}{b_2}\sqrt{\frac{(b_1 b_2 - d_1 d_2)d_3}{d_1 k_1 k_2}}, \frac{(b_1 b_2 - d_1 d_2)}{b_2 k_2} \right)$

The Jacobian of the system in equation (3.1) is given as follows:

$$Jacobian = \begin{pmatrix} -d_1 & b_2 & 0 \\ b_1 - k_2 x_3 & -d_2 & -k_2 x_1 \\ k_1 x_2 & k_1 x_1 & -d_3 \end{pmatrix} \tag{7.7}$$

Now these fixed points are put in the Jacobian to determine the parametric conditions for stability of the fixed point. The Fixed Point 2 and Fixed Point 3 show invariance under the transformation $(x, y, z) \to (-x, -y, -z)$ and the same results are obtained for having the same behavior and conditions of stability.

7.2.1.1   *Case I*

For fixed point the Jacobian is derived as follows:

$$Jacobian = \begin{pmatrix} -d_1 & b_2 & 0 \\ b_1 & -d_2 & 0 \\ 0 & 0 & -d_3 \end{pmatrix}$$

For this the characteristic equation is given as follows:

$$\lambda^3 + e_1\lambda^2 + e_2\lambda + e_3 = 0$$

where

- $e_1 = (d_1 + d_2 + d_3)$;

- $e_2 = (d_2 d_1 + d_1 d_3 + d_2 d_3 - b_1 b_2)$;

- $e_3 = (-d_3)(b_1 b_2 - d_1 d_2)$.

From Routh-Hurwitz criteria for stability at fixed point $(0, 0, 0)$ it is required that

$$b_1 < \left(\frac{d_1 d_2}{b_2} \right) = b_\alpha$$

The system is asymptotically stable when $b_1 < b_\alpha$, critically stable when $b_1 = b_\alpha$ and unstable when $b_1 > b_\alpha$.

7.2.1.2 Case II

The fixed point

$$\left(\sqrt{\frac{(b_1 b_2 - d_1 d_2)\, d_3}{d_1 k_1 k_2}}, \frac{d_1}{b_2} \sqrt{\frac{(b_1 b_2 - d_1 d_2)\, d_3}{d_1 k_1 k_2}}, \frac{(b_1 b_2 - d_1 d_2)}{b_2 k_2} \right)$$

and

$$\left(-\sqrt{\frac{(b_1 b_2 - d_1 d_2)\, d_3}{d_1 k_1 k_2}}, -\frac{d_1}{b_2} \sqrt{\frac{(b_1 b_2 - d_1 d_2)\, d_3}{d_1 k_1 k_2}}, \frac{(b_1 b_2 - d_1 d_2)}{b_2 k_2} \right)$$

show invariance and so have the same conditions of stability. The Jacobian for these fixed points are as follows:

$$Jacobian = \begin{pmatrix} -d_1 & b_2 & 0 \\ b_1 - k_2 \frac{(b_1 b_2 - d_1 d_2)}{b_2 k_2} & -d_2 & -k_2 \sqrt{\frac{(b_1 b_2 - d_1 d_2) d_3}{d_1 k_1 k_2}} \\ k_1 \frac{d_1}{b_2} \sqrt{\frac{(b_1 b_2 - d_1 d_2) d_3}{d_1 k_1 k_2}} & k_1 \sqrt{\frac{(b_1 b_2 - d_1 d_2) d_3}{d_1 k_1 k_2}} & -d_3 \end{pmatrix}$$

The characteristic equation for the fixed point is given as follows:

$$\lambda^3 + e_1 \lambda^2 + e_2 \lambda + e_3 = 0$$

where

- $e_1 = (d_1 + d_2 + d_3)$;

- $e_2 = \left(\frac{d_3 (d_1^2 + b_2 b_1)}{d_1} \right)$;

- $e_3 = 2(d_3)(b_1 b_2 - d_1 d_2)$.

Thus, for stability it is required that

$$b_\alpha < b_1 < b_\kappa$$

where

- $b_\alpha = \left(\frac{d_1 d_2}{b_2} \right)$;

- $b_\kappa = \frac{(d_1+d_2+d_3)(d_1{}^2)+2(d_1{}^2 d_2)}{b_2(2d_1-(d_1+d_2+d_3))}$;

- b_κ is the threshold critical value of b_1.

The system is asymptotically stable when $b_\alpha < b_1 < b_\kappa$, critically stable when $b_1 = b_\kappa$, and unstable at $b_\kappa < b_1$, which finally leads to chaos.

From the stability analysis it is evident that as the values of parameter b_1 vary the stability of the fixed points vary and finally $b_\kappa < b_1$ chaos begins, leading to randomness in the system.

7.2.2 Phase Space Analysis

A mathematical space where each of the variables needed to describe the instantaneous state of the system dynamics is represented by the orthogonal coordinate directions is known as phase space. Phase space analysis is a method of analyzing the direction of flow in which the system evolves. Phase portrait is plotted between the system variables and evolution of the trajectories is then studied with variation in parameter values for the stability of fixed points. This explains how with time stability shifts from one equilibrium state to another. The transfer of stability from one equilibrium state to another determines the dynamics of the system in terms of which system variable will dominate and which will lose significance.

Numerical simulation of the above system is carried out for different values of the fixed parameters $a_1 = 1$, $a_2 = 5$, $a_3 = 1$, $b_2 = 6$, $c_1 = 2$, $c_2 = 1$; it should be $d_1 = 5$, $d_2 = 1$, $d_3 = 1$, $b_2 = 6$, $k_1 = 2$, $k_2 = 1$ as per equation (7.1)-(7.3) and varying parameter b_1. For the fixed parameter values, one gets

$$b_\alpha = \left(\frac{a_1 a_2}{b_2} \right) = 0.83$$

while

$$b_\kappa = \frac{(d_1 + d_2 + d_3)\left(d_1{}^2\right) + 2(d_1{}^2 d_2)}{b_2(2d_1 - (d_1 + d_2 + d_3))} = 11.5$$

For different values b_1 of the following conditions are observed:

- **Case I**: $b_1 = 6$, the condition $b_1 > b_\alpha$ and $b_1 < b_\kappa$ is satisfied and system is observed to be in stable state at point $(x_1, x_2, x_3) = (1.8,\ 1.1,\ 5.2)$.

- **Case II**: $b_1 = 11$, the condition $b_1 > b_\alpha$ and $b_1 \approx b_\kappa$, so critically stable state is observed at point $(x_1, x_2, x_3) = (\pm2.5,\ \pm2.0,\ 10.2)$.

- **Case III**: $b_1 = 16$, the condition $b_1 > b_\alpha$ and $b_1 > b_\kappa$, so the system is in chaotic state at point $(x_1, x_2, x_3) = (\pm3.0,\ \pm2.5,\ 15.2)$.

In Figure 7.2, the transition of dynamic state from stable to chaotic phase can be observed as the parameter b_1 is varied. Thus, choosing b_1 as the varying bifurcation parameter plotting the bifurcation plot will be helpful in understanding the evolution of dynamic states of the system with the variation in parameter b_1.

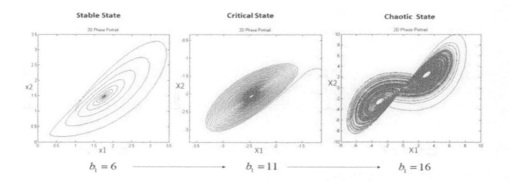

Figure 7.2   The different dynamic states observed in 2D phase space.

7.2.3   Time Series Analysis

Time series analysis is a method of analyzing the evolution of variable values with respect to time. This analysis is quintessential in explaining how the variables are separately evolving with time. Phase portrait gives the idea of how the variables together evolve but the evolution of individual variables is hard to decipher only on the basis of phase portraits, especially when chaos or state of uncertainty is encountered.

In Figure 7.3, the combined times series graph for the viral class, vulnerable class and the protected class of system are shown for the stable, critical and chaotic state of dynamics as observed in phase space analysis for $b_1 = 6$, $b_1 = 11$ and $b_{1} = 16$ respectively.

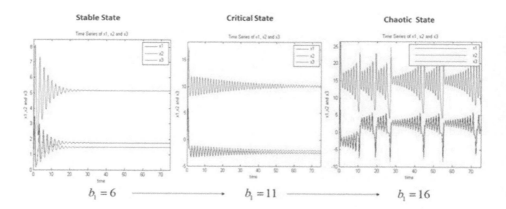

Figure 7.3   Combined time series plots for different dynamic states.

It is evident from the figure that as b_1 parameter is varied, reduction in persistence in the time series can be observed. As the dynamics state of the system enters chaotic phase the persistence of the time series that reduces the randomness gets introduced in the time series. One of the effective ways to observe the increase in anti-persistent behavior of the time series is to calculate the Hurst exponent (H). As a measure of long-term memory of a given time series, Hurst exponent is calculated. Hurst exponent relates to the autocorrelations for time series and the rate at which it reduces with the increase in the lag between the pair of values. If H is between 0.5 and 1.0 the time series is said to be persistent with long-term positive autocorrelations, implying that a high value in the time series will be followed by another high value for a long time in the future. On the other hand, if H is between 0 and 0.5 it implies switching between high and low values in adjacent pairs for the long term. If $H = 0.5$, then it implies that the time series is completely uncorrelated for which the value of autocorrelation can be positive or negative at small time lags with an exponential decay of the absolute value of autocorrelation quickly to zero.

In this study the Hurst exponent (H) is determined for the time series at $b_1 = 6$, $b_1 = 11$ and $b_1 = 16$ using dispersion analysis method. Dispersion analysis is one of the ways to calculate the Hurst exponent and involves calculation of standard deviation or variance at different group levels in which the time series is divided. Firstly, the time series is divided into groups of size m. The mean for each group is determined and its standard deviation is calculated. One proceeds and keeps calculating till the number of group is $n \leq 4$. Once the standard deviation of the means for each group is determined for different size groups a plot is made between the log values of the standard deviation to log value of the corresponding group size and its slope by power law gives the Hurst exponent.

For time series obtained at $b_1 = 6$ the Hurst exponent (H) comes to be 0.65. As b_1 is increased to the value $b_1 = 11$, H becomes 0.53. Finally, when b_1 is set to the value 16 the criteria $b_\kappa < b_1$ gets satisfied and systems become chaotic, which becomes evident with the high amount of random fluctuations in the time series for which the $H = 0.34$. This shows that as $b_\kappa < b_1$ the system transits to chaotic state.

Thus, it is important to do the bifurcation analysis as $b_\kappa < b_1$ chaos begins and Hopf bifurcation is connected to the route to chaos, in which a limit cycle evolves beginning from a fixed point. On carrying out a bifurcation analysis the parametric condition for b_1 can be determined at which the occurrence of Hopf bifurcation is possible, leading the dynamics of the system to a chaotic random phase.

7.2.4 Bifurcation Analysis

Bifurcation analysis is known as the mathematical study of the variation in the topological or qualitative structure of a given family which can be a solution of a family of differential equations or integral curves of a family of vector fields. For studying the dynamical systems with nonlinearity such studies are applied. The term "*bifurcation*" in mathematics was first introduced by Henri Poincaré in 1885. The diagram of the equilibrium or steady-state solutions of a dynamical system in terms of a varying parameter is known as a bifurcation diagram and the parameter is known as a bifurcation parameter.

A bifurcation occurs when an arbitrary continuous change introduced to the parameter values chosen as the bifurcation parameter of a system lead to an abrupt variation in topological behavior of the system quantitatively. Local and global bifurcations are the two broad categories into which bifurcations are divided.

Local bifurcations are studied entirely through the changes in the local stability properties of the equilibria, periodic orbits or other invariants as the bifurcation parameters cross through the critical threshold value. The local bifurcation takes place when the stability of the fixed or equilibrium point of system changes with the change in bifurcation. For a continuous system this implies that the real part of the eigenvalue passes through zero for the equilibrium point. As the parameter value is moved closer to the bifurcation point the topological variations in the phase portrait of the system get confined to an arbitrary small neighborhood of the bifurcating fixed point and hence the bifurcation is called local bifurcation. Now, as the real part of the eigenvalue becomes zero, local bifurcation occurs. If the eigenvalue is nonzero and purely imaginary then it is known as Hopf bifurcation, while if the eigenvalue is zero then it is known as steady-state bifurcation. Besides Hopf bifurcation, local bifurcations are further categorized into saddle, transcritical, pitchfork, flip or period doubling. If the modulus of the eigenvalue of the Jacobian is equal to 1 then it is either saddle, transcritical or pitchfork. If eigenvalue is -1 then it's period doubling and otherwise it is Hopf bifurcation with purely imaginary eigenvalues.

On the other hand, when a larger invariant set of systems collide with each other or with equilibria of the system, global bifurcation occurs. Contrary to the case of local bifurcations, the topological changes are not confined to a small neighborhood of the bifurcating fixed point and hence it is called global bifurcation. Global bifurcations cannot be detected just by the stability analysis of the equilibrium point as they involve complicated sets of chaotic attractor. Global bifurcations are further classified into homoclinic, heteroclinic, infinite period and blue sky catastrophe bifurcation. In the case of limit cycle colliding with a single saddle point, then it is homoclinic bifurcation. If two saddle points collide with the limit cycle then the bifurcation is heteroclinic. When stable node and saddle point simultaneously occur on a limit cycle then it is infinite period bifurcation. A blue sky catastrophe type of global bifurcation occurs when limit cycle collides with a non-hyperbolic cycle.

In the previous section three fixed points of the system were determined and through numerical simulation in phase space it was observed that as b_1 exceeds the threshold critical value

$$b_\kappa = \frac{(d_1 + d_2 + d_3)\,(d_1{}^2) + 2(d_1{}^2 d_2)}{b_2(2d_1 - (d_1 + d_2 + d_3))}$$

the system transits to chaotic states. The critical value acts as the point at which the Hopf bifurcation occurs, leading to chaos.

7.2.4.1   Case I

For Fixed point 1 $(x_1, x_2, x_3) = (0, 0, 0)$ the characteristic equation is as follows:

$$(\lambda + d_3)\left[\lambda^2 + (d_1 d_2)\lambda + (d_1 d_2 - b_1 b_2)\right] = 0$$

From the above equation the eigenvalue $\lambda_1 = -d_3$ and the other two eigenvalues are $\lambda_{2,3} = \frac{-(d_1+d_2)\pm\sqrt{D}}{2}$, where $D = d_1{}^2 + d_2{}^2 - 2d_1 d_2 + 4b_1 b_2$. Complex eigenvalues arise D is negative for which $b_1 < \frac{(2d_1 d_2 - d_1{}^2 d_2{}^2)}{4b_2}$. Along with this, if $d_3 = 0$ and $d_1 + d_2 = 0$ then Hopf bifurcation is possible as the eigenvalue $\lambda_1 = 0$ and $\lambda_{2,3} = \frac{\pm i\sqrt{D}}{2}$.

Now, for the system under consideration the decay rates have nonzero positive finite values due to which Hopf bifurcation is not possible for the fixed point $(x_1, x_2, x_3) = (0, 0, 0)$. For $b_\alpha = \left(\frac{d_1 d_2}{b_2}\right)$ the system is asymptotically stable at fixed point $(0, 0, 0)$ when $b_1 < b_\alpha$, critically stable when $b_1 = b_\alpha$ and unstable when $b_1 > b_\alpha$. As no Hopf bifurcation is possible for this fixed point for $b_1 < b_\alpha$ or $b_1 > b_\alpha$ no chaotic state is observed.

7.2.4.2   Case II

For the fixed point

$$\left(\sqrt{\frac{(b_1 b_2 - d_1 d_2)\,d_3}{d_1 k_1 k_2}}, \frac{d_1}{b_2}\sqrt{\frac{(b_1 b_2 - d_1 d_2)\,d_3}{d_1 k_1 k_2}}, \frac{(b_1 b_2 - d_1 d_2)}{b_2 k_2}\right)$$

and

$$\left(-\sqrt{\frac{(b_1 b_2 - d_1 d_2)\, d_3}{d_1 k_1 k_2}}, \ -\frac{d_1}{b_2}\sqrt{\frac{(b_1 b_2 - d_1 d_2)\, d_3}{d_1 k_1 k_2}}, \ \frac{(b_1 b_2 - d_1 d_2)}{b_2 k_2} \right)$$

the characteristic equation is given as:

$$\lambda^3 + \lambda^2 (d_1 + d_2 + d_3) + \lambda \left[\frac{d_3(d_1{}^2 + b_2 b_1)}{d_1} \right] + 2d_3(b_1 b_2 - d_1 d_2) = 0$$

To determine the parametric condition for Hopf bifurcation let us assume $\lambda = i\mu$ or purely imaginary and put it in the above-mentioned characteristic equation. The substitution leads to the following equation:

$$-i\mu^3 - \mu^2(d_1 + d_2 + d_3) + i\mu \left[\frac{d_3(d_1{}^2 + b_1 b_2)}{d_1} \right] + 2d_3(b_1 b_2 - d_1 d_2) = 0$$

On equating the real and imaginary

$$\mu = \pm \sqrt{\frac{2d_3(b_1 b_2 - d_1 d_2)}{d_1 + d_2 + d_3}}$$

and also

$$b_1 = \frac{(d_1 + d_2 + d_3)\,(d_1{}^2) + 2(d_1{}^2 d_2)}{b_2(2d_1 - (d_1 + d_2 + d_3))}$$

which is the same as the threshold critical value b_κ crossing in which chaos in the dynamic state of the system is observed. So, as $b_1 > b_\kappa$ the Hopf bifurcation takes place and system is routed towards chaotic state. Further, the Hopf bifurcation is linked to the second route to chaos, period doubling being the other route. As for the system under study and the considered parameters $2d_1 > (d_1 + d_2 + d_3)$ the bifurcation is subcritical, implying that the fixed points absorb an unstable periodic orbit and in return lose their stability. The trajectories crossover for $b_1 > b_\kappa$ on one side of the stable manifold of the origin which leads to their spiraling on the other side.

In Figure 7.4, the transition of dynamic state from stable to chaotic phase can be observed through the bifurcation diagrams for variation in b_1.

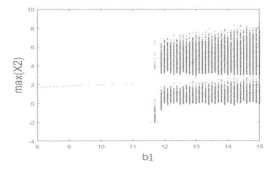

Figure 7.4　Bifurcation diagram for variation in b_1 parameter.

The bifurcation diagram validates the findings of stability analysis, phase space analysis and times series analysis. However, the last and one of the most powerful tools to identify occurrence of chaos in the system dynamics is Lyapunov exponent, which is dealt with in the next section.

7.3   Lyapunov Exponent and Chaos

For a deterministic system that exhibits sensitive dependence on initial conditions, the aperiodic long-term behavior of the system is defined as chaos. The most effective way of identifying the occurrence of chaos in the dynamic state of the system is by determination of the values of Lyapunov exponent. The Lyapunov exponent is named after the Russian mathematician A. M. Lyapunov, who addressed the problem in his 1892 research work proposing two methods, one of which deals with Lyapunov exponent based on linearization of the equation of motion. One of the key components of chaos dynamics is the rate at which nearby trajectories diverge. Lyapunov exponent measures the rate of contraction and expansion and so far proves to be the best technique available to researchers for validating chaos present in dynamics of nonlinear systems.

Lyapunov exponents are a generalization of the eigenvalues of a fixed point. The linearized equation for the system is equation $\frac{dv}{dt} = f(v)$, where $v \in D \subset R^n$ with sensitive dependence on initial conditions can be written as:

$$\frac{dy}{dt} = \frac{\partial f}{\partial v}(\phi(v_0))y$$

where $v_0 = v(t = 0)$. For this system the solution can be stated as:

$$y(t) = V_{v_0}^t y_0$$

where for the linearized equation $V_{v_o}^t$ is the fundamental matrix satisfying the chain rule $V_{v_0}^{t+s} = V_{v_0}^t \circ V_{v_0}^s$. For $t \to \infty$ the following exponent can characterize the asymptotic behavior of the fundamental matrix:

$$\lambda(V^k, v_0) = \lim_{t \to \infty} \ln \frac{V_{v_0}^t e_1 \wedge V_{v_0}^t e_2 \wedge \dots \wedge V_{v_0}^t e_n}{\|e_1 \wedge e_2 \wedge \dots \wedge e_k\|}$$

Eigenvalues of the solution are represented as $p_1(t), .., p_n(t)$. Now, as

$$\frac{dy}{dt} = A(x_o)t \Rightarrow y(t) = e^{A(x_0)t}$$

where $A(x_0) = \frac{\partial f}{\partial v}(x_0)$.

For x_0 the Lyapunov exponent is stated as $\lambda_i(x_0) = \lim_{t \to \infty} \frac{1}{t} \ln |p_i(t)|$ whenever the limit exists.

Near the fixed point the rate of expansion ($\lambda_i > 0$) or contraction ($\lambda_i < 0$) are indicated by Lyapunov exponent as they are equal to real parts of eigenvalues of the critical point.

It can be mathematically interpreted that for a dynamical system Lyapunov characteristic exponent or Lyapunov exponent is a measure that characterizes the rate at which infinitesimally close trajectories get separated. If the initial separation in phase space between two trajectories is represented by δX_0 then δX_0 diverges by a rate

$$|\delta X(t)| \approx e^{\lambda t} |\delta X_0|$$

where λ represent the Lyapunov exponent.

For differentiating between dissipative and conservative system, Lyapunov exponent is employed as a criterion as it measures the rate of contraction and expansion. If $\sum_{i=1}^{n} \lambda_i = 0$ the system is conservative, as in phase space the volume of the solution remains conserved. In the case of $\sum_{i=1}^{n} \lambda_i < 0$ then the phase space is contracted, which indicates the system is dissipative in nature. It is a noteworthy fact that an attractor for a dynamical system occurs only when $\sum_{i=1}^{n} \lambda_i \leq 0$, as for $\sum_{i=1}^{n} \lambda_i > 0$ the system is expanding and so in that case the system will never be able to reach any attractor in its course of evolution.

Lyapunov exponents play a crucial role in characterizing different types of attractors of a dynamical system. If the system of study is one-dimensional and dissipative then only one attractor is possible for a negative Lyapunov exponent, which in phase space is represented by equilibrium point. In the case of a dissipative two-dimensional system, two Lyapunov exponent values are considered. A point-like attractor occurs if both the Lyapunov exponents are negative. If one Lyapunov exponent is zero and the other is negative, then limit cycle is observed in phase space which corresponds to periodic solution.

Three types of solutions are possible when considering a three-dimensional dissipative system. A point-like attractor occurs when all the Lyapunov exponents are negative. If one Lyapunov exponent is negative and the other two are zero, then two-frequency quasi-periodicity occurs; and if one Lyapunov exponent is zero while the other two are negative, then the limit cycle appears in phase space. In the case of one Lyapunov exponent being positive, the other one being zero and the last one being zero, trivial attractors arise if

$$\sum_{i=1}^{n} \lambda_i \leq 0$$

Strange attractors arise when all the Lyapunov exponents are positive and if at least one of the Lyapunov exponents is positive, the solution is known to be chaotic.

For the blockchain VVP model, the details of the Lyapunov exponent are given as follows:

- **Case I**: $b_1 = 6$, Lyapunov exponents are $\lambda_1 = -0.21$, $\lambda_2 = -0.21$, $\lambda_3 = -6.58$ and the system is observed to be in stable state at point $(x_1, x_2, x_3) = (1.8, 1.1, 5.2)$.

- **Case II**: $b_1 = 11$, Lyapunov exponents are $\lambda_1 = -0.04$, $\lambda_2 = -0.04$, $\lambda_3 = -6.91$, so critically stable state is observed at point $(x_1, x_2, x_3) = (\pm 2.5, \pm 2.0, 10.2)$.

- **Case III**: $b_1 = 16$, Lyapunov exponents are $\lambda_1 = 0.40$, $\lambda_2 = -0.00$, $\lambda_3 = -7.40$, so the system is in chaotic state at point $(x_1, x_2, x_3) = (\pm 3.0, \pm 2.5, 15.2)$.

So, the system transits from stable point like attractor at $b_1 = 6$ to limit cycle at $b_1 = 11$ and finally the route to chaos at $b_1 = 16$. The Lyapunov exponent plot for stable state at $b_1 = 6$, critical state at $b_1 = 11$, and chaotic state at $b_1 = 16$ are shown in Figure 7.5.

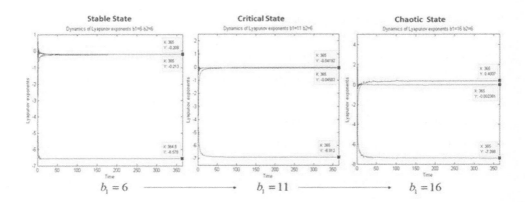

Figure 7.5   Lyapunov exponent plot for different dynamic states.

7.4   Controlling of Chaos

From the determination of Lyapunov exponent it is clearly evident that chaos occurs for the model as $b_1 > b_\kappa$. Now, the next part of the problem is to control chaos and restore system stability. Getting out of the chaotic state is essential for a malware propagation model with viral, vulnerable and protected class of computers connected in a blockchain network, as during the chaos there are random fluctuations that occur in a number of viral types, vulnerable computers, and protected computers. In such a state of randomness or uncertainty it is possible for hackers to take advantage of the situation and break into the system and successfully achieve their purpose like cryptocurrency theft.

Many schemes and methods are available for synchronization but the master-slave scheme has been the most used scheme while active control has been the most widely used method to control chaos. The purpose is to synchronize two identical systems at different states and parameter values so that stability of the chaotic system is restored by linking it to a master in stable state. For synchronization, the error system is derived by taking the difference of two identical systems, one in stable state and another in chaotic state, that are considered under the master and slave scheme, equations for which are described as follows:

This error system gives the differential equation of evolution of system errors. For synchronization of the two systems it is necessary to stabilize the error system for which the Lyapunov function is determined as follows:

Using Controller 1 and Controller 2 the master and slave system are synchronized for controlling of chaos.

From Figure 7.6 it is evident that the Controller 1 and Controller 2 derived from Condition 1 and Condition 2 of synchronization between master and slave system are perfectly synchronizing and controlling chaos.

It is further observed that Controller 1 is faster than Controller 2 by three time units due to presence of more migration terms. This highlights the importance of encounters in stabilizing the population levels ensuring stability of the system.

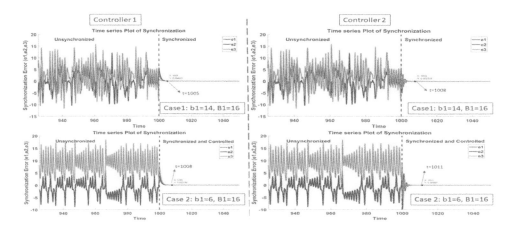

Figure 7.6 Synchronization in Case 1 and synchronization with chaos control of chaos in Case 2 on activation of Controller 1 and Controller 2 at $t = 1000$.

7.5 Conclusion

In this chapter, the problem of modeling of blockchain system using analogies from biological and epidemiological models is dealth with. A Virus-Vulnerable and Protected (VVP) model is proposed where the Type I interactions between the malware viral class, the vulnerable and protected class of computers are considered for modeling the system of study. The model accounts for rapid removal of the malware virus from the existing network, replacing it with its new kind and also the decay rate of the computers both in vulnerable and protected class. In contrast to other cybervirology models, the developed model takes into account the change in malware viral class population level. After development of the model, it is analyzed using different methods of nonlinear analysis. Using stability analysis the equilibrium points or steady-state solutions of the system are derived. The trivial equilibrium and endemic equilibrium solutions are observed to exist. No worm-free equilibrium state is observed for the system studied.

From stability analysis the parametric condition for stability of different fixed points are determined, which are validated by carrying out numerical simulation to obtain phase plots using fourth-order Runge-Kutta method in phase space analysis. The critical threshold value of parameter b_1 is evaluated and defined as b_k. The moment the parameter b_1 exceeds the value b_k the dynamics of the system enters into chaotic phase. The stable, critical and chaotic state of dynamics are clearly observed in phase plots. By calculation of Hurst exponent (H) under time series analysis the gradual rise of anti-persistence behavior in time series for the system variable is witnessed with the transit of system dynamics towards chaos. The bifurcation analysis confirms the existence of Hopf bifurcation for $b_1 > b_K$ and transition of dynamics from stable to chaotic state, as also observed in the bifurcation plot. The final confirmation of occurrence of chaos is obtained by determining the Lyapunov exponent. Once the chaos is confirmed the restoration of stability of the model controlling of chaos is carried out. Using Lyapunov stability theory, the controllers are designed which synchronize the two identical blockchain systems in different dynamic states and are synchronized through master-slave scheme applying active control.

Once the synchronization between the identical systems in different dynamic states is achieved by application of multistate controllers, the chaos is controlled in chaotic blockchain system by synchronizing it to an identical system in stable state. Two controllers are designed, out of which Controller 1 is observed to be faster than Controller 2 in controlling chaos due to presence of more interaction terms between the malware viral class and protected class of computers in the network, which has effective antivirus to counter malware attacks. It can be concluded that such encounters play a crucial role in stabilizing the population levels and restoring the stability of the system which is susceptible to fluctuations due to cyber malware attacks.

Future Scope of Work

In this chapter, a three-dimensional model based on the interaction of the viral class of malware, vulnerable class of computers, and the protected class of computers has been considered. The system can be extended to four- or higher-dimensional models on inclusion of recovered, exposed, and other classes of computers. In the present model, Type I interactions have been assumed in the first stage of modeling the blockchain system. Other types of interactions can be considered, which can lead to a study of different kinds of systems and phenomena all together. Similarly, a vast amount of research can be carried out on studying the effect of other parameters on the dynamics of malware propagation. Active control design under master-slave scheme has been used to develop the controllers for synchronizing the systems in chaotic phase and its control in the present study. Besides active control, other mechanisms like scalar coupling, hybrid synchronization and adaptive control mechanism can be used to control chaos. Based on these methods new controllers can be developed and compared to obtain controllers which effectively control chaos in minimum time post activation.

Acknowledgment

For providing financial support and research facilities, the authors are thankful to Guru Gobind Singh Indraprastha University, Delhi, India.

REFERENCES

1. Kephart, J. O., White, S. R., & Chess, D. M. (1993). Computers and epidemiology. *IEEE Spectrum*, 20-26.

2. May, R. M., & Lloyd, A. L. (2001). Infection dynamics on scale-free networks. *Physical Review E*, 64, 066112-1-066112-3.

3. Newman, M. E. J., Forrest, S., & Bathrop, J. (2002). Email network and the spread of computer virus. *Physical Review E*, 66, 035101-1-035101-4.

4. Zhou, C. C., Gong, W., & Towsley, D. (2003). Worm propogation modelling and analysis under dynamic quarantine defence. In *Proceeding of ACM CCS Workshop on Rapid Malcode*, ACM, 51-60.

5. Keeling, M. J., & Eames, K. T. D. (2005). Network and epidemic models. *Journal of Royal Society Interface*, 2(4), 295-307.

6. Yuan, H., & Chen, G. (2008). Network Virus epidemic model with point-to-group information propagation. *Applied Mathematics and Computation*, 206(1), 357-367.

7. Drief, M., Ganesh, A., & Massouili. (2008). Threshold of virus spread on network. *The Annals of Applied Probability*, 18(2), 359-378.

8. Picqueria, J. R. C. (2009). A modified epidemiological model for computer viruses. *Applied Mathematics and Computations*, 213(2), 355-360.

9. Ham, X., & Tan, Q. (2010). Dynamical behavior of computer virus or internet. *Applied Mathematics and Computations*, 217(6), 2520-2526.

10. Mishra, B. K., & Prajapati, A. (2014). Cyber warfare: Worms transmission model. *International Journal of Advanced Science & Technology*, 63, 83-94.

11. Memon, R. A., Li, J. P., & Ahmad, J. (2019). Simulation of blockchain using queuing theory. *Electronics*, 8, 234.

12. Saito, K., & Iwamura, M. (2018). How to make a digital currency on a blockchain stable. *ArXiv, abs/1801.06771.*

13. Li, G., & Zhen, J. (2004). Global stability of an SEI epidemic model with general contact rate. *Chaos Solitons and Fractals*, 23, 997-1004.

14. Kim, J., Krishana, R., & Jang, J. (2006). Cost optimization in SIS model of worm infection. *ETRI Journal*, 28(5), 692-695.

15. Lorenz, E. N. (1963). Deterministic nonperiodic flow. *Journal of the Atmospheric Sciences*, 20(2), 130-141.

16. Das, S., Srivastava, M., & Leung, A. Y. T. (1997). Hybrid phase synchronization between identical and nonidentical three dimensional chaotic systems using the active control method. *Nonlinear Dynamics*, 73, 2261-2272.

17. Kyprianidis, I. M., Volvos, C. H., Stouboulos, I. N., & Hadjidemetrious, J. (2006). Dynamics of two resistively coupled duffing-type electrical oscillators. *International Journal of Bifurcation & Chaos*, 16(6), 1765-1775.

18. Tiam, L., Xu, J. & Sun, M. (2007). Chaos synchronization of energy resource chaotic system with active control. *International Journal of Nonlinear Science*, 3(3), 228-234.

19. Heo, Y. S., Jung, J. W., Kim, J. M., Jo, M. K., & Song, H. J. (2012). Chaotic dynamics of a Chua's system with voltage controllability. *Journal of Korean Physics Society*, 60(7), 1140-1144.

20. Yang, S. J., Li, C. D., & Huang, T. W. (2014). Impulsive control and synchronization of memresistor based chaotic circuits. *International Journal of Bifurcation & Chaos*, 24(12), 1450162.

21. Goksu, A., Kocamaz, U. E., Uyaroglu, Y., & Taskin, H. (2016). Synchronization of chaotic supply chain systems using a single controller based on Lyapunov function. *Academic Journal of Science*, 5(1), 181-188.

22. Ma, J.H., & Chen, Y.S. (2001). Study for the bifurcation topological structure and the global complicated character of a kind of nonlinear finance system (I). *Applied Mathematics & Mechanics*, 22(11), 1240-1251.

23. Bai, E. W., & Lonngren, K. E. (1997). Synchronization of two Lorenz systems using active control. *Chaos, Solitons and Fractals*, 8(1), 51-58.

24. Bhowmick, S. K., Hens, C., Ghosh, D., & Dana, S. K. (1997). Mixed synchronization in chaotic oscillators using scalar coupling. *Physics Letter A*, 376, 2490-2495.

25. Sundarapandian, V., & Sivaperumal, S. (2012). Anti-synchronization of four wing chaotic systems via sliding mode control. *International Journal of Automation & Computing*, 9, 274-279.

26. Ablay, G., & Aldemir, T. (2009). Synchronization of different chaotic systems using generalized active control. *International Conference on Electrical & Electronics Engineering - ELECO 2009 Brusa*. II-182-II-185.

27. Daszkiewicz, M. (2017). Chaos synchronization of identical Sprott systems by active control. *Advances in Theoretical and Applied Mechanics*, 10(1), 21-32.

28. Bodale, I., & Oancea, V. A. (2015). Chaos control for Williamowski-Rossler model of chemical reactions. *Chaos, Solitons and Fractals*, 78, 1-9.

29. Ucar, A., Lonngren, K. E., & Bai, E. W. (2006). Synchronization of unified chaotic system via active control. *Chaos, Solitons and Fractals*, 27, 1292-1297.

30. Volos, C. K., Pham, V. T., Vaidyanathan, S., Kyprianidis, I. M., & Stouboulos, I. N. (2015). Synchronization phenomena in coupled Colpitts circuits. *Journal of Engineering Science and Technology*, 8, 142-151.

CHAPTER 8

BLOCKCHAIN AND BITCOIN SECURITY

K. Murugeswari,[1] B. Balamurugan[2] and G. Ganesan[3]

[1] Department of Computer Science and Engineering, Kalasalingam Academy of Research and Education, Srivilliputhur, Tamil Nadu, India

[2] Galgotias University, School of Computer Science and Engineering, Greater Noida, Delhi, India

[3] Department of Computer Science and Engineering, KLN College of Information Technology, Sivagangai, Tamil Nadu, India

Corresponding authors: murugeswari.k@klu.ac.in; kadavulai@gmail.com; ganesan.g@klncit.edu.in

Abstract

Bitcoin is the world's first virtual currency, which was introduced in 2008. After only 10 years, that is in January 2018, its value reached 18k. This slow progress is owing to security violations like hacking and theft, which happened in the past 10 years. This chapter aims to show the strength of Bitcoin value, despite its many security threats. With the help of a case study, the major contributing security breach which caused a drop in the value of Bitcoin is identified. Also, there is a focus on the prediction of future value of Bitcoin.

Keywords: Bitcoin, security, blockchain

8.1   Introduction

Bitcoin was introduced in 2008 by Satoshi Nakamoto [1]. Bitcoin was an enhanced version of cryptocurrency, which was introduced in 1999 by Wei Dai. It is a currency system without any central control. Bitcoin was launched after the financial crisis of 2007-2008, which was a motivating factor for its creation. Bitcoin transactions can be done internationally without any fees or low fees. It also needs no personal information and it is transparent to each user. Each party who participates has a copy of the ledger called blockchain, which is secured by a cryptographic algorithm. The two major challenges of Bitcoin are volatility and degree of acceptance.

Ciaian *et al.* made an attempt to make Bitcoin a global currency by analyzing its characteristics [2]. Kleineberg and Helbing showcased how it can sustain digital diversity [3]. Chambers and Helbing insisted on the need for a robust currency by identifying the security and technology needed for manufacturing it [4]. Sompolinsky *et al.* introduced a faster cryptocurrency protocol which confirms the transactions in seconds instead of minutes [5]. After India's demonetization move in November 2016, people started to move towards digital currency such as bitcoin, which doesn't have any control over centralized decisions (see Figure 8.1).[1]

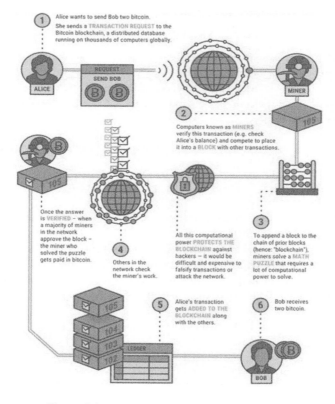

Figure 8.1   Understanding a Bitcoin transaction.

---

[1] https://twitter.com/diioannid/status/989417621400453120

8.2   Security Threats to Bitcoin

For a better understanding of the security threats to Bitcoin, the working idea of bitcoin needs to be understood first. Hence, it has been the focus of researchers in recent years and the subject of in-depth studies [6]. Other nontechnical factors affecting the value of Bitcoin are; government legislation and the strength of traditional currencies. This chapter will aim at identifying which factors mentioned here will cause major fluctuations in the Bitcoin currency value.

8.3   Working Idea of Bitcoin

Bitcoin was based on the peer-to-peer transactions principle; the owner only knows the complex public address and a private key. It means that the transaction takes place between peer-to-peer without the intervention of a third party financial institution by utilizing the network for hashing the timestamp of transactions. Then all hashes are added and form a chain of hashes called Blockchain. It now acts as a permanent record/ledger of transactions witnessed on the network, which is the backbone of bitcoin network. It uses SHA-256 algorithm to generate cryptographic data. Each transaction is signed by the private key of the owner of that particular bitcoin. Hence, third party tampering is prevented.

For doing Bitcoin transactions, two items are mandatory:

1. Bitcoin address and

2. Private key known only to the owner.

These two items form an asymmetric key pair. The bitcoin address is a random sequence of numbers and letters which act as a public key. If user A wants to send bitcoins to user B, first the input (source of transaction and amount) is signed with the private key of A and the output is the public key of user B, then it is sent as a private message to user B. Finally, the bicoins are sent to user B's wallet. It requires a number of independent confirmations, which takes approximately 10 minutes. These confirmations will be provided by the Bitcoin miners. Mining is the process of providing confirmation to the bitcoin transactions by the shared consensus system on the network. Miners are the core of bitcoin system and they are responsible for confirming the validity of all transactions on the bitcoin network.

For each generation of new bicoins, a block is added to the blockchain by using hash function.

Bitcoin is the first cryptocurrency beyond any centralized control such as monetary power. However, this decentralized nature leads to the following limitations:

- Public ledger maintained by every user

- No central authority to validate distributed transactions

- Anonymity of bitcoin creation

- Dynamic nature of bitcoin exchange values

Decentralization is felt by the users by having the transparency of validation of code used for services.

8.4 Case Study for Analyzing the Reason for Fall in Bitcoin Value

In 2017, Fraser and Bouridane listed the possible security threats to Bitcoin and they analyzed the causes for the fall in Bitcoin value [7]. They are as follows:

8.4.1 Security Threats to Bitcoin Protocol

Since Bitcoin is purely an online product, risks are always around. Bradbury identified a security flaw and named it the "51% attack," in which an individual or group of users can have control over more than half of the bitcoin network [8]. They also double spend bitcoins. This problem is mentioned by Bonneau *et al.* [9]. He also elaborated that this kind of problem is impossible with the current size of bitcoin network (millions of nodes). However, threat to bitcoin is minimal, it cannot be fully discounted. Bitcoin values are also affected by public concern.

8.4.2 Security Threats to Bitcoin Services

As the use of Bitcoin was popularized, the services utilizing it were also being increased. Bohme *et al.* surveyed Bitcoin digital wallet services and currency exchanges in the two public sectors which hold and trade the bitcoins respectively [10]. They define digital wallet as an electronic version of accounts, transactions and private keys which are necessary to transfer or spend the bitcoin values.

Bohme also states individuals can obtain bitcoin through Bitcoin exchange without going through the complex mining process. Moore and Christin further investigated and reported that many bitcoin users lost money due to hacking of Bitcoin exchanges [11].

Compared to Bitcoin protocol, the above-mentioned Bitcoin services are more vulnerable to all kinds of cyberattacks.

8.4.3 Security Threats by Other Factors

In addition to security breaches, financial decisions and government legislation are other factors which affect the value of Bitcoin. Basically, Bitcoin is a kind of currency; hence, whatever problems occur with traditional currencies will also be applicable to bitcoin.

8.5 Analyzed Report

In this section, seven cases of Bitcoin values dropping against the U.S. dollar were analyzed. The U.S. dollar is the commonly accepted standard currency around the world. Data investigated for these seven cases are from 2008 only. The standard drop value taken here is $150. The investigated results are mapped out for any one of these three categories:

- Security threats to Bitcoin protocol

- Security threats to Bitcoin services

- Security threats by other factors

From 2013 to 2017, at different intervals, the highest and the lowest bitcoin values and their differences are recorded in Table 8.1.[2]

Table 8.1   Bitcoin value changes against the U.S. dollar and their reasons.

Dates	Highest value ($)	Lowest value ($)	Value change against USD ($)	Proposed reason for drop in value	Category	Score
10/04/14 – 15/04/13	230.00	68.00	-162.00	A fork in the Bitcoin Blockchain [12-14]	Flaw in the Bitcoin Protocol	70.43
04/12/13 – 19/12/13	1230.68	553.48	-677.20	The closure of Silk Road [12, 15-16]	Flaw or Breach of Bitcoin Service	55.02
02/02/14 - 17/02/14	945.00	279.11	-665.89	The collapse of Mt. Gox [15, 17-18]	Flaw or Breach of Bitcoin Service	70.46
05/03/14 - 11/04/14	666.62	383.17	-283.45	Chinese Government Intervention [12, 19-20]	Other Factor	42.52
19/06/16 - 23/06/16	769.99	600.22	-169.77	Brexit [21-23]	Other Factor	22.05
29/07/16 - 02/08/16	657.41	503.46	-153.95	Breach of Bitfinex [2-25]	Flaw or Breach of Bitcoin Service	23.42
05/01/17 - 13/01/17	1118.53	787.59	-330.94	Chinese regulation fears [22, 26, 27]	Other Factor	29.59

For each record, the reason for the fall in the value is identified and fit into one of the three categories of reasons. Finally, average percentage of reduction in value is calculated for each category. The reason having the highest percentage is concluded to be the most influential factor which affects the value of bitcoin.

From Figure 8.2 we concluded that security threats to bitcoin protocol were the most influential factor. We also claimed that their methodology was deemed to be the best way for identifying the most significant factor affecting the value of bitcoin.

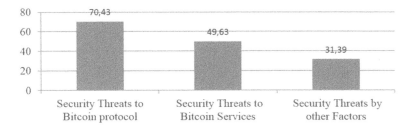

Figure 8.2   Average percentage of the Bitcoin value drop.

[2]https://www.statista.com/statistics/326707/bitcoin-price-index/

8.6   Rise of Bitcoin Value

Even though there are frequent fluctuations in Bitcoin value, it still retains the number one position. The year 2019 was a great one for Bitcoin, with more people starting to believe in the technology and starting to invest. By mid-2019 its value started to reach $20,000. Around the world there are only 21 million bitcoins ready for circulation. Among those, only 17 million are already mined and the remaining 4 million are yet to be mined, which will hike the bitcoin value more. Countries like the U.S, Japan and South Korea have shown interest in using bitcoin and other cryptocurrencies.

From the Nasdaq report shown in Figure 8.3, it can be seen that Bitcoin value was expected to reach up to $23,499 by the end of the year 2019 [14, 27-28]. Hence, 2019 was a bullish year for Bitcoin.

Figure 8.3   Bitcoin price prediction.

8.7   Conclusion

The purpose of this chapter was to show the strength of bitcoin value. From the case study, it is observed that security threats in the Bitcoin services mostly affect the value of bitcoin. Bitcoin's pros have outweighed its cons. Hence, Bitcoin has gained popularity around the world and its technology has attracted the major countries. A Nasdaq report also revealed that by the end of the year 2019, its predicted value will have reached $23,499. It's a good beginning for Bitcoin. A careful elimination of security breaches and flaws in bitcoin services and protocol will result in a reduction in the volatility of Bitcoin value.

REFERENCES

1. Nakamoto, S. (2008). Bitcoin: A Peer-to-Peer Electronic Cash System.

2. Ciaian, P., Rajcaniova, M., & Kancs, D. (2016). The digital agenda of virtual currencies: Can BitCoin become a global currency? *Information Systems and E-Business Management*, 14(4), 883-919.

3. Kleineberg, K. K., & Helbing, D. (2016). A social bitcoin could sustain a democratic digital world. *European Physical Journal Special Topics*, 225(17-18), 3231-3241.

4. Chambers, J., Yan, W., Garhwal, A., & Kankanhalli, M. (2014). Currency security and forensics: a survey. *Multimedia Tools and Applications*, 74(11), 4013-4043.

5. Sompolinsky, Y., Lewenberg, Y., & Zohar, A. (2016). SPECTRE: A Fast and Scalable Cryptocurrency Protocol [Cryptology eprint archive]. Retrieved from https://eprint.iacr.org/2016/1159.pdf.

6. Ahmad, F. A., Kumar, P., Shrivastava, G., & Bouhlel, M. S. (2018). Bitcoin: Digital decentralized cryptocurrency. In *Handbook of Research on Network Forensics and Analysis Techniques* (pp. 395-415). IGI Global.

7. Fraser, J. G., & Bouridane, A. (2017, September). Have the security flaws surrounding bitcoin effected the currency's value?. In *2017 Seventh International Conference on Emerging Security Technologies (EST)* (pp. 50-55). IEEE.

8. Bradbury, D. (2013). The problem with bitcoin. *Computer Fraud and Security*, 2013(11), 5-8.

9. Bonneau, J., Kroll, J., Felten, E., Narayanan, A., Clark, J., & Miller, A. (2015). Research perspectives and challenges for bitcoin and cryptocurrencies. Presented at the IEEE Symposium on Security and Privacy.

10. Böhme, R., Christin, N., Edelman, B., & Moore, T. (2015). Bitcoin: Economics, technology, and governance. *Journal of Economic Perspectives*, 29(2), 213-238.

11. Moore, T., & Christin, N. (2013, April). Beware the middleman: Empirical analysis of Bitcoin-exchange risk. In *International Conference on Financial Cryptography and Data Security* (pp. 25-33). Springer, Berlin, Heidelberg.

12. Popper, N. (2015). *Digital Gold: Bitcoin and the Inside Story of the Misfits and Millionaires Trying to Reinvent Money*. HarperCollins.

13. Decker, C., & Wattenhofer, R. (2013). Information propagation in the bitcoin network. In *IEEE P2P 2013 Proceedings*.

14. Batabyal, A. (2019, July 12). Bitcoin Price Prediction 2019, 2020, 2025- Latest BTC to USD Forecast. Retrieved from https://coinswitch.co/news/bitcoin-price-prediction-2019-2020-2025-latest-btc-price-prediction-bitcoin-news-update.

15. Eyal, I., & Sirer, E. G. (2018). Majority is not enough: Bitcoin mining is vulnerable. *Communications of the ACM*, 61(7), 95-102.

16. Kleiman, J. A. (2013). Beyond the silk road: unregulated decentralized virtual currencies continue to endanger US national security and welfare. *American University National Security Law Brief*, 4(1), 59-78.

17. Trautman, L (2014). Virtual currencies; Bitcoin & what now after Liberty Reserve, Silk Road, and Mt. Gox? *Richmond Journal of Law and Technology*, 20(4), 1-108.

18. Hern, A. (2013, October 3). Bitcoin price plummets after Silk Road closure. Retrieved from https://www.theguardian.com/technology/2013/oct/03/bitcoin-price-silk-road-ulbricht-value.

19. Turpin, J. B. (2014). Bitcoin: The economic case for a global, virtual currency operating in an unexplored legal framework. *Indian Journal of Global Legal Studies*, 21(1).

20. Kristoufek, L. (2015b).What are the main drivers of the bitcoin price? Evidence from wavelet coherence analysis. *PLOS One*. https://doi.org/10.1371/journal.pone.0123923.

21. Kristoufek, L. (2015a). What are the main drivers of the bitcoin price? *PLOS One*, 10(4).

22. Chester, J. (2016, July 14). How Brexit is affecting the bitcoin and blockchain industries. Retrieved from https://www.forbes.com/sites/jonathanchester/2016/07/14/how-the-brexit-is-affecting-the-bitcoin-and-blockchain-industries/#22f601ed7493.

23. Bovaird, C. (2016, July 17). Will the Brexit and China Continue to Influence Bitcoin Prices? Retrieved from https://www.coindesk.com/brexit-china-bitcoin-prices-2016.

24. Bovaird, C. (2016, December 20). From Brexit to Bitfinex: What shaped Bitcoin's price in 2016. Retrieved from https://www.coindesk.com/brexit-bitfinex-shaped-bitcoins-price-2016

25. Redman, J. (2016, August 3). Bitcoin price dives 22% after $60 million Bitfinex hack. Retrieved from https://news.bitcoin.com/bitfinex-hack-bitcoin/

26. Baldwin, C., & Poon, H. (2016). Bitcoin worth $72 million stolen from Bitfinex exchange in Hong Kong. Reuters, last accessed (16.01. 2017) at: http://www. reuters. com/article/us-bitfinex-hacked-hongkong-idUSKCN10E0KP.

27. Justina Lee, T. C. (2017, January 6). Through rally or crash, Heres why bitcoin buyers are nervous about China. Retrieved from https://www.bloomberg.com/news/articles/2017-01-06/bitcoin-buyers-eye-beijing-nervously-as-prices-slide-from-record.

28. Titcomp, J. (2017, January 5). Bitcoin price falls by 20pc in dramatic crash. Retrieved from https://www.telegraph.co.uk/technology/2017/01/05/bitcoin-price-falls-20pc-dramatic-crash/

PART II

CRYPTOCURRENCIES AND BLOCKCHAIN APPLICATIONS

CHAPTER 9

APPLICATIONS WITH BLOCKCHAIN TECHNIQUE

L. Godlin Atlas,[1] C. Magesh Kumar,[1] Rajakumari,[1] P. Hamsagayathi[2]

[1] Department of Computer Science and Engineering, Sri Shakthi Institute of Engineering and Technology, Coimbatore, Tamil Nadu, India

[2] Department of Electronics and Communication Engineering, Bannari Amman Institute of Technology, Sathyamangalam, India

Corresponding authors: godlin88@gmail.com; mageshchinna@gmail.com; rajakumaricse@siet.ac.in; palanisamy.hamsagayathri@gmail.com

Abstract

Blockchain technologies can be used to develop a lot of applications which are similar to the internet. The information recorded on a blockchain can take on any form, whether it is denoting a transfer of money, ownership, a transaction, someone's identity, an agreement between two parties, or even how much electricity a light bulb has used. It can be done by getting conformation from several devices, such as a computer, on the network. No one can remove or alter the data without the knowledge and permission of those who made that record, as well as the wider community. Rather than keeping information in one central point, as is done by traditional recording methods, multiple copies of the same data are stored in different locations and on different devices on the network, such as computers or printers, which is called a peer-to-peer network. If one point of storage is damaged or lost, multiple copies remain safe and secure elsewhere, and if one piece of information is changed without the agreement of the rightful owners, there are countless other examples in existence where the information is true, making the false record obsolete.

Blockchain owes its name to the manner in which it works and how data is stored, which means the information is packed into blocks which link to form a chain with similar blocks. Normally, each block contains the data it is recording. It will also include a digital signature linked to the account that made the recording and a unique identifying link, in the form of a hash (think of it as a digital fingerprint), to the previous block in the chain. It is this link that makes it impossible for any of the information to be altered or for a block to be inserted between two existing blocks. In order to do so, all following blocks would need to be edited too. As a result, each block strengthens the previous block and the security of the entire blockchain because it means more blocks would need to be changed to tamper with any information. When combined, all of these create an unquestionable storage of information, one that cannot be disputed or declared to be untrue.

Keywords: Blockchain, cryptocurrencies, bitcoin, decentralization

9.1 Introduction

9.1.1 Overview

Blockchain technology is one of the most innovative technologies of this century. The primary association of this technology lies in cryptocurrencies and bitcoin. The rate of change in notation happens rapidly. Decentralization and transparency is the major potential benefit which attracts industries to its core. Blockchain technology is a chain of blocks containing data of value without any central supervision. These blocks contain immutable data which is secured cryptographically [27]. It allows the digital information to be distributed and owned by only one owner. It can be called a digital ledger stored in distributed networks.

Blockchain technique uses two important data structures called pointers and linked lists.

- *Pointers*: Pointers are variables in programming which stores the address of another variable. Usually normal variables in any programming language store data.

- *Linked Lists*: A linked list is one of the most important items in data structures. Figure 9.1 shows what a linked list looks like.

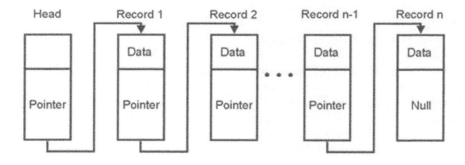

Figure 9.1 Linked list.

It is a sequence of blocks, each containing data which is linked to the next block via a pointer. The pointer variable contains the address of the next node in it and hence the connection is made [32]. The last node has a null pointer, which means that the pointer has no value.

The pointer inside each block contains the address of the next block. Here the first block can be called the "genesis block" and its pointer lies out in the system itself [40]. The representation is given below in Figure 9.2.

Figure 9.2 Hash function.

Here, a hash pointer contains the hash of previous blocks. So the structure of blockchain technique is based on a pointer in the linked list, as shown below in Figure 9.3.

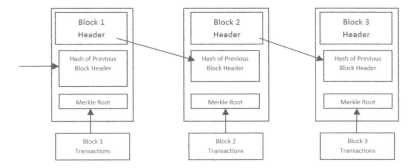

Figure 9.3 Simplified Bitcoin blockchain.

The Blockchain is a linked list which contains data and a hash pointer. The hash pointer points to its previous block in order to create the chain. As previously mentioned, the hash pointer is where the hash of data inside the previous block is stored. This concept makes the blockchain technique amazing, reliable and trailblazing [40].

The decentralization and immutability aspects of Blockchain technology are described below:

9.1.2 Decentralization

A network contains a common client-server structure. The normal client-server model consists of a centralized server, which is represented in Figure 9.4.

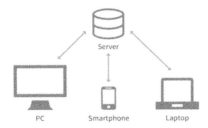

Figure 9.4 Client-Server model.

Everyone in the network can connect with the server by sending a query to get the required information. But the issue with this model is that the entire system depends upon the server, which is critical for the server to be functioning all the time for the system to work. Suppose if the main server stops working, everyone in the network will be affected [28]. More than that, security is another issue with this model since the server handles all the sensitive data of clients. Anyone can hack the server and get sensitive pieces of information. Moreover, censorship is an issue.

In order to counter all these issues, a different kind of network architecture is introduced which partitions its entire work load among participants called peers, who are all equally privileged. Here, the important concept is that there won't be a central service hereafter, instead there will be several distributed and decentralized peers. This is called peer-to-peer network [31].

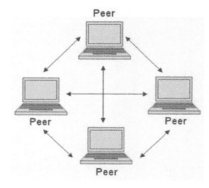

Figure 9.5   Peer-to-peer connection.

People use peer-to-peer networks, as shown in Figure 9.5, for file sharing, which is also called torrenting. Downloading the data directly using client-server architecture is usually extremely slow and depends upon the server.

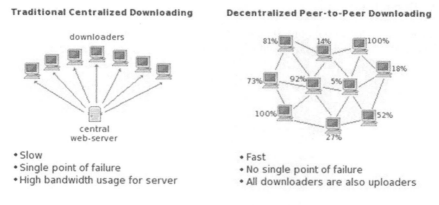

Figure 9.6   Centralized vs. Decentralized downloading.

So, in peer-to-peer systems there is no central authority and they function well even if one of the peers goes out of the race; and the systems are not prone to censorship. This is why blockchain technology functions in a decentralized manner [12].

9.1.3 Immutability

Immutability, in the context of the blockchain, means that once something has been entered into the blockchain, it cannot be tampered with. The reason why the blockchain has this property is due to cryptographic hash function.

In simple terms, hashing means taking an input string of any length and giving out an output of a fixed length. In the context of cryptocurrencies like bitcoin, the transactions are taken as an input and run through a hashing algorithm (bitcoin uses SHA-256) which gives an output of a fixed length [29], as shown below.

INPUT	HASH
Hi	3639EFCD08ABB273B1619E82E78C29A7DF02C1051B1820E99FC395DCAA3326B8
Welcome to blockgeeks. Glad to have you here.	53A53FC9E2A03F9B6E66D84BA701574CD9CF5F01FB498C41731881BCDC68A7C8

As can be seen in the case of SHA-256, no matter how big or small your input is, the output will always have a fixed 256-bits length. This becomes critical when you are dealing with a huge amount of data and transactions [28]. So, basically, instead of remembering the input data which could be huge, you can just remember the hash and keep track.

A cryptographic hash function is a special class of hash functions which has various properties, making it ideal for cryptography. There are certain properties that a cryptographic hash function needs to have in order to be considered secure [19].

The important property which we focus on is the Avalanche Effect, which means that even if we make a small change in our input data, the changes that will be reflected in the hash will be huge [37].

An example of a test done with SHA-256 is shown below.

INPUT	HASH
Hi	3639EFCD08ABB273B1619E82E78C29A7DF02C1051B1820E99FC395DCAA3326B8
Welcome to blockgeeks. Glad to have you here.	53A53FC9E2A03F9B6E66D84BA701574CD9CF5F01FB498C41731881BCDC68A7C8

Even if we change the case of the first alphabet of the input it will affect a lot of the entire hash function. The blockchain is a linked list which contains data and a hash pointer which points to its previous block, hence creating the chain. Here, an interesting feature of blockchain which makes it reliable and trailblazing is that if a hacker is trying to attack block 3 and tries to change the data, then the hash will be changed automatically, which in turn changes the data of the previous block and so on; this will completely change the chain, which is impossible. This is exactly how blockchain attains immutability.

9.2 Applications of Blockchain Technology

9.2.1 Blockchain Technology in the Food Industry

In the modern era, Blockchain plays a great role in various fields. The primary application is the food industry, which is a primary source of the food needed by living beings. The most fundamental thing we should know regarding food is the source from which it comes. People are becoming indifferent to the food they eat. This problem starts both at the customer as well as supplier side.

According to an October 6, 2006 report, multiple states in the U.S. suffered a major *E. coli* outbreak caused by spinach. Around 199 people were affected, 22 of whom were children under five years old. Of those affected, 31 of the 199 developed a type of kidney failure called hemolytic-uremic syndrome. Ultimately, three people died in the outbreak, one of whom was a 2-year-old child.

As a result of this, pandemonium broke out in the entire food industry. People were desperately trying to trace the source of the infected spinach. Everyone immediately pulled spinach from the market. It took the Food and Drug Administration a total of two weeks to find the source of the contaminated spinach, and for two weeks there was no spinach on the market.

One lot from one farm to one supplier is all it took to shut down the entire industry for two weeks, the results of which are depicted in Figure 9.7. For two weeks, farmers whose entire livelihood depended on spinach were left penniless.

Figure 9.7   Photo showing the effects of the ban on spinach due to the *E. coli* outbreak.

All this would have been avoided if there was a better way to trace the spinach. Here traceability and transparency is the key process of identifying the affected spinach. But traceability is a long process and before the source is identified, entire industries may be shut down and livelihoods ruined. So, the primary process which we can implement is transparency. In order to tackle this problem the process should be monitored from beginning to end until it reaches the market place.

Here is where the blockchain technology can be implemented in order to tackle this problem. It maintains the complete details of food records.

Remember that the blockchain is an open ledger and the data in it is open to everyone and there is no central authority taking charge of the records. This is shown in Figure 9.8. This greatly reduces the time that may be wasted going through endless red tape and the hierarchy. In fact, having these data on the blockchain will reduce the waiting time from weeks to mere seconds.

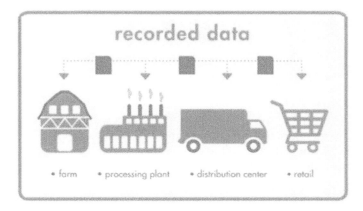

Figure 9.8 Flow of supply process.

Walmart has already done two test runs with IBM, one with Chinese pork and the other with Mexican mangoes. Walmart and IBM used "Hyper Ledger," a blockchain originally built by IBM and now housed under the Linux Foundation's Hyperledger group for these tests.

As the blockchain gets more and more integrated into the food industry it will make the whole process more transparent and safer. The advantages of a transparent food system are that it.

- Greatly enhances food safety.

- Ensures fresher food since no one will risk sending "non-fresh" food in an open system.

- There is less food waste because every single piece of food is accounted for.

- Stops food fraud because the system is open for everyone to see.

- Another advantage of an open system is that it promotes responsibility among the food producers since they now know that they can't get away with underhand dealings.

9.2.2 Cybersecurity

Figure 9.9 is a general representation of the cybersecurity system. On September 7, 2017, Equifax, one of the world's largest consumer credit reporting agencies, shocked the world when they revealed that they had just faced a massive cybersecurity breach.

Figure 9.9   Representation of cybersecurity.

They faced unauthorized data access from mid-May through July 2017, which they discovered on July 29. Around 145.5 million consumers were at risk of having their personal information stolen which included:

- Names

- Social Security numbers

- Birth dates

- Addresses

- Driver's license numbers

However, this was definitely not the first time that a major cybersecurity breach happened to a well-known company. Back in 2016, search engine giant Yahoo faced a major attack and around one billion Yahoo accounts were compromised. Attackers were able to get the following data:

- Names

- Passwords

- Telephone numbers

- Answers to security questions

Unfortunately, this wasn't the first instance of Yahoo getting hacked either since there are tons of DIY guides online on how to hack Yahoo. Imagine how compromised the security of a company is when there are DIY guides on how to hack that specific company floating online.

When security companies like Verizon did their research they found certain trends. Apparently, 65% of the data breaches were because of weak, default, or stolen passwords. Which is a significant number despite it being less than the previous year's of (95%). According to their research, the main reason why most of these attacks happen is that of the gullibility of the people themselves.

Time and again people fall for phishing attacks and they keep on giving away sensitive data such as usernames, passwords, and credit card details. In fact, Verizon's report states that 23% of the people keep opening phishing email and half of them even open the attachments which come along with it. To know the depth of this we can calculate the amount spent on cybercrime per year, which is more than $400 billion annually.

Here, we want to know how blockchain technology helps people prevent these types of attacks. There are three blockchain features that help to prevent cyberattacks, which are listed below:

- *Trustless System*: According to a Richtopia article, blockchain runs without the concept of human trust.

- *Immutability*: The blockchain allows one to store data and secure it using various cryptographic properties such as digital signatures and hashing. One of the best features of this is that as soon as data enters a block in a blockchain it cannot be tampered with. This is called "immutability."

- *Decentralization and Consensus*: The blockchain technology is a decentralized distributed system which is made of a lot of nodes. The majority of the nodes need to come together to build a consensus and make a decision. So, instead of a central authoritative figure, we have a democratic system which is an important concept in blockchain technique.

9.2.3 Voting

In a democracy, voting is the essential tool which is the most important factor that makes a government for the people and by the people. However, many countries around the world are still using the traditional paper ballot system, which has lots of issues. The concept is simple, you put your vote on a piece of paper and put it in a ballot box. At the end of the election, the votes are counted and whoever gets the most votes is the winner. However, as simple as it may sound, there are a lot of issues that can happen due to the traditional paper balloting system.

Figure 9.10 shows the general structure of a voting system.

Figure 9.10 Representation of voting technology using blockchain.

Following are the problems associated with the traditional paper ballot system:

- The system cannot be automated and is extremely tedious. From actually physically going to the venues where the ballot boxes are kept to waiting in long lines, the entire process is extremely time-consuming.

- The amount of time taken to count the votes is too high.

- The election can be hijacked via the insertion of bogus ballot papers.

- More powerful parties can use intimidation tactics at the venues to rig the election in a certain way.

- The amount of paper wastage can cause harm to the environment.

- There is no historical record possible to keep track of each and every vote made.

- The cost of expenditure on paper ballots is very high.

- It is impossible to keep track of your vote.

- Once you have cast a vote you cannot change it.

To counter the disadvantages mentioned above, a digital voting system was introduced which was employed by countries like Estonia. According to the survey, Estonia has had electronic voting since 2005. During the 2015 parliamentary elections, 30.5% of the votes were cast digitally.

There were some possible issues in the system shown in Figure 9.11, which were pointed out by *The Economist*.

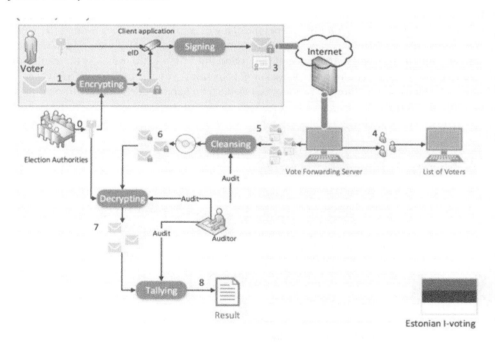

Figure 9.11 Representation of voting system.

- Firstly, the client-side machine could develop a malware which reads each and every vote cast and changes the vote to the other candidate.

- An attacker can directly infect the servers through malware placed on the DVDs used to set up the servers and transfer the votes.

While these issues were criticized and contested by the Estonian Information Systems Authority, the fact remains that having a centralized server taking care of the votes can be susceptible to multiple attacks and hacks.

The solution to the above issues is given by Blockchain technology.

Here, companies like Follow My Vote are using blockchain technology and elliptical curve cryptography to bring voting into the 21st century. Their goal is simple, make the election process as transparent as possible. Here, by integrating blockchain the casting of votes can be hidden. Any potential voter can securely login using their webcam and government-issued ID card. After they are done voting, anyone can use their voting ID to track their votes and check that it has been cast correctly. On top of that, voters even have the ability to change their votes any number of times till the deadline.

Elliptical curve cryptography (ECC) is used to create these votes. ECC is a form of asymmetric cryptography. Asymmetric cryptography uses two keys (a public key and a private key) to encrypt and decrypt data. ECC is basically what Bitcoin and Ethereum use for their cryptography. One thing to note, the private key should not be revealed to anyone but the user and the public key generates a public address which is shared with everyone.

During voter registration, the voter creates two ECC key-pairs. The voter reveals their identity to a verifier who certifies the first key-pair. Once that is done, the voter registers their second key-pair anonymously as belonging to the first pair. The first key-pair is called "identity key-pair" while the second is called "voting key-pair."

The voter can then create a transaction, which is basically their vote, and sign off on it with their voting private key. Once the vote is cast, anyone can verify whether the signature is valid or not and make sure that none of the votes have been tampered with. They can simply verify using the voter's public key to check whether it is indeed the voter who did the voting or not.

9.2.4 Land Registry

India has looked into the blockchain technology as a possible solution to their land registry problems. Property fraud is one of the biggest issues in India.

Consider this for a second; in 2013, New Delhi alone had 181 reported cases of property fraud while Mumbai came a close second with 173 cases. So, to counter this issue, the governments of Andhra Pradesh and Telangana have partnered up with the Swedish startup ChromaWay to put their land registry on the blockchain.

The execution is going to be extremely straightforward. The system will have a blockchain back-end and a web app front-end. The front-end will aid in the overall system abstraction. ChromaWay will be using their own database platform called Postchain. One of the many interesting innovations that they possibly could be doing is the introduction of cryptographically secure, digital fingerprints.

This is how it can possibly work:

- A hash is taken of the geo-coordinates along with a polygonal description of the land. This hash is tied to the owner's ID and the result is hashed again and added to the blockchain.

- Since the hash is always a unique value, everyone will have a unique ID. Plus, because of the blockchain's immutability, no one can tamper with the records.

9.2.5 Blockchain Applications in Healthcare

Blockchain technology has the potential to disrupt the healthcare industry's centralized operations, opening the door for optimized business and service delivery. The distributed ledger technology (DLT) is an innovation rife with the possibility of improved transparency, security, and efficiency. Smart contracts on the blockchain operate automatically without third-party personnel needed to verify documents or specific steps using pen-and-paper processes. With automation comes a reduction in the notorious bureaucracy that currently stands in the way of patients receiving the best care possible.

Immutable data stores that can be analyzed and updated in real time are working to reshape the healthcare landscape entirely. Existing centralized models have proved to be inefficient in delivering affordable quality healthcare to populations. When a community is healthier, we all win. Highly efficient blockchain-based applications are ready to be deployed to redefine how healthcare institutions operate from national healthcare systems to privatized hospitals. Not only can direct healthcare interventions be improved, so can prescription compliance and healthcare insurance models. The list goes on.

As DLT works to dramatically improve the transparency and efficiency of outdated industry, even parties beyond patients and providers benefit. Regulation and auditing become easier to manage. Introducing top-of-the-line technology also improves business operations and gives key healthcare players a clear advantage over private sector competitors.

When our existing healthcare framework is slow, expensive, and requires ten different intermediaries, we know there is a problem. Governments and hospitals want to provide comprehensive care that is affordable to administer as it is easy for the public to access. Now with blockchain technology the tools are in place to make that mission a reality. Small startups and larger companies that are early adopters are figuring out ways to cut overhead, deliver better care, streamline insurance coverage processes, and therefore improve the overall quality of life and extend life expectancy for the greater population.

9.2.5.1 The Pitfalls of Centralized Healthcare Systems

The centralized healthcare system as we know it today varies from country to country. Most countries have a national healthcare system that distributes care centrally through the government. The U.S. has a privatized for-profit healthcare system with government programs for low-income individuals and the elderly. National healthcare systems, government administered programs, and privatized for-profit healthcare all share similar pain points as a result of decentralization and outdated technology. Here are some of the main issues with centralized health care delivery:

- Information sprawl

- Data insecurity

- General inefficiency

- Expensive

- Slow

- Opaque operations and pricing

9.2.5.2 The Benefits of Decentralizing Healthcare

Deploying distributed ledger technology can improve the healthcare supply chain in countless ways. Healthcare is incredibly data heavy, and when critical information becomes lost in the shuffle, it can dramatically alter patient outcomes. As discussed in the prior section looking at the pitfalls of centralized healthcare operations, it is this misuse of technology and lack of proper technological infrastructure that stands in the way of successful healthcare delivery. The flaws mainly rest in the health institution's inability to create linear information stores for patient data that would allow for fast and easy information sharing and improved patient access. Central administration becomes moot in a decentralized tech landscape, since all users take equal ownership and have equal access to information without sacrificing security.

Here are the potential ways blockchain integration could revolutionize the healthcare industry:

- *Interoperability*: More sophisticated and robust APIs could allow for electronic health record (EHR) interoperability, meaning that health information systems can work together across organizational boundaries to deliver more advanced and effective healthcare interventions. The blockchain network serves as an ideal platform for interoperability and could help to resolve the issue of informational patient data sprawl plaguing the industry.

- *Improved Data Stores and Analytics*: Blockchain can help create a patient-first environment where the populations can control their data on a permissioned blockchain. Identity can be removed from actual healthcare data to improve statistics while still providing real-time, tamper-proof analytics for improved healthcare interventions.

- *Immutability*: When a single immutable document exists for every patient, the data is then tamper-proof, and accuracy is guaranteed. When data is more accurate, data analysis becomes nearly error proof as a direct result. Immutability also helps to secure documentation and prevent fraudulent behavior and malpractice.

- *Tighter Security:* Decentralized data storage and payment platforms are automatically more secure by nature of their design. Servers and cloud storage are more vulnerable, and all information is centralized, ready to hack in one fell swoop. Blockchains are difficult to hack as they rely on cryptography and asymmetrical private key systems to safeguard transactions. These encrypted personal signatures are incredibly difficult to manipulate. Additionally, when data is decentralized it is no longer stored in a singular place with one point of entry, it is in multiple copies on a peer-to-peer network that is innately more difficult to penetrate.

- *Reduced Costs*: Blockchain technology works to streamline expensive multistep processes. In the case of healthcare, there are endless bureaucratic hoops patients and providers jump through to implement even the most basic healthcare intervention successfully. Eliminating go-betweens and unnecessary steps that separate patients from receiving timely and effective care will additionally work to reduce costs. When fraud and duplicates are reduced using blockchain technology everyone in the supply chain can save money.

- *Faster Care Delivery*: Decentralizing the healthcare industry can help reduce delays for both patients and providers. When data is made more available and shared on a public ledger, and the referral process between primary care doctors, health insurers, and specialists becomes abridged, patients can receive care faster. Improving back-office operations will generally make all areas of the industry operate more smoothly.

- *Transparency*: When all actors in the healthcare industry have equal access to tamper-proof information on the blockchain, there is a surge in transparency. Decentralized technology becomes the great equalizer that affords access to those previously left in the dark. A more transparent healthcare system is a more affordable healthcare system.

9.2.5.3   Main Industry Areas for Blockchain Applications in Healthcare

Healthcare isn't just limited to the doctor's office; there are countless agencies, direct care professionals, and patients involved in a single healthcare ecosystem. Healthcare ecosystems also vary from country to country. In the United States, there is a much wider net cast when the term "healthcare" is used. There is an intricate web of pharmaceutical companies, health insurers, primary care providers, in-network specialists, private hospitals, public hospitals, Medicare, and Medicaid. All of these must work in harmony to provide the general population with adequate care.

Here is a list of some of the main areas where blockchain applications could improve overall healthcare delivery ecosystem:

- Health insurance

- Pharmaceuticals

- Private healthcare providers

- National healthcare systems

- Medical research

- Nursing homes and elder care

- Dentistry

- Healthcare administration

9.2.5.4   Blockchain Applications in Healthcare Use Cases

Here is a list of more popular proposed blockchain applications in healthcare use cases, some of which are already in development:

- *Electronic Medical Records*: Electronic medical records on the blockchain are the #1 use case for blockchain applications in healthcare. Why? Because a single, longitudinal and tamper-proof patient record could be made possible thanks to distributed ledger technology. This would place all vaccines, lab results, treatment strategies, and prescription history in a central linear ledger stored on a decentralized peer-to-peer network.

- *Tokenized Healthcare*: Users can share, learn, and earn with their personal medical information. Prevention or treatment could be incentivized for patients through tokenization. Using tokens to motivate community members to improve public health outcomes not only helps in building a healthier general population, it additionally becomes an income stream for participants and stimulates the economy.

- *Prescription Medicine Compliance*: Millions are spent annually on prescription medicine incidences due to improper patient compliance. Medication adherence problems are endemic and costly for individual patients who suffer and the healthcare system as a whole. Incentive for improved medication adherence could be tokenization through APIs that help gamify the prescription-taking process (see the previous use case). Adherence information stored on the blockchain can be a more accessible place for doctors and patients to communicate and follow up with pharmaceutical interventions over time.

- *Automated Health Insurance (Claims Adjudication)*: With the use of smart contract programming on the blockchain, claims can be verified via a P2P network and executed automatically. Without a biased central authority claims fraud could be eliminated through the trustless blockchain environment, which will also help to speed up the claims process.

- *Personalized Care*: The blockchain can facilitate more personalized treatments for individuals based on improved EHRs. When superior, easy-to-share data is in place over time it can even import family medical histories to encourage more tailor-made interventions. No two patients are the same, and healthcare providers know this, but do not have the current resources available to have even the most routine checkups be personalized.

- *Medical Product Supply Chain Tracking*: Companies that vend products to patients through the medical care system have to navigate an incredibly complex supply chain, especially when prescriptions are involved. When items or medication need to be recalled it is difficult to trace the products back to their origins. When blockchain applications are used to record the exchange of goods and services a neat and linear audit trail is created. The transaction history can authenticate products automatically to decrease counterfeiting and better recall medications with harmful side effects.

- *Telehealth Provider Credentialing*: As telehealth becomes a more viable remote-care option, patients are looking for verification that online care providers are the real deal. Introducing blockchain to auto-verify licensure and send out updates to users could help keep telehealth costs down. Notifications could also be sent when there is a new health practitioner on the roster accepting patients.

- *Patient Consent Management*: All patient consent paperwork could be verified on the blockchain, instead of relying on office personnel to authenticate. Prior to visiting the doctor's office, patients can use blockchain portals to record their symptoms and give their consent to treatment immutably. These timestamped and secure documents have the potential to settle malpractice lawsuits in a more timely and affordable fashion.

- *Blockchain Payment Platforms*: Payment platforms on the blockchain are more secure and faster. Health insurance on the blockchain can automatically release funds held in a smart contract when a trigger event (like a patient getting a lab test) occurs. Users can hold their own funds in a smart contract tucked away for medical emergency co-pays for automatic out-of-pocket payments.

9.2.6 Blockchain Applications in Internet of Things (IoT)

Blockchain technology is the missing link to settle scalability, privacy, and reliability concerns in the Internet of Things. According to Cisco, 50 billion devices are due to come online by 2020. With so many connected devices all sending, receiving and processing instructions to turn on, dial down and move up, the sheer amount of data due to come on-stream could come with unprecedented costs. Other issues include how exactly we can track and manage billions of connected devices, storing the metadata that these devices produce, and do it all reliably and securely. Before mainstream IoT consumer adoption can really take hold, these issues will need to be resolved.

Blockchain technologies could perhaps be the silver bullet needed by the IoT industry. Blockchain technology can be used in tracking billions of connected devices, enable the processing of transactions and coordination between devices, and allow for significant savings for IoT industry manufacturers. This decentralized approach would eliminate single points of failure, creating a more resilient ecosystem for devices to run on. The cryptographic algorithms used by blockchains would also help to make consumer data more private. The benefits of decentralizing IoT are numerous and notably superior to current centralized systems. However, blockchain is a newer invention and, similar to IoT, current applications sometimes fall short when it comes to scalability and integration. As tech professionals start to troubleshoot issues and further innovate applications and solutions that are blockchain or IoT industry based, they have quickly realized the potential for blockchain to support IoT and relieve many of the glaring pain points current systems suffer from. Many tech professionals view blockchain and IoT as a perfect match.

9.2.6.1 What Is the Internet of Things (IoT)?

Devices, vehicles, home appliances, hand-held electronics, thermostats, mobile phones, and sensors are denoted by the word "things" when referring to the Internet of Things (IoT). Basically, the Internet of Things it is an umbrella phrase used to address the growing amount of digital devices that are able to connect to a larger communication network.

The Internet of Things was first discussed as a network of smart devices as early as the 1980s. Now it encompasses AI, real-time analytics, machine learning, sensors, tracking systems, and cloud storage. Home and wearable automation ushered in more devices for daily personal use and corporate use than we have ever had before. As more and more technological innovations get added to the list, the way the devices interact with each other becomes more layered and complicated, yet increasingly intertwined.

The IoT industry aims to connect these physical things to enhance our existing infrastructure and operational systems. Most of these previously listed devices can connect to the Internet or go offline and be controlled and monitored remotely. Now, as we introduce more and more automated *things,* the web continues to spread and the responsibility the network acquires increases.

Facility management, highway systems, and manufacturing equipment all fall under IoT. Many industry-specific functions require high-functioning interaction between these physical things. While IoT might sound like a tech-exclusive term, it is a very broad term which refers to even blenders and washing machines or a pair of headphones – anything that can be connected to the internet – though it can be narrowed to define objects that communicate with each other online.

Harnessing IoT has opened the door for near endless combinations and possibilities of ways to leverage the connectivity in order to build a cohesive and optimally functioning IoT network. While the future looks bright for IoT, it is important not to overlook the problem areas that must be ironed out.

9.2.6.2 Issues IoT Currently Faces

Since it was first conceptualized in the 1980s, IoT has come a long way to the bleeding of edge technology we are standing at today, where there is even an Internet of Self-Driving Cars. The number of IoT devices projected to be a part of the average household is expected to jump from around 10 to near 500 by 2022.

Here are the most significant problems with centralized IoT:

- *Security*: This issue is brought up time and time again when it comes to IoT. With so many connected devices it makes it difficult for users to secure their personal data and use patterns. The more devices that are connected the more vulnerabilities and security threats. It also creates more gateways for companies to suffer hacks.

- *Cloud Attacks*: As stated in the intro to this section, most IoT has cloud architecture. This means that large, and often sensitive, amounts of data will be stored on the cloud. This makes cloud providers easy targets for hackers. Where there is centrally consolidated data in an obvious location there are looming cybersecurity threats.

- *Expensive*: Not only is IoT currently expensive to manage and deploy efficiently, the World Economic Forum has estimated that if one cloud provider was hacked it could cost $50 billion to $120 billion dollars in damages. Integration is expensive and it is likely that the cost of devices with IoT capabilities will also rise.

- *Privacy and Data Storage*: Companies will be responsible for massive amounts of consumer data that they can either sell or leave in insecure centralized repositories. Being able to harness that data, store, and adequately protect it is an insurmountable challenge and hoarding it in the cloud has proven to be an incredibly risky strategy. Centralized IoT ramps up the personal identity information (PII) sprawl crisis that consumers fall victim to daily.

- *Consumer Skepticism*: Adoption for centralized IoT has been slow and it is clear that all involved parties have valid concerns about moving forward. Regardless, IoT is a runaway train as manufactuers continue to create IoT devices. Consumers are skeptical that IoT service providers will protect them and also don't necessarily trust the IoT devices themselves and their ability to store and transmit data securely.

- *Inadequate Infrastructure*: There are major connectivity issues with IoT and the server-client model that facilitates connection. While it does work presently, it lacks long-term scalability. Looking at the numbers predicted for 2022 for how many IoT devices will need network support, it is hard to imagine a functioning network supported by current, already inefficient and insecure centralized models.

9.2.6.3   Benefits of IoT from Decentralization

Centralized services might be working for now, but they are not a sufficient long-term IoT solution to support device design of the future on a massive scale. Moving data and backend services away from centralized servers will be the key to IoT capabilities reaching their full potential in a secure way.

Decentralized IoT will make device connectivity and data storage trustless through nodes that can operate without a centralized authority. A distributed model is more efficient, secure, affordable, and will unlock even unforeseen residual benefits for IoT that have yet to be predicted.

Here is a list of the top benefits of decentralizing IoT:

- *Improved Security*: Blockchain offers devices unparalleled security infrastructure that blows cloud-based storage out of the water. Distributed networks lack a single point of entry or vulnerability for hackers to enter. Cryptographic signatures make hacking incredibly difficult; any messages originating from anywhere other than the authentic origin will be null and void on the network.

- *Tamper-Proof Data*: Decentralized applications carry a much lower risk of falling victim to tampering and fraudulent activity. Why? Because distributed ledger technology (DLT) uses asymmetrical cryptography to timestamp and immutably store transaction data and other related information on the ledger.

- *More Affordable*: When security vulnerabilities are removed through placing IoT on distributed networks and storing data via distributed ledger technology and blockchains, IoT becomes more affordable. Service providers currently have a monopoly on IoT and the cost of supporting devices. Decentralization will make IoT more accessible and damage costs from hacks can be more easily prevented or avoided all together. Intermediaries that operate centralized IoT systems and all associated costs will also be eliminated through decentralizing IoT.

- *Trustless*: Trust between all parties and devices using IoT will use the distributed ledger to verify and smart contracts to automate, never having to place trust in a centralized service provider or other actors to store data or be in control of their device connectivity. DLT can automate services through code to act as the intermediary for data flow.

- *Autonomy*: Blockchains enable smart devices to act independently and self-monitor. These mini "Distributed Autonomous Corporations" could be comprised of a decentralized IoT that is able to operate on its own according to the predetermined logic of a specific household or industry. This could completely remove intermediary players and central authority to have completely automated financial services or insurance settlement distribution, for example.

9.2.6.4 Blockchain Internet of Things (IoT) Use Cases

In blockchain, IoT applications have the potential to penetrate nearly every part of daily life. As we become increasingly dependent on the devices, we become more dependent on IoT. As IoT shifts to a decentralized, blockchain-based future, blockchain applications in IoT will be something we use every hour without even realizing we are engaging with "blockchain applications in IoT." Where there is data to be gathered from devices and deployed, there is IoT. Creating cryptographically secure databases for these hubs of device connectivity will be at the center of the use cases for blockchain IoT we explore below.

Some innovative use cases for blockchain applications in IoT are presented below.

9.2.7 Vehicle Industries

The auto industry has many use cases for blockchain because it is a part-intensive industry. The centralized supply chain and trust-based distribution is the current model for how we manufacture and obtain vehicles for daily use. IoT could be used to automatically update blockchain-based ledgers to keep a transparent and immutable vehicle record. This would work to increase transparency across the industry and make purchasing a "lemon" near impossible. Parts are sourced from so many different vendors and implementing blockchain applications and IoT to help track these moving pieces in a tamper-proof and authenticated system would improve the way vehicles are bought, sold, manufactured, and distributed.

9.2.8 Smart Appliances

Smart appliances are the wave of the future. Newer houses and buildings all have appliances that can connect to other appliances, mobile phone apps, and the internet. Rather than storing this data in a central server or cloud-based storage solution, smart appliance data could be stored on the blockchain. This would help to secure personal information and keep home IoT webs secure. Data could be used to improve things like energy costs for an entire grid without linking the information to the person or specific home using public/private key cryptographic to parse out identity from data, while maintaining the data is authentic.

9.2.9 Supply Chains

The global supply chain is multilayered and involves hundreds of parties across time zones. Moving the supply chain to the blockchain is often discussed by distributed ledger enthusiasts. From food distributors to pharmaceutical enterprises, many supply chains could benefit from using a combination of IoT and blockchain to streamline processes. Device authentication through numbering parts and creating provenance and history could help supply chains become trustless. Transfer of ownership and location could be tracked in real time between IoT instruments, the freights themselves or each object individually. Using the "things" in the Internet of Things ability to connect and migrating the connection and related data to the blockchain automates supply chain verification and transactions.

9.3 Conclusion

Blockchain applications are not limited to cryptocurrency and can affect way more sectors than just the finance sector. The revolutionary technology of Blockchain holds a high potential for applications in many different industries and sectors. While some industries have already started adopting blockchain in their businesses, many are still exploring the best possible ways to begin. Blockchain is a new name in the world of technologies but it is definitely the one to last. Even in the early stages, the technology has gained huge popularity starting with its very first application of cryptocurrencies. More areas of applications are being discovered and tested with each passing day. Once the technology is adopted and accepted on a global level, it will transform the way we live today.

REFERENCES

1. Sharma, K., Rafiqui, F., Attri, P., & Yadav, S. K. (2019). A two-tier security solution for storing data across public cloud. *Recent Patents on Computer Science*, 12(3), 191-201.

2. Sharma, K., & Shrivastava, G. (2014). Public key infrastructure and trust of web based knowledge discovery. *Int. J. Eng., Sci. Manage.*, 4(1), 56-60.

3. Shrivastava, G., Kumar, P., Gupta, B. B., Bala, S., & Dey, N. (Eds.). (2018). *Handbook of Research on Network Forensics and Analysis Techniques*. IGI Global.

4. Ahmad, F. A., Kumar, P., Shrivastava, G., & Bouhlel, M. S. (2018). Bitcoin: Digital decentralized cryptocurrency. In *Handbook of Research on Network Forensics and Analysis Techniques* (pp. 395-415). IGI Global.

5. Srivastava, S. R., Dube, S., Shrivastaya, G., & Sharma, K. (2019). Smartphone triggered security challenges – Issues, case studies and prevention. In *Cyber Security in Parallel and Distributed Computing: Concepts, Techniques, Applications and Case Studies*. (pp. 187-206). Wiley-Scrivener.

6. Amit, R., & Zott, C. (2015). Crafting business architecture: The antecedents of business model design. *Strategic Entrepreneurship Journal*, 9(4), 331-350.

7. Stevenson, T. (2002). Anticipatory action learning: conversations about the future. *Futures*, 34(5), 417-425.

8. Inayatullah, S. (2006). Anticipatory action learning: Theory and practice. *Futures*, 38(6), 656-666.

9. Coghlan, D. (2019). *Doing Action Research in Your Own Organization*. SAGE Publications Limited.

10. Reason, P. (2006). Choice and quality in action research practice. *Journal of Management Inquiry*, 15(2), 187-203.

11. Tsoukas, H., & Shepherd, J. (Eds.). (2009). *Managing the Future: Foresight in the Knowledge Economy*. John Wiley & Sons.

12. Ramos, J. M. (2006). Dimensions in the confluence of futures studies and action research. *Futures*, 38(6), 642-655.

13. Floyd, J. (2012). Action research and integral futures studies: A path to embodied foresight. *Futures*, 44(10), 870-882.

14. Bell, E., Bryman, A., & Harley, B. (2018). *Business Research Methods*. Oxford University Press.

15. Yin, R. K. (2017). *Case Study Research and Applications: Design and Methods*. Sage Publications.

16. Nakamoto, S. (2008). Bitcoin: A Peer-to-Peer Electronic Cash System. [Online]. Available at https://bitcoin.org/bitcoin.pdf

17. Yli-Huumo, J., Ko, D., Choi, S., Park, S., & Smolander, K. (2016). Where is current research on blockchain technology?- a systematic review. *PloS One*, 11(10), e0163477.

18. Vukolic, M. (2015, October). The quest for scalable blockchain fabric: Proof-of-work vs. BFT replication. In *International Workshop on Open Problems in Network Security* (pp. 112-125). Springer, Cham.

19. Christidis, K., & Devetsikiotis, M. (2016). Blockchains and smart contracts for the Internet of Things. *IEEE Access*, 4, 2292-2303.

20. Baliga, A. (2016). *The Blockchain Landscape*, Persistent Systems.

21. Sirmon, D. G., Hitt, M. A., Ireland, R. D., & Gilbert, B. A. (2011). Resource orchestration to create competitive advantage: Breadth, depth, and life cycle effects. *Journal of Management*, 37(5), 1390-1412.

22. Adner, R., & Kapoor, R. (2010). Value creation in innovation ecosystems: How the structure of technological interdependence affects firm performance in new technology generations. *Strategic Management Journal*, 31(3), 306-333.

23. Demil, B., & Lecocq, X. (2010). Business model evolution: in search of dynamic consistency. *Long Range Planning*, 43(2-3), 227-246.

24. Johnson, M. W., Christensen, C. M., & Kagermann, H. (2008). Reinventing your business model. *Harvard Business Review*, 86(12), 57-68.

25. Osterwalder, A., & Pigneur, Y. (2010). *Business Model Generation: A Handbook for Visionaries, Game Changers, and Challengers*. Hoboken, NJ, USA: Wiley.

26. Chesbrough, H. (2010). Business model innovation: opportunities and barriers. *Long Range Planning*, 43(2-3), 354-363.

27. Zott, C., & Amit, R. (2013). The business model: A theoretically anchored robust construct for strategic analysis. *Strategic Organization*, 11(4), 403-411.

28. Messerschmitt, D., & Szyperski, C. (2003). *Software Ecosystem: Understanding an Indispensable Technology and Industry*. Cambridge, MA, USA: MIT Press.

29. Samdanis, K., Costa-Perez, X., & Sciancalepore, V. (2016). From network sharing to multi-tenancy: The 5G network slice broker. *IEEE Communications Magazine*, 54(7), 32-39.

30. Wang, J., Conejo, A. J., Wang, C., & Yan, J. (2012). Smart grids, renewable energy integration, and climate change mitigation – Future- electric energy systems. *Applied Energy*, 96, 1-3.

31. Pereira, A. C., & Romero, F. (2017). A review of the meanings and the implications of the Industry 4.0 concept. *Procedia Manufacturing*, 13, 1206-1214.

32. Smit, J., Kreutzer, S., Moeller, C., & Carlberg, M. (2016). *Policy Department A: Economic and Scientific Policy – Industry 4.0*. European Parliament, EU, 1-94.

33. Wang, A., Yu, L., Mudesir, A., Zhu, D., Zhao, B., & Siew, T. S. (2017). *5G Unlocks a World of Opportunities: Top Ten 5G Use Cases*. Huawei Technologies Co., Shenzen, China.

34. DotEcon Ltd and Axon Partners Group. (2018). *Study on Implications of 5G Deployment on Future Business Models*. Vol. 18, pp. 1-116. BEREC.

35. Suthar, P. (2017). *5G Technology Components – Building Blocks of 5G Networks*, Nokia, Helsinki, Finland.

36. Panetta, K. (2017). Top trends in the gartner hype cycle for emerging technologies, 2017. *Smarter With Gartner*, 5.

37. Pazaitis, A., De Filippi, P., & Kostakis, V. (2017). Blockchain and value systems in the sharing economy: The illustrative case of Backfeed. *Technological Forecasting and Social Change*, 125, 105-115.

38. Turk, Z., & Klinc, R. (2017). Potentials of blockchain technology for construction management. *Procedia Engineering*, 196, 638-645.

39. Huckle, S., Bhattacharya, R., White, M., & Beloff, N. (2016). Internet of things, blockchain and shared economy applications. *Procedia Computer Science*, 98, 461-466.

40. Eze, P., Eziokwu, T., & Okpara, C. (2017). A triplicate smart contract model using blockchain technology. *Circulation in Computer Science, Special Issue on Disruptive Computing, Cyber-Physical Systems (CPS), and Internet of Everything (IoE)*, 1-10.

41. Benet, J. (2014). Ipfs-content addressed, versioned, p2p file system. *arXiv preprint arXiv:1407.3561.*

42. Dieterich, V., Ivanovic, M., Meier, T., Zapfel, S., Utz, M., & Sandner, P. (2017). Application of blockchain technology in the manufacturing industry. Frankfurt School Blockchain Center, Germany, 1-23.

CHAPTER 10

IMPACT OF APPLICATION OF BIG DATA ON CRYPTOCURRENCY

SANDEEP KR. SHARMA,[2] RAJIV KUMAR MODANVAL,[2] N. GAYATHRI,[2] S. RAKESH KUMAR[2] AND C. RAMESH[1]

[1] Bannari Amman Institute of Technology, Sathyamangalam, India
[2] Galgotias University, Greater Noida, Uttar Pradeshâ^, India

Corresponding authors: sandeepsharma097@gmail.com; gupta.rajiv0703@gmail.com; n.gayathri@galgotiasuniversity.edu.in; s.rakeshkumar@galgotiasuniversity.edu.in; rameshc@bitsathy.ac.in

Abstract

The popularity of cryptocurrency lies in its colossal applications and technologically advanced architecture. Cryptocurrency uses blockchain technology which replaces the traditional cryptographic methods. Although there is still a lot of research going on to find its applicability in various other domains, in this chapter we will discuss the workings of cryptocurrency with its key applications in big data and its impact on it. The world is heading towards the information age where "data is the new gold" and with this rapid production of diverse data, its processing and management becomes chaotic. Thus, big data technology comes in handy that is effective enough to deal with such humongous data (from its processing till its storage), after which there is a dire need for security which can be easily handled by blockchain. Blockchain, whose architecture was designed to address some of the primary concerns like decentralization, privacy, identity, trust and ownership of data and its unique architecture provides some superior features that can effectively manage those concerns. This chapter provides an outlook on big data and blockchain individually from viewpoints of various situations in which both big data and blockchain coexist to ensure data quality in various sectors, including web, health, education and government, by means of diagrams, workings and inner implementations. We will also discuss the importance of Blockchain and Big Data in national development with its various aspects in Industry 4.0 and some other future aspects that need to be addressed. This chapter is designed to give insights into various facets of cryptocurrency, blockchain and big data and how they are combined to perform certain operations pertaining to the tasks of any organization or institution that may be private or public. Also, the various advantages of using this combination for the overall development of any business or nation's economy are discussed.

Keywords: Blockchain, artificial intelligence, smart and sustainable

10.1   Introduction

Cryptocurrency and big data have been trending topics over the past decade so it's a matter of fact that they have emerged to become one of the greatest centers of interest of researchers, inventors and also developers in the past several years. Cryptocurrency and big data combine enormous technological power and on a global scale they are also attracting investments in values ranging from billions to trillions of dollars. Cryptocurrency uses blockchain technology which is also in full swing, and thus it can be stated that both blockchain and big data are complementary technologies and thus they can coexist. So, using the blockchain technology can add an additional layer to the big data analytics procedure.

The blockchain can act as the heart of all other computer technologies. It is cryptographically secure and robust, and acts like distributed database for processing, transmitting, receiving and storing the data. A record in the database is known as a "block" that contains details of transaction, date, time and a reference to its previous block.

The key component of the blockchain is its property of decentralization [45], in which there isn't any central party or institution to keep control of the data and its form, although checks are made continuously by many computers on the network. The same data can be held by different machines. Also, corrupted or manipulated data on one machine cannot enter in the chain of blocks as it will fail to match the same data held by the other computers. So, we can simply say that as long as it is connected to the network the information remains in the same state.

Blockchain does not have any centralized ledger to store transactions. In the blockchain network every user verifies the transaction block after which it is added in the chain to process so that data stored is invariant and no one can modify it.

The ledger or records data in the blockchain can be related to trades, real estate and dozens of other such domains. As big data analytics is highly used and practiced in Industry 4.0 (focused on data) and blockchain is transparent, the combination can lead to enhanced procedures for data analysis in a transparent manner. For example, it can be used for market fraud detection and prevention, as blockchain technology allows all the individuals on the same network to capture each and every transaction on a real-time basis. Thus, instead of searching for the fraud records that already happened and analyzing them, the fraudulent or risky transactions can be filtered out so as to prevent the fraud from happening. In this way we can prevent fraud before it happens. There has been a lot of cryptocurrency news lately around fraud and volatility, but the impact of big data and real-time analysis could change that in upcoming days.

10.2   Related Studies

Blockchain and big data are emerging technologies of the 21st century and are so popular that they carry a huge range of applications, many of which are under research in various practical and scientific scenarios. Since these are top trending as well as interesting technologies, there is ample research going on due to which the internet is full of information related to these topics. If blockchain and big data are independently very interesting, then what happens when they converge?

The answer to this question is found in this chapter, in which you will be briefed on some of the case studies and proposals related to cryptocurrency with big data, along with its introduction, how it works, its applications, and its future.

The next big cryptocurrencies will be a combination of big data, cyrptocurrency and blockchain technology working in coordination with each other so as to achieve the common goal with utmost accuracy and efficiency. An interesting application like managing health records and securing them with a keyless signature using blockchain can be found along with its related work in [46].

Some recent reviews in application of blockchain in big data are referenced in [40]. As mentioned in various sources, blockchain and big data are the top topics in their fields and highly efficient alone. So, what will happen if they converged with each other; will the end result be superior or just better? The answer to this question will be seen in the upcoming topics.

Before we start, let's analyze the following graph. It is pretty clear that there is unconstrained data growth which is seen from GBs to ZBs. This graph is according to AWS Amazon cloud services.

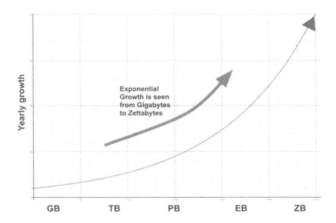

Figure 10.1   Growth of big data from GBs to ZBs.

10.3   Cryptocurrency

Cryptocurrency is one of the trending technologies of the 21st century which uses blockchain, another emerging technology of this era. It is a digital currency in an encrypted format that uses cryptographic techniques for its security. Satoshi Nakamoto [8] invented the first cryptocurrency named Bitcoin in 2008 and it has been in circulation since 2009. Bitcoin is the most celebrated cryptocurrency on the market since 2009 and has become an icon of cryptocurrency [4].

Cryptocurrency transactions are untraceable, anonymous and have created a barrier for illegal transactions like illegal drug trade and illegal purchases, etc. Because the currency has no central storage, bitcoin accounts and its payment processes have no jurisdiction. For cryptocurrency supporters, the primary strength of this technology is its obscurity, despite the potential for illegal abuse, as it enables the transferring of power from institutions to individuals.

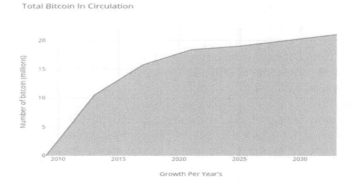

Figure 10.2   Expected growth of bitcoins based on past data.

Figure 10.2 shows the the number of bitcoins in circulation on the market and its growth over the last few years. Bitcoin was invented in 2008 but has been in circulation since 2009 and is growing every day.

10.3.1   How Does a Cryptocurrency Transaction Work?

In a cryptocurrency transaction, the sender creates an e-coin in a series of hash codes. It is then circulated among the other users (connected using blockchain) on the network. Every user then retransmits the e-coin to another user by digitally signing it with the public key of the next user and hash code of the previous transaction then adds this at the last e-coin. For verification of chain of possession a beneficiary has an option to verify the digital signature. One big problem is that the beneficiary is not able to verify whether a user spends the e-coin two times or not. Here's a solution to this problem: Cryptocurrency holders can make a central monitoring team which keeps track of all transfers of e-coin for double-spending. When the transaction is completed the e-coin will returned to the issuer or authority for issuing a new e-coin. The e-coins that are only issued by the central authority directly guarantee the misuse of e-coin. This solution leads to a system where all the transactions go through a central authority owned by a company, just like banking systems. We need to find a way in which the beneficiary can check whether the previous user signed on any earliest transaction or not. The only way to verify that the transaction is not present is to have all the sensitive info about all the transactions. In this model, the central authority has knowledge about all the transactions, like which happened first or last, etc. To implement this model without any trusted third party, the ledger is available for the public, and we need to make a system in which all the owners are in agreement on the transaction in the same order of transactions in which they were received. We need to ensure that the time when the first transaction is received and then the maximum nodes are agreed upon. [17]

10.3.2   The Cryptocurrency Market

The cryptocurrency market emerged in 2008 when the economic crisis affected the whole world and forced investors to search for other options that could guarantee that their money was in safe hands. Before 2008, people were investing their money in banks, expecting it to be safe and growing; but the main problem in the banking system is that the banks also invest our money in various places and give loans to other people to earn money. In some instances, banks face terrible losses which they can't repay or simply declare bankruptcy. In that case, in India investors only get up to 1 lakh including interest from the Reserve Bank of India, and it doesn't matter how much you invested. Due to all these problems, investors started looking for a new field where they could invest without any risk of losing money. When the cryptocurrency called Bitcoin first came on the market, investors started taking interest in it, which was the key reason for the boost in its growth. Once the market for cryptocurrencies started growing, there was no going back. At the present time, there are 2,322 cryptocurrencies on the market with market value of 349 billion US($); and the top 10 cryptocurrencies having a market value of 282 billion US($). Bitcoin leads the cryptocurrency market with a worth of 203.7 billion US($) (as of July, 8, 2019) [42]. Apart from that, the bitcoin is much more popular than other cryptocurrencies. According to data, at the present time a total of 17,951,237.5 bitcoins are in existence; the number of bitcoins keeps changing every 10 minutes until new blocks are mined, each block having 12.5 bitcoins. According to a report, 144 new blocks are mined everyday. This means that 1800 new bitcoins come on the market every day, with a total of 3,048,762.5 bitcoins left to be mined [41]. Market value of one bitcoin reached 20,000 (US)$ at the end of 2017 and an average value of 8000 (US)$ is maintained at the present time [1].

Many researchers are now looking for the parameters of cryptocurrency and have considered many factors like regulation, ambiguity in policy [18], economic process [19], world uncertainty [20], the price of production [21], user characteristics [22], monetary laws [23], and monetary stress [24].

10.3.3   Future of Cryptocurrency in a Country Like India

The new peer-reviewed commercialism through cryptocurrency in the Republic of India competes for a vital role in encouraging individuals to form investments and earn profits. The monetary services system's most significant role is the allocation of economic capital between totally different economic activities. Essentially, due to Bitcoin's commercialization individuals from every financial background have earned a great deal. In India, Bitcoin is one of the types of digital cash. It has been listed as the foremost type of cryptocurrency. This digital cash isn't controlled or regulated by the central government; however, it is managed and controlled by its developers. Bitcoins have gained quality and a sharp increase in their worth over a short span of time. However thanks to a number of its limitations its future cannot be foretold with certainty. Currently, this kind of digital cash has begun to be accepted with some caveats. Because of its high volatility the Indian government has issued three warnings (in December 2013, February 2017 and December 2017) to individuals not to invest in bitcoins [26].

A statement released by the financial institution (RBI) stated that [25]: *"Technological innovations, including those underlying virtual currencies, have the potential to improve the efficiency and inclusiveness of the financial system. However, Virtual Currencies (VCs), also variously referred to as crypto currencies and crypto assets, raise concerns of consumer protection, market integrity and money laundering, among others. Reserve Bank has repeatedly cautioned users, holders and traders of virtual currencies, including Bitcoins, regarding various risks associated in dealing with such virtual currencies. In view of the associated risks, it has been decided that, with immediate effect, entities regulated by RBI shall not deal with or provide services to any individual or business entities dealing with or settling VCs. Regulated entities which already provide such services shall exit the relationship within a specified time. A circular in this regard is being issued separately."*

10.4 Blockchain

As its name suggests, blockchain is a chain of blocks which was implemented in 1991 by a group of researchers. It is an increasing list of records or ledgers called blocks. All the blocks are interconnected using cryptography technique, with every block having transaction data, a timestamp and a hash code of the previous block generated using cryptography technique. Blockchain is the trending technology nowadays, and it's the backbone of cryptocurrency. Satoshi Nakamoto adopted blockchain in 2009 and using this technique he invented bitcoin as the first cryptocurrency. After the implementation of bitcoin, many other organizations adopted blockchain to produce new cryptocurrencies, the result of which is that there are approximately 2,322 cryptocurrencies now being traded with total market value of 349 billion US($) (as of July 9, 2019). The top 10 cryptocurrencies capture 85% of the total market value [8].

Cryptocurrency and its impacts are tightly linked to blockchain technology [10], which governs how Bitcoin works and the basic behavior of the other digital forms of cryptocurrencies. As per reference [9], the distributed ledger technique was adopted by Blockchain that allows buyers and sellers to directly use cryptocurrencies for their transactions, which are permanently stored in the form of a distributed ledger digitally without involvement of any central authorities so as to make it easily accessible to the public. As this technique provides so much transparency it is harder to deny the transaction, also the details of each and every transaction is timestamped (the encoded information in the form of a sequence of characters identifying the occurrence of any event, usually the date, time, etc.) and saved, which makes it nearly impossible to manipulate the content or delete it. So, technically, each and everyone in the peer-to-peer network acts as the authority and their activities are stored in an irreversible way so as to ensure the integrity of transactions and make them least susceptible to damage and tampering [11].

How Blockchain Works

Blockchain is nothing but an increasing list of records known as blocks. These blocks are connected using standard cryptographic techniques, which is a set of processes that are encrypted at the source and decrypted at the destination to guarantee a secure communication of data. Most cryptocurrencies use blockchain technology. Satoshi Nakamoto was the guy who adopted blockchain in 2008 and invented the very first cryptocurrency called *"Bitcoin."* As Blockchain uses distributed ledger technique for processing and keeping transactions, the record is distributed among the blocks connected inside the blockchain. Once data (status of transaction) is written, i.e., transaction is complete, then it is not possible to modify the status or manipulate the data. The way in which it works can be seen as an electronic affidavit. In Blockchain, to avoid annealing of information, a timestamp is used, which is nothing but encoded information in the form of a sequence of characters identifying the occurrence of any event, usually the date, time, etc.

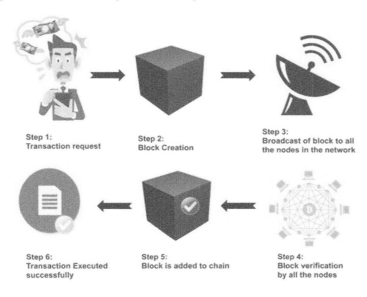

Step 1:
Transaction request

Step 2:
Block Creation

Step 3:
Broadcast of block to all
the nodes in the network

Step 6:
Transaction Executed
successfully

Step 5:
Block is added to chain

Step 4:
Block verification
by all the nodes

Figure 10.3   Schematic of how a blockchain works.

As shown in Figure 10.3, if a client wants to initiate a transaction then the client needs to request the block for that transaction, as shown in the second step. The block is then broadcast to all other nodes connected to the network; once the nodes receive the block they certify it, after which the block is added in the chain for execution.

10.5 Big Data

10.5.1 Introduction

"Big Data is a field that treats ways to analyze, systematically extract information from, or otherwise deal with data sets that are too large or complex to be dealt with by traditional data-processing software" [27].

The term "big data" refers to massive amounts of data that are mostly real-time and still growing at an exponential rate without maintaining any proper format. The term, which was popularized by John Mashey, has been used since the 1990s. Big data plays a very broad role in processing and analyzing humongous amounts of data that is not within the reach of any normal software or tool. One more thing that makes this a super-effective technology for dealing with huge data is its ability to process and analyze any type of data whether it is structured, semi-structured or unstructured. It can efficiently do its work. Briefly, big data is so voluminous and complicated that none of the normal tools and software, like database management systems, are capable enough to process it and store it expeditiously. According to a report by Forbes, each and every minute around the world, internet users watch 4.15 million YouTube videos, 456,000 tweets are tweeted on

Twitter, 46,740 photos are sent on Instagram, and about 510,000 comments and 293,000 status updates are made on Facebook! Billions and trillions of bytes of data are created daily at a rate which is rapidly increasing. One of the technologies responsible for creation of such data is the internet of things (IoT), in which each and every device connected to the internet captures, shares and processes data in real time at very high rates.

The graph below shows the exponential growth of big data research studies by various people in different formats. As seen from the graph, research has grown higher and higher and continues to be reflected in research papers.

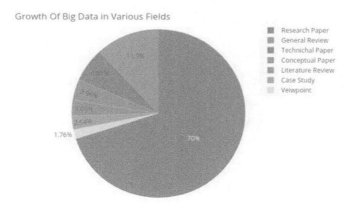

Figure 10.4   Growth of big data research studies by various people in different formats.

10.5.2 Importance of Big Data

Big data in itself has great value, due to which it is basically changing the way we work, think and live. The importance of big data in various fields is described below.

10.5.2.1 *Importance in the Development of a Nation*

We live in the age of data, where data is the most valuable asset. We conduct about 63,000 Google searches per second. Broadly speaking, the use of IoT devices, internet, emerging IT technology and cloud technology are a great source of data which is being created at exponential rates. To manage and process this much data we need some new types of data structures, the design of which is becoming more complex every day. So, there is the need for deep analysis [44] and utilization of big data, which will lead to the continuous growth of a country's economy and increase competition among companies.

10.5.2.2 *Aspects of Industry 4.0*

Industry 4.0 is often said to be the fourth industrial revolution. Data is the focus of this revolution and it is popularly said that "data is the new oil," which means it is the greatest asset any company has. Also, this version of industry is more concerned about or focused on the technologies that use data as a fuel. For example, in machine learning data is used for training and testing the model, in IOT data is created and processed via the cloud and big data, and lots of other applications directly or indirectly use data as a primary source. Since there's a massive amount of data, Big Data technology is of great importance as it is the most effective way to play with such amounts of data up until now.

Figure 10.5 below displays the digital transformation of Industry 4.0 and demonstrates how the current version of industry is operating and the percent revenue increase and cost reduction by the use of upgraded methodologies in the industry.

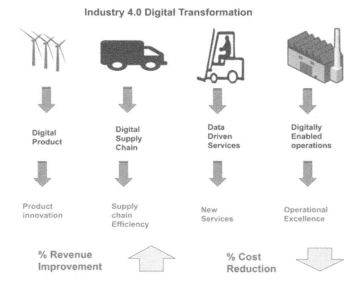

Figure 10.5   Digital transformations in Industry 4.0 using Big Data.

10.6   Coexistence of Big Data and Blockchain

Big Data and cryptocurrency converge in mutual ways as a way to coexist. Implementation of big data in cryptocurrency businesses can lead to new possibilities, which is why the latest industry trends are continuously changing. Data has been collected in the past and will continue to be collected in the future, but now is the time to utilize data for predicting the future. New startups and businesses are now harnessing the ability of such humongous data to make choices concerning where the market is heading.

Currently, the world is facing a vast increase in the amount and variety of digital or virtual data that is synthesized by users and machines; and research scientists are actively looking for the most effective ways of storing and organizing data, in which technologies like big data and blockchain will play a vital role. Some of the most common applications like localized management of personal data, virtual property resolution, IoT communication [43], and public organizations, have a need for the benefit that blockchain in association with big data can bring [28].

The era of big data has brought big challenges along with extensive benefits to the world. Progress and innovation in a wide variety of fields have been prompted by the analytics process of big data; examples of some of the fields of application are crime [30], relation analysis [31], power/energy [32], weather forecasting [33], and banking [37]. Hassani *et al.* describe how big data analytics is helping the banking sector in their security management, risk factor management, client relationship management, and sales, which has considerably optimized their operation potency and profits [37]. As the fastest growing business in the past decade, cryptocurrencies are closely joined to big data in a countless number of ways [34]. Some of the recent reviews of blockchain and its applications in Big Data can be found in [35], in which selective reviews are presented on a couple of applications up until 2016.

10.6.1 Ensuring Data Quality Using Blockchain and Big Data

Cryptocurrencies such as Bitcoin and Ethereum are digital forms of currencies, thus they have digital information associated with them that makes it possible to use them with big data to increase overall quality and security. The digital nature of currency and its transaction procedures are transparent in nature without any centralized institutions that make transactions more secure. This combination can be used for numerous purposes, for instance, let's take hospitals for example. A hospital can use the technique to make sure the patient's records are safeguarded with all the privacy intact and up-to-date information. By using blockchain with big data the hospital can maintain the health and disease database to make sure that all the employees have single mode and immutable access to all the records and data. In this way the hospital can eliminate the risk of patients being misdiagnosed or treated incorrectly due to loss or corruption of test results. Also, two different doctors who are treating the same patient have access to his/her entire medical history so as to write proper prescriptions.

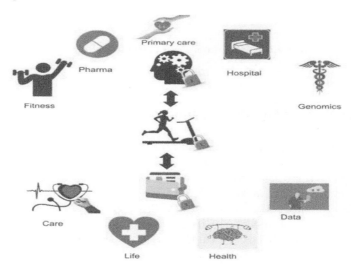

Figure 10.6   Use of blockchain and big data in health facilities.

Because of the nature of cryptocurrencies, they can make a great combination with blockchain and big data technology and this combination not only makes it possible to make future predictions but also can be used for enhancing overall system security and work efficiency. The technology has the power to track suspicious data items with utmost accuracy and can predict 51% of the cyberattacks before they actually happen.

The technology powered by bitcoin and other cryptocurrencies and the combination of blockchain and big data has the potential to change the world we live in. That's why many researchers and scientists are working on organizing large datasets for use with this combination. Some projects like Filecoin, Sia [38], and many others are also working on finding the best solutions for storing vast sets of data that can be accessed efficiently.

10.6.2   Where Can Cryptocurrency with Big Data Be Used?

10.6.2.1   In Education Sector

Universities, colleges, schools and other educational bodies carry huge amounts of data related to their faculties, students and employees which is increasing exponentially day by day, so there's a keen need to use the latest technology for processing and storage. This is where big data comes into the picture since it is an efficient enough technique to deal with such an enormous amount of data. As the data is stored in the servers, it also requires fool-proof security and transparency within institutions in order for higher authorities to prevent data manipulation by any external or internal agents. Data analytics also plays a significant role in analysis of data to improve the operational effectiveness of the educational institutions. Combining the three leads us to cryptocurrency with big data, which can be used to easily store, manage and secure such important data that these institutions possess like students' information, results, teachers' information, etc. As security is the pillar of any storage system, blockchain is the best option to easily eliminate the risk of privacy and data misuse cases, like manipulating student results, attendance and class records, etc. The reason behind that much security lies in the workings of blockchain technology that uses the concept of distributed ledger to provide extra security that is far better than other cryptographic techniques [35].

10.6.2.2   In Government Sector for Preventing Corruption and Securing Confidential Information

Corruption is the biggest issue for developing countries as it directly affects the economy of that country. The root of corruption can be broadly spread across the sector if no action is taken. Many countries are suffering from their inaction in this matter and are trying hard to overcome this issue. So, how does corruption happen? In developing countries, data is stored either in traditional filing systems or in an unorganized manner on computers. Even confidential information is stored using traditional methods. As governments store the most confidential information, it must be secured with updated tools and technologies.

So, how can cryptocurrency with big data solve this problem? To solve this problem, first we need to store the data in an organized manner, as the data is so massive that only big data technology can be used to deal with it, in which the data is processed and stored in an effective manner to provide extra security blockchain that can coexist with big data so as to solve the problem of corruption and provide full-fledged security of confidential records. However, it will require some extra effort to access such important information. The method is very simple: If someone wants to access some credential information they need to raise a request which leads to a block, the block is then transferred to all connected nodes. If all of the nodes allow that request then this request goes for further processing. If any corrupt officer wants to approve any file that is related to the public interest, they need to follow the impenetrable process of blockchain.

10.6.2.3   In Websites to Prevent Cyberattacks

With the advancement of technology and digitization, there's a rapid increase in cyber-crimes. With this increase in crime, there's a need for some effective solutions that can ensure impenetrable security aspects.

Nowadays, websites are generally hosted on centralized servers, making it easy for attackers to enter and access the credentials of the websites to steal and manipulate the data stored in respective servers. To ensure extra safety with higher efficiency in the storage and processing of such websites the developers can use cryptocurrency with big data, which can easily handle the overall processing and storage of data of websites with an extra layer of security using blockchain.

10.7   Future Aspects of Cryptocurrency with Big Data

Those in the financial sector are continuously looking for the future of different markets and make predictions accordingly. Despite the interest in short-term and long-term goals, effective models are always required that can make future predictions more effectively. As the market is growing, with this growth Big Data has found its own place that is being utilized to gain better insights into the world of cryptocurrency, which is estimated to grow to 6.70 USD billion by 2025 at a CAGR of 31.3%. Doing so would make it another flourishing technology of this century.

In this section we will look at the future aspects of cryptocurrency with big data so as to uncover the secrets lying behind it that can make a drastic change in the current scenario of the market. Predicting upcoming market trends has been of great concern to those in the financial world, so there has been a very rapid increase in building effective models to predict future scenarios in the market. As it continues to grow, so does the use of big data to gain insights into the cryptocurrency market. So, it is true to say that cryptocurrency with big data can itself take a large share of the market with a growth expectancy of 6.70 billion US dollars by 2025 and a CAGR of about 31%. This data is analyzed on the basis of evolvement of tools used for forecasting by the financial technology (FinTech) industries as well as their individual growth. Now, let's look at the insights of big data being used to predict the cryptocurrency market.

Cryptocurrency with big data, which is the interaction of big data and cryptocurrency, is seen as one of the research topics, which is why there isn't a clear roadmap to its execution or the adoption of technologies like blockchain [39]. The majority of the research in this field is focused on the use of big data for extracting knowledge, enhancing an extra layer of security by using both technologies together, managing access controls in big data, risk analysis and preventive measures, etc. However, there are many stones unturned in this field that can provide great opportunities to explore more in future research. One of the problems that should be pointed out is the lack of using application programming interfaces (API), due to which transaction records are not fully utilized. Some major drawbacks of cryptocurrency like computational scalability, energy inefficiency of the model, barriers in market entry level, and official or governmental challenges, can find effective solutions by the use of big data analytics in combination with cryptocurrency. Other such aspects can be found in workshops, news, conferences, etc.

We know that the coexistence of cryptocurrencies and big data is generally under research, so there's no proper information about the use of cryptocurrencies as the mainstream currencies and use of blockchain with it [39]. Some of the topics being researched are the use of big data for knowledge extraction and to understand market volatility; and enhancement of big data management using cryptocurrency and big data for additional security enhancement. There are a lot of possibilities still remaining and can be researched further in future studies. For example, transaction records have not been well explored through cryptocurrency and big data. This may be due to the participants having less interest in these domains or having lesser knowledge about these scenarios. Some of the disadvantages of cryptocurrencies like inefficient energy, entry barriers in markets, scalability in terms of computation, and various other authoritarian challenges can be solved through the big data analytics process. There are also flaws in academic research on such topics, many of which are due to publication in seminars, media news, workshops and conferences. So, it can be seen as a topic that covers a wide range and can easily find applications in upcoming research.

10.8 Conclusion

So, now we have arrived at the end of this chapter but this journey is not over yet. It's time to summarize what we have discussed so far. In this chapter, we went through the key findings of cryptocurrency and got to know how it works, along with its applications in the market and its future. Then we discussed the workings of blockchain and its architecture for the implementation of cryptocurrency. We then introduced the concept of big data and discussed its importance in national development and various aspects in Industry 4.0. Finally, we discussed the coexistence of big data and blockchain and how this combination is used to solve some of the real-life problems that are hard to be handled by the traditional techniques, which include maintaining data quality and security for the various sectors of the economy like health, education, government, and websites.

Apart from these, other future work includes the use of big data for extracting knowledge, enhancing an extra layer of security by using both technologies together, managing access controls in big data, risk analysis, and preventive measures, etc. However, there are many stones left unturned in this field that can provide great opportunities to explore more in future research.

REFERENCES

1. Hassani, H., Huang, X., & Silva, E. (2018). Big-Crypto: Big data, blockchain and cryptocurrency. *Big Data and Cognitive Computing*, 2(4), 34. DOI: 10.3390/bdcc2040034

2. Angel, J. J., & McCabe, D. (2015). The ethics of payments: Paper, plastic, or bitcoin?. *Journal of Business Ethics*, 132(3), 603-611.

3. Weber, B. (2014). Bitcoin and the legitimacy crisis of money. *Cambridge Journal of Economics*, 40(1), 17-41.

4. Mourdoukoutas, P. (2018). Bitcoin, Ethereum and Litecoin Are the Most Popular Cryptocurrency Investments Among Millennials. Available online: https://www.forbes.com/sites/panosmourdoukoutas/2018/03/25/bitcoin-ethereum-and-litecoin-are-the-most-popular-cryptocurrency-investments-among-millennials/1a20855876dd (accessed on 30 August 2018).

5. Bhme, R., Christin, N., Edelman, B., & Moore, T. (2015). Bitcoin: Economics, technology, and governance. *Journal of Economic Perspectives*, 29(2), 213-38.

6. Frisby, D. (2014). *Bitcoin: The Future of Money?*. Unbound Publishing.

7. Paul, V., & Michael, C. (2018). *The Age of Crytocurrency: How Bitcoin and Digital Currency Are Changing the Global Economic Order*. Picador.

8. Nakamoto, S. Bitcoin: A Peer-to-Peer Electronic Cash System. Available online: https://bitcoin.org/bitcoin.pdf (accessed on 30 August 2018).

9. https://finance.yahoo.com/news/top-10-cryptocurrencies-market-capitalisation-160046487.html (accessed on September 2019)

10. https://zycrypto.com/regulators-finally-conclude-blockchain-and-bitcoin-are-inseparable/ (accessed on September 2019)

11. https://enterprisersproject.com/sites/default/files/the_truth_about_blockchain.pdf (accessed on September 2019)

12. Narayanan, A., Bonneau, J., Felten, E., Miller, A., & Goldfeder, S. (2016). *Bitcoin and Cryptocurrency Technologies: A Comprehensive Introduction*. Princeton University Press.

13. European Central Bank. Virtual currency schemes. Preprint https://www.ecb. europa.eu/pub/pdf/other/virtualcurrencyschemes201210en.pdf (2012).

14. Clark, J., & Essex, A. (2016). *Financial Cryptography and Data Security*. Springer-Verlag Berlin An.

15. Grinberg, R. (2012). Bitcoin: An innovative alternative digital currency. *Hastings Sci. & Tech. LJ*, 4, 159.

16. Plassaras, N. A. (2013). Regulating digital currencies: bringing Bitcoin within the reach of IMF. *Chi. J. Int'l L.*, 14, 377.

17. https://bitcoin.org/bitcoin.pdf (accessed on September 2019)

18. Demir, E., Gozgor, G., Lau, C. K. M., & Vigne, S. A. (2018). Does economic policy uncertainty predict the Bitcoin returns? An empirical investigation. *Finance Research Letters*, 26, 145-149.

19. Ciaian, P., Rajcaniova, M., & Kancs, D. A. (2016). The economics of BitCoin price formation. *Applied Economics*, 48(19), 1799-1815.

20. Bouri, E., Gupta, R., Tiwari, A. K., & Roubaud, D. (2017). Does Bitcoin hedge global uncertainty? Evidence from wavelet-based quantile-in-quantile regressions. *Finance Research Letters*, 23, 87-95.

21. Hayes, A. S. (2017). Cryptocurrency value formation: An empirical study leading to a cost of production model for valuing bitcoin. *Telematics and Informatics*, 34(7), 1308-1321.

22. Yelowitz, A., & Wilson, M. (2015). Characteristics of Bitcoin users: an analysis of Google search data. *Applied Economics Letters*, 22(13), 1030-1036.

23. Pieters, G., & Vivanco, S. (2017). Financial regulations and price inconsistencies across Bitcoin markets. *Information Economics and Policy*, 39, 1-14.

24. Bouri, E., Gupta, R., Lau, C. K. M., Roubaud, D., & Wang, S. (2018). Bitcoin and global financial stress: A copula-based approach to dependence and causality in the quantiles. *The Quarterly Review of Economics and Finance*, 69, 297-307.

25. https://rbi.org.in/scripts/BS_PressReleaseDisplay.aspx?prid=43574 (accessed on September 2019)

26. https://www.academia.edu/38109797/CRYPTOCURRENCY_EVOLUTION_IMPACTS_AND _FUTURE_IN_INDIA (accessed on September 2019)

27. http://en.wikipedia.org/wiki/Big_data (accessed on September 2019)

28. Karafiloski, E., & Mishev, A. (2017, July). Blockchain solutions for big data challenges: A literature review. In *IEEE EUROCON 2017-17th International Conference on Smart Technologies* (pp. 763-768). IEEE.

29. http://refhub.elsevier.com/S2214-5796(15)00007-6/bib4D617965433133s1 (accessed on September 2019)

30. Hassani, H., Huang, X., Silva, E. S., & Ghodsi, M. (2016). A review of data mining applications in crime. *Statistical Analysis and Data Mining: The ASA Data Science Journal*, 9(3), 139-154.

31. Hassani, H., Huang, X., & Ghodsi, M. (2018). Big data and causality. *Annals of Data Science*, 5(2), 133-156.

32. Hassani, H., & Silva, E. S. (2018). Big Data: a big opportunity for the petroleum and petro-chemical industry. *OPEC Energy Review*, 42(1), 74-89.

33. Hassani, H., & Silva, E. S. (2015). Forecasting with big data: A review. *Annals of Data Science*, 2(1), 5-19.

34. Chuen, D. L. K. (Ed.). (2015). *Handbook of Digital Currency: Bitcoin, Innovation, Financial Instruments, and Big Data*. Academic Press.

35. Karafiloski, E., & Mishev, A. (2017, July). Blockchain solutions for big data challenges: A literature review. In *IEEE EUROCON 2017-17th International Conference on Smart Technologies* (pp. 763-768). IEEE.

36. Jin, X., Wah, B. W., Cheng, X., & Wang, Y. (2015). Significance and challenges of big data research. *Big Data Research*, 2(2), 59-64.

37. Hassani, H., Huang, X., & Silva, E. (2018). Digitalisation and big data mining in banking. *Big Data and Cognitive Computing*, 2(3), 18.

38. https://www.forbes.com/sites/shermanlee/2018/06/08/blockchain-is-critical-to-the-future-of-data-storage-heres-why/#280a5a0e33e9 (accessed on September 2019)

39. Mendling, J., Weber, I., Aalst, W. V. D., Brocke, J. V., Cabanillas, C., Daniel, F., ... & Gal, A. (2018). Blockchains for business process management-challenges and opportunities. *ACM Transactions on Management Information Systems (TMIS)*, 9(1), 4.

40. Karafiloski, E., & Mishev, A. (2017, July). Blockchain solutions for big data challenges: A literature review. In *IEEE EUROCON 2017-17th International Conference on Smart Technologies* (pp. 763-768). IEEE.

41. https://www.buybitcoinworldwide.com/how-many-bitcoins-are-there/ (accessed on September 2019)

42. https://finance.yahoo.com/news/top-10-cryptocurrencies-market-capitalisation-160046487.html (accessed on September 2019)

43. Kumar, P., Shrivastava, G., & Tanwar, P. (2020). Demistifying Ethereum technology: Application and benefits of decentralization. In *Forensic Investigations and Risk Management in Mobile and Wireless Communications* (pp. 242-256). IGI Global.

44. Shrivastava, G., Kumar, P., Gupta, B. B., Bala, S., & Dey, N. (Eds.) (2018). *Handbook of Research on Network Forensics and Analysis Techniques*. IGI Global.

45. Ahmad, F. A., Kumar, P., Shrivastava, G., & Bouhlel, M. S. (2018). Bitcoin: Digital decentralized cryptocurrency. In *Handbook of Research on Network Forensics and Analysis Techniques* (pp. 395-415). IGI Global.

46. Nagasubramanian, G., Sakthivel, R. K., Patan, R., Gandomi, A. H., Sankayya, M., & Balusamy, B. (2018). Securing e-health records using keyless signature infrastructure blockchain technology in the cloud. *Neural Computing and Applications*, 1-9. DOI: 10.1007/s00521-018-3915-1.

CHAPTER 11

A NEOTERIC SMART AND SUSTAINABLE FARMING ENVIRONMENT INCORPORATING BLOCKCHAIN-BASED ARTIFICIAL INTELLIGENCE APPROACH

M. Afshar Alam, Mohd Abdul Ahad, Sherin Zafar, Gautami Tripathi

Department of Computer Science & Engineering, School of Engineering Sciences & Technology, Jamia Hamdard, New Delhi, India

Corresponding authors: zafarsherin@gmail.com; gautami1489@gmail.com; aalam@jamiahamdard.ac.in

Abstract

The rapid increase in the global population has resulted in an estimated increase of 70% in agricultural production by 2050 to meet the ever-increasing demands of people. To develop cost-effective agricultural solutions, 90% intensification of technological farming is required for achieving agricultural inputs and market demands. Today, the agricultural sector is affected by various factors like increased labor costs, increased population, crop failures, unpredictable yields, extreme weather, climate change, market fluctuations, etc. All these factors have directly or indirectly affected the socioeconomic status of farmers. With such a large number of challenges and increasing demands there is a need to implement an artificial intelligence-based approach for developing smart farming environment for the real-time monitoring and management of agricultural issues. According to a UN report, two-thirds of the world population will migrate to urban areas, resulting in a major decline in the agricultural workforce.

This chapter proposes a smart farming environment based on artificial intelligence (AI) and blockchain technology (BCT). Artificial Intelligence can be harnessed to automate and manage the agricultural and related tasks while blockchain technology can help in intensifying agri-food and supply chains. A sensational AI-based approach will help in developing the smart farming environment that can efficiently gather and monitor data for the real-time monitoring to address the uncertain issues faced by the agricultural community.

BCT can handle issues related to the increased demands for agricultural products with transparency and trust. It will also accompany a variety of certifications schemes on branded agricultural products that face issues related to claims, labels and adulterations. BCT can prove to be an efficient solution for agricultural products' safety, quality and sustainability. It will ensure the permanency of records during data sharing. The use of ICT in the agricultural sector will provide more efficient solutions for effective water and land usage resulting in maximum agricultural yields. This chapter proposes a neoteric smart and sustainable farming environment incorporating blockchain-based artificial intelligence approach.

Keywords: Blockchain, artificial intelligence, smart and sustainable

11.1 Introduction

Agriculture is considered to be the prime revenue generator for the Indian economy but the conditions of the farmers across India and the world still remain quite uncertain and totally dependent on weather and other related conditions. Around 13.7% of gross domestic product (GDP) of India comes through agriculture, which is relatively low, with India as an agriculture country providing 7.6% of total agricultural output across the world. Also, agriculture sustains 60% of the total population, with India being the 7th largest exporter of agriculture across the world. With 52% of the population of India involved in agricultural production, the GDP contribution is only 13.7% from the agricultural sector. All the above statistical analysis reveals that the agriculture sector needs to be transformed into e-agriculture by utilizing the current smart technologies. In the last two decades it has been observed that around 3 hundred thousand of the population involved in the agricultural sector have committed suicide and also every day around 2,000 people are changing their minds and shifting towards other sources of income, leaving the agriculture sector [1, 2].

Farmers in India and across the world suffer financial distress due to huge financial instability prevailing in the agriculture sector caused by market risks, climate changes, production aspects and fluctuating prices. Crops of farmers suffer from unfavorable climate scenarios, the erratic nature of weather, rainfall characteristics and inadequate and poorly distributed supply. Also, water for irrigation is heavily unavailable and crop failures occur gradually due to reduction in size of lands and inadequate holdings of lands. An area of 140 million hectares of agriculture land with around 80% small lands and 60% of large farmlands all suffer from droughts and flood calamities. Due to less holdings, land farmers get less income and the prices of their crops are not realized properly, and the poor farmers are not able to sell their crop yields into irregular markets to get decent prices.

The farmers suffer losses as the middlemen get profits due to supply chain inefficiency and lack of failure transparencies. Also, if a farmer gets a high yield, the storage facilities are quite inadequate as 30-40% of yield gets damaged due to the insufficiency and unavailability of cold storage systems. Around 90% of Indian farmers face indebtedness and commit suicide. Credit system access is lacking for about 60% of farmers so they get caught in the trap of money lenders who charge heavy rates of interests of around 40-60%. Also, the cooperative-based credit system also has high rates of interest, so the farmers are unable to repay the loans. Farmers face huge indebtedness as the prices of agricultural inputs are increasing rapidly and production prices are falling. Crops fail repeatedly and farmers are not able to access credit systems. Since the money lenders provide high interest rates, farmers rush towards government support but the changing government policies have led to withdrawal of assistance for farmers [3, 4].

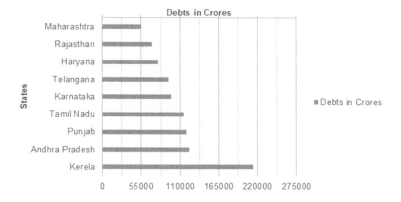

Figure 11.1   Farmers across various states caught in the cycle of agricultural debt.

To a large extent, family unit obligations are considered to be a critical reason for the problems of farmers, the utilization of certain unlimited obligation will help to improve crop efficiency, living conditions, and lower suicide rates of farmers. About 52% of India's 90 million agriculture-dependent families are utilizing the obligation alleviation programs that neglect to give legitimate help to small farmers who rely upon cash from moneylenders, as the farmer is landless and does not approach the bank for loans [5, 6]. Hence, all the above difficulties and drawbacks require an e-agriculture approach for dependent farmers. An e-agriculture scenario focuses on achieving the following:

1. Better credit offices.

2. Better quality and less expensive data sources required for yields.

3. Provide valuable climate data to farmers for the auspicious design of their harvests.

4. Wipe out mediators by connecting farmers directly to customers/retailers.

5. Improve cultivating productivity to guarantee the budgetary strength of farmers.

Farmers need a straightforward, trusted and reliable wellspring of data which can provide the ability to legitimately interface with the market, banks and buyers and dispense with brokers who do profiteering at their expense because of absence of straightforwardness in the system.

The above points and conditions have led to the specifications of the current chapter, "A Neoteric Smart and Sustainable Farming Environment Incorporating Blockchain-Based Artificial Intelligence Approach," which deals with the concepts of both artificial intelligence for making agriculture industry smart and blockchain methodology to incorporate trust of farmers back into this sector. The upcoming sections of this chapter deal with "Artificial Intelligence Technology and Its Impact on Agriculture" in Section 11.2, followed by "Blockchain Technology and Its Impact on Agriculture" in Section 11.3. Section 11.4 specifies the scenario of the proposed work with specifications and simulation analysis. Lastly, the conclusion and future work in Section 11.5 provides complete analysis of this chapter followed by references.

11.2   Artificial Intelligence Technology and Its Impact on Agriculture

Expanded use of technology is considered to be a prerequisite for better crop yields, which is one of the fundamental reasons why robots are called for in horticulture. This has persuaded farmers to develop cultivation activities, which has given an upward push to the prerequisite of computerizing cultivating tasks. Man-made intelligence, commonly known as artificial intelligence (AI), with reproduced algorithmic models mirrors human conduct that can be utilized for various complex tasks. In this procedure an introduced application guides farmers through the process of developing, sowing, reaping and clearance of produce. Artificial intelligence can be adjusted to continuously execute tasks usually performed by humans, as it doesn't require consistent supervision [7]. There are huge advantages to AI being used in agriculture; for example, in the agribusiness sector AI has been used in mechanical technology for crop and soil cultivation. Artificial intelligence and algorithmic models store explicit crop dampness requirements and survey the dampness content in the fields by utilizing satellites. It also contacts farmers through instant messaging about water prerequisites implemented through an auto-water system. Computer-based intelligence makes even-minded evaluations of interest and supply based on crop intensity and local harvest arrangements. This innovation helps ranchers in upgrading their harvest yield and items quality by investigating and connecting a substantial amount of organized and unstructured information from numerous sources into noteworthy bits of knowledge for improving yields. In Tanzania, AI found ailments with 98% precision and conveyed mechanical technology to remove weeds [8].

11.2.1   Future of Artificial Intelligence in Agriculture

As indicated by an examination, computerized cultivating and associated farm administrations can affect 70 million Indian farms in 2020, hence adding US$ 9 billion to farmer wages. In 2017, the Global AI in horticulture showcase measure was 240 million US$ and it is estimated to achieve 1100 million US$ before the end of 2025 and a CAGR of 20.8% from 2018-2025. In this way, activities to increase advanced proficiency in provincial areas can be viewed as a weapon in multiplying farmers salaries in the not so distant future. Driving sales of AI in the agriculture market are Ag Leader Technology, Trimble, John Deere, Iteris, AGCO, aWhere, Gamaya, Granular and Raven Industries. The promise of artificial intelligence is key to an agricultural revolution in a world where more food must be delivered using fewer assets. A technology is being developed and researched at NatureFresh Farms, a 20-year-old company growing vegetables on 185 acres between Ontario and Ohio, in which a robotic lens zooms in on the yellow flower of a tomato seedling and images of the plant flow into an AI algorithm that predicts precisely how long it will take for the blossom to become a ripe tomato ready for picking, packing, and shipping to market. According to Keith Bradley, IT Manager for NatureFresh Farms, knowing exactly how many tomatoes will be available to sell in the future makes the job of the sales team easier. This is only one case of AI changing farming, a developing pattern that will lead to a transformation of agriculture. From detecting pests to predicting which crops will yield the best returns, artificial intelligence can enable mankind to defy one of its greatest difficulties: feeding an extra 2 billion individuals by 2050, even as climate change disrupts developing seasons, transforms arable land into deserts, and floods once-rich deltas with seawater [9].

> *"Farming is on the cusp of a major change."* – Gayle Sheppard, vice president and general manager of Intel® AI.

The farming industry will be changed by information science and computerized reasoning through AI. Farmers will have the devices to maximize each acre of land. Getting the most from each acre isn't a scholarly issue. The United Nations estimates that food production will have to increase by some 50% by the middle of the century. From 1960 to 2015, agricultural production increased significantly as the world's population grew from 3 billion to 7 billion people. While innovations in pesticides, composts, and machines contributed to agricultural gains, most of these gains can be attributed to plowing more land, cutting forests and diverting fresh water to fields, orchards and rice paddies [10].

> *"The industry will be transformed by data science and artificial intelligence. Farmers will have the tools to get the most from every acre."* – Gayle Sheppard, vice president and general manager of Intel$^{\circledR}$ AI.

11.2.2 AI vs. Grasshoppers

Farmers have always been plagued by pests. Nearly ten thousand years after the innovation of agriculture, beetles, grasshoppers, and other harvest-eating bugs still eat into profits by eating grains that would otherwise feed people. However, AI gives producers a weapon against grain-eating bugs. Not long ago, a farmer in Texas checked the direction of the wind and figured a swarm of grasshoppers was probably going to descend on the southwest corner of his fields. But before he could check his fields, he got an alert on his smartphone from the AI company he hired to monitor his farm. Comparing new satellite images against those taken of the same area over a five-year time frame, an AI algorithm recognized that the grasshoppers had descended on another corner of the farmer's field. The farmer investigated the area, confirmed the warning was correct and expelled the costly pests from his field of nearly ripened corn. At NatureFresh Farms, the nursery tomatoes develop in a bed of ground-up coconut husks. It's a supplement free condition that enables the producers to totally control what goes into the plant. Sensors screen the natural product's advancement toward ripeness, changing light to quicken or moderate the pace of development. This sort of cultivation requires impressive preparation, and NatureFresh Farms utilizes Intel$^{\circledR}$ Xeon$^{\circledR}$ processors to control its AI calculations [11-13].

> *"Within excess of 2,500 hubs, the nurseries are a look into the eventual fate of cultivating."*– Keith Bradley, IT Manager for NatureFresh Farms.

11.3 Blockchain Technology (BCT) and Its Impact on Agriculture

Originally designed as a technology to support and reform the financial sector, Blockchain today has changed the way security solutions are being designed and implemented. The blockchain technology is based on the concept of allowing digital information to be distributed without being copied. The implementation of blockchain technology involves a list of records called blocks that keeps on growing with the addition of new information. These blocks are linked together using cryptographic hash functions, where each block contains the hash of the previous block, thus forming a chain. The information provided in this way is available for anyone to see, thus ensuring the transparency and accountability of the information that passes in a secured manner. Whenever a new block is added to the chain, it is verified by millions of distributed users. When the newly created block is verified by the users it is then added to the existing chain using the cryptographic principles [14].

The major aspects of blockchain technology that makes it the choice today are:

- *Its Distributed Nature*: The distributed nature of the blockchain technology allows storing information in a decentralized manner, thus facilitating a peer-to-peer system that allows everyone to be the owner of the information.

- *Transparency*: Another fascinating aspect of blockchain technology is transparency along with user privacy. Blockchain uses public addresses for all transactions, thus securing the real identity of the user.

- *Immutability*: Another aspect of BCT that makes it secure is its immutable nature. The blocks once added to the chain cannot be tampered with. This is made possible with the use of the cryptographic hash function [15].

11.3.1 Types of Blockchain

Blockchains can be broadly divided into three categories, namely public, federated and private, as depicted in Figure 11.2. Public blockchain networks can be accessed by anyone without any participation permissions. Everyone is allowed to add blocks to the chain. Some of the notable features of the public blockchains are transparency, mutability, distributed nature and immutability. The federated blockchains, also known as the consortium blockchains, are controlled by a group of leaders. These are decentralized systems where everyone does not have the right to join and participate, rather the process requires proper permissions. Private blockchains are like a centralized system. There are ongoing debates on the status of the private blockchains as some people are of the view that they don't follow the very nature of blockchains. The private blockchain networks like federated ones require proper permission to access the network [16].

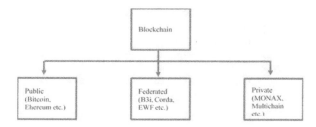

Figure 11.2 Types of blockchain.

11.3.2 Generations of Blockchain Technology

Since its inception in 2008, the blockchain technology has continuously evolved and has created a niche in the industry across multiple sectors, as depicted in Table 11.1. Although the technology is only a decade old it has already seen three generations with a fourth generation in line to be launched. The first generation of the blockchain consisted of bitcoins. It was based on the proof-of-work algorithms. The idea was to enhance the existing monetary system using a P2P, distributed system that is anonymous and transparent at the same time. The second generation of blockchain was introduced after the creators realized that besides money, several other trust-based transactions can benefit from the blockchain.

It was in 2015 that the second generation of blockchain emerged with the introduction of Ethereum. A digital ecosystem was introduced that could be used to benefit several decentralized projects. It was in the second generation that initial coin offerings (ICO) came into the picture. Smart contracts were introduced that made it possible to handle complicated trust agreements in a safe, secure, fair, quick and automatic way without the need of any third party. Despite the benefits provided by the first two generations of blockchain they had many issues, including the scalability.

Table 11.1 Generations of blockchain.

	First generation	**Second generation**	**Third generation**
Examples	Bitcoin, lite coin	Ethereum,	IOTA
Advantages	Secured monetary system	Smart Contracts	Highly Scalable
Limitations	No Scalability	No Scalability	High Cost
Applications	Cryptocurrencies	Initial coin offerings (ICO)	High speed scalable applications

To overcome this, the third generation of blockchain came into the picture. It provides higher scalability and cross-chain transactions. The proof-of-work consensus mechanism was replaced by the proof-of-stake mechanism [17].

11.3.3 Blockchain in Agriculture: A Boost to Smart Agriculture

In the last decade the agricultural sector has adopted modern technological reforms to automate and enhance its key functions, as depicted in Figure 11.3.

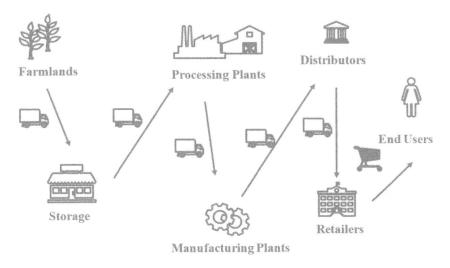

Figure 11.3 Major components of the global agricultural blockchain.

The use of smartphone-based applications has further facilitated the remote monitoring and control of farmlands and other equipment. The use of ICT in the agriculture sector has helped farmers and other stakeholders in the areas of better management and warning systems, monitoring and resource management. The introduction of blockchain technology in the agriculture sector can lead to enhancing the product supply, pricing, product tracking, etc. Starting with the buying of the seeds to the time the crops are actually harvested and sold, everything can be put on the blockchain. Since the blockchain records are highly secured and cannot be tampered with, it can help the agricultural stakeholders to monitor and control risks and minimize the distress of farmers in developing nations like India [18, 19].

Some of the major applications of blockchain in agriculture include:

- *Food Safety*: Today, with increased suspicion about the quality of food that we consume there is an immediate need to develop a mechanism that can track and monitor food safety. With the increase in food-related allergies and other health hazards, customers are demanding assurance for the quality of food they are consuming. The global food industry is also suffering losses at the hands of food frauds. Today, big food chains and other agriculture-based industries are looking out for technological reforms that can solve this issue. Blockchain technology can prove to be a one-stop solution to ensure the quality, authenticity, accountability and tracking of food products. Blockchain has great potential in the food quality and maintenance area [20, 21].

- *Authenticity of Raw Materials or Agricultural Inputs*: The theft of agricultural inputs is costing big agricultural input-based industries millions of dollars and also affects their brand image negatively. The blockchain technology can help to ensure the authenticity of the inputs. All the products right from the manufacturer to the end buyer can be traced for their authenticity. The farmers with the help of their smartphones can scan the blockchain barcode to know about the source of the products they are buying. This can help in ensuring the removal of fake products from the entire process.

- *Food Supply Chain*: Blockchain can be incorporated in the food supply chain to achieve efficiency, transparency, security and fast transactions. Blockchain technology can bring together all the stakeholders of the food supply chain, including the farmers, logistics providers, retailers, consumers, etc., and ensure the auditing of the entire process. Right from the initial phase the farmers can put all information related to the crops on the blockchain that can be received by the food processing industry where they can add onto it. This process can continue till the food reaches the end users. The end users can then ensure the safety of the food they are consuming by tracking the food supply chain.

- *Logistics and Payments*: Logistics and payments play a major role in the agricultural supply chain, especially for the cases where perishable crops are involved in uncertain conditions. In such cases a lot of money is at stake. Implementation of blockchain into the supply chain can simplify the delivery process to a great extent. Firstly, the intermediaries can be removed from the picture. Secondly, the unnecessary delay can be eliminated and on-time payments to farmers can be ensured.

- *Government Subsidies*: In a country like India, the agricultural sector is highly dependent on government subsidies. The government is spending a significant amount of their annual budget for subsidies. In the year 2017-18, the Indian government gave around 32,000 Crore rupees for agricultural-related subsidies to the farmers. The increase in the government subsidies every year on one hand and the deteriorating conditions of the farmers on the other hand raise the question of whether these subsidies are actually reaching the needy. Today, a burning question is how much of this help is actually reaching its actual destination. Governments across the world are searching for mechanisms to monitor and track the entire process of disbursements of subsidies and other forms of government aid. With the introduction of blockchain technology this entire process can be put on the blockchain for easy tracking of the distribution process in a transparent way.

- *Marketing and Sales*: The blockchain technology has the potential to bring together the producer and consumers and redefine the entire process of selling and buying that currently involves several middlemen. The uniting of the sellers and buyers will remove the middleman from the process and minimize the difference between the price paid to the farmers and the price paid by the end consumers for the commodity. Blockchain can help to create a favorable environment where the farmers can directly deal with the consumers with minimum involvement of the middleman [21, 22].

Besides all the above advantages, blockchain can also revolutionize the way land records are maintained. The authorities can use blockchain for all types of record keeping and bring transparency to the whole process. The state of Andhra Pradesh in India has already taken steps in this direction by joining hands with ChromaWay, a Swedish startup, to build solutions for land record keeping [24, 25]. With the rising concerns of the consumers and other stakeholders towards food safety and authenticity of other by-products, blockchain technology can come to the rescue by catering to the challenges presently faced by the agricultural community, as depicted in Figure 11.4.

Figure 11.4   Challenges facing blockchain methodology.

11.4 A Neoteric Smart and Sustainable Farming Environment Incorporating Blockchain-Based Artificial Intelligence Approach

The proposed approach utilizes the two most popular and response-oriented methodologies, AI and Blockchain technologies, for providing sustainable farming or e-agriculture. The diagrams of the AI and blockchain approach to revolutionize farming methodology is depicted in Figure 11.5 and Figure 11.6, respectively.

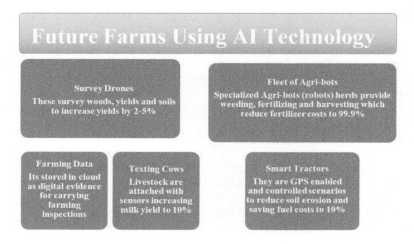

Figure 11.5   Artificial intelligence approach to revolutionize farming methodology into sustainable farming and e-agriculture.

The proposed methodology will provide a huge number of benefits for the farmers which include:

- Precision farming

- Livestock monitoring

- Smart greenhouses

- Crop monitoring

- Smart logistics

- Smart irrigation

- Asset monitoring

- Soil quality monitoring

- Weather forecasting

The proposed AI and blockchain methodologies for e-agriculture focus on achieving the following:

1. Improve small producers by providing them exchanges as expert associations.

2. Strengthen foundation in retail outlets, entire deal markets and acquisition fixates with a push for cleanliness.

3. Link farmers with purchasers through an aggregate-promoting system dependent on contract cultivating, actualized through smart contracts and encouraging virtual sell-offs, store network money and protection of all in the BCT-enabled smart contract contract.

4. Create an information and communications technology (ICT) foundation from farmers to purchasers incorporating all delegates.

5. Integrate AI-based internet of things (IoT)-driven quality testing and investigation for comprehensive bits of data stored along the entire network.

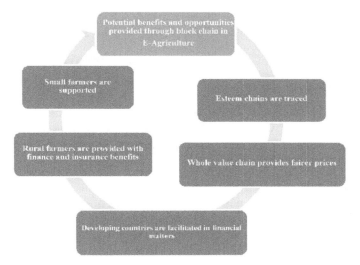

Figure 11.6 Potential benefits and opportunities provided through blockchain in e-agriculture.

Blockchain and e-agriculture help in achieving central value chains to get the following benefits:

- Getting the different partners together and arranging agricultural business linkages is the fundamental capacity of a value chain.

- Effective co-appointment of choices and their trade is required for various members in the value chain to cooperate.

- The administration of the esteem chain covers the guidelines directing coordination among the partners.

- Increasing the estimation of the value chain is conceivable just by expanding the shopper request.

- Beyond satisfying the customer's needs the members of the value anchor should be the focus.

- To maintain aggressiveness the value anchor needs to be continuously developed.

- For the value chain to be economical in the market and build up convincing linkages the chain needs to circulate benefits among the different members.

- Differentiates items.

- Continuously enhances, advances, oversees, and showcases various items for appropriateness.

- Creates higher value.

- Uses hierarchical components to accomplish proficiency.

- Forms partnerships and accomplishes co-appointment.

- Showcases exchanges and incorporates contract systems and supply chains.

- Introduces practices to meet ecological and social duty concerns.

The key steps of low value chains are:

1. *Value Chain Prioritization*: Prioritization of value chains is dependent on various criteria; for example, neglected market request, number of focused makers/endeavors in the esteem chain and the nearness of offices to put resources into their relations for increasing definite investigations.

2. *Value Chain Examination*: A value chain map which graphically presents the partners and their shared connections is readied. Imperatives in the market, innovation/item improvement, executives/association, framework and so forth should be analyzed. Systems of governance, co-appointment, guideline and control in the value chains are analyzed.

3. *Identification of Market-Based Solutions*: Financially reasonable arrangements that can add to value chain aggressiveness need to be addressed. Interest-driven updating of knowledge, skills, technology and support services will be examined.

4. *Assessment of Market-Based Solutions*: The conveyance of pay and work benefits among the chain partners and expenses and edges should be evaluated. Lead firms that could give arrangements in a maintainable way are distinguished and challenges in giving the arrangements inspected.

5. *Identification of Assistance Exercises*: A system of help exercises for supporting difficulties proposed by the lead firms are analyzed through partner meetings.

6. *Structuring Joint Effort and Estimating Execution*: The venture exercises are organized dependent on a causal model that gathers yields; results and effects are a joint effort through memorandum of understanding; money-related and specialized help will be set up. Figure 11.8 shows how the data generated at different stages of the agricultural supply chain through the proposed work can be hashed into a block, forming a blockchain for the entire process. This blockchain can serve multiple purposes as per the needs and requirements of the different stakeholders.

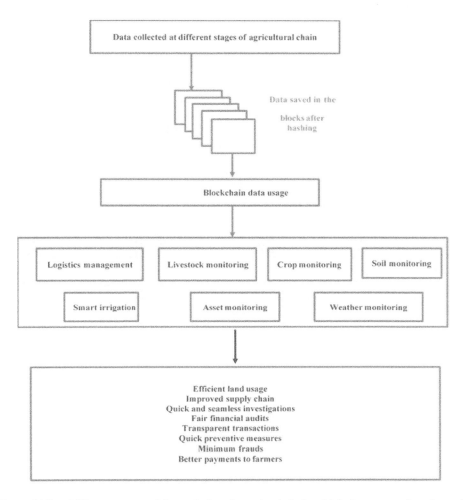

Figure 11.7   Different stages of the agricultural supply chain in which the proposed work can be hashed into a block forming a blockchain.

Blockchain technology (BCT) and artificial intelligence strategies offer enormous chances to improve store-network straightforwardness, recognizability and decrease exchange costs. Blockchain utilizes cryptographic trust that is inalienably detectable, timestamped, and restriction resistant; and a disseminated ledger that is close-continuous. Further enhancements in this innovation have enabled algorithm-based smart contracts which empower a mix of legally binding connections and exchanges through self-confirmation and self-execution understandings. IBM has reported collaborating with Maersk Line, the largest container shipping company on the planet, for shippers, ports, traditional workplaces, banks, and different partners in worldwide supply chains to track cargo utilizing BCT. China-based Dianrong and FnConn have reported the dispatch of Chained Finance, which empowers a store-network fund to convey required money to network providers and give expansive worldwide makers upgraded desirability and straightforwardness utilizing BCT. A few new businesses like Provenance, Monegraph, Skuchain, GateChain, Hijro, Wave, Ripple, and R3 CEV have begun actualizing a progression of ventures and some of them have effectively graduated into adult items and administrations. IBM and a group of driving food organizations are taking a noteworthy stride towards making food supply chains progressively straightforward with BCT.

The proposed approach utilizing BCT and AI methodology will help in achieving the use cases described below:

- *BCT and AI-based methodologies to deal with data preparing and contract handling in e-agriculture*: Important store network exercises for e-agriculture in a customary inventory network have been conducted. Order preparing, delivery and material stream, charging and invoicing and installment are considered. The purchaser's purchase order, products accessibility check and supplier's sales order are the means in the request handling layer. The provider's delivery document, transfer request demonstrating source stockpiling and goal stockpiling, supplier's sales order, carrier's bill, buyer's goods receipt document coordinated with supplier's delivery document and buyer's purchase order are the means in agriculture-based shipping and material stream. The provider's billing due note dependent on supplier's delivery document and supplier's sales order is dispatched to purchaser. A three-route confirmation between buyer's purchases order, buyers good's receipt and supplier's invoice is coordinated and buyer's account charged. Purchaser chooses payment procedure and bank installments are made dependent on approved supplier invoices.

- *BCT and AI-based production network has incorporated various layers, including multivendor contracts, data and financing of supply money streams*: BCT and AI-based incorporated store-network supply chain request prepares a purchase order (PO) from the purchaser. PO from buyer with enrolled conveyance records, bill of lading from carrier and so on could be consequently coordinated through a smart contract. The approved seller's invoice triggers installment exchanges and comprises smart contracts. The total mix of item streams with the data stream could be accomplished through AI-based IoT framework, which is complete in itself. Financing of supply money streams and exchange receivables is significant for fruitful business nowadays. Contrasted with the outdated letter of credit, the supply chain finance currently includes exchange fund instruments like figuring, turnaround calculating, payable financing and dynamic limiting. The purchaser drives the multi-financial specialist securitization process in an enterprise resource planning (ERP) procedure. The beginning stage is the hidden exchange between the purchaser and provider. When the purchaser has endorsed the payable he transfers the receipt to the provider that can be held up until the installment term terminates and the purchaser pays the receipt. On the off chance that the early installment choice is received by the issuing and paying specialists a note is issued by the clearing house. If securities are effectively settled, installment for the limited receipt sums would be prescribed by the special purpose vehicle (SPV). After this, the provider allots the receivable to the SPV and the merchandise is warehoused. At the point when the concurred installment term between the provider and purchaser terminates the purchaser makes an installment to the proprietor of the receipt, i.e., the SPV.

- AI-based IoT and BCT-based agri-food store network cover data preparation and multi-merchant contracts take care of recognizability.

- AI-based IoT and BCT investigation coordinate start to finish delay (end-to-end delay) multi-party coordination and store-network biological system for virus chain in agriculture, fish, meat and so forth.

11.5 Conclusion and Future Work

This chapter showed that AI-based blockchain innovation needs to be utilized in agricultural activities that are intended to set up a demonstrated, straightforward and progressively economical production network, incorporating key partners into the inventory network. There are numerous issues that should be understood in specific situations. The proposed AI-based blockchain innovation was demonstrated to be simpler for farmers to use, collecting all the significant blockchain forms applicable to food for cultivation and horticulture. To lessen the disadvantages of its utilization, governments ought to put more into research and advancement, so as to deliver proof of the potential advantages of this innovation. There is a necessity to see government progress towards the utilization of the AI-based blockchain, taking note of the way that administrations and their applicable divisions ought to watch and comprehend specific situations. From an arrangement point of view, different moves can be made; for example, enabling the development of AI-based blockchain, supporting the innovation as a major aspect of the general objectives of enhancing the aggressiveness and guaranteeing the supportability of the agri-food production network, and planning a reasonable administrative structure for blockchain usage. Summing up, AI-based blockchain is a promising innovation towards a straightforward inventory network; however, numerous challenges still exist which have great prominence among farmers and food supply frameworks. In the distant future it's important to recognize how these difficulties could be handled by administrative and private endeavors, so as to build up blockchain innovation as a protected, dependable and straightforward approach to guarantee sanitation and trustworthiness.

Artificial intelligence-based BCT is still at an incipient phase of improvement; however, there are signs that it is leaving the promotion cycle of burgeoning desires and entering an increasingly sensible and serious period of investigation. The wide methodology discussed in this chapter is to be embraced for its procedural enhancements and for making new value chains for the agricultural and food sectors. The key evaluation criteria should concentrate on giving the partners straightforwardness, profitability, cost investment funds, speed, quality and trust in order to eliminate the pitfalls and special incentives for fair esteem dissemination. Making progress toward such execution requires examination and evaluation of the real dangers to administrative conditions like security and consistency. To adapt to extensive methodologies requires partners cooperating with the country and the network administration to drive them towards this novel change.

REFERENCES

1. Aglionby, J. (2018). Kenya's 4G Capital Plans Tokenised Bond via Cryptocurrency. *Financial Times*, 16.

2. Ahmad, F. A., Kumar, P., Shrivastava, G., & Bouhlel, M. S. (2018). Bitcoin: Digital decentralized cryptocurrency. In *Handbook of Research on Network Forensics and Analysis Techniques* (pp. 395-415). IGI Global.

3. Becker, J., Breuker, D., Heide, T., Holler, J., Rauer, H. P., & Bhme, R. (2013). Can we afford integrity by proof-of-work? Scenarios inspired by the Bitcoin currency. In *The Economics of Information Security and Privacy* (pp. 135-156). Springer, Berlin, Heidelberg.

4. Shrivastava, G. *et al.* (2018). *Handbook of Research on Network Forensics and Analysis Techniques*. IGI Global.

5. Bentov, I., Gabizon, A., & Mizrahi, A. (2016, February). Cryptocurrencies without proof of work. In *International Conference on Financial Cryptography and Data Security* (pp. 142-157). Springer, Berlin, Heidelberg.

6. BitFury Group. (2015). Proof of Stake versus Proof of Work. *White Paper*.

7. Bunge, J. (2017). Latest Use for a Bitcoin Technology: Tracing Turkeys from Farm to Table. *The Wall Street Journal*.

8. Capizzi, G., Lo Sciuto, G., Napoli, C., Tramontana, E., & Woźniak, M. (2016). A novel neural networks-based texture image processing algorithm for orange defects classification. *International Journal of Computer Science & Applications*, 13(2).

9. Clark, F. (2003). *Striking Hypothesis*, Human Sci. & Tech. Press, Changsha.

10. Dharmaraj, V., & Vijayanand, C. (2018). Artificial intelligence (AI) in agriculture. *International Journal Curr. Microbiol. Apply Science*, 7(12), 2122-2128.

11. Hanson, A. J., Anyafulude, J., & Francis, J. N. (2017). Plant leaf disease detection using deep learning and convolutional neural network. *International Journal of Engineering Science*, 5324.

12. Hopfield, J. J. (1982). Neural networks and physical systems with emergent collective computational abilities. *Proceedings of the National Academy of Science of the United States of America*. Vol.79: 2554-2558.

13. Karmokar, B. C., Ullah, M. S., Siddiquee, M. K., & Alam, K. M. R. (2015). Tea leaf diseases recognition using neural network ensemble. *International Journal of Computer Applications*, 114(17).

14. Eyal, I., Gencer, A. E., Sirer, E. G., & Van Renesse, R. (2016). Bitcoin-NG: A scalable blockchain protocol. In *13th USENIX Symposium on Networked Systems Design and Implementation (NSDI 16)* (pp. 45-59).

15. Gupta, V. (2017). *Building the Hyperconnected Future on Blockchains*. World Government Summit.

16. Allison, I. (2016). Skuchain: Here's How Blockchain Will Save Global Trade a Trillion Dollars. *International Business Times*.

17. Besnainou, J. (2017). Blockchain and Supply Chain Financing. A Conversation with Skuchain. *CleanTech Group*.

18. Kamilaris, A., Kartakoullis, A., & Prenafeta-Bold, F. X. (2017). A review on the practice of big data analysis in agriculture. *Computers and Electronics in Agriculture*, 143, 23-37.

19. Khaqqi, K. N., Sikorski, J. J., Hadinoto, K., & Kraft, M. (2018). Incorporating seller/buyer reputation-based system in blockchain-enabled emission trading application. *Applied Energy*, 209, 8-19.

20. White, M., Killmeyer, J., & Chew, B. (2017). *Will Blockchain Transform the Public Sector?. Blockchain basics for government*, A report from the Deloitte Center for Government Insights, Deloitte UniversityPress.

21. Wunsche, A.(2016). *Technological Disruption of Capital Markets and Reporting*.

22. Lee, H. L., Mendelson, H., Rammohan, S., & Srivastava, A. (2017). *Technology in Agribusiness: Opportunities to Drive Value*. Stanford Graduate School of Business.

23. Levitt, T. (2016). Blockchain technology trialled to tackle slavery in the fishing industry. *The Guardian*.

24. Lin, Y. P., Petway, J., Anthony, J., Mukhtar, H., Liao, S. W., Chou, C. F., & Ho, Y. F. (2017). Blockchain: The evolutionary next step for ICT e-agriculture. *Environments*, 4(3), 50.

25. Love, J., & Somerville, H. (2018). Retailer Carrefour using blockchain to improve checks on food products. Reuters.

26. Manski, S. (2017). Building the blockchain world: Technological commonwealth or just more of the same? *Strategic Change*, 26(5), 511-522.

27. Markets and Markets Research (2016). Food Traceability Market worth $14 Billion by 2019.

28. Maslova, A. (2017). Growing the garden: How to use blockchain in agriculture. *Cointelegraph Bitcoin & Ethereum Blockchain News*.

29. Patil, A. S., Tama, B. A., Park, Y., & Rhee, K. H. (2017). A framework for blockchain based secure smart green house farming. In *Advances in Computer Science and Ubiquitous Computing* (pp. 1162-1167). Springer, Singapore.

30. Sharma, S. (2017). Climate Change and Blockchain. ISO 690.

31. Tayeb, S., & Lago, F. (2018). Blockchain technology: between high hopes and challenging implications. *MENA Business Law Review*, First quarter.

32. Tian, F. (2017). A supply chain traceability system for food safety based on HACCP, blockchain & Internet of things. *International Conference on Service Systems and Service Management (ICSSSM)*. IEEE.

33. Tschorsch, F., & Scheuermann, B. (2016). Bitcoin and beyond: A technical survey on decentralized digital currencies. *IEEE Communications Surveys & Tutorials*, 18(3), 2084-2123.

34. Tse, D., Zhang, B., Yang, Y., Cheng, C., & Mu, H. (2017). Blockchain application in food supply information security. *International Conference on Industrial Engineering and Engineering Management (IEEM)* (pp. 1357-1361). IEEE.

35. Srivastava, S. R., Dube, S., Shrivastaya, G., & Sharma, K. (2019). Smartphone triggered security challenges - Issues, case studies and prevention. In *Cyber Security in Parallel and Distributed Computing: Concepts, Techniques, Applications and Case Studies*, 187-206.

36. Sharma, K., & Shrivastava, G. (2014). Public key infrastructure and trust of Web based knowledge discovery. *Int. J. Eng., Sci. Manage.*, 4(1), 56-60.

37. Sharma, K., Rafiqui, F., Attri, P., & Yadav, S. K. (2019). A two-tier security solution for storing data across public cloud. *Recent Patents on Computer Science*, 12(3), 191-201.

CHAPTER 12

THEORIES OF CRYPTOCURRENCY, BLOCKCHAIN AND DISTRIBUTED SYSTEMS AND ENVIRONMENTAL IMPLICATIONS

P. Mary Jeyanthi

Business Analytics & Information Systems, Institute of Management Technology, Nagpur, Maharashtra, India

Corresponding author: pmjeyanthi@imtnag.ac.in / dr.maryprem@gmail.com

Abstract

Blockchain is fundamentally a distributed database and open source where anyone can change the underlying code and see the current status of an operation. It is actually a peer-to-peer network. Think of it as a massive global database that runs on zillions and zillions of computers. It doesn't require any controlling intermediaries to authenticate the transactions. Cryptocurrency and blockchain technology are the most disruptive technologies of the contemporary e-era. The scope of blockchain has the potential to disrupt key barriers to efficiency, commitment and scaling. It could record any structured information end to end. In the case of settling trillions of real-time transactions in banks, blockchain extensively supports settlement systems.

The aim of this chapter is to provide concrete knowledge about cryptocurrency, the state-of-the-art of cryptography, blockchain and distributed systems, and to emphasize the synthetic sketch of environmental issues raised by the development of new disruptive technologies. There are key challenges to be focused on if the blockchain is to work in the environmental sector; for example, blockchain systems, especially the use of cryptocurrencies, are enormously energy-intensive. Moreover, there are many natural resources and environmental services considerations that are relevant to low- and middle-income countries while engaging these in a global framework.

Keywords: Cryptocurrency, blockchain technology, energy consumption, Bitcoin, environmental implications, distributed systems

12.1 Introduction

Bill Gates opined that "Banking is essential, banks are not." The early 21st century has seen a proliferation of financial technology and analytics firms, providing a wide and varied array of services, from payments and local and international money transmission to financing through P2P lending and crowdfunding. Venture capital funding in the U.K. for financial technology-related business has increased to more than US $500 million in 2014, while the sector is estimated to contribute more than GBP20 billion to the economy.[1] Many countries have quantified their purpose to create an ecosystem in which such businesses can grow, which can only mean the continued growth of the sector in the predictable future. Simultaneously, the friction of making payments and transfers in fiat currency is reduced, facilitated by e-money, which will raise the bar of virtual currency and the cryptocurrency market.

As per Satoshi Nakamoto, the unknown person or people who developed Bitcoin, a cryptocurrency is nothing but an electronic payment system based on cryptographic proof instead of trust, allowing any two willing parties to transact directly with each other without the need for a trusted third party. New coins are created by an algorithm with the insertion of cryptography. Cryptocurrencies have come a long way from their relatively ambiguous origins.

While the financial institutions have concerns about digital currencies as tools for criminals, terrorists or rebellious individuals frustrated with traditional money, the industry has significantly progressed in establishing their legitimate potential. As of 2019, the trend of digital asset and payment systems has picked up due to decentralized peer-to-peer network.

In 2017, Japan became the first country in the world that legalized cryptocurrency such as Bitcoin and Ethereum at the official level. That allowed many online stores across the country to accept payments in tokens. Other countries also didn't want to refrain from this global trend. The G20 is currently working on the possibility of cyrptocurrency market regulation. However, there are some countries that ban cryptocurrencies in their territories. For example, financial firms in China are not allowed to hold cryptocurrency or lead any initial coin offerings (ICOs). In Venezuela, cryptocurrency miners are prosecuted.

One of the greatest inventions in the world is electricity. Now, more and more, the usage of electricity is extended to a greater level. Most of our electricity is generated from nonrenewable sources that pollute our air and water. As the demand for electricity increases, the damage to our planet also increases. Even though we care about our world, we are not willing to give up the luxuries of electricity. Cryptocurrency mining demands an extremely high and ever-increasing amount of electricity. Green energy production is one of the missions of the world, especially for Blockchain and cryptocurrencies marketers.

One of the major problems is still not being effectively addressed, namely, the energy consumption of transacting across many of the biggest Blockchain networks in the industry. This issue, which has grown exponentially over the past few years, shows no signs of slowing down and continues to cause environmental degradation along the way. Despite being called a hoax by figures such as Jamie Dimon, Bitcoin has continued to grow to over US $1800. On top of being feared as a bubble or a tool for criminals, cryptocurrency has also generated considerable concern for environmentalists. Despite its virtual nature, Bitcoin mining requires a massive amount of processing power and in turn, energy.

---

[1] Investment Trends in FinTech report by SVB, available at http://www.svb.com/News/Company-News/ 2015-FinTech-Report–Investment-Trends-in-FinTech/?site=U.K.

According to *Digiconomist*,[2] Bitcoin's estimated annual electricity consumption as of March 17th 2020 was 77.78 TWh (see Figure 12.1). To put that into perspective, if Bitcoin's network were a country, it would rank 60th in terms of global energy consumption, on par with the nation of Bulgaria. The energy used by a single Bitcoin transaction could power the average U.S. household for eight days.

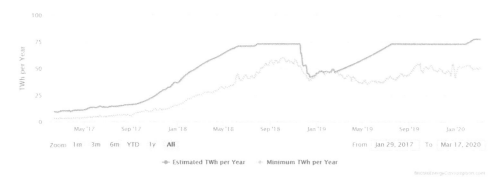

Figure 12.1   Bitcoin energy consumption index.

This daily consumption of power translates to 118.36 kg of CO_2 being emitted per transaction, or 11083 kilotons annually. If we follow the EPA's estimate that the average car emits 4.7 metric tons of CO_2 each year, then Bitcoin has the same environmental impact as approximately 2.358 million cars annually. These statistics have caused many environmentalists to fear the rise of Bitcoin and other cryptocurrencies, as they are creating emissions and hindering the fight against global climate change (see Figure 12.2).

Figure 12.2   Photographic depiction of the relation between cryptocurrencies and the environment.

The blockchain is the backbone of the digital currency of the world. The energy required for mining cryptocurrencies is significant. Most of the current mining farms are using electricity from nonrenewable, greenhouse gas-emitting sources (coal, petroleum-based fuels, and other fossil fuels). The utilization of Blockchain technology should not be synonymous with environmental degradation and high energy costs. We need to enrich ourselves with technological innovation and creation without the detrimental effects on air and water. It is ultimately the responsibility of those developing innovative cryptocurrency

[2]https://digiconomist.net/bitcoin-energy-consumption

and blockchain projects to create a profitable solution which allows Blockchain to build a greener, more sustainable future. Using green energy and renewable powered data mining centers on a self-financing network, we have the responsibility of not just providing innovative solutions for cryptocurrency mining, but for green and sustainable energy in all forms. Currently green energy and environmental sustainability sectors have been investing in Green Energy real assets and incubating innovation by promoting, encouraging and financing research and development into new renewable technologies and sustainable practices to make the world a safer place to live in the future. It is providing a bridge between the existing regulatory environment and Blockchain ecosystems. Blockchain and cryptocurrencies have paved the way for this generation's industrial revolution, and we must give it the best opportunity to survive if we're to pass on the baton to the millennial generation for it to thrive.

The emphasis of this chapter is on current tendencies in the growth of cryptocurrency as well as the implications of environmental issues. It also aims to explore the limits of blockchain and distributed system. In addition to the implications and applications of cryptocurrency and blockchain being described, the concept is elaborately discussed along with the theories of cryptocurrency, blockchain and distributed system and futuristic advancements and their implications.

12.2 Literature Review

According to Unites States Senator Thomas Carper, "Virtual currencies, perhaps most notably Bitcoin, have captured the imagination of some, struck fear among others, and confused the heck out of the rest of us." While the issue of environmental sustainability of cryptocurrencies is under debate in the media (*The Guardian*, November 2017), academia has been relatively slow to address this urgent issue. Only a couple of papers have discussed the impact of the growth of these digital asset classes on the environment. Sustainability in the context of environmental and economic aspects have been analyzed by Vranken [45], and the results provide an opposite conclusion to the popular belief of the developments in Bitcoin mining hardware that briefly outline alternative schemes that are less energy demanding. He finally looks at other Blockchain applications and argues that energy consumption is not a primary concern of his study. Harwick [21] states that the sustainability of cryptocurrencies is dependent upon an amalgam of environmental, economic, financial and ethical aspects.

Figure 12.3   The environmental impacts of Bitcoin.

Despite these issues, the major drawback for China continues to be the electrical costs. This has been the case for several years as the average national rates in both India and China have hovered at approximately 8 cents per kWh, which is significantly lower than other countries such as Denmark at 41 cents per kWh. While Moses Lake in Washington State has made headlines for its 1.7 cents per kWh rates which have attracted numerous pools, in China, some commercial operators can get electricity for 3 cents per kWh. Out of all currently deployed consensus algorithms, proof-of-work achieves the highest degree of trust minimization [2]. In the future, however, cryptocurrencies might thrive in such an environment because, unlike the paper-money alternatives, they allow users to make digital payments. In Kenya, where many people are unbanked but have cell phones, Vodafone's M-Pesa system has taken off [8]. If incumbent money were especially unstable, such users might opt to use their phones to transfer cryptocurrencies. O'Dwyer and Malone [5] looked at the energy consumption of bitcoin mining and considered if and when bitcoin mining would be profitable compared to the energy cost of performing the mining, and concluded that specialist hardware is usually required to make bitcoin mining profitable. They have reported that the power currently used for bitcoin mining is comparable to Ireland's electricity consumption. Rogojanu and Badea [38] explored the advantages and disadvantages of Bitcoin and compared it with other alternative monetary systems.

Ciaian, Rajcaniova, and Kancs [11] examined Bitcoin price formation by focusing on market forces of supply/demand and specific factors of digital currencies. A few studies have emerged with the view that Bitcoin presents an alternative to conventional currencies in times of weak trust, such as during the global financial crisis in 2008, thus referring to Bitcoin as digital gold [37, 38]. Others have examined the benefits of including Bitcoin in an equity portfolio [15, 17]. Baur, Lee, and Hong [3] argued that Bitcoin is a hybrid between precious metals and conventional currencies. They also highlighted its role as a useful diversifier (i.e., uncorrelated with traditional assets) and an investment. If Bitcoin is regarded as an investment, then we need to know more about its properties and particularly about its relation to other assets. However, what renders an asset interesting is its diversification and impact on environmental issues and energy consumption.

12.3 Theories of Cryptocurrency, Blockchain and Distributed Systems

12.3.1 The Theory of Blockchains

> *"The blockchain is an incorruptible digital ledger of economic transactions that can be programmed to record not just financial transactions but virtually everything of value."* – Don & Alex Tapscott, authors of *Blockchain Revolution*.

A blockchain is, in the simplest of terms, a timestamped series of immutable record of data that is managed by a cluster of computers not owned by any single entity. Each of these blocks of data (i.e., block) are secured and bound to each other using cryptographic principles (i.e., chain).

The industry-disrupting capabilities of blockchain is that it does not have the central authority.

Since it is a shared and immutable ledger, the information in it is open for anyone and everyone to see. Hence, anything that is built on the blockchain is by its very nature transparent and everyone involved is accountable for their actions. A blockchain caries no transaction cost; but there is an infrastructure cost.

Blockchain is defined as a ledger of facts. In this, several computers are assembled in a peer-to-peer network. Communication inside this network obeys cryptography. Members of this network are called nodes.

12.3.2   Definition of Blockchains

The technical definition of blockchain is that a blockchain is a linked list that is built with hash pointers instead of regular pointers.

A sociopolitical-economic-semi-technical libertarian definition is that a blockchain is an open, borderless, decentralized, public, trustless, permissionless, immutable record of transactions.

The financial-accounting definition is that a blockchain is a public, distributed ledger of peer-to-peer transactions.

A blockchain is a growing list of records, called blocks, which are linked using cryptography. Each block contains a cryptographic hash of the previous block, a timestamp, and transaction data (generally represented as a Merkle tree).

By design, a blockchain is resistant to modification of the data. It is an open, distributed ledger that can record transactions between two parties efficiently and in a verifiable and permanent way.

Figure 12.4   Simple blockchain model.

Distributed ledger technology defines a distributed ledger as a consensus of replicated, shared digital data spread across multiple sites, countries, or institutions. There is no central administrator or centralized data storage.

12.3.3   Distributed Ledger Technology (DLT) vs. Blockchain

A distributed database is spread across several nodes or computing devices which are involved in the replication of transactions/data across the nodes. Distributed ledger technology is decentralized and has different types of consensus mechanisms (see Figure 12.5).

The first fully functional distributed ledger technology combines the existing mature concepts of distributed database and cryptography. It is a chain of blocks that provides secure and valid distributed consensus and has an append-only data structure in DLT. Blockchain technology is therefore well-suited for recording events, managing records, processing transactions, tracing assets, and voting.

Figure 12.5   Distributed ledger technology (DLT).

12.3.4   Evolving Terminology with Evolved Technology: Decentralized vs. Distributed

As we all may be aware, the term "*decentralize*" has grown in popularity over the years with increased excitement around bitcoin and increased understanding of technology without central points of control or failure.

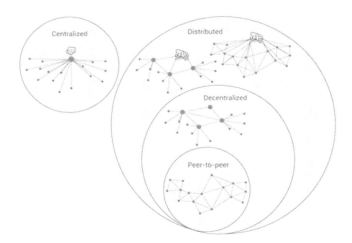

Figure 12.6   Distributed communications networks.

The illustration in Figure 12.6 attempts to convey and momentarily modify the use of the terms "*decentralized*" and "*distributed*."

12.3.4.1   Why Blockchain Will Change the World

- Enhanced security: Blockchain resists hacking by decentralizing the data storage layer. It spreads the data thin, making it more difficult to attack. It is easier to attack a single central database than to attack numerous copies of the decentralized database.

- There are no updates and deletes, making it an immutable record of historical facts. Provides proof of stake.

- Can be used to store anything of value that can be digitized.

- Improves efficiencies in transaction clearing, especially when dealing with multiple agencies.

- Lowers transaction fees.

- No central authority means no central trust. The blockchain itself provides digital trust. It is trustless.

- Open and transparent. All transactions in history can be seen, tracked, and validated by anyone.

- May become the ultimate proof of value ownership, bypassing governments, corporations, individuals, and criminals.

- Provides powerful audit trails.

12.3.4.2   *Where Is Blockchain?*

- It is decentralized.

- Nodes on the network hold copies of the blockchain (not all nodes need to have the entire copy).

- When a new block is relayed, the other nodes validate it and add it to their blockchain.

- You can think of it as nodes (participants) each having a copy of the entire database of transactions.

- Any attempt to tamper with the history of the database will be evident to all other nodes and they will immediately reject the change.

- All nodes abide by the same consensus rules that govern the creation and validation of transactions. Otherwise other nodes will reject the offending transaction (see Figure 12.7).

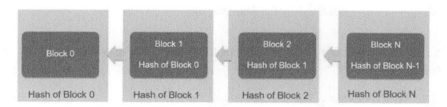

Hash ~ Fingerprint

Figure 12.7   Blockchain structure.

12.3.4.3 Proof of Stake

The proof of stake in Blockchain includes:

- Existence: system of record with timestamp.

- Ownership: who owns what.

- Integrity: no double-spending of digital assets.

- Provenance: history of owners.

- Traceability: trail of movements.

12.3.4.4 How Is a Blockchain Built?

Alice sends Bob a transaction. The transaction is broadcast through the blockchain network to other nodes. Nodes validate transactions. If the transaction is valid, the nodes propagate it further. A (volunteer) node collects valid transactions and puts them into a block. The block contains a hash (fingerprint) of the previous block. The block is then broadcast to the network. Other nodes validate and append their blockchain with the new block. The blockchain can only be appended. Changes to the history of the blockchain are tamper evident and in some cases tamper proof. Everyone in the network now knows that Alice has sent Bob a transaction (see Figure 12.8).

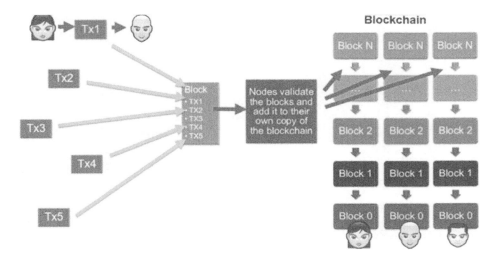

Figure 12.8   How blockchain works.

12.3.4.5 Bitcoin: "In Us We Trust," "In Code We Trust"

Bitcoin is a brilliant invention. It combines several advances in technology in a totally unique way, as shown in Figure 12.9.

Figure 12.9   Diagram of the combined technological advancements of Bitcoin.

On October 31, 2008, at 2:10 pm Eastern Standard Time, Satoshi Nakamoto published the Bitcoin whitepaper to the cryptography mailing list (Figure 12.10). The service used was a pipermail message service hosted on metzdowd.com run by a group of cypherpunks. The mailing list message title was called "Bitcoin P2P e-cash paper" and Nakamoto explained that he had been "working on a new electronic cash system that's fully peer-to-peer, with no trusted third party." The anonymous creator also revealed that the paper was hosted on the website bitcoin.org.

Figure 12.10   The November 1, 2008 online post of Satoshi Nakamoto announcing the white paper that became Bitcoin.

12.3.5   Main Bitcoin Properties: A Peer-to-Peer Electronic Cash System

▪ Double-spending is prevented with a peer-to-peer network.

- No mint or other trusted parties.

- Participants can be anonymous.

- New coins are made from Hashcash style proof-of-work.

- The proof-of-work for new coin generation also powers the network to prevent double-spending.

Digital Signatures: We define an electronic coin as a chain of digital signatures. Each owner transfers the coin to the next by digitally signing a hash of the previous transaction and the public key of the next owner and adding these to the end of the coin. A payee can verify the signatures to verify the chain of ownership (see Figure 12.11).

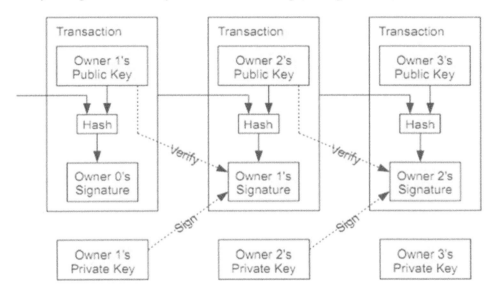

Figure 12.11   Digital signatures.

Ordering Facts: Members of Blockchain network exchange facts. Peer-to-peer (P2P) networks solve a difficult concept of reconciliation. Relational databases offer relational integrity. An ordering of facts guarantees integrity over a P2P network. Blockchain implements proof-of-work consensus using blocks.

Blocks: Blocks order facts in a network of peers. When facts are grouped in blocks, only a single chain of it replicates in the entire network. Each preceding block refers to the previous one.

Mining: The process of looking for blocks is called mining. Block mining brings some form of money. Those who run nodes in a blockchain are called "Miners." It's a voluntary process to a turn node into a miner node.

Money and Cryptocurrencies: Each miner node in a Blockchain tests thousands of random strings to form a new block. Reading facts is easy but storing facts in Blockchain comes with a price.

Each Blockchain has its own cryptocurrency. It is called Bitcoin in the Bitcoin network, and Ether in the Ethereum network. Blockchain generates its own money. Cryptocurrency can be readily converted into real money.

Contracts: The blockchain is capable enough to execute programs. A few blockchains allow each fact with a mini-program. These programs are replicated together with facts. Contracts and database are replicated across all the nodes.

Preprogrammed conditions when interfaced with the real world and broadcasted to everyone are known as a "Smart Contract." It is technically enforceable. Eventually, smart contracts extend to smart property and other smart things.

How does it work?: Blockchain mainly relies on three concepts (see Figure 12.12):

- Peer-to-peer network

- Distributed consensus

- Public-key cryptography

It is the combination of these three concepts that enable a computing breakthrough.

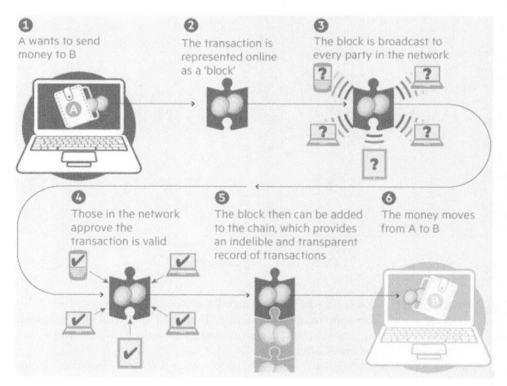

Figure 12.12   How a blockchain works.

12.3.5.1 Transactional Networks: A Blockchain Future

Blockchains are distributed ledgers, a database we each keep an up-to-date copy of. In private blockchains, such as that underlying the Venezuelan "*petro*" or that proposed by UBS for bank transactions, a centralized authority decides who can record new "*transactions*"; there's not much that is novel here from the perspective of economic theory, although there are important technical advances that make private blockchains more efficient than existing distributed ledger technologies. Most casual interest is in public blockchains, which are decentralized and in which participants are anonymous. These blockchains are the main technological advancement underlying cryptocurrencies such as Bitcoin or Ethereum.

For this process to generate a stable, usable blockchain successful miners must always want to attach their new block to the longest existing blockchain. In principle, miners could choose to attach their block to an alternative blockchain; perhaps the most recent block contains a transaction in which I spent all my money on pizza, a decision I now regret and would like to eliminate by instead returning to the shorter blockchain that does not include this transaction. This is the second challenge of public blockchains, ensuring that everyone sticks to the existing chain of transactions. We distinguish between two reasons for not sticking to the existing chain, (i) malicious, like double-spending and tampering, to which we will return later, and (ii) benign, based on widespread disagreements, to which we turn now. Proof-of-work appears to almost perfectly solve the first, but only partially the second (see Figure 12.13).

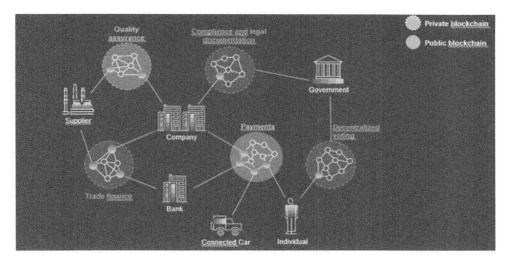

Figure 12.13   Published blockchain and private blockchain.

Theorists in Economics instead view miners as rational profit-maximizers and analyze their incentives to follow an equilibrium of coordinating on the longest existing blockchain [4]. They find that coordination on the longest existing blockchain is a Markov perfect equilibrium, but this equilibrium is not unique, with other equilibria representing forks of the blockchain. In a simple model environment such forks only occur due to some random outside event, a sunspot shock. Extending the model environment to allow for the realistic elements of information delays, and mining software updates creates the possibility of forking equilibrium, without the need for sunspot shocks.

There are two important economic forces at play in the blockchain that determine whether miners attach their new blocks to the longest existing chain. First, miners' actions are strategic complements: under the assumption that the value of a blockchain depends on it's being stable and credible, and that miners are rewarded in the cryptocurrency based on that blockchain, it follows that miners should focus on a single blockchain. Miners do this by playing the "longest chain rule" strategy, as suggested by Nakamoto [33], and the resulting coordination on a single blockchain is a Pareto-optimal equilibrium. However, if for any reason (e.g., a sunspot shock) a miner thinks that other miners will coordinate on a different chain, then the optimal strategy is also to follow that other chain, resulting in a fork, and all miners now coordinate on that other chain. Hence, multiple equilibria are possible, and while a stable blockchain is one of these equilibria, forks of this are another. Examples of such forks arising from widespread disagreement among miners about the future of Bitcoin include Bitcoin Gold[3] and Bitcoin Cash.[4]

The second important economic force is vested interest: miners cannot immediately spend the cryptocurrencies they receive as a reward for successful mining. This means some miners will necessarily hold cryptocurrency whose value is tied to the blockchain on which they were mining remaining active. This blunts the incentive of previously successful miners to create new forks. It also means that if a fork does occur then some miners will have incentives to continue mining on the preexisting, now minority, chain. This creates the possibility that after a fork there will be multiple existing blockchains, and that these will persist. Unlike temporary forks that rely only on coordination motives and would arise with atomistic miners, equilibria with persistent forks rely on some miners being large enough that they take into account the impact of their actions on the value of the blockchain. In practice, there exist pools of miners, such as AntPool and BTC.com,[5] who each represent more than 10% of computing power, and who likely exhibit such strategic behavior.

12.3.5.2 Proof-of-Work vs. Proof-of-Status

The standard approach of public (decentralized) blockchains to allocating who gets to update the blockchain, adding new blocks of transactions, is by "*proof-of-work.*" All miners attempt to solve problems that are computationally difficult and when a miner finds a solution they get to add a block; the problems are such that their solution is easily verifiable by other miners. For miners solving these problems, the more computing power they have the more problems they will solve, but the difficulty of the problems is determined so that the greater the combined total computing power of all miners the more difficult the problems. Since the same number of blocks are being created in a given time, and since computing power is expensive, both in terms of the cost of electricity and the associated carbon emissions, it is in society's interest to use the minimum amount of electricity necessary. For an individual miner, using more computing power increases their chance of successful mining. Any one miner using more computing power means that the total computing power increases, and so everyone else's chance of successful mining decreases: a negative externality on everyone else. This negative externality leads to overuse of computing power, and wasted resources. If all the miners could agree to sign a binding agreement to all use less computing power they would want to do so.

What alternatives are there to proof-of-work? One is centralized blockchains, but these are really a different concern. The main suggested alternative for decentralized blockchains is proof-of-status. Proof-of-status works by allocating the right to add a new block to the chain randomly to current holders of cryptocurrencies based on their current holdings of the currency. Blocks would be added at regular time intervals and, for example, someone who held 5% of all existing currency would have a 5% chance of being chosen to be the one who adds the new block. The main problem with conceptual objection is that there is

---

[3]https://bitcoingold.org/
[4]https://www.bitcoincash.org/
[5]https://btc.com/stats/pool/AntPool

nothing at stake, so if a fork occurs then there is no reason not to keep contributing block to both the blockchains, rather than settling on one "true" blockchain. The worry is that this leads to a proliferation of different blockchains, which for cryptocurrencies would dilute their value, and for other blockchain applications would render them useless.

Theories exist in both economics and computer science that explore the conditions under which a proof-of-stake mechanism for allocating the right to edit would work; for example, Saleh [41] shows that under the assumption that eventually everyone would agree on a single blockchain then proof-of-status will quickly lead to everyone agreeing on that blockchain, but this largely glosses over the nothing-at-stake problem by ignoring the possibility that the alternative blockchains exist forever. The Ethereum currency has long discussed switching to proof-of-status, and Peercoin[6] has implemented a cryptocurrency based on proof-of-status. However, existing implementations have remained marginal. Implementing a practically useful proof-of-status implementation, or other decentralized alternative to proof-of-work, such as proof-of-contribution or proof-of-network-centrality, would solve many of the inefficiencies resulting from excess electricity use and the major environmental objection to cryptocurrencies, and decentralized blockchains more generally.

12.3.5.3 *Blocksize and Transaction Costs*

As of early 2018, the number of transactions that Bitcoin is able to process is limited to just 3-4 per second, compared to the 30,000 credit card transactions per second by Visa. Since the demand for Bitcoin transactions is greater than this (self-imposed) limit, transaction fees have emerged to determine which transactions get processed. In 2017 the total amount of transaction fees paid on Bitcoin transactions was US$277.1 million.

The limited number of Bitcoin transactions is self-imposed due to the maximum size of each block, which is currently set to around 2mb. There is no reason this could not be changed, so that each block took up more storage space and so could record more transactions. It would simply require a technical adjustment to the code implementing the Bitcoin protocol, and this change is periodically proposed, needing only a simple majority of miners to adopt it. (Such changes are sometimes made; in fact, prior to 2010 the blocksize was 36mb.) The main argument against it is that any increase in the blocksize would make the blockchain much larger and more expensive to store, as well as increasing bandwidth requirements. This is especially true as the number of transactions is linear in the blocksize, so an increase from 2mb to 20mb per block would increase from 3-4 to 60-80 transactions per second. To those who wish to view Bitcoin as money this is problematic, but is not a problem for those who view Bitcoin as a digital alternative to gold.

The limited supply of transactions, combined with an increased demand for transactions, has led directly to the existence and growth of transaction fees which miners charge to include a given transaction in a block. These transaction fees match the demand for Bitcoin transactions with the fixed supply, and increase during periods when there is high demand for transactions [14]. While these transaction fees do match the demand to the supply by reducing the quantity demanded it is worth repeating that they do not help to increase the quantity supplied, as this is strictly limited by the blocksize which is coded into the protocols implementing Bitcoin. The transactions fees do, however, increase the returns to mining, resulting in more computing power being used to process the same number of transactions; the difficulty of the numerical problems solved by miners increases to

---

[6]https://www.peercoin.net/

ensure that the rate at which blocks are added does not change in response to the increased mining.

This use of transactions fees to decide which transactions to process was foreseen and is a deliberate part of the Bitcoin protocols. The idea is that in its early days Bitcoin would reward successful miners by giving them bitcoins, but that the size of this reward would decrease over time to ensure that the number of bitcoins in existence would eventually level out, and the rewards to successful miners would instead come in the form of the transaction fees they could charge.

These issues around transaction fees in principle exist in essentially all public (decentralized) blockchain implementations, as they involve fixed limits on the size of each block and the rate at which new blocks are added to the blockchain. In principle, transaction fees could be avoided by adjusting the blocksize or arrival rate of new blocks in response to the demand for transactions (which are placed in a queue in the "*mempool*") in much the same way that the protocols currently automatically adjust the difficulty of the numerical problems in response to mining effort. Economic theory suggests that rewarding miners with coin, rather than transaction fees, is more efficient, as it spreads the same cost over a wider base – all transactions in the memory pool, rather than just those that are processed – and so is less distorting [10]. Although transaction fees do have the efficiency advantage of reducing processing delays for those transactions that are highest priority, that is, those for which people are willing to pay to reduce the delay [26]. Which effect would dominate depends how large the queue of transactions to be processed is.

12.3.5.4   *The Threat of Double-Spending: Avoiding Tampering*

Alice sends Bob a selfie photo. Alice sends Charlie the same selfie photo. Alice has double spent her selfie jpg files! For a currency to succeed, there must be no double spends. How can a digital asset not be double spent!.

Figure 12.14   The threat of double-spending.

The most important breakthrough in Nakamoto's invention is the solution to the double-spending problem without the need for a trusted intermediary (no arbiter). Previous attempts at digital currencies needed a central service to validate transactions and to prevent double spends.

This innovation can then be extended to other non-currency assets, e.g., land titles.

Since the coins in any cryptocurrency are not physical objects it is possible to send the same coin to two different people. However, the transaction record will only end up showing one of these transactions, the other will be illegitimate. Double-spending involves doing exactly this, using one coin to make two purchases, only one of which will end up being legitimate and so only one of the two sellers will ever get paid. A useful cryptocurrency will have to prevent such attacks. In 2013, GHash.io used double-spending to steal about US$100,000 worth of bitcoin from the gambling site Betcoin Dice.[7] They paid for a bet by making a bitcoin transaction, if they won the bet they simply did nothing, but if they lost the bet then they initiated a double-spending attack. This was possible both because Betcoin Dice didn't wait to settle the transaction, and because GHash.io accounted for 35% of all mining at that time and so would often win the right to add new blocks.

To execute a double-spending attack in a blockchain-based cryptocurrency you would spend a coin, which would be recorded in a block, and then respend the same coin and replace the previous block recording the first spend with a new block recording the second spend. The difficulty in pulling off a double-spending attack is that you have to get the right to edit that block. For a blockchain in which the right to edit is allocated by proof-of-work this means that pulling off a double-spending attack is more difficult if there are lots of miners (if your own computing power is small relative to total computing power of all miners), and number of blocks since the first spend (you have to replace all of them to become the longest chain). The payoff to a successful double-spending attack is bigger the larger the size of the payment (the payoff to spending the same $10 twice is $10, the payoff to spending the same $100 twice is $100).

Chiu and Koeppl [10] provide a more detailed description. Defense against double-spending comes in two main forms, waiting until some time has passed since the transaction was added to the blockchain so that a double-spending attack would have to edit more blocks, and the blockchain having more miners so pulling off a double-spending attack is more costly. Technical changes that make double-spending easier to detect and so more difficult to pull off have also been proposed (see Figure 12.15).[8]

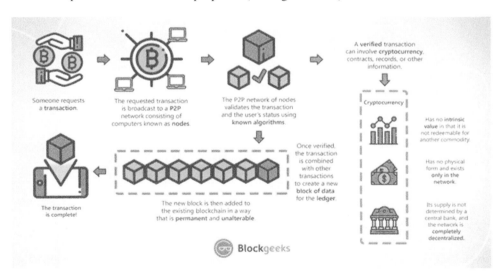

Figure 12.15   What is blockchain technology?

Let's define a good cryptocurrency as one in which transactions can be processed quickly and at the minimum expense (less waiting and less mining), but which prevents double-

[7]https://www.bitcoinsportsbooks.com/reviews/betcoin-dice/
[8]https://blockgeeks.com/guides/what-is-blockchain-technology/

spending (more waiting and more mining). This leads to a few guidelines for a good cryptocurrency, and for what transactions a cryptocurrency is best suited. A good cryptocurrency rewards mining effort with new coin, rather than transaction fees. This way the cost of paying to encourage mining is shared by all transactions, rather than just successful ones, which discourages double-spending. Cryptocurrencies are best for processing small transactions, as processing large ones means there are greater incentives to double spend and so settling large transactions takes longer. Based on this, Chiu and Koeppl [10] estimate that a cryptocurrency that issued new coins at an annual money growth rate of 2% could be competitive with existing payment systems for processing retail purchases in terms of transactions costs and processing times.

This theory focuses on the "*economic*" and transactional aspects of the blockchain, rather than the code and computing aspects.

By allowing digital information to be distributed but not copied, blockchain technology created the backbone of a new type of internet.

In Figure 12.16, we built a linked list using hash pointers. We're going to call this data structure a blockchain. Whereas in a regular linked list you have a series of blocks, each block having data as well as a pointer to the previous block in the list, in a blockchain the previous block pointer will be replaced with a hash pointer. So, each block not only tells us where the value of the previous block was, but it also contains a digest of that value that allows us to verify that the value hasn't changed. We store the head of the list, which is just a regular hash pointer that points to the most recent data block.

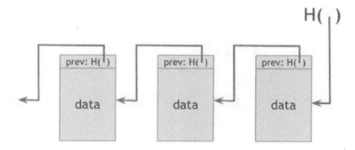

Figure 12.16   Blockchain: A blockchain is a linked list that is built with hash pointers instead of pointers.

12.4   Environmental Implications of the Cryptocurrency Market

Even a single transaction uses a huge amount of power. Take bitcoin, for example. A Bitcoin Energy Consumption Index, which tracks the energy consumption of digital currency, has been put together by *Digiconomist*. According to BECi, each bitcoin transaction consumes 251 KWh of electricity. That is enough energy to power 8.49 U.S. homes for a full day. Given that there are around 300,000 bitcoin transactions every day, this equates to a lot of homes that could be powered.

12.4.1   Key Stats

- 42.67 TWh: The annual energy consumption of Bitcoin and Ethereum combined.

- 0.19%: The percentage of the world's electricity used by Bitcoin and Ethereum.

- 8.49: The number of U.S. households that could be powered for a full day with the same energy as a single Bitcoin transaction.

Bitcoin well and truly pricked the mainstream consciousness in 2017. Thanks to an incredible 11-fold rise in value in 2017, everyone is suddenly talking about Bitcoin and cryptocurrencies. It's easy to see why the phenomenon has grabbed the world's attention – anything that goes from $1,000 in value to $11,000 in value inside 12 months is clearly big news. It's a meteoric trajectory, and one that has triggered talk of an impending bubble, the inevitability of regulation, and an uncertain future.

It has been widely reported that the Bitcoin mining network now consumes more electricity than 159 countries of the world. The huge energy consumption is down to the way bitcoin and other cryptocurrencies operate. In order to avoid fraud, there is no centralized authority validating transactions. Instead, they are validated by miners who process blocks of cryptocurrency transactions in return for a reward in the form of coins. Processing the blocks involves solving difficult computational problems which can only be undertaken by powerful computing systems. And, of course, the more powerful a computing system, the more energy it will use. Every cryptocurrency transaction works in this way, meaning every transaction requires a lot of electricity (see Figure 12.17).

Figure 12.17　Environmental implications of the cryptocurrency market.

For the cryptocurrency Ethereum, which is second in popularity after bitcoin, the energy usage is still extremely high. Overall it uses 11.07 TWh of electricity, which is just over a third of that of bitcoin. Although one third sounds good, each Ethereum transaction still uses enough juice to power 1.77 U.S. homes. When you combine the energy consumption of bitcoin and Ethereum, it works out to be more annually than Hong Kong. Critics of cryptocurrencies point out that equivalent payment systems, such as Visa, operate at a fraction of the consumption rate. But that fact isn't going to stop people from using the new method.

If this is the current energy consumption of cryptocurrencies, what does the future hold? As more and more people rush to get involved in the new market, the amount of miners will only increase, along with the amount of energy consumed. Is it possible to make cryptocurrencies sustainable?

There are some potential solutions being mooted for the energy problem. Austrian startup HydroMiner is using renewable hydropower to operate its mining servers. Similarly, NastyMining is using solar and wind energy to mine for bitcoin in a green way. Then there is the Harvest Project,[9] which is using wind energy to mine cryptocurrency that will then be used for climate change research. These solutions work on a small scale, but given the fact that most major bitcoin mining centers are based in China, where they are powered with electricity that is produced largely by burning fossil fuels, then it is probably not a cure-all solution.

Reducing the amount of energy that each cryptocurrency transaction uses is another way to make it more sustainable. This is something that Ethereum is working towards by switching to a different model of verification. The Bitcoin community is also working on the lightning network which will enable more transactions on the network without using more power. Yet, neither of these changes are imminent, meaning that for now energy consumption rates are locked-in at a high level.

The gold rush on cryptocurrency isn't showing any signs of abatement. Even if the bitcoin bubble bursts there will still be energy-intensive mining taking place. It's not an easy problem to solve, and it's one that is here to stay.

12.4.2 Energy Consumption

Mining is the process of adding transaction records to Bitcoin's public ledger of past transactions. The blockchain serves to confirm transactions to the rest of the network as having taken place. Bitcoin nodes use the blockchain to distinguish legitimate Bitcoin transactions from attempts to respend coins that have already been spent elsewhere. This process is energy-intensive and often causes power consumption issues (see Figure 12.18 and Table 12.1).[10]

Table 12.1 Bitcoin energy consumption.

Description	Value
Bitcoin's current estimated annual electricity consumption* (TWh)	70.64
Bitcoin's current minimum annual electricity consumption** (TWh)	40.47
Annualized global mining revenues	$8,240,907,582
Annualized estimated global mining costs	$3,531,763,005
Current cost percentage	42.86%
Country closest to Bitcoin in terms of electricity consumption	Colombia
Estimated electricity used over the previous day (KWh)	193,521,261
Implied Watts per GH/s	0.118
Total Network Hash rate in PH/s (1,000,000 GH/s)	68,297
Energy footprint per transaction (KWh)	530
Number of U.S. households that could be powered by Bitcoin	6,540,302
Number of U.S. households powered for 1 day by the electricity consumed for a single transaction	17.93
Bitcoin's electricity consumption as a percentage of the world's electricity consumption	0.32%
Annual carbon footprint (kt of CO_2)	33,552
Carbon footprint per transaction (kg of CO_2)	251.94

---

[9]https://www.harvestproject.org/
[10]http://bitcoinenergyconsumption.com/

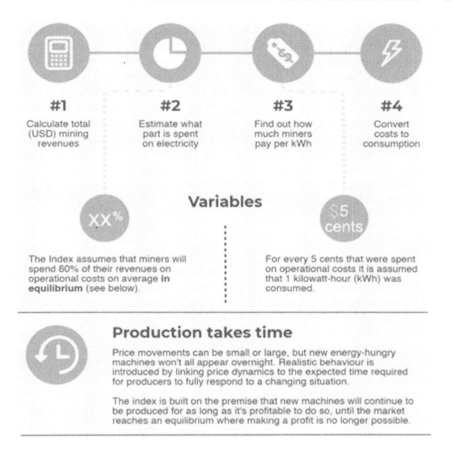

Figure 12.18   Steps to determine Bitcoin's energy consumption.

12.4.3   What's Next?

Block propagation has been heavily optimized with the relay networks that the miners use and compact blocks for ordinary node users. Still, researchers are working to remove overhead from the system to make it as streamlined as possible. Only once developers are satisfied that width requirements are as low as possible for the current amount of throughput, will increasing throughput be on the table. Blockchain technology is fascinating and exciting. It has enormous potential to replace all the intermediaries. Now is the crucial time to invest in Blockchain.

The technology behind blockchain employs advanced cryptography, performance optimization, and custom network protocols. The blockchain is the backbone of the digital currency of the world. The energy required for mining cryptocurrencies is significant. Most of the current mining farms are using electricity from nonrenewable, greenhouse gas-emitting sources (coal, petroleum-based fuels, and other fossil fuels). The utilization of Blockchain technology should not be synonymous with environmental degradation and high energy costs. We need to enrich ourselves with technological innovation and creation without the detrimental effects on air and water. It is ultimately the responsibility of those creating innovative cryptocurrency and blockchain projects to create a profitable solution which allows blockchain to build a greener, more sustainable future using green energy and renewable powered data mining centers on a self-financing network. We have the responsibility of not just providing innovative solutions for cryptocurrency mining, but for green and sustainable energy in all forms. Currently, Green Energy and Environmental Sustainability sectors are investing in green energy real assets and incubating innovation by promoting, encouraging and financing research and development into new renewable technologies and sustainable practices to make the world a safer place to live in the future. It is providing a bridge between the existing regulatory environment and Blockchain ecosystems. Blockchain and cryptocurrencies have paved the way for this generation's industrial revolution, and we must give it the best opportunity to survive if we're to pass the baton to the millennial generation for it to thrive.

12.5 Conclusion

The blockchain is the backbone of the digital currency of the world. The energy required for mining cryptocurrencies is significant. Most of the current mining farms are using electricity from nonrenewable, greenhouse gas-emitting sources (coal, petroleum-based fuels, and other fossil fuels). The utilization of Blockchain technology should not be synonymous with environmental degradation and high energy costs. We need to enrich ourselves with technological innovation and creation without detrimental effects on air and water. This is ultimately the responsibility of those creating the innovations in cryptocurrency and blockchain projects. A profitable solution needs to be created which allows blockchain to build a greener, more sustainable future. Using green energy and renewable-powered data-mining centers on a self-financing network, we have the responsibility of not just providing innovative solutions for cryptocurrency mining, but for green and sustainable energy in all forms. Currently, Green Energy and Environmental Sustainability sectors are investing in green energy real assets and incubating innovative technology by promoting, encouraging and financing research and development into new renewable technologies and sustainable practices to make the world a safer place in the future. It is providing a bridge between the existing regulatory environment and Blockchain ecosystems. Blockchain and cryptocurrencies have paved the way for this generation's industrial revolution, and we must give it the best opportunity to survive in order to pass the baton to the next generation, where it can thrive.

REFERENCES

1. de Vries, A. (2018). *Digiconomist*. [Online]. Available: https://digiconomist.net/bitcoinenergy-consumption.

2. Baron, J., O'Mahony, A., Manheim, D., & Dion-Schwarz, C. (2015). The current state of virtual currencies. In *National Security Implications of Virtual Currency: Examining the Potential for Non-state Actor Deployment*. (pp. 5-22). Rand Corporation.

3. Baur, D. G., Lee, A. D., & Hong, K. (2015). Bitcoin: Currency or Investment?.

4. Biais, B., Bisiere, C., Bouvard, M., & Casamatta, C. (2019). The blockchain folk theorem. *The Review of Financial Studies*, 32(5), 1662-1715.

5. Bhme, R., Christin, N., Edelman, B., & Moore, T. (2015). Bitcoin: Economics, technology, and governance. *Journal of Economic Perspectives*, 29(2), 213-38.

6. Bonneau, J., Miller, A., Clark, J., Narayanan, A., Kroll, J. A., & Felten, E. W. (2015, May). Sok: Research perspectives and challenges for bitcoin and cryptocurrencies. In *2015 IEEE Symposium on Security and Privacy* (pp. 104-121). IEEE.

7. Bouri, E., Jalkh, N., Molnr, P., & Roubaud, D. (2017). Bitcoin for energy commodities before and after the December 2013 crash: diversifier, hedge or safe haven?. *Applied Economics*, 49(50), 5063-5073.

8. Burns, S. (2015). Mobile money and financial development: The case of M-PESA in Kenya. Available at SSRN 2688585.

9. Chapron, G. (2017). The environment needs cryptogovernance. *Nature News*, 545(7655), 403.

10. Chiu, J., & Koeppl, T. V. (2017). The economics of cryptocurrenciesbitcoin and beyond. Available at SSRN 3048124.

11. Ciaian, P., Rajcaniova, M., & Kancs, D. A. (2016). The economics of BitCoin price formation. *Applied Economics*, 48(19), 1799-1815.

12. Corbet, S., Lucey, B., Urquhart, A., & Yarovaya, L. (2019). Cryptocurrencies as a financial asset: A systematic analysis. *International Review of Financial Analysis*, 62, 182-199.

13. De Vries, A. (2018). Bitcoin's growing energy problem. *Joule*, 2(5), 801-805.

14. Easley, D., O'Hara, M., & Basu, S. (2019). From mining to markets: The evolution of bitcoin transaction fees. Journal of Financial Economics.

15. Gasser, S., Eisl, A., & Weinmayer, K. (2014). Caveat Emptor: Does Bitcoin Improve Portfolio Diversification? Doctoral dissertation, WU Vienna University of Economics and Business.

16. Farell, R. (2015). An analysis of the cryptocurrency industry. *Wharton Research Scholars*. 130.

17. Gandal, N., & Halaburda, H. (2014). Competition in the cryptocurrency market. *Bank of Canada Working Papers*.

18. Giungato, P., Rana, R., Tarabella, A., & Tricase, C. (2017). Current trends in sustainability of bitcoins and related blockchain technology. *Sustainability*, 9(12), 2214.

19. Glaser, F., Zimmermann, K., Haferkorn, M., Weber, M. C., & Siering, M. (2014). Bitcoin-asset or currency? revealing users' hidden intentions. *Revealing Users' Hidden Intentions*. ECIS.

20. Guadamuz, A., & Marsden, C. (2015). Blockchains and Bitcoin: Regulatory responses to cryptocurrencies. *First Monday*, 20(12-7).

21. Harwick, C. (2016). Cryptocurrency and the problem of intermediation. *The Independent Review*, 20(4), 569-588.

22. Hileman, G., & Rauchs, M. (2017). Global cryptocurrency benchmarking study. *Cambridge Centre for Alternative Finance*, 33.

23. Hive Blockchain Technologies. (2018). *Hive Financial Reporting*. [Online]. Available: https://www.hiveblockchain.com/investors/reporting.

24. Hoy, M. B. (2017). An introduction to the blockchain and its implications for libraries and medicine. *Medical Reference Services Quarterly*, 36(3), 273-279.

25. https://www.coinspeaker.com/new-york-state-now-wants-levy-tax-bitcoin-mining/

26. Huberman, G., Leshno, J. D., & Moalleni C. (2017). Monopoly without a monopolist: An economic analysis of the bitcoin payment system. *Research Discussion Papers* 27/2017. Bank of Finland.

27. Iwamura, M., Kitamura, Y., & Matsumoto, T. (2014). Is bitcoin the only cryptocurrency in the town? Economics of cryptocurrency and Friedrich A. Hayek. *SSRN Electronic Journal*. DOI: 10.2139/ssrn.2405790.

28. Krafft, P. M., Della Penna, N., & Pentland, A. S. (2018, April). An experimental study of cryptocurrency market dynamics. In *Proceedings of the 2018 CHI Conference on Human Factors in Computing Systems* (p. 605). ACM.

29. Lim, J. W. (2015). A facilitative model for cryptocurrency regulation in Singapore. In *Handbook of Digital Currency* (pp. 361-381). Academic Press.

30. Luther, W. J. (2016). Bitcoin and the future of digital payments. *The Independent Review*, 20(3), 397-404.

31. Krause, M. J., & Tolaymat, T. (2018). Quantification of energy and carbon costs for mining cryptocurrencies. *Nature Sustainability*, 1, 711-718.

32. Jiansheng, M. (8 March 2017). China Smart Grid. [Online]. Available: http://www.chinasmartgrid.com.cn/news/20170308/622441.shtml.

33. Nakamoto, S. (2008). Bitcoin: A peer-to-peer electronic cash system.

34. O'Dwyer, K.J., & Malone, D. (2014). Bitcoin mining and its energy footprint.

35. Poelstra, A. (22 March 2015). On stake and consensus. [Online]. Available: https://download.wpsoftware.net/bitcoin/ pos.pdf.

36. Popper, N. (2015). *Digital Gold: Bitcoin and the Inside Story of the Misfits and Millionaires Trying To Reinvent Money*. HarperCollins.

37. Rogojanu, A., & Badea, L. (2014). The issue of competing currencies. Case study-Bitcoin. *Theoretical & Applied Economics*, 21(1).

38. Rysman, M. (2009). The economics of two-sided markets. *Journal of Economic Perspectives*, 23(3), 125-43.

39. Das, S. (2018). CCN. [Online]. Available: https://www.ccn.com/australian-blockchainfirm-strikes-190-million-crypto-mining-deal/.

40. Saleh, F. (2019). Blockchain without waste: Proof-of-stake. Available at SSRN 3183935.

41. Swanson, T. (2014). Bitcoins: made in China. *Bitcoin Magazine*, 12.

42. Tiwana, A., Konsynski, B., & Bush, A. A. (2010). Research commentary – Platform evolution: Coevolution of platform architecture, governance, and environmental dynamics. *Information Systems Research*, 21(4), 675-687.

43. Truby, J. (2018). Decarbonizing Bitcoin: Law and policy choices for reducing the energy consumption of Blockchain technologies and digital currencies. *Energy Research & Social Science*, 44, 399-410.

44. Vranken, H. (2017). Sustainability of bitcoin and blockchains. *Current Opinion in Environmental Sustainability*, 28, 1-9.

CHAPTER 13

BLOCKCHAIN TECHNOLOGY: A PARADIGM SHIFT IN INVESTMENT BANKING

R. Vedapradha,[1,*] Hariharan Ravi,[1,*] Arockia Rajasekar[2]

[1] Department of Commerce and Management, St. Joseph's College of Commerce (Autonomous), Bangalore, Karnataka, India

[2] Department of Commerce, St. Joseph's College (Autonomous), Trichy, India

*Corresponding author: vedahariharan@gmail.com; hari712@gmail.com

Abstract

Purpose: Blockchain technology can have ramifications across the investment banking ecosystem due to their cryptographic distributed ledger. The aim of this chapter is to evaluate the adaptation feasibility and predict its performance for a regulatory framework when Blockchain technology is applied by investment banks.

Design/Methodology/Approach: Random sampling is used with a sample size of 50 respondents from investment banks operating in urban Bangalore based on the primary data collected. Statutory impact (SI), compliance policy (CP), fiscal policy (FP), competitive edge (CE), and service-level agreement (SLA) are the variables. SPSS and SPSS AMOS are the statistical software used to test the structural equation model (SEM) with confirmatory factor analysis (CFA), multiple linear regression analysis and one-way ANOVA (analysis of variance).

Findings: The model fits perfectly based values to fit indices. SI is the most influencing variable and has a greater impact on acceptability with beta value 0.899 at 0.001 percent significant level with Chi-square value being 3.14 and the estimated reliability post-adoption is 81 percent. SI, CP, SLA, and CE are the significant predictors of performance with a greater association between the performance of the banks and regulatory framework indicators with significance at 0.01 percent level.

Originality/Value: The technology can reduce the operating cost from the middle and backend, improves transparency, and prevents money laundering, as it is tamper-proof and accessed by all the parties at the same time.

Keywords: Service-level agreement (SLA), anti-money laundering (AML), investment banking cycle, competitive edge

13.1 Introduction

Blockchain technology facilitates investment banks to create a cryptographic distributed ledger amongst the various parties involved in investment banking to validate the transactions. The transactions consist of the data, which is very prevalent and constantly creates more efficient information transactions, enhances regulatory controls, and improves reliability by eliminating the intermediaries. It can be applied in KYC (*Know Your Customers*) of clients, AML of data sharing, collateral management, trading and settlements of trades, and clearing through a transaction cloud.

Blockchain technology can help banks reduce their infrastructure cost as a network of computers maintains the transactions on the internet platform without any approval from the central authority. It also helps in reducing the operational cost based on their back-office processes such as clearing, trade support, compliance and settlement of securities, as it can remove the reconciliation since the transactions are distributed and virtually tamper proof.

Banking costs can be reduced with integrated database management by the investment banks as they invest a tremendous amount of money in the maintenance of databases. Databases are created to store, validate, and transform information regarding clients, financial transactions, and documents. Blockchain technology plays a pivotal role in rendering quality service with more transparency and efficiency by offering a centralized platform to the database, permitting access to data between the counterparties along with a highly secured access system [1].

13.1.1 Evolution of Technology

The concept of the technology has created an edge for the various industries to improve efficiency, productivity and channelize a game plan to sustain in the long run. Wei Dai is the eminent researcher who launched the digital money concept through Bitcoin, which focused on offering solutions to various issues on a technological platform that can also generate money based on decentralized consensus. Satoshi Nakamoto created a revolution in the digital world by familiarizing the world with Blockchain technology in 2008 in the form of cryptocurrency, where it is a peer-to-peer electronic cash system. It was developed to design a decentralized ledger that works on trustable sources of networks which are not controlled by individuals. The preferred languages to be used for this technology are C++, Java, Python, Solidity, and Ruby. Initially, the concept of Bitcoin was only in the news but it began to transform due to the enormous opportunities it offered and it started creating a buzz post-2014, finally gaining importance post-2017 [2].

13.1.2 Scope of Applications

The application of this transforming technology is suitable for all possible industries and can be customized based on their requirements. The infrastructure creates a database through which data can be shared, stored, and transferred through a mechanism, as it has various levels of permissions. These tasks performed by the users can only be accessed to read and execute, but some can just read the transactions, promoting security and privacy.

Some of the areas of its magical applications which are creating a greater impact are discussed below. In addition to financial institutions, it is applicable in many more industries as well. Here, a few of the applications are discussed in detail based on Figure 13.1.

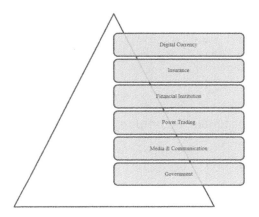

Figure 13.1   Applications of blockchain technology.

- *Digital Currency*: Bitcoin was limited in its usage due to the failures in the regulatory framework. However, the advanced technology creates room for the next level where the reliability of the digital identity has been approved, applied and tested for knowing the customers based on online authentication standards across the service industries.

- *Financial Institutions*: Banks and other financial institutions are highly prone to money laundering, identity theft, digital transfer of funds and many more attacks that can hamper customer relationships and affect the services rendered. Now, financial institutions are being transformed by a robust technology, enabling them to reduce costs, increase efficiency, and provide more secure transactions.

- *Insurance*: Insurance protection against uncertain damages can put a business in trouble by collapsing in a second if there is no coverage for the same. The insurance companies are vulnerable to illegal claims and manipulation of data. Hence, blockchain technology can be a boon to them as it facilitates in the streamlining of the documentation process and the payments of premiums and claims, due to complete digital transformation which reliably handles data in the form of documents.

- *Government Bodies*: There are often setbacks in government systems due to corruption and nonproductive operations as a result of various political and economic factors. In order to render better civil services to civilians, blockchain technology can be used to create a transparent platform connecting the governing authorities with the general public through the digital world, thereby processing transactions which promote the conversion of ineffective services into effective public service delivery along with the promise of optimum utilization of resources.

- *Media and Communications*: Internet of things (IoT) has opened the gates to countless users easily accessing the information from the internet platform, which calls for protection of the different parties involved in the development of the arts and mass media, like research authors, actors, musicians, singers, and theater artists whose work and contributions are pirated without permission or acknowledgment. Blockchain technology can solve this problem of access and use by bringing all the parties in direct contact with consumers.

- *Power Trading*: Various commodities are traded across the exchanges by industries, from products to asset classes, involving cash transactions and digital documents during the process of transfer of ownership to ensure transparency. Blockchain technology is applied to the settlement process for trading and transferring resources flawlessly.

13.1.3   Merits of Blockchain Technology in Banks

Blockchain is one the most robust disruptive technologies that can facilitate in revamping the entire business of the banks. Figure 13.2 shows some of the merits of adopting this technology.

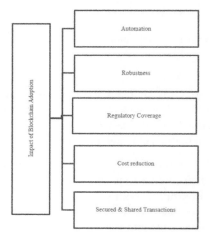

Figure 13.2   Blockchain technology for better customer experience.

Blockchain technology can help to increase transparency and effectiveness at a larger scale due to the following attributes:

- *Robustness*: It can improve the quality of transactions with strong reliability due to the distributed ledger based on cloud transactions.

- *Regulatory Framework*: It enables creating better transparency and security with "know-your-customer" documentation which prevents money laundering activities.

- *Cost Reduction*: It can reduce cost by utilization of resources and streamlining few operational processes in the areas of middle-office and back-office segments.

- *Automation*: The added advantage of blockchain technology is that it has better implications for creating innovative and customized products and services for better customer relationship management.

- *Secured and Shared Transactions*: The transactions are based on the validation from all the parties involved and are tamper-proof unless approved by all. It ensures better data security due to cloud computing [3].

13.1.4 Investment Banks

Specialized banks often focus on the operations of offering asset management, wealth management, advisory services, and consultancy service to various clients ranging from financial institutions through central banks to manage their portfolios under three segments, namely front-end, middle and back-end operations. It is one of the most critical divisions in banking apart from commercial and retail because they promote capital formation, generate foreign exchanges, facilitate foreign direct investments, and create employment opportunities. Some of the key players of this division are financial institutions, financial markets, authorized brokers, clearing houses, and legal agencies. They are investing a lot of money on the middle and back-end operations by setting up a captive firm across emerging countries to obtain a cost advantage and time lag. Some of the leading banks, like Morgan Stanley,[1] Goldman Sachs,[2] Northern Trust,[3] State Street,[4] and Wells Fargo,[5] have their headquarters based in the U.S., U.K., and various other European countries [4].

13.1.5 Theoretical Framework

Investment banks play a pivotal role in capital formation, generating foreign direct investments, and promoting foreign exchange reserves of a nation. They have proved to be a ray of hope in the development of emerging countries moving in the direction of growth and development. An investment bank has various operational services offered at different levels to multiple clients, which are front-end, middle, and back-end operations. The theoretical framework of an investment bank is shown in Figure 13.3.

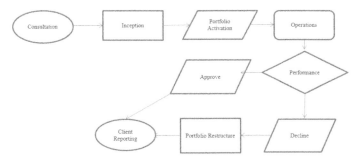

Figure 13.3   Theoretical framework of investment banks.

[1] https://www.morganstanley.com/
[2] https://www.goldmansachs.com/
[3] https://www.northerntrust.com/
[4] https://www.statestreet.com/home.html
[5] https://www.wellsfargo.com/

- *Consultation*: The clients are mostly financial institutions, central banks, and high-net-worth individuals who approach these banks to avail the asset management services. Some clients seek the guidance of only consultation services. Most of them look forward to investments at this stage. They often come in direct contact with the front-end desk through productive interaction.

- *Inception*: The marketing consultants create an avenue to the clients who are interested in the investments. The concerned staff assists the clients in going through the initial document verification before proceeding. There is effective integration of different departments responsible for the initialization, who are involved during the decision-making process to validate and evaluate the activation. The client will confirm the percentage of the portfolio comprised of different proportions of asset classes to be invested.

- *Portfolio Activation*: The portfolio manager designs a customized portfolio for the clients based on their requirements with suitable currency, quantum of the amount, base currency, and local currency. All departments will be informed to ensure preparations are made before the fund gets traded in the financial markets.

- *Operations*: It consists of reconciliation of the portfolio, preparation of accounting statements, calculation of net asset value (NAV), making accounting adjustments in the accounting systems for the authentic proof of the record kept between the custodian and the IBs.

- *Performance*: The performance of the portfolio is calculated in comparison with the benchmark or index, like S&P and NIFTY 50, to examine the portfolio floated by the IBs across the asset class. There are two major types of strategies, namely Active strategy and Passive strategy. An active strategy is adopted when the portfolio floated by the IB is expected to outperform or reflect results above the level of the benchmark of the market portfolio. A passive strategy focuses on balancing the portfolio drafted by the investment bank only to mimic the market index.

- *Approve/Decline*: When the portfolio performance matches the expected market index's performance, the portfolio manager approves the results for further reporting. In the case of the reverse situation, then the manager declines the reporting immediately.

- *Portfolio Restructures*: The portfolio manager rearranges the combination of different asset classes in the current portfolio structure when the expected performance of the fund is less than (in case of active strategy) and above (in case of passive strategy) the performance of the market index.

- *Client Reporting*: The final report is generated and formatted as per the requirements of the clients based on SLA, like weekly, quarterly, monthly, semi-annually or annually, and dispatched to the clients, which gives them a summarized view of their investments, fund allocation, portfolio combination, and revenue generation [5].

13.1.6   Investment Banking Operational Levels

The banks are broadly divided into various operational levels, namely front-end, middle and back-end operations, based on the nature of service rendered. These levels are interconnected, where the output of the first level becomes the input of next level.

13.1.6.1 *Front-End Operations*

This level is confined to direct interaction between the authorized personnel of banks with clients who seek advice and guidance for their investments. They approach the new business team who are involved in the promotion of the customized products and services offered by the banks. Professional staff briefs the various clients about the products and services. Once after the client's confirmation, they proceed towards verification of their KYC documents to process further. The papers are either approved or rejected based on their reliability and authenticity status. The last step is to incept the portfolio once the reports are legally authorized.

Figure 13.4 reflects the flow of the operations at the front-end desk.

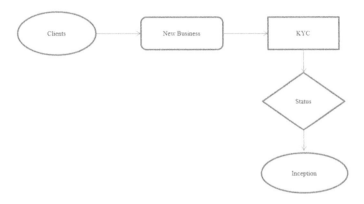

Figure 13.4   Process in front-end operations.

13.1.6.2 *Middle Operations*

The inception portfolio designed as per the requirements of the clients is further processed by the portfolio administration department, who are responsible for activation of the fund, trading to integrate with trade and shareholder service departments. Figure 13.5 shows the trade department intimates the custodian and brokerage firms for all the trades booked (buy & sell) so that the custodian keeps the physical stock and cash ready during the settlements. Brokerage firms are responsible for executing the trades as an authorized agent who charges a specific fee for the service rendered.

The risk management department always thrives on monitoring the risk associated with the transactions arising across the portfolios to protect the banks from going bankrupt, portfolios getting overdrawn, idle cash and many more measures. The department plays a significant role in promoting the smooth functioning of the activities. The shareholder's service department is responsible for record keeping of the cash contributions and withdrawals made by the clients from their portfolio. The clients will contribute a specific quantum of cash for a portfolio traded live in the financial market for the first time. This amount is based on the currency of the client's domicile country towards the fund activation. These activities are of a different nature involving multiple services rendered by the banks to their clients playing a significant role in the business. However, it also is very challenging and risky if there is any negligence by the analysts or risk management team. Examples of risky situations could be idle cash in the portfolio contributed by the client without being invested or overtrading, or evaluating the cash balances available in the portfolio at the closure of the markets. A large risky transaction consists of a large quantum of the amount with globally accepted currencies like US Dollar, Euro, British Pound, Japanese Yen still not settled at the clearing houses, a failed trade due to insufficient funds at the third party and many more.

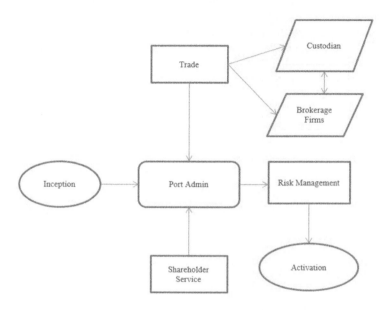

Figure 13.5   Process in middle operations.

13.1.6.3 Back-End Operations

Figure 13.6 reflects the flow of back-end operations, which is one of the most important and robust levels of services where the banks can generate efficiency and transparency that leads to approved client reporting. Once the portfolio is activated, there must be a reconciliation performed within the portfolio at different currency and security levels to check the accuracy of transactions and books of accounts maintained between custodian and IBs. NAV reconciliation follows after the portfolio reconciliation on the reconciliation tool in accounting systems.

Banks maintain their accounting systems based on the contractual whereas the custodian reflects the transaction based on actual settlements. Hence, there will always be the difference in settlement of transactions between custodian and banks due to reasons like failed trades, delay at a third party, and time lag. Portfolio reconciliation is concerned with operations related to cash and stock. NAV reconciliation is confined to computing the total NAV of the portfolio based on each security level, currency level, trades, and income separately between custodian records and IB's records. The portfolio administration department confirms the NAV after closing the books of the accounts on the last working day of every month. Performance of the fund will be computed to verify the results have matched, outperformed or underperformed the market index. The portfolio manager adjusts the composition of the securities in the fund to match the requirements of the clients. Client reporting is the last phase of the operation where the summary of the investments and the performance of the portfolio created for the clients will be dispatched to them to meet the requirements of the SLA [6].

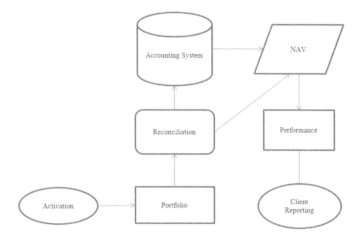

Figure 13.6   Process in back-end operations.

13.1.7 Conceptual Framework

Blockchain technology can transform the business process with a strategic, operational model finely tuned within the regulatory framework. It has the potential to replace the current infrastructure by adopting the distributed ledger process focused on improving the operational process either in the short-term or long-term goals. A dedicated team must be approved to learn the new technologies, explore their potential and evaluate the positive results upon implementation. The banks must prioritize their immediate pain points by studying the feasibility and preparedness of transforming processes that can create an edge. A blueprint must be developed and simulated in measuring the possible success or failures to ensure the maximum scalability and reduce the disruptions towards clients, operations and players of the market. Most of the banks are spending an exorbitant amount on the activities in the areas of middle and back-end operations to take advantage of the resources, cost element, and availability of labor that is also forcing them to set up subsidiary units or captive firms in the developing nation. This technology is still at the acceptance stage since there is anonymity at the other end when there are smart contracts entered between the parties traded on the financial markets, and identification becomes very challenging. Hence, the scope of its application must be validated before implementation and looking forward towards the execution.

Figure 13.7 describes the conceptual framework of an investment bank. Some software companies are working towards developing a foolproof mechanism to overcome the barrier of identity [7].

The flowchart in Figure 13.7 reflects the conceptual framework of the application when adopted; it has higher acceptability through its implications on curbing the client-related process, money laundering, compliance, and legal practices, which are prone to various challenges. The drawbacks can be changed into opportunities if the investment banks chalk up their ground-level research to addressing the obstacles, and will definitely face

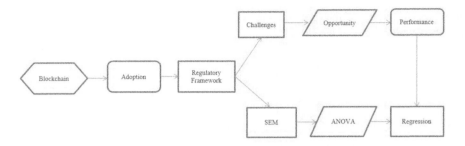

Figure 13.7   Flowchart representation of a conceptual framework.

difficulties in the short run but can surely prove to be effective. Hence, this study attempts to test the model of adaptability through the structural equation model, verifying the results through one-way ANOVA and Multiple Linear Regression models towards the overall performance of the banks' post-implementation [7].

13.1.8 Challenges

Every opportunity creates room for challenges to be faced and addressed, prompting the achievement of goals. Adoption of Blockchain technology consists of a few problems that have to be analyzed before implementation. Some of them are as follows:

- *Standards*: The route of software calls for identification of rules as authorized operating technology within the framework by combining the authority and responsibility.

- *Governance Models*: There must be a well-structured model developed and tested before the actual implementation of the technology to validate the challenges and consequences to ensure the suitability and scalability.

- *Transfer of Assets*: The logical transactions of the assets in the market when there are dual flows off and on between the parties, the management of which must be answered and decided.

- *Regulators*: There must be a balanced plan designed to ensure both privacy and transparency among the transactions of the players.

- *Acceptance*: Most of the employees do not accept the changes due to structural changes, technological changes and their efforts towards the training and development. There may be a few employees who always are reluctant to take the changes. The banks must address these issues.

- *Positioning*: Identification of the perfect time and process which is most suitable for the technological implementation must be forecasted and tested, and only then must be adopted, which requires time, cost and energy.

- *Location*: The area of improvement that facilitates a process, resulting in cost-effectiveness and optimization of resources, must be analyzed and placed in the right process by a suitable strategy.

- *Digital Talent*: Hunting down suitable talented employees for investment banks is very challenging as they are expected to be acquainted with both technology and investment banking concepts.

- *Client Experience*: The clients may have mixed reactions towards the acceptance of this technology as they might not be aware of it and might feel it is redundant when compared to an earlier technology or process, and it is an arduous task for banks to convince their clients to have confidence in the technology.

- *Cloud Concept*: The banks must be willing to move towards the cloud concept where all the transactions are secure and transparent, which means no hidden cost can be applied to the client's service charges.

- *Research*: Research and development is the lifeblood of any business, and investment banks are always striving to create new products and services to gain an edge on the competition. It involves cost, time and resources [8].

13.2   Literature Review

Researchers have attempted to explore whether the impact of implementing integrated cloud and blockchain platforms will deliver better solutions to citizens by establishing a smart collaboration between them and their local government by offering a secure communication platform in a smart city [9]. The application of innovative technologies in the Internet of Things offers services which have been tested for their performance using cloud technology to enhance storage capacity, payment systems and ensure that transactions are tamper-proof [10]. Data can be stored and secured through networked cloud-based systems to ensure the validation of transactions. The computer networks operate with innovative infrastructures for companies and individuals to handle and manage their data. Data plays a pivotal role in cloud computing and promotes safety with a combination of hardware and software to better safeguard records, especially in commercial and military groups. A study by Liang *et al.* showed that a blockchain-based data provenance architecture in cloud environment ensured data operations and enhanced the security and privacy of users [11]. It enables dealing with smart contracts, offering better security and transparency with the third party during the transactions, promoting lower cost of operations, and better cybersecurity, especially when applied in industrial sectors with scalability and improved efficiency [12]. A disruptive technology has been proposed which is capable of revolutionizing the transportation industry with road network planning and facilitating drivers by offering security measures and comfortable driving based on the network models used to build an intelligent, secure and self-determining transport system for optimum utilization of resources. The authors have proposed that the vehicle network architecture operate in a smart city [13].

Tosh *et al.* have stated that there are practical concerns during the adaptation process of the technology based on the cloud concept and its performance handling the security concerns within the structured framework. The technology assures that data is secure and private through the cloud platform that enhances the performance [14]. A study be Stanciu attempted to evaluate distributed and hierarchical control systems based on smart contracts at the monitoring level, integrating the edge nodes at a micro-level in service architectures [15]. E-government is the emerging concept adopted to ensure decentralized and standardized models to facilitate in addressing the nation's issues based on the cloud infrastructure in combination implementation which promotes effective and optimal resource management that focuses on analyzing the national data centers [16]. The introduction of an intelligent vehicle trust point mechanism applied in communication focuses on improving credibility, reliability and data accuracy. It has resulted in a better legal consensus due to the reward-based system in the communications [17].

Singh and Lee propose that emerging innovative technologies can be applied in meeting the standards of service-level agreement in business which ensures data accuracy, security and better improves the quality of standards. The comparative study has offered a solution to security concerns through a trusted third party [18]. Risk management, money laundering, and many other problems are addressed with the integration of active and eminent systems for improving authentication, validation and security across the financial institutions [19]. Kocsis *et al.* highlight the implementation of the technology applied to various complex systems to evaluate the performance outcome, attempting to venture into the novelty of hyperledger fabric services [20]. Experiments were conducted to confirm the secured and shared transactions that can also facilitate useful trades by various players in the market based on the Paillier cryptosystem to assure the confidentiality of data sharing [21]. Smart contracts have proven to be very influential in decentralized sharing of information among the various parties involved in trading, securing the information in consensus with application of this innovative technology which enables sustainable financial markets covering the vast area of economic performance retaining the quality of the data [22]. Biais *et al.* tested the application of technology in the form of a protocol game to evaluate the strategies of rational and strategic miners in the chain, ensuring the retention of foundational technological concepts resulting in orphaned and persistent divergence chains with excessive calculation ability [23]. Data can be stored and secured through networked cloud-based systems to ensure the validation of transactions. The computer networks operate with innovative infrastructures for companies and individuals to handle and manage their data [24-28].

13.3 Statement of the Problem

Investment banks are vulnerable to theft of critical data related to clients, money laundering, settlements and clearance of the securities, which plays a crucial role in the risk management and auditing that creates a benchmark in the industry. The regulations are stringent to arbitrate and mitigate frauds and risk of a trade or when a counterparty fails. Banks must adhere by law to perform KYC before bringing the clients on board. Hence, adopting the proposed technology can curb many regulatory-related obstacles and improve the performance of the investment banks, promoting better customer relationship management. It also ensures a reduction in operating cost and resources with maximum productivity.

13.3.1 Objectives

The study focuses on the below objectives:

- Evaluation of adaptability of Blockchain technology on a regulatory framework by investment banks.

- Assessment of performance by investment banks with the implementation of Blockchain technology.

13.3.2 Hypothesis

- H_0: There is no association between the adaptation and regulatory framework by investment banks.

- H_0: There is no significant impact of adoption on performance in investment banks.

13.3.3 Sampling

Random sampling technique has been implemented to obtain the sample size of 50 respondents based on the probability.

13.3.4 Data Collection and Source

The research is exploratory and based on the primary data obtained through a standard questionnaire. The respondents are the employees of various foreign investment banks operating in urban Bangalore.

13.3.5 Variables and Statistical Tools Used

Statutory impact, compliance policy, fiscal policy, auditing, and service-level agreement are the variables. Statistical package for social science (SPSS) and SPSS AMOS (analysis of moment structures) are the statistical software applied for the study. Structural equation model (SEM) with confirmatory factor analysis (CFA), multiple linear regression analysis and one-way ANOVA (analysis of variance) are the statistical tests performed.

13.3.6 Limitations

The research is limited within the geographical location of urban Bangalore based on the foreign investment banks. There is the further scope of venturing into comparative study pre- and post-implementation of artificial intelligence, machine learning and cloud computing technology enabled techniques of operations in back office and middle office.

13.4 Results

Structural equation modeling (SEM) is one of the multivariate analysis techniques applied to evaluate the structural relationship between the dependent and the independent variables. The model designed is based on the conceptual framework to test the adaptability of the Blockchain technology within their regulatory framework.

Table 13.1 reveals the components of a model fit based on the adaptability in the investment banks. Since all the parameters of model fit reflect the value within the threshold values, it is a perfect model to evaluate the adaptability of innovative technology. SEM model reflects the calculated value of P is 0.535 (> 0.05), reflecting the model fits perfectly. The Goodness of Fit Index (GFI) value is 0.975 and Adjusted Goodness of Fit Index (AGFI) is 0.906, confirming a good fit. The computed Normed Fit Index (NFI) value is 0.959, and the Comparative Fit Index (CFI) value is 1.000. It also shows that the Root Mean Square Residual (RMR) value is 0.020 and Root Mean Square Error of Approximation (RMSEA) value is 0.000.

Table 13.1 Model fit summary of the structural equation model of adaptability of blockchain technology in investment banks.

Indices	Value	Suggested value
Chi-square Value	3.141	–
DF	4	–
P value	0.535	> 0.05 (Hair et al., 1998)
Chi-square Value/DF	0.785	< 5.00 (Hair et al., 1998)
GFI	0.975	> 0.90 (Hu and Bentler, 1999)
AGFI	0.906	> 0.90 (Hair et al., 1998)
NFI	0.959	> 0.90 (Hu and Bentler, 1999)
CFI	1.000	> 0.90 (Daire et al., 2008)
RMR	0.020	< 0.08 (Hair et al., 1998)
RMSEA	0.000	< 0.08 (Hair et al., 1998)
Source: Computed based on primary Data		

Figure 13.8 shows the SEM model applied for the testing of the goodness of fit in the adaptability in their regulatory framework to create more transparency in the business transactions. This model consists of 5 observed variables, namely RF1 (*Statutory impact*), RF2 (*Compliance policy*), RF3 (*Competitive edge*), RF4 (*Fiscal policy*) and RF5 (*Service-Level Agreement*) measuring the construct variable regulatory framework. The measurement error represents other variations for a particular observed variable and their estimation. A factor loading represents the relationship between the factor and its indicator. e_1 (*Legality*), e_2 (*Ownership*), e_3 (*Cost*), e_4 (*Access*), and e_5 (*Clients*) represent that those factors having an impact are treated as error terms by running the model.

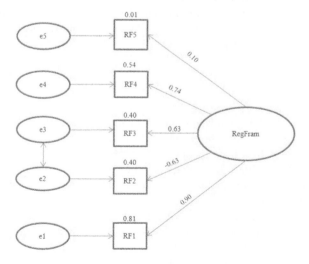

Figure 13.8 Path diagram with standardized estimates displayed based on the regulatory framework in investment banks.

A variance in Statutory Impact of 81 percent is accounted for by the Regulatory framework; the rest of the difference of 19 percent is due to the unique factor legality (e_1). Hence, 0.81 is the estimated SI reliability of the banks adopting the technology. A variance of 40 percent in Compliance policy is accounted for by the Regulatory framework; the deviation of 60 percent is due to the unique factor ownership (e_2). Hence, 0.40 is the estimated reliability of CP if the banks adopt the technology. A variance of 63 percent in Competitive edge accounts for the Regulatory framework, the balance of the variation 37 percent is due to the unique factor cost (e_3). Hence, 0.60 is the estimated reliability of CE if the banks adopt the technology. A variance of 74 percent in Fiscal policy is accounted for by the Regulatory framework; the remaining variance of 26 percent is due to the unique factor access (e_4). Hence, 0.74 is the estimated reliability of FP if the banks adopt the technology. A variance of 10 percent in Competitive edge is accounted for by the Regulatory framework; the other variance of 90 percent is due to the unique factor clients (e_5). Hence, 0.10 is the estimated reliability of SLA if the banks adopt the technology.

Adaptability defining factors statutory impact (81%), fiscal policy (74%), competitive edge (63%) and compliance policy (40%) reflect successful and higher levels of acceptance when the investment banks implement Blockchain technology. However, the factor client-based reliability towards acceptance and adaption by these banks is just 10%. Hence, it can be concluded that the overall adaptability is 65%, offering a platform that is reliable and secure networks to ensure better customer relationships and transparency.

The results in Table 13.2 show that unstandardized coefficients (B) based on RF1 is 1.000, RF2 is 0.948, RF3 is 0.878, RF4 is 1.112, and RF5 is 0.104. The p values of RF1, RF2, RF3, and RF5 are significant at 0.001 percent level and have a positive impact on the adaptability of the technology. However, RF2 shows a negative impact as the banks are expected to permit access to their customers, creating ownership to view their financial data which can be shared by them across banks and financial institutions to avail better services and deals. As per the standardized coefficient (Beta) values from Table 13.2 below, statutory impact has the maximum effect with 0.899, which is the most influencing factor in the model, followed by fiscal policy (0.737), competitive edge (0.633), SLA (0.104), and least influencing factor is compliance policy (-0.632).

Table 13.2 Confirmatory factor analysis of the impact of the adoption of technology on the performance based on the SEM model.

Name	Application	Product
NYIAX	Advertising	Ad exchange platform
MetaX	Advertising	Digital fraud can be avoided
Accenture	Marketing	New commercial capabilities using blockchain
Brave	Token transaction	Browser
Blockstack	Data privacy using DApps	Allows user to visit sites with their data privacy
Snovio	Data privacy	Gives access of information to the publishers for a limited time
MadHive	HubDSP/advertising	Blockchain for Digital video content sites
BitClave	Business and activity watch	Decentralized search engine

RF3 predicts 87.8 percent, RF4 predicts 112 percent, and RF5 predicts 10.4 percent, and RF2 diverges from the impact prediction because of the compliance policy which discloses the trades performed by the employees in the banks. RF1 predicts 100 percent success post-adaptation.

RFW reflects the regulatory framework which is considered as the latent construct variable on the acceptance of the technology.

ANOVA is a statistical tool applied to estimate the difference of variances among the group means of the variables selected for the study based on the sample size. The results from Table 13.3 show that there is a more significant association between the performance of the investment banks and regulatory framework, indicating variables when Blockchain technology is adopted, which are significant at 0.01 level in regard to RF1, RF3, RF4, and RF5.

Table 13.3   Regulatory framework and performance on the adaptability of the blockchain.

Regulatory Framework	Performance	Sum of Squares	Mean Square	F	Sig.
RF1	Between Groups	8.603	0.478	4.337	(0.000) **
	Within Groups	3.417	0.110		
	Total	12.020			
RF2	Between Groups	10.147	0.564	1.178	0.335
	Within Groups	14.833	0.478		
	Total	24.980			
RF3	Between Groups	30.513	1.695	3.633	(0.001) **
	Within Groups	14.467	0.467		
	Total	44.980			
RF4	Between Groups	15.745	0.875	2.074	(0.036) **
	Within Groups	13.075	0.422		
	Total	28.820			
RF5	Between Groups	8.080	0.449	3.479	(0.001) **
	Within Groups	4.000	0.129		
	Total	12.080			
**Significant at 0.01 per cent level. Source: Computed from primary data					

One-way ANOVA was executed to compare the ramification of regulatory variables with the performance of the investment banks. The outcome reflects that there is significant effect of the mentioned technology, RF1 ($F = 4.337$, $p = 0.000$), RF3 ($F = 3.633$, $p = 0.001$), RF4 ($F = 2.074$, $p = 0.036$), RF5 ($F = 3.479$, $p = 0.001$). However, RF2 is not significant as the p value is 0.335, and the F value is 1.178. Hence, there is a higher level of association between the regulatory variables based on technology and the performance of the banks.

A linear regression model is used to predict the dependent variables based on the independent variables to evaluate and predict the linear relationship existing between the variables chosen for the study.

Table 13.4 shows the model fit summary details of the multiple linear regression model evaluated for testing the impact of performance on the banks when innovative technology of Blockchain is adopted. Hence, 77 percent of the prediction of the dependent variable can be successful based on the known independent variables.

Table 13.4 Model fit summary of the multiple linear regression model.

Particulars			Change	
Model	R	R Square	F	Sig.
1	0.773	0.597	13.027	(0.000) **
Dependent Variable. Performance. Source: Computed from primary data. **Significant at 0.01 per cent level.				

Table 13.5 reflects the performance predictors in the regression model adopted to test the performance of these investment banks based on the independent variables, namely statutory impact, compliance policy, competitive edge, fiscal policy, and service-level agreement. The dependent variable is the performance of the bank.

Table 13.5 The performance predictors in the regression model.

Variables	Unstandardized Coefficients (B)	Beta	t	Sig.
(Constant)	16.790	-	1.916	0.062
X_1	5.594	0.483	4.284	(0.000) **
X_2	4.311	0.537	4.846	(0.000) **
X_3	1.631	0.273	2.171	(0.035) **
X_4	-.463	-0.062	-0.514	0.610
X_5	3.908	0.339	2.879	(0.006) **
Source: Computed from primary data. **Significant at 0.01 per cent level.				

Performance is the dependent variable while the independent variables of the regulatory framework are X_1, X_2, X_3, X_4, and X_5. The prediction was based on the model of regression developed using "*Enter*" method as per Table 13.5. A multiple linear regression equation was applied to forecast the performance of the banks based on technology-enabled indicating variables. The following is the equation:

$$Y = 16.790 + 5.594X_1 + 4.311X_2 + 1.631X_3 - 0.463X_4 + 3.908X_5. \qquad (13.1)$$

Where,

- Y = Dependent variable, X_1, X_2, X_3, X_4 and X_5 are independent variables.

- X_1 = Statutory impact

- X_2 = Compliance policy

- X_3 = Competitive edge

- X_4 = Fiscal policy

- X_5 = Service-level agreement

Y reflects the performance of the investment banks and 16.790 is the constant value. A significant regression equation was $(F(5, 44) = 13.027, (p < .000)$, with an R2 of 0.597. Hence, the forecasted performance is equal to 16.790 + 5.594 (Statutory impact) + 4.311 (Compliance policy) + 1.631 (Competitive edge) -0.463 (Fiscal policy) + 3.908 (Service-level agreement).

The performance of the banks increases for every 5.594 strategies of legal decisions, 4.311 compliance strategies, 1.631 competitive advancements, and 3.908 percent of quality reporting as per service-level agreement. However, the quality of decisions based on the fiscal policy is reduced by 0.463 for every decision. The error terms are implementation cost, the reluctance of employees, and resources involved in training the employees to adopt this technology. Hence, statutory impact, compliance policy, service-level agreement, and competitive edge are significant predictors of the bank's performance having a positive impact due to the adoption of a crypto ledger. However, fiscal policy is not a significant predictor as the value of p is 0.612. The impact of execution for the regulatory network has a significant impact on the output performance as the value of R is 0.773.

13.5   Discussion of Findings

The statutory impact has been by the error term e_1 based on the scope for legal identification amongst the counterparties involved in the Blockchain; computer codes generated in the form of smart contracts for the financial assets question its application, raising concerns about the legal entity. Compliance policy influences the error term e_2 which calls for giving ownership to the customers, providing access to their financial data and allowing it to be shared across financial institutions; there are concerns regarding the ownership of non-cryptocurrency-based financial assets being transferred on this platform with certainty.

Banks can create a competitive edge with the adoption of this technology, which can reduce their operating cost by almost 50 percent, but the cost of implementation (e_3) influences the outcome. The cost of training human resource to adapt to the existing systems and implementation cost is expensive. It also depends upon banks being able to afford to invest such a considerable amount in revamping their business. They must consider the cash inflows that pay back their investment.

The fiscal policy of investment banks is focused on generating cash flows through various services rendered to different groups of clients and also consists of their investments for the capital requirements. The artificial intelligence-enabled technology promotes trade settlements; transparent contracts compute the gains or losses, adjusting the collaterals accordingly and increasing transparency. The error term (e_4) influences the adjustability as there are questions related to access and control of the technology based on the ledger versions being kept open or controlled.

SLA is a legal contractual agreement between the service provider and the clients defining the level of service expected, reporting, monitoring, consequences on failing to meet the standards, reliability, service standards, quality, availability, and responsibilities within a specified timeframe. It is affected by the error term (e_5), which can be due to issues like client privacy and security, process speed on scalability, and cyber risks involved when the Blockchain technology is adapted. The impact of technology enabled with Blockchain in the regulatory network has a significant impact on the output performance as the value of R

is 0.773. The ANOVA test has proved that there is a more significant association between the adaptability and the performance. Regression analysis has confirmed that statutory impact, compliance policy, service-level agreement, and competitive edge are indeed significant predictors of the bank's performance. The SEM model has fitted perfectly within the regulatory framework of the banks. All the parametric tests performed have proved positively that the adaptation of the technology is very impressive and brings a tremendous change in the operations of the investment banks.

13.6 Conclusion

Blockchain is a promising technology for reducing the cost of operations, infrastructure, and human capital in the service industry. It has an enormous implication on the compatibility of infrastructure, expertise skill sets, computing power, and datacenter management. Hence, this chapter has shown that the investment banks can adopt this technology in their regulatory framework because data sharing, secured transactions, and contracts for tamper-proof digital agreements which promote authenticity. Blockchain improves with time based on the scalability of the technology.

REFERENCES

1. Are you exploring the Blockchain technology for your investment bank? (2019). Retrieved from https://www.accenture.com/in-en/insight-perspectives-capital-markets-blockchain.

2. Narayanan, V. (2018). A brief history in the evolution of Blockchain technology platforms. Retrieved from https://hackernoon.com/a-brief-history-in-the-evolution-of-blockchain-technology-platforms-1bb2bad8960a.

3. Accenture Consulting Report. (2017). Top 10 challenges for Investment banks. (Accessed on 4th February 2019). https://www.accenture.com/t20180418T063906Z__w__/us-en/_acnmedia/Accenture/Designlogic/16-3360/documents/Accenture-2017-Top-10-Challenges-10-Distributed-Ledgers-Blockchain.pdf.

4. Vedapradha, R., et al. (2016). Investment banking - A panacea for economic development in banking sector. *International Journal of Business Quantitative Economics and Applied Management Research*, 3(4), 46-48.

5. Guo, Y., & Liang, C. (2016). Blockchain application and outlook in the banking industry. *Financial Innovation*, 2(1), 24.

6. Vedapradha, R., & Ravi, H. (2018). Application of artificial intelligence in investment banks. *Review of Economic and Business Studies*, 11(2), 131-136.

7. Nead, N. (June). The Impact of Blockchain on Investment Banking. Retrieved from https://investmentbank.com/blockchain/.

8. Shrivastava, G., Kumar, P., Gupta, B. B., Bala, S., & Dey, N. (Eds.). (2018). *Handbook of Research on Network Forensics and Analysis Techniques*. IGI Global.

9. Biswas, K., & Muthukkumarasamy, V. (2016, December). Securing smart cities using blockchain technology. In *High-Performance Computing and Communications; IEEE 14th International Conference on Smart City; IEEE 2nd International Conference on Data Science and Systems (HPCC/SmartCity/DSS)*, 2016 IEEE 18th International Conference (pp. 1392-1393). IEEE.

10. Samaniego, M., & Deters, R. (2016, December). Blockchain as a service for IoT. In *Internet of Things (iThings) and IEEE Green Computing and Communications (GreenCom) and IEEE Cyber, Physical and Social Computing (CPSCom) and IEEE Smart Data (SmartData)*, 2016 IEEE International Conference (pp. 433-436). IEEE.

11. Liang, X., Shetty, S., Tosh, D., Kamhoua, C., Kwiat, K., & Njilla, L. (2017, May). Provchain: A blockchain-based data provenance architecture in cloud environment with enhanced privacy and availability. In *Proceedings of the 17th IEEE/ACM International Symposium on Cluster, Cloud and Grid Computing* (pp. 468-477). IEEE Press

12. Ahram, T., Sargolzaei, A., Sargolzaei, S., Daniels, J., & Amaba, B. (2017, June). Blockchain technology innovations. In *Technology & Engineering Management Conference (TEMSCON)*, 2017 IEEE (pp. 137-141). IEEE.

13. Sharma, P. K., Moon, S. Y., & Park, J. H. (2017). Block-VN: A distributed block chain based vehicular network architecture in smart city. *Journal of Information Processing Systems*, 13(1), 84.

14. Tosh, D. K., Shetty, S., Liang, X., Kamhoua, C., & Njilla, L. (2017, October). Consensus protocols for blockchain-based data provenance: Challenges and opportunities. In *Ubiquitous Computing, Electronics and Mobile Communication Conference (UEMCON)*, 2017 IEEE 8th Annual (pp. 469-474). IEEE.

15. Stanciu, A. (2017, May). Blockchain based distributed control system for edge computing. In *2017 21st International Conference on Control Systems and Computer Science (CSCS)* (pp. 667-671). IEEE.

16. Chibuye, M., & Phiri, J. (2017). Blockchain – it's practical use for national data centres. *Zambia ICT Journal*, 1(1), 57-62.

17. Singh, M., & Kim, S. (2017, November). Introduce reward-based intelligent vehicles communication using blockchain. In *SoC Design Conference (ISOCC), 2017 International* (pp. 15-16). IEEE.

18. Singh, I., & Lee, S. W. (2017, November). Comparative requirements analysis for the feasibility of blockchain for secure cloud. In *Asia Pacific Requirements Engeneering Conference* (pp. 57-72). Springer, Singapore.

19. Cong, L. W., & He, Z. (2019). Block chain disruption and smart contracts. The *Review of Financial Studies*, 32(5), 1754-1797.

20. Kocsis, I., Klenik, A., Pataricza, A., Telek, M., De, F., & Cseh, D. (2018). Systematic performance evaluation using component-in-the-loop approach. *International Journal of Cloud Computing*, 7(3-4), 336-357.

21. Zhang, Y., Deng, R., Liu, X., & Zheng, D. (2018). Outsourcing service fair payment based on blockchain and its applications in cloud computing. *IEEE Transactions on Services Computing*.

22. Cong, L. W., & He, Z. (2018). Blockchain disruption and smart contracts (No. w24399). National Bureau of Economic Research.

23. Biais, B., Bisiere, C., Bouvard, M., & Casamatta, C. (2019). The blockchain folk theorem. *The Review of Financial Studies*, 32(5), 1662-1715.

24. Ahmad, F. A., Kumar, P., Shrivastava, G., & Bouhlel, M. S. (2018). Bitcoin: Digital decentralized cryptocurrency. In *Handbook of Research on Network Forensics and Analysis Techniques* (pp. 395-415). IGI Global.

25. Sharma, K., & Shrivastava, G. (2014). Public key infrastructure and trust of Web based knowledge discovery. *Int. J. Eng., Sci. Manage.*, 4(1), 56-60.

26. Srivastava, S. R., Dube, S., Shrivastaya, G., & Sharma, K. (2019). Smartphone triggered security challenges – issues, case studies and prevention. In *Cyber Security in Parallel and Distributed Computing: Concepts, Techniques, Applications and Case Studies*. (pp. 187-206). John Wiley & Sons.

27. Sharma, K., Rafiqui, F., Attri, P., & Yadav, S. K. (2019). A two-tier security solution for storing data across public cloud. *Recent Patents on Computer Science*, 12(3), 191-201.

28. Kumar, P., Shrivastava, G., & Tanwar, P. (2020). Demistifying Ethereum technology: application and benefits of decentralization. In *Forensic Investigations and Risk Management in Mobile and Wireless Communications* (pp. 242-256). IGI Global.

CHAPTER 14

TRADING ENERGY AS A DIGITAL ASSET: A BLOCKCHAIN-BASED ENERGY MARKET

Claudia Pop, Marcel Antal, Tudor Cioara, Ionut Anghel

Technical University of Cluj-Napoca, Cluj-Napoca, Romania

Corresponding authors: claudia.pop@cs.utcluj.ro; tudor.cioara@cs.utcluj.ro; marcel.antal@cs.utcluj.ro; ionut.anghel@cs.utcluj.ro

Abstract

In this chapter we address the smart energy grid decentralization problem by proposing a blockchain-based energy market allowing the energy to be traded among prosumers in a peer-to-peer fashion. We discuss how the blockchain technology could facilitate implementation in such a market, allowing the transformation of energy into a digital asset which could be tracked and traded. The main advantages brought by the blockchain technology, such as energy provenance, transactions privacy and immutability, are discussed and details on their implementation in our envisioned energy market are provided. To implement the energy market management operations, such as prosumers registration and permission control, bid/offer matching and financial settlement self-enforcing smart contracts are used. At the same time, prosumer-level smart contracts are used to automatize the bids and offer registration and monitor their energy generation and demand. This is an ongoing research effort and the proof of concept implementation of such an energy market will be tested in selected micro-grid in the coming months.

Keywords: Blockchain, energy market, energy as digital asset, transactions privacy, permission control, smart contracts, P2P energy trading

14.1   Introduction

The architecture of energy distribution systems needs to be redesigned to undertake the increasing complexity of operations and new decentralized management models need to be adopted [1-4]. In fact, centralized energy systems do not consider local conditions and cannot be easily optimized from the user needs perspective, usually providing no incentives to consumers. Nowadays, the centralized energy systems are adopting low-carbon, co-operative and decentralized policies, where energy management may effectively take place at the local level, while simultaneously offering valuable services to the main grid for avoiding grid reinforcement and facilitating voltage management in longer lines and network balancing. Energy price, improved economics and available technologies of the distributed energy prosumers are encouraging alternatives to more local-oriented organization of energy systems, which may simultaneously combine increased energy autarky and self-supply for a local community by providing effective services to the main grid; and hence may generate and combine local and grid-level value streams, with a view to render more affordable local management of energy and, accordingly, lower upstream investment cost for local communities procurement and operation of local energy systems [8-10]. In this way, decentralized market-based coordination of smart local grid prosumers [5-7] makes it possible to self-supply local energy demand and opens up the possibility of considering local communities as the key to still missing stakeholders.

At the same time, from an ICT (information and communication technology) perspective, the blockchain technology has attracted research and industry attention in the past years, due to its huge potential to decentralize complex energy systems management. Currently, P2P (peer-to-peer) trading platforms are considered effective ways for reducing transaction costs and at the same time letting small suppliers compete with larger ones. P2P energy trading may be conveniently used for those markets featuring high demand variability and diversity [11]. P2P trading systems include centralized P2P systems, with a central authority in the middle between supplier and procurers of service (such as Uber and Airbnb), to fully decentralized P2P systems, with no middleman in charge of managing transactions. Energy trading platforms offer different value streams, namely: energy matching for the coordination of complementary flexibility assets where a market mechanism can consider prosumers' individual preferences, uncertainty reduction due to the aggregation of flexibility and capturing preference satisfaction better. Even if electricity was considered a homogeneous asset, recently prosumers exhibit preferences (beyond economical ones), such as environmental and local community ones [12, 13]. In this context, P2P trading platforms can be considered heterogeneous preferences of individual prosumers and community-level stakeholders [14], offering a new business model for trading energy that considers issues such as privacy, autonomy, trust, control and coordination. In this scenario, a dynamic coalition of prosumer-based mechanisms are envisaged as being highly automated and are also the subject of current research [15-17]. At the same time, several energy trading pilot projects are currently being developed which incentivize the creation of rural microgrids in developing countries as an interesting potential application [18]. Blockchain distributed ledger provides an immutable tamper-proof decentralized data storage, which may bring P2P trading systems market transparency, transaction traceability, and transaction verification, resulting in making the same information on the flexibility bid available to all participating stakeholders at the same time [19]. A smart contract is a piece of software running on blockchain network of participating prosumers nodes, managing and executing energy transactions between prosumers and between prosumers and aggregators and/or power network operators, without and/or under the supervision of a trusted third party. Indeed, energy tokenization and smart contracts implicitly include billing and financial transaction settlement, and minimal transactions are feasible, thus resulting in a reduced transaction cost. Public blockchain smart contracts have been defined to allow prosumer energy trading without the involvement of a trusted third party [20]. Existing startups are working on developing blockchain-based solutions for decentralized energy markets but none of them is mature enough; these include SolarCoin [21], Grid Singularity [22] and Grid+ [23]. Still, multiple technical problems must be solved, mainly in terms of data privacy, mining and validation, scalability, etc.

In this chapter, we present the H2020 eDREAM project [24] vision of implementing a P2P energy market for the exchange of energy among prosumers and a decentralized model for maximizing use of locally produced renewable energy (microgrid level). Our goal is to show how the blockchain technology could help in implementing such a market, allowing the transformation of energy into a digital asset which could be tracked and traded. We propose an energy market implementation based on energy tokens and address the main technological advantages: the energy provenance tracking, transactions privacy, and permission control. The energy market operation as well as prosumer actions for energy trading are implemented via self-enforcing smart contracts. The chapter has the following structure: Section 13.2 details a blockchain-based P2P energy market, Sections 13.3 and 13.4 address the challenges and blockchain technological solutions for implementing such a market, while Section 13.5 summarizes the information previously presented in the chapter.

14.2   Blockchain-Based P2P Energy Market

The envisioned energy marketplace will enable any prosumer to directly participate in the market auction (see Figure 14.1).

Figure 14.1   Blockchain-based P2P energy market.

This is of utmost importance in the context of integrating many small-scale distributed energy prosumers in order to provide opportunities for competitive or cooperative procurement models. The market will match consumers with energy producers and will rely on green energy tokens as a reward for using renewable energy. For creating energy tokens, we propose the use of ERC-721 open standard which allows representing the energy asset as a non-fungible token in the blockchain system. The tokens will be generated in proportion to the predicted production of renewables at local system level, thus energy becomes a transactable asset. Prosumers will then use tokens when participating in the electricity market sessions.

The market will leverage on the self-enforcing smart contracts to implement the potential P2P prosumers energy trading. These contracts are distributed for each prosumer enrolled within the marketplace and will stipulate the expected energy production/demand levels, energy price in tokens or the associated token-based incentives for rewarding the prosumers for consuming renewable energy when available, etc. During a market session each prosumer will submit bids and offers (i.e., from their contracts) representing the amount of energy they are willing to buy or sell. The use of smart contracts will allow them to automatically submit bids/offers, and the validity is checked to ensure that market session rules are respected by being done by the smart contract themselves.

A market-level smart contract will programmatically deal with market operation processes such as the match among bids and offers and energy clearing price calculation per session. For clearing price calculation, the market-level smart contract aggregates and sorts, ascending the energy supply offers and descending the energy demand bids. The intersection point between the two curves gives the market-clearing price. The bids/offers are matched as follows: the offers (supply) with the price lower than the clearing price and the bids (demand) with the price greater than the clearing price. Prosumers may accept or reject the matched offers/bids. If an offer/bid is accepted, then the market participant is committed to get/provide the energy amount agreed upon in the offer/bid (or the corresponding share for partial acceptance) in a specific time window. As a result, energy transactions are generated, replicated in all the nodes and validated, but they are not fully confirmed until a new block containing them is added to the blockchain.

The market financial settlement takes advantage of the consensus-based validation. Once issued, the energy transactions are registered in future blockchain blocks across the network nodes. The blockchain consensus mechanisms know these changes and can validate the existing state updates. Thus, instead of single authority and centralized energy transactions (DSO; distributed system operator), in the blockchain version every network peer node has an equal. Each transaction is tracked and validated by each peer locally before unanimously accepting it in the history, the market using a highly reliable and completely replicated decentralized validation process, where network nodes are responsible for integrity checks of the market actions: tokens issued, bids, offers, clearing price computation, monitored values, settled price, green energy consumer rewards and brown energy consumer penalties. The results of each prosumer node computation will determine whether the actions contained in the block are valid and whether the block will be added as a valid block in the chain history.

For energy market implementation we have considered the blockchain architecture featuring three layers [25]: Application, Network and Protocol. At the Protocol layer resides the software implementation that runs at a prosumer node, and includes all the rules that govern the energy market distributed ledger, establishing the protocol for the actual blockchain creation process: block of energy transactions initialization, configuration, evolution, etc. The Network layer is responsible for creating a peer-to-peer network of prosumers over the protocol layer, where each prosumer peer in the network joins and becomes a participant in the marketplace. The top layer, the Application layer, consists of the energy trading smart contracts that are built and run over the network layer, providing the possibility of defining and implementing the specific business rules of energy domain.

14.3   Distributed Ledger for Energy Tracking

The blockchain distributed ledger consists of immutable transactional energy data stored in linked packages called blocks [26]. In the context of electrical grid, we consider that the digital asset traded in the network is a virtual representation of the actual energy traded in real life. The distributed ledger eliminates the need for a central authority in the network being built over a peer-to-peer network of nodes, where all the nodes are equal. In the case of the energy grid, a graph of peer nodes can be modeled where each node may represent a prosumer interested in trading energy, or other stakeholders such as energy aggregators or DSOs. Energy transactions and blocks are distributed and replicated in the network from node to node (see Figure 14.2).

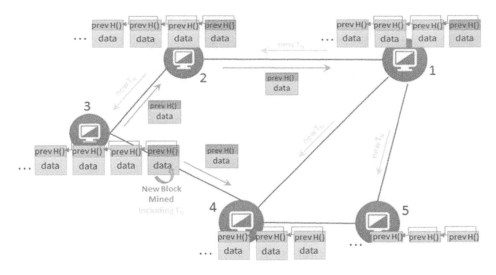

Figure 14.2   Example of P2P network distributed ledger [26].

Whenever a new prosumer joins the blockchain network, a new node (i.e., light or full) might be created and will connect to a predefined list of seed nodes. These seed nodes will provide information about all the prosumers' peers they know about, and the process repeats with the newly discovered peers until the new node builds its own list of peers. The nodes can be light or full, depending on the amount of information they store. The most common nodes are the full nodes which keep the entire blockchain locally (i.e., replicated) and can make the block and transaction validations on their own, without relying on any other instance of the network. Moreover, they are nodes that actively participate in the consistency and integrity of the blockchain by participating in the consensus algorithms. However, due to the fact that the entire blockchain requires a very large memory space, the light nodes (also called simplified payment verification nodes) do not hold the entire blocks (e.g., Node 5), but only their headers, reducing the storage space by 1000 times. When a new energy transaction is registered, the issuer node (e.g., Node 1 in Figure 14.2) it will propagate it to all its peers (Node 2, Node 4, and Node 5 in Figure 14.2). In turn, the nodes receiving the transaction will validate and forward it to their own peers, and so on, until the transaction is known by all the nodes in the network. Similarly, when a node manages to mine a block of energy transactions (e.g., Node 3 in Figure 14.2) it will propagate it to its peers (e.g., Node 2, Node 4) and each receiving node will validate it, before sending it further. A node can decide not to forward a transaction if it has already been registered in order to not generate loops in the whole network.

14.3.1 Energy Provenance and Immutability

The provenance property enables tracking energy transactions back to the moment of their creation in the blockchain. This property is ensured by the data structure used to create the blockchain. The distributed ledger is a collection of blocks, linked using hash pointers, where a set of valid transactions are stored in each block (see Figure 14.3). This data structure is an append-only linked list. If a change appears in previously registered nodes, then inconsistencies are generated (the block hash pointer should also change). In this context, if the previous node must be changed, all the following nodes need to be rehashed and linked to have consistency. This way the data structure is tamper-proof for all block transactions. Also, being an append-only type of data structure (new blocks are always added at the head of the chain), this structure offers reliable historical information and also the prevailing order in which the energy transactions are registered. The probability of an attacker modifying the value of the transacted energy asset in a block decreases proportionally to the following block's number.

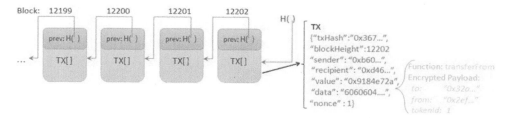

Figure 14.3   Energy transactions registered in blockchain.

The prosumer who generates energy can register energy assets in the distributed ledger, based on the information provided by the associated power meter, by signing a registration transaction having as a receiver the address of the asset-managing smart contract. The flow of energy between prosumers will then be represented in blockchain as energy transactions between prosumers' accounts (see Figure 14.3). To make an energy transaction, the contract managing the producer's account will issue an operation of type transfer and specify the producer's address, the asset to be transferred and the receiving counterpart, which is the consumer's address. To prove the ownership of the energy the prosumer provides the hash pointer to previous transactions showing that the asset belongs to him/her and signs the current transactions to validate the transfer.

Three hash function properties make them suitable for storing the energy transactions data in a secure, tamper-proof manner in the distributed ledger:

- *Collision-Free Property*: For any two input energy transactions T_X and T_Y there is a very high probability of having two different hash values $H(T_X) \neq H(T_Y)$. Collisions are possible, since the input data size is greater than the output data size; however, a good hashing function is designed such that by knowing the hash code there are no better ways to find the input value, other than trying all the possibilities. This property has a very important consequence for the security of the stored data on energy transactions. Considering that an attacker has knowledge of the hash code of an energy transaction, $H(T_X)$, the probability of determining the actual transactional information T_X is extremely low, since it would take an unfeasibly long time to try all the possibilities.

- *Data Concealing Property*: Allows any prosumer entity to hide its energy transactions data by providing a hash of that data (considering that it is improbable for an attacker to provide another piece of data to have the same hash).

- *Data Binding Property*: A binding agreement between the hash code and the input data in energy transactions allows the prosumer entity to prove the origin and ownership of the energy data at any time in the future by applying the hash function on the original piece of data. Hash values can be further used to identify and verify data integrity. When retrieving the data based on a specified hash pointer one can check that the data has not changed since the creation.

The energy market may feature many P2P energy transactions that may occur over a short amount of time. A good solution from a performance aspect is to use Merkle trees to aggregate more transactions in a single block (see Figure 14.4).

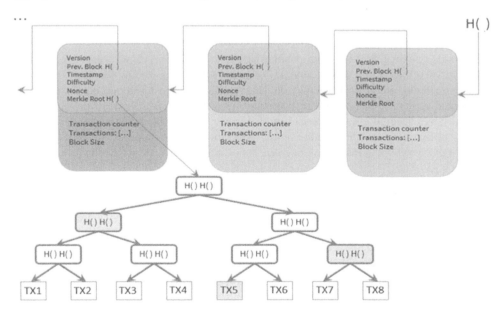

Figure 14.4 Merkle tree for storing multiple energy transactions and Merkle path.

Thus, a block's energy transactions are paired two-by-two while the transactions' hashes are used to create the Merkle tree in a bottom-to-top fashion (leaves contain energy transactions). The upper levels are generated by pairing hashes of two elements from an inferior level. If the total number of transactions considered is an odd number, then the last transaction will be duplicated. After constructing such a binary hash tree, any changes in an inferior level, will trigger updates up to the root of the Merkle tree.

By encoding the energy transactions in the Merkle tree root hash one can ensure validity and integrity of the recorded transactions in time. The Merkle tree root hash is added in the block header and used to create a block hash which is further used to identify a block in the blockchain. Also, the block is never saved in the blockchain storage and instead is always calculated by each node using the header information. However, for performance reasons the hash of the block can be stored in another table for fast indexing. Another way to identify a block is by the height of the block in the chain. This is given by the distance from the genesis block, which is considered the block at height zero. A third party willing to modify a block energy transaction value needs to rehash the entire block in order to provide the correct Merkle tree root of the data. To recompute the hash of the block requires an immense amount of power and currently would take years for a single node to compute it. Even if the attacker manages to change the block, the new recomputed hash of the block needs to be referenced by the following block in the linked list. Changing the reference would require changing the hash of the next block, and similarly all the following blocks need to be rehashed, which requires an immense amount of computational power, which is not possible with the current processors.

The Merkle trees are used to provide a digital footprint of the set of energy transactions stored in each block of the blockchain. The hash of the tree root provides a smaller footprint, which is important for small energy prosumers that do not have the necessary computing capabilities. This kind of prosumer node will store only the block's header and the actual energy transactions are remotely stored. Also, such light prosumer nodes may ask other nodes if an energy transaction was mined and to find the block where the actual transaction is stored. Since the network may contain both honest and dishonest nodes, the light node cannot rely on simple positive answers, but it will request proof that energy transaction is mined in a specific block. Rehashing the entire tree to obtain the root node hash is a good method to verify that an energy transaction is stored in a block. When the computed root node hash is equal to the one from the header of a small prosumer node block, then a specific energy transaction was successfully mined. Considering that many energy transactions can be included in the block, the verification process can be improved by using a Merkle path instead of an entire set of transactions.

14.3.2   Energy Transactions Privacy

In a blockchain P2P energy market, the transactions are duplicated and shared in the peer nodes of the network. Thus, it is of maximum importance to use solid methods for preserving the privacy of market registered prosumers. The prosumer's energy production/consumption patterns should not be visible to other peers in the network. The privacy of the energy profiles and transactions is of utmost importance, since they are considered personal data that can further be used to extract information regarding different daily patterns of the prosumer. The public-key cryptography is very important to assure the energy data ownership, the security of all energy transactions as well as the authentication and authorization. Prosumers will use their private key to sign their own energy transactions, which will be accessed in the network only through their public key. Cryptographic signature uses mathematical functions for public-keys computation, but it is unfeasible to compute the private key by using the public one, thus ensuring non-repudiation in a blockchain energy market. To enforce energy asset ownership, each entry of an energy transaction is linked to the identity of a prosumer that must own at least a public-private key pair. By applying several hashing and encoding algorithms over the public key the prosumer's identity is generated as a 34-character string. Since the energy transaction is guarded by cryptographic scripts, the only method to prove energy ownership and execute a transaction is to own the paired private key. At the same time, an authentication and authorization mechanism in the distributed ledger is constructed using the private-public key pair. The traded energy assets part of a transaction are not sent directly to the address of the receiving prosumer but rather to a locking script/smart contract which contains the public key of the recipient. The locking script/smart contract contains a set of rules that must be enforced whenever the energy asset is transitioned again in the future. Thus, the energy assets are locked and the next energy transactions involving them must provide the required signature created using the private key through an unlocking script. The transactions traded energy assets are locked with locking scripts using public keys of the corresponding prosumer recipients and to unlock them, a cryptographic signature is required that can only be provided by a prosumer peer holding the paired private key. Once the transaction is mined, the recipient prosumers are given ownership over the energy assets.

Zero-knowledge proof methods can be used to assure privacy preservation in a P2P energy market. They allow a verifier to check if the prover has secret information in a manner in which the prover won't divulge the information [27]. Zero-knowledge proofs have been used by digital currencies to create anonymous transactions without the need of third parties by unlinking transactions from the origin of the payment, but still reveal payment amounts and destinations [28]. It is our belief that the zero-knowledge proof mechanisms, mainly the zkSnarks, can be adapted to ensure the privacy of transactions on energy tokens. zkSnarks relies on three different functions that allow:

- *G - key Generator*: Key generator function G has as input a lambda parameter and the program function F is used to validate the secret. As output, the generator issues two keys: the proving key (p_k) used by the prover to run the program F and to issue the proof that it holds the correct secret, and the verification key (v_k) used by the verifier to validate that the public value is indeed corresponding to the proof validating the undisclosed secret.

$$G(lamda, F) \Rightarrow (p_k, v_k) \tag{14.1}$$

- *P - Prover*: Prover function P is used by the prover to generate the proof that it indeed holds the secret. The prover must provide as input the proving key, p_k, generated by G, the public information H and the secret s, which will be checked against H. If the program F is successful, the proof is generated.

$$P(p_k, H, s) \Rightarrow proof \tag{14.2}$$

- *V - Verifier*: Verification function V is used by any player of the network to check the integrity of the public information. The function receives as input the verification key, v_k, together with the public information H that will be validated against the proof published by the prover.

$$V(s_k, H, proof) \Rightarrow true/false \tag{14.3}$$

The ERC standards [30] state that the token contract contains mapping between the holder's address and the amount of energy tokens. To represent the energy assets, the

P2P energy marketplace should provide privacy over the energy tokens owned by the prosumers as well as privacy over the transferred values that occurs between the prosumers' accounts. For a transfer, information about the sender, the receiver and the amount of energy transacted is required, but it this type of information that can be linked with energy consumption/production patterns of prosumers, which is not desired. A solution is to enhance the functionality of the ERC standard by including the benefits brought by zero-knowledge proofs in terms of transaction privacy. A similar implementation can be found in [29] to allow the integration of zero-knowledge proofs for token transfers. First, the energy token registry must hide the information regarding the balance of the user by using a hashed value. Second, the transfer function can no longer reveal the energy value being transferred between the addresses, so a hashed value is provided together with the balances hashed values obtained after the transfer between the two accounts.

The challenge in this case is to validate the received hashed energy values (transfer value, sender balance and receiver balance). For each transfer of tokens, the condition `balances[_from] >= energyValue` must hold true. Since this is not possible, over the hashed input two generator functions, each with a corresponding set of proving and verifying keys, are used (see Table 14.1).

Table 14.1   Generator functions for zero-knowledge proofs.

Generator function	Generated Keys	F Program	Validation Rules Implementation
$G_S(\lambda, F_{sender})$	senderPK senderVK	F_{sender} (H_{sender}, s)	s.energyValue > 0 && H_{sender}.balance > s.energyValue
			H_{sender}.hashedEnergyValue == sha256(s.energyValue)
			H_{sender}.hashedSenderBalance == sha256(s. senderBalance)
			H_{sender}.hashedUpdatedSenderBalance == sha256(s.senderBalance - s.energyValue)
$G_R(\mu, F_{receiver})$	receiverPK receiverVK	$F_{receiver}$ ($H_{receiver}$, s)	$H_{receiver}$.hashedEnergyValue == sha256(s.energyValue)
			$H_{receiver}$.hashedReceiverBalance ==sha256(s.receiverBalance)
			$H_{receiver}$.hashedUpdatedReceiverBalance == sha256(s.receiverBalance + s.energyValue)

The first function corresponding to the sender prosumer (G_S), is validating that the sent energy tokens value is available and the balance is updated accordingly, and the hashes are correct. The second function corresponding to the receiver prosumer (G_R), validates that the updated balance of the receiver and the hash of the transacted energy value are correct. With H_{sender} and $H_{receiver}$ we depict all the information made public such as hashed energy value, hashed sender or receiver balance, hashed updated sender or receiver balance, etc. To validate this information, the sender/receiver must provide the secret information (the transacted energy value), retrieving the proof and verifying that the information made public is indeed correct.

Once the generator issues the keys for each function, the verification keys are stored in the energy token smart contract so that any miner can check the validation of the hashed public information. The proving keys are issued to the senders/receivers respectively to be used off-chain, and they will acquire the proof of validation by leveraging on the prover function (see Table 14.2).

Table 14.2   Prover and verifier functions for zero-knowledge proofs.

Prover	Prover Function	Prover Output	Verifier	Verifier Function
Sender	$P(senderPK, H_{sender}, s)$	senderProof	Smart Contract	$V(senderVK, H_{sender}, senderProof)$
Receiver	$P(receiverPK, H_{receiver}, s)$	receiverProof	Smart Contract	$V(receiverVK, H_{receiver}, receiverProof)$

Each time a transfer is issued, together with the public information the sender and the receiver must also provide the proof for that information, so that each node has the chance to verify it. If the transaction is successfully validated, the transaction is mined, and the balances are updated according to the hashed values, as depicted in Figure 14.5.

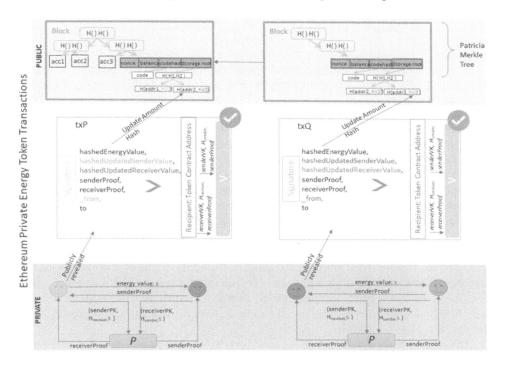

Figure 14.5   Private transaction for energy tokens using zero-knowledge proofs.

14.4   Self-Enforcing Smart Contracts for Energy Market Management

14.4.1   Prosumers Registration and Permission Control

Two types of blockchain infrastructure deployments can be considered for our energy marketplace implementation: public blockchain or private blockchain. The main difference between them lies in the access control of new prosumers from a microgrid to the energy market and in the reading/writing rights they may empower (see Table 14.3).

Table 14.3   Public vs. private blockchain for energy marketplace implementation.

	Public		Private	
	Permission less	Permissioned	Consortium	Enterprise
Access	Any Prosumer	Any Prosumer based on Prior Validation	Based on Owners Group Validation	Based on Administrator Validation
Transactions	Any Prosumer	Owners and Validated Prosumers	Owners and Validated Prosumers	Administrator
Commit to Chain	Any Prosumer	Owners and Subset of Validated Prosumers	Owners and Subset of Validated Prosumers	Administrator

Of course, the DSO's desire to maintain some degree of control on prosumers' registration to the grid and implicitly to the energy marketplace limits the blockchain deployments suitable for our case.

The first alternative is to consider private blockchain deployments as a solution to manage the access rights of prosumers in the energy marketplace and to restrict some of them to a group of owners (e.g., group of large prosumers) of even a single market operator. In this case the energy market can be managed by a group of big prosumers, retailers or aggregators having an important stake in market operation or by a single entity such as the DSO. It is important that the prosumers are known and vetted before given access, this decision having a great impact upon the energy market operation, both in terms of security and consensus. Since the market participants are known, and thus can be held accountable for their actions, the need for high-energy consuming consensus algorithms, such as proof-of-work, are not necessarily justified. In such a private ecosystem, the validators are legally accountable, thus a certain level of trust between the nodes can be considered. Thus, more energy-efficient consensus algorithms can be suitable for private blockchain ecosystems (i.e., Proof of authority [31] or practical Byzantine fault tolerance [32]). However, a private blockchain requires having trusted entities at least for validating new prosumers and issuing new blocks on chain.

The second alternative is to use a public permissioned deployment and to manage the new prosumers registration validation using smart contracts. Prior to their validation the prosumers will be able to read data from the chain, but they will not be able to write new transactions and to mine/validate blockchain blocks. The permissions management is achieved in the public blockchain system, by either validating the prosumer before its registration to the energy market, or by establishing some permissions rules at the level of each decentralized application, by keeping a registry of all the validated users in the smart contracts. Our aim is to change the current energy market operation, thus one of the main requirements is to eliminate the control of the central entities such the DSOs. As a result, the energy market will be decentralized and governed by the decisions and consensus achieved through the collaboration of all the prosumers registered. In this regard the proposed solution considers a public blockchain network, whose robustness and security is intrinsic and does not require a trusted entity to ensure a well-functioning system. We have defined a smart contract (see Figure 14.6) providing access control and permissions for new prosumers joining the energy market.

```
pragma solidity 0.4.24;

import "./MarketSessionBidsOffersMatching.sol";
import "./DEPContract.sol";

contract ProsumersRegistration {

        address private activeMarket;
        mapping(address => address) registry;
        mapping(address => uint) accountReputation;
        uint private reputationLimit;

        modifier onlyValidatedProsumer{
            require(registry[msg.sender] != address(0x0));
            require(accountReputation[msg.sender]>reputationLimit,
            "Only a reputable prosumer can call this function.");
        _;}

        function registerAccount() public returns (address) {
            require(registry[msg.sender] == address(0x0));
            address new_prosumer_address = new DEPContract();
            registry[msg.sender] = new_prosumer_address;
            return new_prosumer_address;
        }
        function validateAccount(address account) public onlyValidatedProsumer{
            accountReputation[msg.sender] = accountReputation[msg.sender] +1;
        }
        function registerBuyOrder(ProsumerEnergyBid _energyBid) public onlyValidatedProsumer{
            MarketSessionBidsOffersMatching m = MarketSessionBidsOffersMatching(activeMarket);
            m.registerBuyOrder.value(msg.value)(_energyBid);
        }

        function registerSellOrder(ProsumerEnergyOffer _energyOffer) public onlyValidatedProsumer{
            MarketSessionBidsOffersMatching m = MarketSessionBidsOffersMatching(activeMarket);
            m.registerSellOrder(_energyOffer);
        }
}
```

Figure 14.6   Smart contract controlling prosumers registration in the energy market.

Firstly, the contract keeps track of all the prosumers' accounts from the grid and registers information about the accounts' reputation. Every new prosumer account that accesses the energy market must be validated by several reputable accounts already registered before being tracked by the account registry function of the smart contract. Once registered, the prosumer account can lose its reputation in the case of prosumers not respecting the bids or offers it makes regarding the energy production/consumption. Considering these restrictions, the smart contract defines the rules regarding the prosumer's rights and for each new energy market action initiated by the prosumer the rules verification is considered a prerequisite. However, the openness of the system rendered in the public chain may be considered as unsuitable for many institutions and enterprises, raising governance and privacy concerns.

14.4.2 Prosumers Energy Trading

The proposed energy marketplace is a democratic and open marketplace offering the possibility to any consumer and producer to participate in the market auction, and consequently acquire energy at lower prices than the ones provided by an energy retailer. This is of utmost importance, since in the past few years the distributed renewable energy resources have multiplied, opening challenges and opportunities for competitive procurement models. At the same time, by matching the small-scale energy producers with consumers in a localized fashion it will contribute to the microgrid energy balance, allowing renewable energy to be consumed as much as possible in the area in which it was produced.

We have defined energy as a non-tangible and non-fungible asset. The fungibility is the property that describes an asset as being indistinguishable from another asset (i.e., interchangeable without any detectable differences). For a given quantity of energy there are several aspects that make it distinguishable from another. For example, the source of energy (solar, wind, fuel, etc.) is an aspect that clearly differentiates future tokens. Furthermore, the timeframe or grid region of energy generation can also be used to differentiate between energy tokens. The Ethereum community has defined several standards regarding the representation of real-life assets using blockchain and specific rules for issuance, tracking, transfer and destruction. However, only one of these standards addresses the non-fungible assets. Thus, we have proposed the adoption of ERC-721 standards [33] for representing the energy asset as a non-fungible energy token in our blockchain-based energy marketplace. The ERC-721-based energy token contract allows the specification and configuration of token properties by providing a description for each token instance through the token URI (see Figure 14.7; left). At the same time, the metadata for each energy token is defined using a JSON schema consisting of information regarding the type of energy produced, generation time as well as the producer's location. In our implementation each token will correspond to 1 Wh energy.

```
pragma solidity ^0.4.24;

import "./ERC721.sol";

contract EnergyToken is ERC721 {

    string internal name;
    string internal symbol;

    mapping (address => uint256) internal ownedTokensCount;
    mapping(address => uint256[]) internal ownedTokens;
    mapping(uint256 => uint256) internal ownedTokensIndex;
    mapping (uint256 => address) internal tokenApprovals;
    uint256[] internal allTokens;
    mapping(uint256 => uint256) internal allTokensIndex;
    mapping(uint256 => string) internal tokenURIs;
}
```

```
"title": "Energy Token Metadata",
"properties": {

    "generation": {
        "type": "string",
        "description" : "The type of energy generated"
    },

    "generation-period": {
        "type": "string",
        "description" : "The time of generation"
    },

    "generation-location": {
        "type": "string",
        "description" : "The geographical location of generation"
    }
}
}
```

Figure 14.7   Energy token based on ERC-721 contract (left) and token metadata (right).

Nowadays, energy markets are based on two types of timeframes: short-term contracts for day-ahead or intraday markets and long-term contracts (e.g., forward, options, derivatives). Our peer-to-peer energy market focuses on the short-term contracts and relies on smart contracts for defining the prosumers actions in day-ahead and intraday market sessions.

Before a market session is opened each producer needs to acquire several tokens proportional to their forecasted energy production. The tokens will act like an obligation, and the price paid for the tokens is set as a guarantee (i.e., stake) in case the obligation is not fulfilled by the producer. According to the forecasted curve, the tokens will be mapped to the corresponding forecasted time of generation. During a market session, using personalized smart contracts, each market registered prosumer will be able to submit energy offers or bids specifying price-quantity pairs for each timeslot defined by the session type (24 hours for day-ahead and 4 hours for intraday). When publishing an offer, a producer will also need to specify the unit price required for selling his/her energy and prove the ownership over the energy tokens. When publishing a bid, a consumer will specify the required amount of energy and the price he/she is willing to pay for each energy token unit. All the energy offers/bids the prosumer registers in a market session are modeled as a smart contract tracked by the blockchain. Figure 14.8 presents such a smart contract for modeling the prosumer-level market actions.

```solidity
pragma solidity 0.4.24;

contract ProsumerEnergyBid {

    address private consumer;
        address private energyTokenContract;
        string private marketSession;

        mapping(uint => uint)  hourlyEnergyBid;
        mapping(uint => uint)  hourlyEnergyPrice;
}
```

```solidity
pragma solidity 0.4.24;

contract ProsumerEnergyOffer {

        address private producer;
            address private energyTokenContract;
            string private marketSession;

        mapping(uint => uint[])  hourlyEnergyTokenOffered;
        mapping(uint => uint)  hourlyEnergyPrice;

        function getEnergyTokens(uint h) public view returns (uint[]){
        return hourlyEnergyTokenOffered[h];
        }
}
```

Figure 14.8   Prosumer-level smart contracts for defining energy bids (left) and offers (right).

The energy market session is also managed via a smart contract which collects all the bids/offers submitted (Figure 14.9).

```solidity
pragma solidity 0.4.24;

import "./ProsumerEnergyBid.sol";
import "./ProsumerEnergyOffer.sol";

contract MarketSessionBidsOffersMatching {

        string private marketSession;
        address private marketSettlementContract;
        mapping(uint => EnergyDemandEntry[]) private hourlyEnergyDemands;
        mapping(uint => EnergyOfferEntry[]) private hourlyEnergyOffers;

        struct  EnergyDemandEntry {
            address consumer;
            uint   quantity;
            uint   unitPrice;
        }
        struct  EnergyOfferEntry {
            address producer;
            uint[]  tokenIds;
            uint   unitPrice;
        }
        function registerBuyOrder(ProsumerEnergyBid _energyBid) public payable{
            for(uint h=0;h<24;h++){
                uint quantity = _energyBid.hourlyEnergyBid(h);
                uint price = _energyBid.hourlyEnergyPrice(h);
                hourlyEnergyDemands[h].push(EnergyDemandEntry(msg.sender,quantity, price));
            }
        }
        function registerSellOrder(ProsumerEnergyOffer _energyOffer) public{
            for(uint h=0;h<24;h++){
                uint256[] memory  tokenIds =_energyOffer.getEnergyTokens(h);
                uint price = _energyOffer.hourlyEnergyPrice(h);
                hourlyEnergyOffers[h].push(EnergyOfferEntry(msg.sender,tokenIds, price));
            }
        }
        function matchOrdersAndUpdateMarketSettlement()  public{ ...
        }
        function energyMarketRulesValidation() private returns (bool) { ...
        }
}
```

Figure 14.9   Smart contract for market session management.

Two mappings are defined. The first mapping keeps track of all energy bids registered in the chain for each hour while the second one in a similar fashion on energy offers. Whenever a new prosumer energy bid is registered in the energy market session the consumer is required to deposit an amount of energy tokens proportional to the quantity requested and the price the consumer is willing to pay. The coins will be locked in the smart contracts until the end of the market session. Before the session ends, each bid must be validated against the operator's market rules and an algorithm for determining the energy clearing price is run. The energy supply offers are ascending sorted while the energy demand bids are descending stored. The intersection point between the two curves gives the market session clearing price. This is the price at which all the matching actions will be traded. The bids/offers matching considers the energy offers (supply) with the price under the clearing price and the energy bids (demand) with the price over the clearing price. For every energy bid or offer not matched in the current market session the deposit energy tokens are unlocked and returned to the corresponding prosumer. For the matched ones, only the difference between the energy tokens deposited and transacted energy cost at the established clearing price will be returned and the rest will be safeguarded by the contract until the transaction's settlement moment (i.e., when the actual energy is produced, monitored delivered and the proof is registered in the blockchain).

Once the bid and offers are matched, a smart contract for market session settlement is responsible for verifying that the promises are held, and the energy transactions are conducted accordingly (see Figure 14.10). The producer proves that it holds the locked energy asset agreed to be produced by providing the specific token IDs and the consumer address is required as a recipient of energy tokens transfer. Upon successful energy monitoring and registration in the blockchain, the consumers' tokens will be delivered to the producer as payment for the delivered energy.

```solidity
pragma solidity 0.4.24;

contract MarketSettlement {

        address private energyTokenContract;

        mapping(string => uint) marketSessionClearingPrice;
        mapping(uint => MatchedOrder[]) hourlyMatchedOders;
        mapping(uint => MatchedOrder) hourlyMatchedOrders;

        struct MatchedOrder {
                address producer;
                address consumer;
                uint  quantity;
                uint[]  energyTokenIds;
                string marketSession;
        }

        function settleProducerActivity(uint hour, uint monitoredQuantity) payable {...}
        function settleConsumerActivity(uint hour, uint monitoredQuantity) payable {...}
}
```

Figure 14.10   Smart contract for market session financial settlement.

The consumer tokens will remain as proof of the prosumers activity and the type of energy consumed, for future evaluation and validation. However, if there is any deviation from the values promised matched bids and offers, the prosumer will be penalized and required to pay additional fees for the imbalance caused.

14.5   Conclusion

In this chapter the implementation of a blockchain-based peer-to-peer energy market allowing energy to be traded as a digital asset was described. We have discussed the main advantages brought by the blockchain approach in terms of assuring the energy provenance, transactions immutability and security. Also, we have presented a first implementation of such an energy market model relying on smart contracts for implementing the prosumers potential activity as well as the energy market management actions. This is an ongoing research effort and we expect that in coming months the concept implementation of the energy marketplace will be tested in the context of eDREAM pilot microgrids to show its effectiveness.

Acknowledgment

This work was conducted in the context of the eDREAM H2020 project (grant number 774478), co-funded by the European Commission in the H2020 Framework Programme (H2020-LCE-2017-SGS).

REFERENCES

1. Mendes, G., Loakimidis, C., & Ferraro, P. (2011). On the planning and analysis of integrated community energy systems: A review and survey of available tools. *Renew Sustain Energy Rev*, 15(9), 4836-54.

2. van der Schoor, T., & Scholtens, B. (2015). Power to the people: Local community initiatives and the transition to sustainable energy. *Renew Sustain Energy Rev*, 43, 666-75. DOI: 10.1016/j.rser.2014.10.089

3. Frantzeskaki, N., Avelino, F., & Loorbach, D. (2013). Outliers or frontrunners? Exploring the (self-)governance of community-owned sustainable energy in Scotland and the Netherlands. *Renew Energy Gov Lect Notes Energy*, 23, 101-16.

4. Avelino, F., Bosman, R., Frantzeskaki, N., Akerboom, S., Boontje, P., Hoffman, J. & et al. (2014). The (self-)governance of community energy: challenges & prospects. *DRIFT Practice Brief*. DOI: 10.13140/2.1.1297.0242.

5. Burger, C., & Weinmann, J. (2013). *The Decentralized Energy Revolution*. London: Palgrave Macmillan UK.

6. Burger C, & Weinmann J. (2016). European utilities: strategic choices and cultural prerequisites for the future A2. In: Sioshansi, F. P. (Ed.). *Future of Utilities–Utilities of the Future*. (Ch. 16, pp. 303-22). Academic Press, Boston, MA.

7. CSIRO. *Change and Choice: The Future Grid Forum's Analysis of Australia's Potential Electricity Pathways to 2050*. CSIRO Energy.

8. Giotisas, C., Pazaitis, A., & Kostakis, V. (2015). A peer-to-peer approach to energy production. *Technol Soc*, 42, 28-38. DOI: 10.1016/j.techsoc.2015.02.002.

9. Rathnayaka, A. J. D., Potdar, V. M., Dillon, T., & Kuruppu, S. (2015). Framework to manage multiple goals in community-based energy sharing network in smart grid. *International Journal Electronic Power Energy System*, 73, 615-24. DOI: 10.1016/j.ijepes.2015.05.008.

10. Wolsink, M. (2012). The research agenda on social acceptance of distributed generation in smart grids: Renewable as common pool resources. *Renew Sustain Energy Rev*, 16, 822-35.

11. Einav, L., Farronato, C., & Levin, J. (2016). Peer-to-peer markets. *Annual Review of Economics*, 8, 615-635.

12. Yang, Y., Solgaard, H. S., & Haider, W. (2015). Value seeking, price sensitive, or green? Analyzing preference heterogeneity among residential energy consumers in Denmark. *Energy Research & Social Science*, 6, 15-28.

13. Boait, P. J., Snape, J. R., Darby, S. J., Hamilton, J., & Morris, R. (2017). Making legacy thermal storage heating fit for the smart grid. *Energy Build*. 138, 630-640.

14. Da Silva, P. G., Karnouskos, S. & Ilic, D. (2012). A survey towards understanding residential prosumers in smart grid neighborhoods. In *IEEE PES Innov. Smart Grid Technol*. Eur. http://doi.org/chm3.

15. Fleiner, T., Janko, Z., Tamura, A., & Teytelboym, A. (2018). Trading networks with bilateral contracts. Available at SSRN 2457092.

16. Baeyens, E., Bitar, E. Y., Khargonekar, P. P., & Poolla, K. (2013). Coalitional aggregation of wind power. *IEEE Transactions on Power Systems*, 28(4), 3774-3784.

17. Lee, W., Xiang, L., Schober, R., & Wong, V. W. (2014). Direct electricity trading in smart grid: A coalitional game analysis. *IEEE Journal on Selected Areas in Communications,* 32(7), 1398-1411.

18. Robert, F. C., Ramanathan, U., Durga, P., & Mohan, R. (2016, October). When academia meets rural India: Lessons learnt from a MicroGrid implementation. In *2016 IEEE Global Humanitarian Technology Conference (GHTC)* (pp. 156-163). IEEE.

19. Pop, C., Cioara, T., Antal, M., Anghel, I., Salomie, I., & Bertoncini, M. (2018). Blockchain based decentralized management of demand response programs in smart energy grids. *Sensors*, 18(1), 162.

20. Aitzhan, N. Z., & Svetinovic, D. (2016). Security and privacy in decentralized energy trading through multi-signatures, blockchain and anonymous messaging streams. *IEEE Transactions on Dependable and Secure Computing*, 15(5), 840-852.

21. Gogerty, N., & Zitoli, J. (2011). DeKo: An electricity-backed currency proposal. *Social Science Research Network*. Available online: http://ssrn.com/abstract=1802166

22. Grid Singularity, Available online: http://gridsingularity.com

23. Grid +, Available online: https://gridplus.io/

24. eDREAM H2020 project - http://edream-h2020.eu/

25. Hileman Garrick and Rauchs Michel, 2017 Global Blockchain Benchmarking Study , September 22, 2017, Available at SSRN: https://ssrn.com/abstract=3040224

26. Pop, C., Cioara, T., Antal, M., Anghel, I., Salomie, I., & Bertoncini, M. (2018). Blockchain based decentralized management of demand response programs in smart energy grids. *Sensors*, 18(1), 162.

27. Seijas, P. L., Thompson, S. J., & McAdams, D. (2016). Scripting smart contracts for distributed ledger technology. *IACR Cryptology ePrint Archive, 2016, 1156*.

28. Miers, I., Garman, C., Green, M., & Rubin, A. D. (2013, May). Zerocoin: Anonymous distributed e-cash from bitcoin. In 2013 *IEEE Symposium on Security and Privacy* (pp. 397-411). IEEE.

29. https://media.consensys.net/introduction-to-zksnarks-with-examples-3283b554fc3b

30. ERC Token standard, https://theethereum.wiki/w/index.php/ERC20_Token_Standard

31. Why Blockchain Needs 'Proof of Authority' Instead of 'Proof of Stake. Cointelegraph. Dec 2017, https://cointelegraph.com/news/why-blockchain-needs-proof-of-authority-instead-of-proof-of-stake

32. Sukhwani, H., Martnez, J. M., Chang, X., Trivedi, K. S., & Rindos, A. (2017, September). Performance modeling of pbft consensus process for permissioned blockchain network (hyperledger fabric). In *2017 IEEE 36th Symposium on Reliable Distributed Systems (SRDS)* (pp. 253-255). IEEE.

33. ERC-721 Non-Fungible Token Standard, Available online at https://github.com/ethereum/EIPs/blob/master/EIPS/eip-721.md, (accessed on 19 July 2018)

CHAPTER 15

APPLICATION VIEW TOWARDS BLOCKCHAIN: DEMYSTIFYING THE MYTHS

UTKARSH CHITRANSHI AND SUNIL KUMAR CHAWLA*

Computer Science and Engineering, CGC College of Engineering, Mohali, Punjab, India

*Corresponding author: sunil.3550@cgc.edu.in

Abstract

Blockchain is an eccentric technology, at the same time, the most vaunted, least understood and most disrupting technology of the current era. The idea of blockchain is not so old. It is still in its infancy phase. In this chapter, we have tried to view blockchain from an application point of view, throwing some light on mining mechanism, participants of blockchain system, organized and versatile use cases; while demystifying the myths.

Keywords: Blockchain, Bitcoin, myths, applications

Cryptocurrencies and Blockchain Technologies and Applications.
Edited by Gulshan Shrivastava *et al.* Copyright © 2020 Scrivener Publishing

15.1   Introduction

The idea of cryptographically secured currency was first published in the year 1991 in a white paper written by S. Haber and W. S. Stornetta. Following this, the idea of decentralized digital currency came into existence in the late 90s. Then, Satoshi Nakamoto proposed the revolutionary idea of bitcoin [1]. After these successful applications a new renaissance began, which is now spreading in all domains and industries.

This chapter explains the nontraditional view of blockchain in multiple industries and the myths that surround the blockchain arcade. Simply defined, Blockchain gets its name from the way it stores transactional data, i.e., in forms of blocks that are linked together to form a chain of blocks [2]. The number of transactions grows, resulting in the blockchain growth. Various popular cryptocurrencies available on the market are shown in Table 15.1:

Table 15.1   Famous cryptocurrencies around the world.

S. No.	Name	Logo
1	Ethereum	
2	Bitcoin	
3	NEM	
4	Litecoin	
5	NEO	
6	Monero	
7	Ripple	
8	Dash	
9	Vertcoin	
10	Bytecoin	

"Blockchain is shared, immutable ledger that facilitates the process of recording transactions and tracking assets in a business network. An asset can be either tangible (e.g., a house, a car, cash, land) or intangible (intellectual property, patents, copyrights, branding). Virtually anything of value can be tracked and traded on a Blockchain network, reducing risk and cutting costs for all involved" [3].

15.1.1   Problems in the Present System

- Cash dependent.
- The time taken for transactions is too long.

- Third-party validations in the presence of mediators add to disorganization.

- Frauds and cyberattacks.

- Credit card organizations charge a lot.

- Those in third world countries who don't have access to bank accounts can easily do parallel transactions.

- Limited transparency.

- The volumes of transactions worldwide are increasing exponentially, hence causing complexities, vulnerabilities, inefficiencies, and the rising costs of current transaction systems.

15.1.2 Definitions

To understand the subject matter better, let us go through some related definitions.

15.1.2.1 *Web 3.0*

The advantages of Web 3.0 are:

- *Semantic Web*: The Semantic Web along with artificial intelligence (AI) is the foundation of Web 3.0. The Semantic Web helps to understand the machines, what the data means and how it can use the data. The main aim is to create an internet of knowledge across the world which will help process and connect content through search and analysis.

- *Artificial Intelligence*: AI allows sites to screen information and present consumers with the best data analysis possible.

- *3D Graphics*: Web 3.0 is changing the course of the internet, from the old 2D web into a more pragmatic 3D computerized world. Present use cases are online games, e-commerce, real-estate industry; basically every industry where a third party is involved.

- *Ubiquitous*: Web 3.0 exists everywhere, at the same point of time, as defined by the word "ubiquitous."

- *Connectivity*: Information is more connected due to semantic metadata. As a consequence, the experience of a common user advances to a higher level that influences all the accessible information.

15.1.2.2 *Internet of Value (IoV)*

The IoV refers to an online framework or a community in which users can instantly transfer value/money from one node to another, eliminating mediators and reducing the third-party costs. Anything that has financial value or has a social value can be moved between parties, including currency, property shares and even votes.

From a more reasonable perspective, the IoV is totally supported by blockchain paradigm, which is revolutionary technology supporting e-currency. This technology has disrupted how business is conducted in many sectors, such as banking and entertainment, and has started to impact the traditional industrial areas such as real estate and e-commerce. Hence, blockchain is creating a fair playing field between brands, consumers and lenders. The impact of the technology is that high-value transactions will no longer have to go through expensive, third-party mediators for safe authentication of transactions. This is done through the technology, which serves as a clear and distributed ledger, which is not handled by any sole authority and is universally accessible.

Hence, allowing for instant transactions of some entity called value, thus reduces uncertainty, while it also disproves the influence of third-party and middleman costs. From the consumer's viewpoint, the IoV signifies the next echo of the digital age and has the potential to lessen the power of banks, financial lenders and large corporations by giving power to more decentralized and autonomous institutions. In the financial sector, the IoV will shape the fundamentals laid in the wake of the 2007-08 financial crisis, when accessible, short-term lenders filled the financing void that was left after banks chose to tighten their criteria for lending. However, industries and service providers will most likely view the IoV from a different point of view due to the fact that this development has drawbacks in terms of improving profit margins and retaining the current market proportion. After all, it is fair to infer that some service providers (e.g., brokers) will gradually become immaterial in the age of blockchain, while mediators who do survive nowadays will need to seek out fresh revenue streams. The exact impression of the IoV has yet to be seen, of course, but there's no doubt that this evolution will shake up several industries and marketplaces in the long run.

15.1.2.3 *Initial Coin Offering*

For traditional companies, there exist a few means of collecting funds required for their development and expansion such as crowdfunding. A company can initially be a small venture and grow with time as its revenues permit, only being obliged to company owners; but at the same time, they have to wait for funds from external sources to set up. Consequently, companies may see external investors for initial assistance, who provide a rapid inflow of funds but typically come up with the option of giving them a share in the ownership. Other ways in which companies get money is by selling shares in their company and by selling bonds via an initial public offering (IPO). An Initial Coin Offering (ICO) is the cryptocurrency industry's equivalent to an IPO in the conventional investment ecosphere. ICOs act as fundraisers of a kind; moreover, a company looking to create a new coin, app, or service can launch an ICO. Following the launch, interested investors buy the offerings, either with fiat currency or with pre-existing digital tokens like "ether." In exchange, investors acquire a new cryptocurrency token specific to the ICO. Shareholders also expect that the token will perform remarkably well in the future, providing them with a stellar return on investment. The investor funds are used by the company holding the ICO as a means of sponsoring its goals, initiating its product, or starting its own digital currency. The startups use ICOs to dodge the difficult and controlled capital-raising required by venture capitalists or banks.

15.1.2.4 *Significant Terms*

Some related terms of significance are mentioned below:

- *Consensus*: For a transaction to be valid, all participants must agree on its validity.

- *Provenance*: Participants know where the asset came from and how its ownership has changed over time.

- *Immutability*: No participant can tamper with a transaction after it has been recorded to the ledger. If a transaction is in error, a new transaction must be used to reverse the error, and both transactions are then visible.

- *Finality*: A solitary, mutual ledger delivers a unique place to decide the proprietorship of an asset or the accomplishment of a transaction.

- *Distributed and Sustainable*: The ledger is shared, updated with every transaction, and selectively replicated among participants in near real-time. Because it's not owned or controlled by any single organization, the blockchain platform's continued existence isn't dependent on any individual entity.

- *Secure, Private, and Indelible*: Encryption and cryptography check unauthorized access to the network and confirm that contributors are who they claim to be. Confidentiality is preserved through standard cryptographic practices and/or data partitioning methods to give participants selective visibility into the ledger; both transactions and the identity of involved parties can be masked. After conditions are settled to, participants can't tamper with a record of the transaction; errors can be overturned only with fresh transactions.

- *Transparent and Auditable*: Because participants in a transaction have access to the same records, they can validate transactions and verify identities or ownership without the need for third-party intermediaries. Transactions are time-stamped, ordered, and can be verified in near real-time.

- *Consensus and Transactional*: Every related contributor must settle on the legitimacy of the transaction. The use of "consensus-based algorithms" achieves this. The settings required to complete a transaction or to conduct the exchange is set up by each participant.

- *Coordinated and Flexible*: As business rules and smart contracts can be built into the platform, blockchain business networks can evolve as they mature to support end-to-end business processes and an extensive variety of events.

15.1.2.5 *Permissioned Blockchain Offer*

- *Enhanced Privacy*: By using IDs and consents, users can state the transaction details they want other participants to be able to view. Approvals can be prolonged for distinctive users; for example, auditors may require special privileges to additional transaction details.

- *Improved Auditability*: Having shared the ledger that serves as a solitary source of truth, advances the capability to monitor and audit transactions.

- *Increased Operational Efficiency*: The transfer of ownership is streamlined by the wholesome digitization of assets. Transactions can be performed at a pace better inline with the pace of business.

Note: Where third-party oversight is required, blockchain reduces the burden on the regulatory system by making it easier for auditors and regulators to review relevant transaction details and verify compliance.

15.1.2.6   Block Subparts: Purpose Immutability

A block of a typical blockchain has the following three parts, as shown in Figure 15.1:

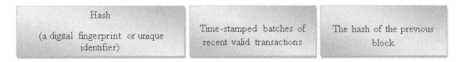

Figure 15.1   Parts of a block in a blockchain.

- Hash (a digital fingerprint or unique identifier)

- Time-stamped batches of recent valid transactions

- The hash of the previous block

15.2   What Blockchain Does Not Replace

Blockchain does not replace:

- Database

- Messaging technology

- Transaction calculus

- Business procedures

Instead, the blockchain provides certified evidence of transactions.

- *Proof of Stake*: To validate transactions, validators must hold a certain percentage of the network's total value. Proof of stake might provide increased protection from a malicious attack on the network by reducing incentives for attack and making it very expensive to execute attacks.

- *Multisignature*: A majority of validators (for example, three out of five) must agree that a transaction is valid.

- *Practical Byzantine Fault Tolerance (PBFT)*: PBFT is an algorithm designed to settle disputes among computing nodes (network participants) when one node in a set of nodes generates different output from the others in the set.

- *State-Based Communication*: Nowadays, banks interconnect through secure messaging platforms, such as SWIFT, to complete the transactions; each party conserving its state of the task locally on their personal servers. By blockchain, they can send communications that denote the shared state of the job on the blockchain, with each message stirring the job to the following state in its life cycle.

- *Peer-to-Peer (P2P) Transactions*: On a blockchain for business network, participants exchange assets directly, without having to process the transaction through intermediaries or a central point of control, thus reducing the costs and delays associated with the use of intermediaries.

- *Consensus*: Instead of mediators, blockchain uses "consensus algorithms" to validate and authenticate the transactions. Participants can conduct business at a speed that's more in-line with that of their commercial and professional choices [10].

15.3 Mining Mechanism

When participants are unidentified (e.g., in the Bitcoin world), commitment is almost unaffordable. "On the Bitcoin network, consensus is reached through proof of work." The network tests each machine that saves a ledger copy with a complex puzzle based on the ledger version. Machines with same ledger copies unite to crack the puzzle they have been asked to solve. The first team to answer the puzzle is the winner, and all other machines update their ledgers to match that of the victorious team. The notion is that the majority wins as it has the highest computing power to solve its puzzle first. Proof of work is valuable on an unrestricted/open blockchain, such as the one used for Bitcoin, but it consumes substantial computing power and electricity, making it an elegant way to reach consensus [5].

15.4 Various Participants of Blockchain System

- *Blockchain Developer*: A blockchain developer is a computer programmer who builds the applications and smart contracts that enable blockchain users to conduct transactions on the blockchain network. Applications serve as a conduit between users and the blockchain

- *Blockchain User*: A Blockchain user is a participant (normally, a business user) with permissions to join the blockchain network and conduct transactions with other network participants. The technology operates in the back-end, so the blockchain user has no awareness of it. There are typically multiple users on any individual business network.

- *Traditional Processing Platforms*: Existing computer systems may be used by the blockchain to augment processing. This system may also need to initiate requests into the blockchain.

- *Blockchain Network Operator*: Those who have special consents and authority power to define, construct, manipulate, and supervise the blockchain network. Each business on a blockchain network has a blockchain network operator.

- *Regulator (R)*: A Regulator is a blockchain user with special permission to oversee the transactions happening within the network. Regulators may be prohibited from conducting transactions.

- *Certificate Authority (CA)*: An individual who issues and manages the different types of certificates required to run an authentic blockchain; for example, certificates may need to be issued to blockchain consumers or to different transactions.

- *Traditional Data Sources (DS)*: Existing data systems that may provide data to influence behavior of smart contracts and help to define how communications and data transfer will occur between traditional applications/data and the blockchain via API calls, through MQ style cloud messaging, or both.

The market capital of different cryptocurrencies can be found out with respect to the transactions performed using those currencies shown in Figure 15.2. The current total market capitalization of leading cryptocurrencies is $323.43 Bn.

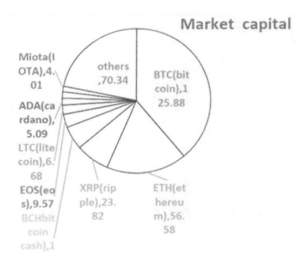

Figure 15.2   The market capital of the main cryptocurrencies; the total market capital presently is $323.43 billion.

15.5   Organized Use Cases

1. International Rule Organization

2. Supply-Chain Administration

   - Food security
   - International trade

3. Healthcare

   - E-medical records
   - Payment authentication

4. Monetary Services

   - Trading
   - Trading settlements
   - International transactions
   - Provides important digital proofs

5. Government

15.6 Hyperledger

Started by the Linux Foundation, Hyperledger is an open source community which is highly suitable for enterprises. Hyperledger Fabric is a specialized blockchain framework for the implementation in which Hyperledger schemes are presented by the Linux Foundation. It is also a container technology which proposes a linked architecture and pluggable, substitutable facilities using modular technology [4].

Other functionalities consist of:

- Decreases expensive calculations involved in proof-of-work concept.

- Creates permissioned and distributed shared ledgers.

- Obeys with acts and rules that exist today.

- Obeys verified identities and private transactions.

- Provides privacy, scaling, performance, security and auditability.

- Chains a wide variety of corporate use cases with sustainable requirements.

Dissimilar to the other blockchain applications, Hyperledger Fabric fulfills all five main fundamentals of a blockchain for private chains:

1. *Programmable*: Influences fixed logic in smart contracts to mechanize business processes across the network.

2. *Permissioned Network*: It shows association and access rights within the business system.

3. *Confidential Transactions*: It gives commerce the elasticity and security to make dealings noticeable to select parties that have a correct cryptological order.

4. *FIPS 140-2*: It is the high-level central information processing protocol which supports the use of blockchain in regulated industries such as government, financial services, and healthcare.

5. *Doesn't Rely on Cryptocurrencies*: Doesn't require mining and complex computations to guarantee transactions.

15.7 Steps to Creating Your Own App

Decentralized applications (DApps) are the apps that run on a peer-to-peer network of nodes rather than a single node, i.e., a computer. They are a type of software program programmed to exist on the internet in such a way that is controlled by a distributed entity.

The steps to creating DApps are:

1. Determining how the Blockchain fits into the industry.

2. Identifying the loopholes in commercial processes.

3. Defining how blockchain can change.

4. Selecting a suitable use case for blockchain application.

5. Determining the goals of the required blockchain network.

6. Identifying dependencies which would play an important role in consumer priorities.

7. Choosing the best blockchain provider and adequate and easy platform.

15.8 Advertising Industry

Blockchain technology is widely used in the advertising industry. A new problem of the 21st century is data theft, i.e., companies are looking for the personal information of users and customers mainly for data analytics, which would increase sales and the market capitalization of the company [8]. The Cambridge Analytica data scandal is the best example of losing control of personal user data. There are three types of advertising:

1. Brand advertising, in which a client pays to have their advertisement in any sort of print or digital media to raise brand awareness.

2. Direct sales advertising, in which a publisher prints/publishes an advertisement in media such as a blog, newspaper, website, or YouTube channel. The process is simple but includes a third component or intrusion into the system, i.e., if one advertiser wishes to sell his mobile phone he contacts the third party, then the third party selects how and where the advertisement will be digitally published, taking into account factors such as where the buyer is most likely to see the product and how easy it will be to buy. The problem with this model is the participation of the third party and high cost of endorsement. The most successful third party is Alphabet, which uses Google search engine and YouTube channels for user products. Google uses search engine optimization (SEO) and other techniques for the listing of top websites [7].

3. Ad exchange platform, which questions why users need to pay extra to the third-party search engines when one can create their own predefined marketing strategy and definite viewers arena that would provide better sales at a very low cost. Ad exchange platforms, like the USAs NYIAX, currently have the biggest market capital and is expanding its platform to also include other countries.

The Know Your Customer system, commonly known as KYC, is a campaign started by many companies so that only verified and authorized users are in the system. We can guarantee a transparent system with blockchain. Many browsers have been developed which allow advertisers to pay a small amount and the viewers who visit the site will be paid an incentive. Blockchain is poised to help media and entertainment companies, as it can create a digital rights database; for example, if an artist creates a music album he/she can directly sell it to the user by means of digital rights. One can use smart contracts to pay the amount to the artist, without the use of a third entity. All this results in far better data privacy over which users have control. Moreover, it creates a true digital identity to use the digital assets. There are ad frauds that are performed by the bots created by other firms just to influence the market. For tackling these kinds of problems one needs a platform, which is free from third-party involvement. The digital media faces an uncontrolled situation which is the fraud performed by the automatic programs called bots. The losses due to Ad fraud by the end of 2017 were around $16.4 billion. This problem has been solved by startups like MetaX and adChain [7].

15.9 Present Day Implementation

There are three main ways to implement blockchain: 1) using an existing code, 2) creating new smart contracts, and 3) creating a developer-friendly framework. Bitcoin, Ethereum and Cosmos SDK are examples of each respectively [11]. Bcoin and Btcd are two other substitutes; also, Inter-Blockchain Communication is another protocol which can be used instead of Cosmos. It's very simple to use; Ethereum uses the solidity programming language and its unit is ether. Ethereum has been a major focus of interest because of its ability to indulge in multipurpose projects; it can even be used by people who are not very aware of programming [13]. The most advantageous feature of Ethereum [3] is that it has the most active and developed community. Microsoft Azure and IBM offer services at a cost which is not very suitable for everyone who aims to use blockchain; hence, development of blockchain technology is quite costly. Microsoft Azure is a game changer which gives free services to beginners so that they can understand how to use it. It has very broad commercial adaptability in almost all the big economies. A user or organization can also pay extra for faster transactions. Proof of work is merely the waste of resources as it uses direct economic state to complete the transaction. It may get transformed to proof-of-stake concept in the future, where there is no such requirement to generate a proof of work. The Enterprise Ethereum Alliance is a group of large IT firms which have joined resources to develop the Ethereum, the main ones are Microsoft, Accenture, Intel, and ING, along with the Indian giant WIPRO [15]. Distributed applications or DApps are a new approach which decentralizes the workload and focuses on sharing of resources, which uses a "gas" model which acts like a token and is used to increase or decrease the speed of transaction [16]. Ethereum consortium is a model which consists of a leader and has submembers; the leader acts like a switch in computer networking which directs the flow of information from one node to another [9]. Plasma smart contracts are very efficient in promotional marketing; it contains the whole contract and the payment model for both the advertiser and the publisher [2].

Table 15.2 gives a detailed understanding of top brands and companies working in the advertising industry that use blockchain [17].

Table 15.2 List of some key players in the advertising industry.

Name	Application	Product
NYIAX	Advertising	Ad exchange platform
MetaX	Advertising	Digital fraud can be avoided
Accenture	Marketing	New commercial capabilities using blockchain
Brave	Token transaction	Browser
Blockstack	Data privacy using DApps	Allows user to visit sites with their data privacy
Snovio	Data privacy	Gives access of information to the publishers for a limited time
MadHive	HubDSP/advertising	Blockchain for Digital video content sites
BitClave	Business and activity watch	Decentralized search engine

15.10   Versatile Use Cases

Blockchain has also shown promise in helping to solve the humanitarian issue of this era– the refugee problem. Datarella has led an effort to solve the problem on the Syrian front. Blockchain technology bypasses the problems created by bureaucracy and international conflicts. This technology acts like a decentralized banking system for people who do not have a bank account. It dispenses with the problem of international socioeconomic distances, as transfer remittances are a very costly way of transferring money in certain remote regions of the world. It makes the transfer of money to migrants very easy.

Voter fraud can be prevented by the use of distributed ledgers, which gives us an unhackable electronic voting technique. It can be a better alternative than the traditional electronic voting machine (EVM). Government efficiency can also be improved. The Government of India should adopt the methods from the UAE government, which aims to implement blockchain in office work and public benefits. By accepting this technology the bureaucracy will banish corruption and fraud will become predictable. Also, some states in India have accepted the proposal of converting all the land records into a single chain. Blockchain has emerged as a very rewarding technology for the field of cybersecurity. Classified data and important records of institutions can now be digitally preserved. Industries that handle highly sensitive information, like defense and aerospace, need a foolproof way to store data; blockchain can be used to do so.

Table 15.3   List of some successful startups using blockchain around the world and their basic field of work.

Name	Sector	Application
TUI	Tourism	Track internal contracts
SWIFT	International payments	22 banks signed for the single platform
Airbus	Manufacturing	Airplane manufacturing
IBM	Blockchain solutions	Non-finance-related blockchain solutions
Webjet	Online travel portal	Find empty hotel rooms
Unilever	Hired IBM	Digital advertising
Nasdaq	Government, finance, advertising	Working In Estonia
Ripple	Payments	International transactions
Enigma	Real estate	Renting of apartments
BitPesa	Donations	For African people
MedRec	Health care	Record management

Other fields of interests are financial (trading, deal organization, equities, settlements, peer-to-peer lending), insurance (claim filings, fraud prediction, telematics and ratings), media (digital rights management, art authentication, ticket purchase, goods tracking, advertisement click frauds using bots, and real-time sale), computer science (DNS, expanse of market, API platform plays), medical (records sharing, compliance, DNA sequencing, prescription sharing), asset titles (diamonds, car leasing and sales, home mortgage payments), government (voting, vehicle registration, copyrights), identity (personal, objects, digital assets, refugee tracking, employee reviews), IoT (device directories, grid monitoring, smart home, operations like water flow), payments (B2B, micropayments, tax payments), consumer (Uber, Apple Pay, P2P, digital rewards, cross company, loyalty rewards tracking), and supply chain management (agriculture food authentication, pharmaceutical tracking, shipping and logistics management) (see Table 15.3).

The revenue trend graph has been significantly increasing throughout the past decade. It's expected to reach $20000 million by the year 2025. Due to the backing up of the internet, blockchain has the upper hand due to the community of this technology, which is very active and supports the development of this project. Projects like the Hyperledger, chain operation standard 1 and R3 consortium are prominent in development and research. Indian entrepreneurs are also working on creating a change after realizing the potential of this technology. Most of them are based in the metropolitan cities. These startups are eager to launch their products in the near future. Indian startups are also working on blockchain-based applications at full force. Recently, New Street Technologies has backed up $2 million funding. A list of a few of the startups [14] is given in Table 15.4:

Table 15.4   The list of some successful Indian startups and their basic application and product.

Name	Application	Product
PrimeChain	Banking, governance, insurance	KYC solution, Loan, contract, API
Sofocole	Smart-contracts, supply-chain, insurance	sofoCap, sofoChain, Sofo Insurance
Caieina	Smart contracts	Smart contract wizard
EzyRemit	Payments, banking, global financing	B2B transactions, EzHedge, EzRemit
Auxesis	Coverage, supply-chain, cross border payments, capital markets	Auxledger, AuxPay, Token Bazaar, Darwin Insurance
KrypC	Information Technology	Krypcore
Records Keeper	Enterprise, Big Data and Analytics	Data security solution
Signzy	Banking, insurance, mutual fund payments cryptocurrency.	Real KYC
GetXS	Property supervision, healthcare, connected marketplace, monetary services	XS
Accubits	Finance, retail, supply chain	ICosys solutions, reinsurance
Elemenbal	Smart contracts, banking, capital market	KYC solution
Somish	Finance, retail, manufacturing	Fortune 500s, governments, startups
StaTwig	Supply chain	Intelligent supply chain

15.11 Myths

- **Myth 1**: There is only one blockchain: No, there are many blockchains like Ethereum, Bitcoin, etc. These are applications of blockchain which create their own chains using the same principles.

- **Myth 2**: Data on blockchain is not secured: The data is totally secured on blockchain because of its versatile and cryptographic features.

- **Myth 3**: Blockchain is synonymous with any other database or is similar to cloud: Blockchain is not a replacement for the database or any cloud system, it is self-proclaimed technology with its pros and cons.

- **Myth 4**: Smart contracts are similar to normal contracts done in real-world exchanges. Smart contracts are a programmed unit of sets of instructions that are specifically meant to be used in blockchain-based DApps.

15.12 Conclusion

In a nutshell, blockchain provides key business benefits of minimizing the time and cost factors involved in a transaction along with tightening the security. Enhanced privacy, improved audibility due to shared ledger, and increased operational efficiency are significant takeaways of the technology. Building trust with blockchain over a network is an important issue to handle. Healthcare, financial services such as banking, government sectors like defense, and pharmaceuticals are some famous application areas of blockchain. A great many areas of blockchain still need to be researched, such as infrastructure, protocols, environment, strategies, and applications. Several issues and challenges are wide open to be worked upon.

REFERENCES

1. Nakamoto, S. (2008). Bitcoin: A peer-to-peer electronic cash system. https:// bitcoin.org/bitcoin.pdf.

2. Poon, J., & Buterin, V. (2017). Plasma: Scalable autonomous smart contracts. *White Paper*, 1-47.

3. Buterin, V. (2014). A next-generation smart contract and decentralized application platform. *White Paper*, 3, 37. https://www.ethereum.org/pdfs/EthereumWhitePaper.pdf

4. Cachin, C. (2016, July). Architecture of the hyperledger blockchain fabric. In Workshop on distributed cryptocurrencies and consensus ledgers (Vol. 310, p. 4). https://www.zurich.ibm.com/dccl/papers/cachin_dccl.pdf

5. Blockchain Investopedia. Archived from the original on 23rd March 2019, https://en.wikipedia.org/wiki/Blockchain.

6. Staff, E. (2016). Blockchains: The great chain of being sure about things. *The Economist*, 18.

7. Web 3.0 [Online] Available: https://www.expertsystem.com/web-3-0/

8. Four Ways the Blockchain could be applied to digital advertising [Online] Available: https://www.econsultancy.com/blog/69712-four-ways-the-blockchain-could-be-applied-to-digital-advertising

9. Technology choices when building your own blockchain [Online] Available: https://blog.cosmos.network/technology-choices-when-building-your-own-blockchain-a15385cf59bd.

10. Blockchain is a new model that makes the existing model obsolete [Online] Available: https://medium.com/future-crunch/blockchain-is-a-new-model-that-makes-the-existing-model-obsolete-8671ee6dd252.

11. Bitcoin vs. Ethereum driven different purposes [Online] Available: https://www.investopedia.com/articles/investing/031416/bitcoin-vs-ethereum-driven-different-purposes.asp.

12. Amazing real world examples how blockchain is changing our world [Online] Available https://www.forbes.com/sites/bernardmarr/2018/01/22/35-amazing-real-world-examples-of-how-blockchain-is-changing-our-world/2/#3fa034bf1232

13. Ethereum Foundation. (2018). Ethereum: Blockchain app platform. [Online]. Available: https://www.ethereum.org/

14. Watchlist Indian Blockchain Startups [Online] Available: https://inc42.com/features/watchlist-indian-blockchain-startups/

15. Jeon, J. H., Kim, K. H., & Kim, J. H. (2018, January). Block chain based data security enhanced IoT server platform. In *2018 International Conference on Information Networking (ICOIN)* (pp. 941-944). IEEE.

16. Yang, Z., Yang, K., Lei, L., Zheng, K., & Leung, V. C. (2018). Blockchain-based decentralized trust management in vehicular networks. *IEEE Internet of Things Journal*, 6(2), 1495-1505.

17. Gu, J., Sun, B., Du, X., Wang, J., Zhuang, Y., & Wang, Z. (2018). Consortium blockchain-based malware detection in mobile devices. *IEEE Access*, 6, 12118-12128.

18. Kumar, P., Shrivastava, G., & Tanwar, P. (2020). Demystifying Ethereum technology: Application and benefits of decentralization. In *Forensic Investigations and Risk Management in Mobile and Wireless Communications* (pp. 242-256). IGI Global.

19. Shrivastava, G., Kumar, P., Gupta, B. B., Bala, S., & Dey, N. (Eds.). (2018). *Handbook of Research on Network Forensics and Analysis Techniques*. IGI Global.

20. Ahmad, F. A., Kumar, P., Shrivastava, G., & Bouhlel, M. S. (2018). Bitcoin: Digital decentralized cryptocurrency. In *Handbook of Research on Network Forensics and Analysis Techniques* (pp. 395-415).IGI Global.

21. Srivastava, S. R., Dube, S., Shrivastaya, G., & Sharma, K. (2019). Smartphone triggered security challenges – issues, case studies and prevention. In *Cyber Security in Parallel and Distributed Computing: Concepts, Techniques, Applications and Case Studies*, (pp. 187-206). John Wiley & Sons.

22. Sharma, K., & Shrivastava, G. (2014). Public key infrastructure and trust of Web-based knowledge discovery. *Int. J. Eng., Sci. Manage.*, 4(1), 56-60.

23. Sharma, K., Rafiqui, F., Attri, P., & Yadav, S. K. (2019). A two-tier security solution for storing data across public cloud. *Recent Patents on Computer Science*, 12(3), 191-201

24. Gupta, M. (2017). *Blockchain for Dummies, IBM Limited Edition*. Wiley Publications, USA, ISBN: 978-1-119-37123-6.

25. Kumar, P., Shrivastava, G., & Tanwar, P. (2020). Demistifying Ethereum technology: Application and benefits of decentralization. In *Forensic Investigations and Risk Management in Mobile and Wireless Communications* (pp. 242-256). IGI Global.

Printed and bound by CPI Group (UK) Ltd, Croydon, CR0 4YY